THE ENCYCLOPAEDIA OF TYPE FACES

THE
ENCYCLOPAEDIA
OF TYPE FACES

W. PINCUS JASPERT
W. TURNER BERRY : A. F. JOHNSON

NEW YORK
BARNES & NOBLE

FIRST PUBLISHED IN 1953

SECOND EDITION (REVISED & ENLARGED) 1958

THIRD EDITION (FURTHER RESTYLED & ENLARGED) 1962

FOURTH EDITION (ENTIRELY RESTYLED & GREATLY ENLARGED) 1970

© 1970 BLANDFORD PRESS LTD, 167 HIGH HOLBORN, LONDON W.C.1

FIRST PUBLISHED IN THE UNITED STATES, 1970
BY BARNES & NOBLE, INC.

SBN 389 04043 6

MADE IN GREAT BRITAIN
Printed and bound by Fletcher & Son Ltd, Norwich
on Bingham Opaque quality paper 118 gsm
supplied by P. F. Bingham Ltd.

CONTENTS

PREFACE TO FOURTH EDITION

THIS NEW EDITION has had a further 400 specimens of new or recently resurrected type faces added to it. There has also been a substantial number of additions of older faces still in use, including in particular a variety from American sources. It had been hoped to include black letter types, but the physical difficulties of obtaining good specimens from founders and matrix suppliers have delayed this plan which will have to await a better opportunity, or possibly even a separate publication.

As in previous editions, almost all the elaborate designs from the latter part of the nineteenth century which were cut and cast in innumerable technically unsatisfactory variations and copies have been omitted. Those wishing to use such type designs are advised to look at the various style books now issued by photolettering studios.

Phototypesetting faces as such have only been included where they relate to keyboard-operated machines, that is machines which are governed by the limitations and restrictions of mechanical composition, whether by hot metal or photography. The numerous photo display alphabets available nowadays cannot claim to be subject to the disciplines of the typefounder's craft.

The introduction of the British Standard 2961:1967 classification system, now applied (and partly reprinted by kind permission of the British Standards Institute in London), should help considerably in classifying types. There are, however, still some types that defy any classification. These are found principally amongst those romans which originated during the Victorian era, together with others of more recent vintage from this century, including some which have basically lineale style but also scripts and "manuscript" designs. The classification of types was done by Helen Wodzicka.

The new, greatly enlarged format of this handbook is intended to enable users to keep the volume as a desk book in which annotations can easily be made. By arranging types alphabetically under three main sections—Romans, Lineales & Scripts, it is hoped to make the location of type faces easier for quick reference.

Typefounders and their agents, composing machine and matrix manufacturers, have once again given very considerable assistance and practical help in preparing this edition. However, in this issue we have again had to reproduce several designs from printed specimens because of the impossibility of obtaining actual specimen alphabet settings from readily available sources. Where the setting of specimens appears out of style, this is because of the difficulty of reconciling material from many different sources, including reproductions from type, slugs, electros, line blocks and even metal and plastic stereos.

It would not have been possible to revise this new edition without the very active help and advice of a number of people, Alan Hutt and A. D. B. Jones, both of London, Matthew Carter, New York, and in particular Dr G. W. Ovink, of Amsterdam. They provided notes of substantial value and have especially helped in clarifying references to source material and historical links.

I am also grateful to James Mosley, Librarian of the St. Bride Printing Library, for the Index to Designers and for his general cooperation.

Much valuable help was also given by readers in many countries who provided information and corrections, suggestions and type specimens for reference.

Physically, the production of this book would have been extremely difficult but for the friendly assistance of Jerry Kuehl in Paris, and Roy Knightley in London, to whom my personal thanks are due.

The majority of type faces shown in this book are copyright designs, and may not be copied without permission from the appropriate foundry or owner of the design.

W.P.J.

TECHNICAL TERMS USED
IN THE DESCRIPTIONS

ARM: The projecting horizontal strokes on such letters as **T, E.**

ASCENDER: The part of a lower-case letter which projects above the mean-line, as in **b, h, l,** etc.

BASE LINE: The imaginary line on which the base of capital letters rests.

KERN: That part of a type which overhangs the body.

LIGATURE: The connecting link between two letters that are joined together. Often misused in the sense of logotype, that is, two or more letters cast on one body, generally comprising such characters as *fi, ff, fl, ffi, ffl, ct, st, ll, tt, sp.*

LOOP: The lower part of **g,** also called the tail.

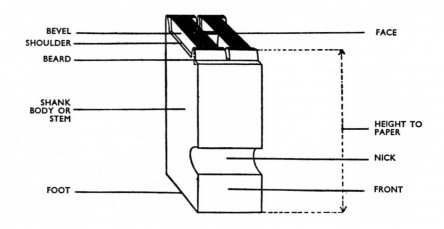

BEVEL · SHOULDER · BEARD · SHANK BODY OR STEM · FOOT · FACE · HEIGHT TO PAPER · NICK · FRONT

BOWL: The rounded part of such letters as **P, B** and the upper part of **g** to distinguish it from the lower part known as the loop or tail.

CAP-LINE: The imaginary line which rules along the top of capital letters.

COUNTER: The enclosed parts of a letter, such as lower-case **p, q.**

CURSIVE: Literally, resembling hand-writing; flowing rather than formal.

DESCENDER: Those parts of such letters as **g, p, q** which descend below the base line.

EAR: The projecting stroke on the bowl of the **g.**

EYE: The enclosed part of the lower-case **e.**

MEAN-LINE: The imaginary line that runs along the top of lower-case **a, n, x,** etc.

POINT OF MAXIMUM STRESS: The thickest part of curved letters, like **O, e,** etc.

SHORT-RANGING FIGURES: Numerals which range on the base line.

SPUR: The small beak on the end of arcs, as in **G.**

SWASH LETTERS: Flourished italic letters as **A, C, D, E, I, P, S,** etc.

UNCIALS: Rounded capital letters from which are derived lower-case letters, such as **e, u** etc.

X-HEIGHT: The face of the lower-case letters without ascenders and descenders.

INTRODUCTION

THIS SELECTION OF TYPE FACES has been compiled to provide a reference
book for all those who use type—typographers, printers, publishers, advertisement designers and the business man who takes some interest in the choice of
type for his stationery and publicity. It may also be of value to the lettering artist, the
signwriter, and the engraver, who in consequence of the limitations of their own books
of alphabets, often turn—we trust with a little uneasiness of conscience—to printers'
type for inspiration.

Some explanation of the terms used in the descriptions of type faces seems to be
required. This is not the place to enter into technical details on the making of types or
to attempt a description of the cast type itself. We are concerned with the superficial
impression made by the type when pressed on to paper, though, of course, many of the
terms applied to the impression are originally used of the metal type itself. As we shall
describe some types which are several centuries old, it may be as well to refer briefly to
the existence of such things as punches and matrices. A letter is in the first place cut in
reverse on the end of a steel punch, which in turn is driven into a matrix. The matrix
receives an impression of the letter the correct way round, and from this is cast,
again in reverse, the metal type actually set by the compositor. When a text is said
to be composed in original CASLON type, this is a convenient shorthand. The type is,
of course, more or less newly cast, but is derived from the original punches. Punches
are all but indestructible, and, in fact, a number have survived from the fifteenth
century.

The body of the type is the whole of the superficial area, which is not, of course,
completely filled by any letter. What are called full-bodied letters occupy the whole
height of the body, e.g. Q. Small letters like a, m, o, occupy the middle part of the body
only. Ascending letters, like b, d, l, occupy the upper and middle parts, and descending
letters, like p, q, the middle and lower parts. These three parts vary much in their proportions. When we speak of a type of small face we mean that the middle part is short
in relation to the ascenders and descenders. The length of the ascenders and descenders
is one of the principal points to be noted in describing a type. We speak also of bold-faced
and light-faced types, referring to the thickness or thinness of the strokes of the letter.
The face of a type is the same thing, then, as the impression of the letter. Types may also
vary in width, laterally. Proportionally narrow types are called condensed. If the letters
fill the body laterally, or fill it as nearly as possible, then the letters when set in line will
have very small spaces of white between each other. The "set" is said to be close. This
is a second point in which there is much variation among types. CASLON, for example,
is a type which has a wide set, and a comparatively small face. The inside white spaces
of the letters are called the counters, a term borrowed from the processes of punch
cutting. From the seventeenth century onwards the sunk part of the letter, that is, the
part which would be left in white, was made by driving into the punch another bar on
which this area was engraved. This bar was called the counter-punch.

IMPORTANCE OF SERIFS

In the designing of formal letters, not cursive or script characters, unconnected strokes are finished off by the addition of short cross-lines called serifs. These seemingly insignificant little lines have a surprising effect on the appearance of the face of a type and are therefore of great importance in typographical classification and description. They may be horizontal on the top, or inclined; they may be thick or thin, and of varying size in proportion to the main stem. On the underside they may be connected to the main stem by a triangular piece or in a curve, and are then described as bracketed; on the other hand the under-part may be entirely cut away, leaving a flat, unbracketed serif. In the case of foot serifs the bracketing, if any, is, of course, on top. Inclined serifs are normally confined to the lower case, on the m, n, p, r, u's, etc. Even when these are inclined those on the tops of the ascenders may be horizontal. The form of the foot serifs should also be noted.

Types were originally copied from manuscript letters written with broad-nibbed pens, or quills. The earliest printed books were in fact made to resemble contemporary manuscripts as nearly as possible. When a broad-nibbed pen, held at right angles to the paper, is used, it is clear that a vertical stroke will be of the same thickness as the pen's edge, and that a horizontal stroke will be a thin line, while curved strokes will vary in thickness from the one extreme to the other. In an "o" the two thickest parts will be directly opposite each other—due east and west, so to speak. In such a letter we describe the distribution of the thicks and thins, or the distribution of weight as vertical; we speak of the vertical colouring, stress, or shading. Holding the pen at right angles to the paper is a strained attitude, and we find that an angle of 45 degrees or less was more usual. This gives a diagonal shading; for example, the thickest parts of the "o" are diagonally opposite—north-east and south-west, or in some cases even north-east-north by south-west-south. Such shading is characteristic of early romans and of most of the book types in use today. Again, there can be variations in the gradation between thick strokes and thin; the gradation may be gradual and slight, or it may be extreme and abrupt. All book types show some variation of thick and thin; in the fifteenth century it was slight, and gradually became more pronounced, until it reached the extreme in the nineteenth century when they became called hair lines.

VARIATIONS IN DESIGN

All these points of variation so far referred to, differences in the degree and position of the shading or stress, differences in the forms of the serifs, and in the proportions of the different parts of the body, apply to the fount of type in general. Variations in the design of individual letters are perhaps even more helpful in distinguishing one type from another. A summary of the more obvious points to be observed in particular letters may be useful. The apex of A is sometimes pointed, sometimes flat, or again, oblique; the position of the bar varies. In the C the extent to which the circle is completed and the absence or presence of serifs or beaks and their shape, in E, F and L the width of the horizontal strokes or arms, are points to be noted. G is often C with a horizontal lower serif; sometimes the stroke below this serif is vertical, and sometimes there is a small projection on the right, which we call a beard or spur. H varies much in width and in the position of the bar. J was a non-existent letter at the time of the invention of printing, and our form is really the swash I. With the modern face it became a short-ranging letter; variations in the terminal or lower curve are to be noted. In the M the outer strokes may be upright or splayed, the middle strokes may meet on the line or at various points short of the line, while the top serifs vary considerably. The bowl of the P is often not closed. The tail of the Q varies greatly. The final stroke or tail of the R has undergone many changes. It may end in a serif on the line; it may taper to a point, even descending below the line; with the modern face it became curved and more vertical. The relation of the upper and lower curve in the S, and in the T the width of the horizontal stroke and the form of its serifs have varied. V originally did duty for U, which is a form dating from about 1600. For one period in the seventeenth century U assumed the same design as the lower-case u, with a foot serif, and that form has been revived in many recently designed romans. The middle strokes of the W meet at various heights, and when they meet at the top are sometimes without a serif.

Variations in the shape and size of the bowl of the a, in the extent to which the top arc curves downwards and the manner in which this is finished, make this letter useful for our purpose. In the eighteenth century b acquired a foot serif on the left. The foot serif on the d has changed from an inclined position to the horizontal. This applies to the u also. An important letter is e. The "eye" was in early days enclosed by an oblique stroke; when this stroke became horizontal the eye was very small and gradually grew larger, until in the nineteenth century it was as deep as half of the face of the letter. The position of the thickest part of the curve should be observed. g is equally important for the changes in the sizes of the bowl and the curves of the tail or loop. This tail is sometimes not closed. On the bowl is a projection, which we call the ear; this was originally a short horizontal stroke projecting from the right-hand top corner. Later it became curved, and sometimes started from a higher point on the bowl. h has changed little since, with JENSON, it acquired the straight shank, originally a curve. The dot over the i was in some early types not vertically over the stem, but away to the right; in other cases a dash took the place of the dot. The q in some modern faces has a top serif on the right. The height of the t and finish at the top, the cross-stroke, whether bracketed or not, and lastly the tail of the y are noteworthy. For the s and w the points noted in the capitals apply.

Besides the ordinary letters, the fount of roman includes also other sorts, tied letters or ligatures and punctuation marks. The ligatures, or combinations of two and even three letters cast on one body, have survived in a few cases, like the f combinations, ff, fl, etc. In types based on early models the earlier ligatures, such as ct and st, are still found. Full stops have at times been diamond-shaped, and commas have been oblique dashes. The arabic figures, too, are part of the fount. In the early designs 1 and 2 were short letters, 3, 4, 5, 7 and 9, descending letters, and 6 and 8 ascending letters. In the modern face all the figures were cut to range on the line, although there are now non-ranging figures for such types as TIMES ROMAN which look somewhat neater. Several typefounders provide alternative figures for many of their faces, modern or old style, so that the typography of these can best be suited to individual requirements and style preferences of the designer or typographer using them.

THE ITALICS

The italic letters are now also a part of the complete roman fount. Such is the sad fate of this once beautiful letter, originally an independent rival to roman. In origin it is a cursive form of the Italian hand on which roman types were based, and should properly be called *Cursive*, as in fact it is called in Germany, or *Chancery*, a name applied to it bacause it was used in the Papal Chancery at Rome. The earliest italic, that of the Venetian printer, Aldus Manutius, dating from 1501, was a niggardly sort of type devised for pocket editions. Later, under the influence of Italian writing masters like Lodovico Vicentino at Rome and Tagliente at Venice, more formal and graceful designs were produced, which ensured the popularity of italic in the sixteenth century. Such types have been the model for several modern italics, which will be described below. It was long before italic became merely a secondary letter to roman, and even longer before it was cut to harmonise with the roman. Our italics are inclined—this inclination is not essential and some few of the early models were upright—and the difficulty of inclining roman capitals at a uniform angle is evident in many of our old-face italics. Since this cursive letter was less bound by traditional forms than the roman, greater variety of design has been possible, with the result that italics are more easy to distinguish than romans. Not infrequently it is easier to recognise a roman from its accompanying italic than from the roman letter itself. On the other hand, our printers tend to use italic less and less, and one may search a text in vain for a word in italic. In view of the unimportant position which it now occupies, less space will be given in the following descriptions to the secondary letter.

The angle of inclination of an italic is the first characteristic to be observed. In the best early Italian models this angle was slight, and became more pronounced with the old-face group. Recent designs again tend more towards the upright. The lack of consistency of the angle of inclination is another characteristic of the old-face group. In some cases one can hardly imagine that the designer ever intended his italic capitals to combine together. Many italics have second forms for some upper-case letters, script forms, which are known as swash letters. These naturally were not meant to be used in the middle of words, though in fact they frequently are. In the lower case the greatest variation occurs in the serif formation, or rather what corresponds to the serif formation in the roman. It is here that italic especially retained the cursive quality of the hand on which it was modelled. The initial strokes are not serifs, but pen strokes. When deliberate attempts were made in the eighteenth century to harmonise the two designs, the italics did for a time acquire roman serifs, though never in this country. With our founders the calligraphic initial strokes of the Caslon italic degenerated into the pot-hooks of the nineteenth-century design.

W.T.B.
A.F.J.

TYPEFACE NOMENCLATURE

From the earliest days of printing, trade terms have been used which were passed orally from craftsman to apprentice; they related to the physical objects used in typographical printing processes, e.g. metal "types". Since the beginning of this century such terms have been used by designers and others outside the industry but, as they usually have no occasion to use the physical objects, they use the terms in more abstract senses. For example, the term "type face" now commonly refers to the printed character left on the paper by the printing surface ("face") of the physical "type".

Another factor which adds to the confusion is that (as in many other industries) established technical words are made to do service for new concepts that arise from new developments. Such confusion certainly arose after the invention of the pantographic mechanical punch-cutter and the hot-metal composing machine which largely replaced the hand-cut punch and hand composition. Photographic setting might have added to the danger of confusion in terminology, although the issue of the first edition of this standard reduced this to some extent.

Often the context will prevent any misunderstanding of the sense in which a particular word is used, but this is not always the case, and confusion does arise in practice. It is now common practice for publishers, advertisers and other print buyers to give detailed specifications to the printers and it is, therefore, important to define terms in a manner that will avoid embarrassing and costly misunderstandings in commercial transactions.

CLASSIFICATION

The names of groups of type faces now in general use have grown haphazardly over the past 150 years. Some of the names are descriptive but others are historical and, except to those well versed in the history of printing and type design, have little meaning. Since the end of the last century, several attempts have been made to evolve a classification of type faces, but none has found really wide acceptance. It has become increasingly evident, especially during the last ten years, that there is a real need for classification which can be accepted nationally, and preferably internationally, and which will facilitate discussions between type face designers and printers, printers and print-buyers, and teachers of typography and their students.

In 1954, Maximilian Vox, in France, published some proposals which were simpler than any of the earlier attempts. While they were generally welcomed, they were also criticized and were amended later. In 1959, a draft German Standard was issued, giving a classification which related to the principles adopted by Vox, but which was considerably more complex. After considering the comments which they received on this draft, the Deutscher Normenausschuss published a revised classification (DIN 16518) in 1964, which was almost identical to the Vox classification. The Vox classification is widely used in many European countries.

The difficulty arises that if the categories are rigidly defined and limited to a practical number, many type faces elude classification. On the other hand if the categories are loosely defined, each may contain type faces which are fundamentally different although having certain, perhaps arbitrary, factors in common. This classification attempts to limit the possibilities of confusion.

The actual nomenclature must, of course, differ in different countries according to language. The classification in the British Standard is based on the concepts of English-speaking countries.

CLASSIFICATION OF TYPE FACES

I	Humanist	Type faces in which the cross stroke of the lower case e is oblique; the axis of the curves is inclined to the left; there is no great contrast between thin and thick strokes; the serifs are bracketed; the serifs of the ascenders in the lower case are oblique. *Note.* This was formerly known as "Venetian", having been derived from the fifteenth-century minuscule written with a varying stroke thickness by means of an obliquely-held broad pen.	Verona Centaur Kennerley
II	Garalde	Type faces in which the axis of the curves is inclined to the left; there is generally a greater contrast in the relative thickness of the strokes than in Humanist designs; the serifs are bracketed; the bar of the lower case e is horizontal; the serifs of the ascenders in the lower case are oblique. *Note.* These are types in the Aldine and Garamond tradition and were formerly called "Old Face" and "Old Style".	Bembo Garamond Caslon Vendôme
III	Transitional	Type faces in which the axis of the curves is vertical or inclined slightly to the left; the serifs are bracketed, and those of the ascenders in the lower case are oblique. *Note.* Influenced by the letter-forms of the copperplate engraver. It may be regarded as a transition from Garalde to Didone, and incorporates some characteristics of each.	Fournier Baskerville Bell Caledonia Columbia

IV	Didone	Type faces having an abrupt contrast between thin and thick strokes; the axis of the curves is vertical; the serifs of the ascenders of the lower case are horizontal; there are often no brackets to the serifs. *Note.* These are type faces as developed by Didot and Bodoni. Formerly called "Modern".	Bodoni Corvinus Modern Ex- tended
V	Slab-serif	Type faces with heavy, square-ended serifs, with or without brackets.	Rockwell Clarendon Playbill
VI	Lineale	Type faces without serifs. *Note.* Formerly called "Sans-serif".	
	a Grotesque	Lineale type faces with nineteenth-century origins. There is some contrast in thickness of strokes. They have squareness of curve, and curling close-set jaws. The R usually has a curled leg and the G is spurred. The ends of the curved strokes are usually horizontal.	SB Grotesque No. 6 Condensed Sans No 7 Headline
	b Neo-grotesque	Lineale type faces derived from the grotesque. They have less stroke contrast and are more regular in design. The jaws are more open than in the true grotesque and the g is often open-tailed. The ends of the curved strokes are usually oblique.	Edel/Wotan Univers Helvetica
	c Geometric	Lineale type faces constructed on simple geometric shapes, circle or rectangle. Usually monoline, and often with single-storey a.	Futura Erbar Eurostyle
	d Humanist	Lineale type faces based on the proportions of inscriptional Roman capitals and Humanist or Garalde lower case, rather than on early grotesques. They have some stroke contrast, with two-storey a and g.	Optima Gill Sans Pascal
VII	Glyphic	Type faces which are chiselled rather than calligraphic in form.	Latin Albertus Augustea
VIII	Script	Type faces that imitate cursive writing.	Palace Script Legend Mistral
IX	Graphic	Type faces whose characters suggest that they have been drawn rather than written.	Libra Cartoon Old English

Note. The impossibility of placing every type face into one of the categories above is recognized. In cases of difficulty the use of a compound term, e.g. Humanist/Garalde, is suggested.

Extracts from British Standards 2961:1967, on which the classification of type faces in this edition of *The Encyclopaedia of Type Faces* is based.

ROMAN TYPES

THERE ARE THREE PRINCIPAL FEATURES of the roman face which were gradually modified in the three centuries from JENSON to BODONI. In the earliest romans, copied as we have pointed out, from contemporary humanistic manuscripts, the serifs were inclined and bracketed, that is to say, the underpart of the serif was connected to the stem in a curve or by a triangular piece. On the upper case the serifs were often thick slabs extending to both sides of the uprights. In the typical modern face serifs are thin, flat and unbracketed. In between the two extremes various gradations are found. In all early romans the incidence of colour or stress is diagonal, while in the modern face it is vertical. If an O is drawn with a broad-nibbed pen held at an angle to the paper, the two thickest parts of the letter will be diagonally opposite. This was the manner in which the calligraphers of the fifteenth century drew an O; but by the year 1700 the writing masters, whose work was being reproduced on copper-engraved plates, had adopted the method of holding the pen at right angles to the paper, thus producing a vertical stress. The engravers of type who developed the modern face were adapting to typography a style already prevalent among the engravers. The third point in which the design was modified was in the amount of variation between the thick and thin strokes, and in the degree of abruptness of the variation. In the fifteenth century the stress was slight and gradual, in the nineteenth it was extreme and abrupt.

An inline with upper and lower case in which the left strokes are accentuated. In **A, M, N** and **U** the upstrokes are fine and not inline. All letters are condensed and somewhat angular. The serifs are flat.

ACROPOLIS
L. Wagner 1940

iv

Das neue Modeheft REISE NACH ATHEN

ACROPOLIS

Designed by H. Thannhaeuser. An inline sloped roman with minute serifs. The line passes right through the vertical strokes. There is also a set of swash capitals.

ADASTRA
Stempel 1928

ix

Streamers DHER

ADASTRA

ABCDEFGHIJKLM
NOPQRSTUVWXYZ

ADASTRA SWASH CAPITALS

ix

1

AETERNA
or JOST
MEDIAEVAL

Ludwig & Mayer 1927;

Intertype (Berlin)

Designed by Heinrich Jost. Mediaeval in German is used with much the same meaning as our Venetian. The type is of rich colour, has small serifs and short descenders. The capitals vary in width, **E**, **F** and **L** being narrow, corresponding with some well-known Roman inscriptions, *e.g.*, those of the Trajan column. There are two **M**'s and **N**'s, one having no top serifs. **U** has the lower-case design and **W** no middle serif. **e** has the Venetian form, the **g** an odd rectangular ear. The dot on the **i** is diamond-shaped. The italic has capitals consistent with the roman; the inclination is very slight and in the lower case some letters are upright. It is rather like a GOUDY italic. There is also an italic and a bold. AETERNA, as the type is now called, is a slightly revised version.

i

ABCDEFGHIJKLMNOPQRSTUVW
XYZ
abcdefghijklmnopqrstuvwxyz
1234567890

AETERNA ROMAN

i

ABCDEFGHIJKLMNOPQRSTUVW
XYZ
abcdefghijklmnopqrstuvwxyz
1234567890

AETERNA ITALIC

i

ABCDEFGHIJKLMNOPQRSTU
VWXYZ
abcdefghijklmnopqrstuvwxyz
1234567890

AETERNA BOLD

ALBERTINA

Monotype 1965

Designed by Chris Brand. This face is available only as Monophoto matrices, and it was first used for a catalogue of the work of Stanley Morison which was exhibited at the Albertina Library, Brussels, in 1966.

ii

ABCDEFGHIJKLMNOPQRSTUVWXYZ
abcdefghijklmnopqrstuvwxyz
1234567890

ii

ABCDEFGHIJKLMNOPQRSTUVWXYZ
abcdefghijklmnopqrstuvwxyz
1234567890

ALBERTINA

Designed by Berthold Wolpe. A display roman which has thickened terminals rather than serifs. In the M the middle strokes descend only half-way. There is also a second M and two Ws. U has the lower-case design. In the lower case ascenders and descenders are short. The e has a large eye and the g a large bowl. There is no italic. The figures are short-ranging. There is also Albertus Light, a normal weight, and a Bold Titling.

ABCDEFGHIJKLMNOPQRSTUVWXY
abcdefghijklmnopqrstuvwxyz
1234567890
ALBERTUS LIGHT

ABCDEFGHIJKLMNOPQRSTUVWXY
abcdefghijklmnopqrstuvwxyz
1234567890
ALBERTUS

ABCDEFGHIJKLMNOPQRSTUVWXYZ
1234567890
ALBERTUS BOLD

ABCDEFGHIJKLMNOPQRSTU
VWXYZ 1234567890
ALBERTUS TITLING

Letters have a strong vertical stress and are available in five different versions, including an extended one.

ABCDEFGHIJKLMNOPQRSTUVWXYZ
abcdefghijklmnopqrstuvwxyz
1234567890
ALBION

ABCDEFGHIJKLMNOPQRSTUVWXYZ
abcdefghijklmnopqrstuvwxyz
1234567890
ALBION BOLD

ALDUS

Stempel 1954;
Linotype (Frankfurt)

Designed by Hermann Zapf. A roman of old-face design. Serifs are small and only slightly inclined. The **Q** has an external tail. In the lower-case the **g** is particularly good. In the italic the upper case (except **U**) is the roman slightly inclined, but not the lower case.

ii

ABCDEFGHIJKLMNOPQRSTUVWXYZ

abcdefghijklmnopqrstuvwxyz

1234567890

ABCDEFGHIJKLMNOPQRSTUVWXYZ

abcdefghijklmnopqrstuvwxyz

ALDUS

ii

ABCDEFGHIJKLMNOPQRSTUVWXYZ

abcdefghijklmnopqrstuvwxyz

1234567890

ABCDEFGHIJKLMNOPQRSTUVWXYZ

abcdefghijklmnopqrstuvwxyz

1234567890

ALDUS BOOK

ALFRODITA

Nacional

A set of shaded capitals with very small serifs. The shading is formed by four parallel lines.

ix

ABCDEFGHIJKLMNOPQRSTUVWXYZ

ALFRODITA

ALLEGRO

Ludwig & Mayer 1936

Designed by Hans Bohn. A fat face italic of very slight inclination. The bulbous terminals of arcs, as in **a** and **r**, are much in evidence. Most of the bowls are not quite closed.

ix

ABCDEFGHIJKLMNOPQRSTUVWXYZ

abcdefghijklmnopqrstuvwxyz

1234567890

ALLEGRO

Designed by K.F. Bauer and Walter Baum. An italic of heavy weight and almost monotone. The serifs are stubby. There are two lower cases, hence the two names. The first is an inclined roman and the second a script of the brush variety. Ascenders and descenders are generous, more especially in the script.

ALPHA
AND BETA
Bauer 1954

ABCDEFGHIJKLMNOPQRSTUVWXYZ   ix

ALPHA CAPS

abcdefghijklmnopqrstuvwxyz   ix

ALPHA LOWER CASE

abcdefghijklmnopqrstuvwxyz   ix

1234567890

BETA

A modern face with some modifications. The A has an oblique top, **G** a small spur and the **R** is more like OLD FACE. In the bracketing of the serifs and the size of the eye of the **e** it resembles SCOTCH ROMAN.

ALT LATEIN
Schelter & Giesecke 1924

Games and Sports   iv

Buntpapierindustrie und Export
Die Buntpapierfabrikation, eines von den vielerlei
Spezialgebieten in der Papierveredelung, kann auf

ALT LATEIN

Designed by Georg Trump. A very narrow type with short ascenders and descenders, and fine serifs. Rounded letters are slightly angular. The upper curve of the **c** ends in a dot, and the top of the **t** is finely tapered. The dot on the **i** is somewhat elongated. The serifs on the cross beam of the **T** are wedge shaped, and the **A** has a horizontal serif on the top.

AMATI
Weber 1951

ABCDEFGHIJKLMNOPQRSTUVWXYZ   iv

abcdefghijklmnopqrstuvwxyz

1234567890

HOWARD YOUNG GALLERIES

AMATI

Designed by Richard Isbell. Serifs are short and the type is exceptional for its large x-height. Vertical strokes taper to the base and serifs are short.

ABCDEFGHIJKL MNOPQRSTUV WXYZ

abcdefghijklmn opqrstuvwxyz

$£1234567890

AMERICANA

ABCDEFGHIJK LMNOPQRSTU VWXYZ

abcde fghijklmnopqrstuvwxyz

1234567890 $$¢£%,.:------·()[]? ?!""""&*

AMERICANA ITALIC

A roman with small serifs, inclined in the lower case. The round capitals—**C, G, O** and **Q**—are wide. In the **M** the middle strokes stop short of the line.

ABCDEFGHIJKLMNOPQRSTUVWXYZ
abcdefghijklmnopqrstuvwxyz   1234567890
ABCDEFGHIJKLMNOPQRSTUVWXYZ
abcdefghijklmnopqrstuvwxyz   1234567890

ANCIEN

Designed by John Peters as a 4½ pt type face for Bible composition.

When jobs have type sizes fixed quickly margins of error widen unless determining calculations are based on factual rather than hypothetical figures. No variation in the amount of copy can affect the degree of error once that error has been made. If instead of ten point the estimator specifies nine point for the type size whether When jobs have type sizes fixed quickly margins of error widen unless determining calculations are based on factual rather than hypothetical figures. No variation in the amount of copy can affect the degree of error once that error has been made. If instead of ten point the estimator specifies nine point for the type

ANGELUS

Designed by Arno Drescher. This roman, which is very similar to CANDIDA, has little variation of stress. The lower case is wide with short ascenders and descenders. EGYPTIAN 505 is similar.

ABCDEFGHIKLMNOPQRSTUVWXY ZÄÖÜÇÆŒ abcdefghijklmnopqrsſtuv wxyz äöüchckßʒàéîòúçæœ 1234567890

iv/v

ABCDEFGHIJKLMNOPQRS TUVWXYZ abcdefghijklmnopqrstuvwxyz 1234567890

ANTIQUA 505

ABCDEFGHIJKLMNOPQRST UVWXYZ abcdefghijklmnopqrstuvwxyz 1234567890

iv/v

ANTIQUA 505 BOLD

ABCDEFGHIJKLMNOPQRS TUVWXYZ abcdefghijklmnopqrstuvwxyz 1234567890

iv/v

ANTIQUA 505 BOLD CONDENSED

ABCDEFGHIJKLMNOPQ RSTUVWXYZ abcdefghijklmnopqrst uvwxyz 1234567890

iv/v

ANTIQUA 505 EXTRA BOLD

ANTIQUES
Stevens Shanks c. 1860

Antique was one of the early names for an Egyptian. NO. 3 is a Clarendon and a revival of an early design; and No. 5 is a lighter face of the same basic design. No. 6 is a fat Egyptian, also in the English style and, like ANTIQUE No. 3, was taken over from the foundry of V. & J. Figgins.

v

ABCDEFGHIJKLMNOPQRSTUVWXYZ
abcdefghijklmnopqrstuvwxyz
1234567890

ANTIQUE No. 3

v

ABCDEFGHIJKLMNOPQRSTUVWXYZ
abcdefghijklmnopqrstuvwxyz

ANTIQUE No. 5

v

ABCDEFGHIJKLMNOPQRS
TUVWXYZÆŒ
abcdefghijklmnopqrstuvwxyz
ffifflfiffflfiœæ£
1234567890

ANTIQUE No. 6

i

ABCDEFGHIJKLMNOPQRSTUVWXYZ
abcdefghijklmnopqrstuvwxyz
1234567890

ABCDEFGHIJKLMNOPQRSTUVWXYZ
abcdefghijklmnopqrstuvwxyz
1234567890

ANTIQUE OLD STYLE

Designed by Adrian Frutiger. This is the first new type face to be designed specifically for Monophoto filmsetters. One set of matrices covers the entire composition range from 6 to 24 pt. The weight is sufficiently heavy to produce a good impression when printed by photolithography on smooth papers, while at the same time light enough to contrast with the semi-bold version.

ABCDEFGHIJKLMNOPQRSTUVWXYZ

abcdefghijklmnopqrstuvwxyz

1234567890

ABCDEFGHIJKLMNOPQRSTUVWXYZ

abcdefghijklmnopqrstuvwxyz

1234567890

APOLLO

ABCDEFGHIJKLMNOPQRSTUVWXYZ

abcdefghijklmnopqrstuvwxyz

1234567890

APOLLO BOLD

Designed by G.G. Lange. A condensed roman of medium weight with short ascenders and descenders. The serifs are small, oblique and pointed. Numerals range on the line. There are two weights and an italic.

ABCDEFGHIJKLMNOPQRSTUVWXYZ

abcdefghijklmnopqrstuvwxyz

1234567890

ABCDEFGHIJKLMNOPQRSTUVWXYZ

abcdefghijklmnopqrstuvwxyz

1234567890

ARENA

ABCDEFGHIJKLMNOPQRSTUVWXYZÆŒ

abcdefghijklmnopqrstuvwxyz

ARMSTRONG

ABCDEFGHIJKLMNOPQRSTUVWXYZÆŒ

abcdefghijklmnopqrstuvwxyz

ARMSTRONG BOLD

Designed by Otto Arpke. A modified fat face, with thin horizontal serifs. It is more nearly monotone than some designs in this group. The vertical strokes are wedge-shaped, being thinner at the feet. There are no serifs at the top of the **M**, nor on the middle strokes of **W**. In the lower case unconnected strokes are terminated by a thin serif, *e.g.*, the arc of the **a** and the terminals of **e, g** and **t**. There is also a light face and a shaded version.

ix

Edita Horák Praha ZEICHNUNG

ARPKE ANTIQUA

This italic cut for hand composition in 1925 by Plumet in Paris, was designed by Frederic Warde to accompany the Monotype Corporation's CENTAUR, resembles BLADO, but the capitals are narrower and in the lower case the serifs on the ascenders are flat. Warde had already designed as a private face an italic based on an earlier Chancery type of Arrighi, in which the ascenders have calligraphic terminals and with a number of swash varieties.

viii

ABCDEFGHIJKLMNOPQRSTUVWXYZ&
abcdefghijklmnopqrstuvwxyz 1234567890

ARRIGHI ITALIC OR CENTAUR ITALIC

Designed originally for Barnhart Bros. & Spindler by Robert Wiebking. A display roman with heavy, blunt serifs. The lower case is conspicuous for some freakish forms. The arc of the **a** extends beyond the bowl and the **g** has an ear rising out of the top of the bowl and curling backwards. The tail is wider than the bowl. There is an italic and a bold.

ix

Dainty or Lace-like
The Charming Face

ARTCRAFT

Non-Distribution

ARTCRAFT BOLD

Designed by Ashley Havinden. A series of heavy monotone capitals, with very small serifs. The feet of the **A, M** and **Y**, and the tail of the **R** are cut off obliquely. The **M** is pointed at the top and splayed. The **S** is tilted over to the right. There is also a series of ranging figures.

ix

ABCDEFGHIJKLMNOPQRSTU
VWXYZ& 1234567890

ASHLEY CRAWFORD

ix

ABCDEFGHIJKLMNOPQRST
UVWXYZ& 1234567890

ASHLEY CRAWFORD PLAIN

Designed by Francesco Simoncini. A text type designed for book and newspaper work, with clear variation of stress, and a finely cut character.

ABCDEFGHIJKLMNOPQRSTUVWXYZ

abcdefghijklmnopqrstuvwxyz

1234567890

ABCDEFGHIJKLMNOPQRSTUVWXYZ

abcdefghijklmnopqrstuvwxyz

1234567890

ABCDEFGHIJKLMNOPQRSTUVWXYZ

ASTER

ii

ABCDEFGHIJKLMNOPQRSTUVWXYZ

abcdefghijklmnopqrstuvwxyz

1234567890

ASTER BOLD

ii

Designed by Robert Girard. A re-cutting of a baroque face. The bowl of the **P** is not closed, the **G** has no spur, and the tail of the **R** descends below the line. The spur of the lower-case **r** is slightly higher than other lower-case letters. There is an italic, and also special initials. Known as MAZARIN by Stephenson & Blake.

ii

ABCDEFGHI   *ABCD EFGH*

peuples qui firent   *Peuples, quelle ne*

ASTREE OR MAZARIN

Designed by A. Butti, with initials by A. Novarese. A roman with small flat serifs and little variation of stress. **K** and **R** have curved tails. The **M** is splayed. The **C**, **G** and **Q** are almost script forms. The top of the ascenders are thickened. The distinguishing letter is a freak **g** which ends on the line. The figures are short ranging. The italic has serifs slightly inclined. There is also a bold face.

ABCDEFGHIJKLMNOPQRSTUVWXYZ

Œabcdeghijklmnopqrstuvwxyz

1234567890

ABCDEFGHIJKLMNOPQRSTUVWXYZ

Œabcdefghijklmnopqrstuvwxyz

1234567890

ix

ATHENAEUM

ABCDEFGHIJKLMNOPQRSTUVWXYZ

abcdefghijklmnopqrstuvwxyz

1234567890

ATHENAEUM BOLD

ix

ATLANTIC 35
Lanston Monotype 1909–35

A type face first used by the *Atlantic Monthly* in 1909, and based on SCOTCH ROMAN, though the lower case is taller.

iv

ABCDEFGHIJKLMNOPQRSTUVWXYZ&ÆŒ
abcdefghijklmnopqrstuvwxyzæœ   fiflffffiffl $1234567890
ABCDEFGHIJKLMNOPQRSTUVWXYZ&ÆŒ
ABCDEFGHIJKLMNOPQRSTUVWXYZ&ÆŒ
abcdefghijklmnopqrstuvwxyzæœ   fiflffffiffl $1234567890

ATLANTIC 35

ATRAX
Bauer 1926

Designed by Heinrich Jost. Shaded bold roman capitals. The shading passes through the vertical strokes. There are also ranging figures.

ix

NEW YORK RANGERS

ATRAX

AUGUSTEA
Berthold 1905–25

A modern face roman with short ascenders and descenders. The italic has the serifs of the roman. There are two heavier weights. It has no resemblance to the Nebiolo foundry's capitals bearing this name, shown elsewhere. *Cf.* CENTURY.

iv

ABCDEFGHIJKLMNOPQRSTUVWXYZ
abcdefghijklmnopqrstuvwxyz   1234567890

ABCDEFGHIJKLMNOPQRSTUVWXYZ
abcdefghijklmnopqrstuvwxyz

AUGUSTEA LIGHT

iv

ABCDEFGHIJKLMNOPQRSTUVWXYZ
abcdefghijklmnopqrstuvwxyz

AUGUSTEA MEDIUM

iv

ABCDEFGHIJKLMNOPQRSTUVWX
abcdefghijklmnopqrstuvwxyz

AUGUSTEA BOLD

AUGUSTEA
Nebiolo 1951

Designed by A. Butti and A. Novarese. A set of inscriptional capitals and short-ranging figures. The **M**, which is splayed, has no top serifs. **W** has no middle serif.

vii

ABCDEFGHIJKLMNOPQRST
UVXYZWÇÆŒ   1234567890

AUGUSTEA

ABCDEFGHIJKLMNOPQR STUVXYZW 1234567890

AUGUSTEA OPEN

ABCDEFGHIJKLMNOPQRSTUV XYZW
abcdefghijklmnopqrstuvxyzw 1234567890

NOVA AUGUSTEA

Designed by Matthew Carter for phototypesetting and easy enlargement and reduction.

ABCDEFGHIJKLMNOPQRSTUVWXYZ
abcdefghijklmnopqrstuvwxyz   1234567890
ABCDEFGHIJKLMNOPQRSTUVWXYZ
abcdefghijklmnopqrstuvwxyz   1234567890

AURIGA

Designed by Georges Auriol. A calligraphic type with short ascenders and descenders. The pen-drawn qualities are very evident in the upper case. There are white gaps in some strokes. The **M** is curiously designed.

les feuilles éparpillées   1234567890
ABCDEFGHIJKLMNOPQR

AURIOL

Designed by Jackson Burke. This newspaper face was introduced primarily to meet the improved specifications adopted by Canadian news agencies for teletypesetter composition. AURORA of the Weber foundry is quite different and the same as NORMAL GROTESQUE.

ABCDEFGHIJKLMNOPQRSTUVWXYZ

abcdefghijklmnopqrstuvwxyz

1234567890

When it is considered that it was the intention to make the book one of practical instruction, and that it was written with the hope that it might be placed in the hands of each printer's boy on entering the business, I trust this sin of inelegance may [from Savage's Dictionary

AURORA

AUSTIN'S PICA No. 1

Austin c. 1819

iv

Designed and cut by Richard Austin for his own foundry and one of the earliest "modern" faces in Britain.

ABCDEFGHIJKLMNOPQRSTUVWXYZ
ABCDEFGHIJKLMNOPQRSTUVWXYZ
ABCDEFGHIJKLMNOPQRSTUVWXYZ
1234567890

*ABCDEFGHIJKLMNOPQRSTUV
WXYZÆŒ*
*ABCDEFGHIJKLMNOPQRST
UVWXYZÆŒ*

AUSTIN'S PICA NO. 1

BALLÉ INITIALS

Bauer

ix

Designed by Maria Ballé. A series of light, decorated initials, in which the main down strokes are inline.

BALLÉ INITIALS

P. T. BARNUM

American Typefounders

ix

A reversed Egyptian, that is with serifs thicker than the main strokes. In fact the heavy strokes are all in the wrong places. Such types were originally called Italian or French Antique. Barnhart Brothers & Spindler originally issued this type in the nineteenth century and called it FRENCH CLARENDON.

LOR Zero is the figure

P. T. BARNUM

BARBOU

Monotype 1925

iii

Based on one of the first transitional types of the eighteenth-century Paris founder, P.S. Fournier, to provide a bookish type which was narrow without being condensed. A 14-pt size was cut by The Monotype Corporation at the same time as the cutting of the better known FOURNIER, and this was used in several volumes of *The Flenron*, but it was not until 1959 that a 12 pt size was made available for the printing of *The Papers of Benjamin Franklin* by the Lakeside Press, Chicago. Additional smaller sizes have been added to the range.

ABCDEFGHIJKLMNOPQRSTUVWXYZ

abcdefghijklmnopqrstuvwxyz

1234567890

ABCDEFGHIJKLMNOPQRSTUVWXYZ

abcdefghijklmnopqrstuvwxyz

1234567890

BARBOU

Presumably a revival of a nineteenth century design. Capitals only, equal in width. The serifs, which are triangular, resemble those in the design known as LATIN FACE. The inclined version is called BARONESS.

SWAINE AND ADENEY
BARON

REGISTERED INSURANCE COM
BARONESS

The original punches of the types cut by John Baskerville of Birmingham are still in existence. They were sold by Baskerville's widow to Beaumarchais and have descended through various French foundries to Deberny & Peignot. Some of this material survives and is now at the Cambridge University Press. The story has been told by John Dreyfus. Baskerville is a round letter and appears to us to differ little from the old faces, but if compared in detail with CASLON it will be seen why we call it the first of the transitional romans in this country. There is more differentiation of thick and thin strokes, the serifs on lower-case letters are more nearly horizontal and the stress nearer the vertical. The **R** in some sizes has the eighteenth-century curled tail. The **W**, lower-case also, has no middle serif. In the **g** the tail is not closed, and the ear is curled. The

Amongst the feveral mechanic Arts that have engaged my attention, there is no one which I have purfued with fo much fteadinefs and pleafure, as that of Letter-Founding. Having been an early admirer of the beauty of Letters, I became infenfibly defirous of contributing to the perfection of them. I formed to my felf Ideas of greater accuracy than had yet appeared, and have endeavoured to produce a Sett of Types according to what I conceived to be their true proportion.

ABCDEFGHIJKLMNOPQRSTUVWXYZ Æ &
abcdefghijklmnopqrstuvwxyz .,;:!?--—()[] æ fi ff fl ffi ffl
£1234567890 * § ft & f fl « » Qu

ABCDEFGHIJKLMNOPQRSTUVWXYZ
abcdefghijklmnopqrstuvwxyz & 1234567890

ABCDEFGHIJKLMNOPQRSTUVWXYZ
abcdefghijklmnopqrstuvwxyz & 1234567890

DEBERNY & PEIGNOT BASKERVILLE

ABCDEFGHIJKLMNOPQRSTUVWXYZ
abcdefghijklmnopqrstuvwxyz
1234567890

ABCDEFGHIJKLMNOPQRSTUVWXYZ
abcdefghijklmnopqrstuvwxyz
1234567890

MONOTYPE BASKERVILLE

iii

ABCDEFGHIJKLMNOPQRSTU
abcdefghijklmnopqrstuvwxyz 12

MONOTYPE BASKERVILLE BOLD

iii

ABCDEFGHIJKLMNOPQRSTU
VWXYZ
abcdefghijklmnopqrstuvwxyz
1234567890

**ABCDEFGHIJKLMNOPQRSTU
VWXYZ
abcdefghijklmnopqrstuvwxyz
1234567890**

*ABCDEFGHIJKLMNOPQRSTU
VWXYZ
abcdefghijklmnopqrstuvwxyz
1234567890*

ABCDEFGHIJKLMNOPQRSTUVWXYZ &&£

INTERTYPE BASKERVILLE

iii

ABCDEFGHIJKLMNOPQRSTUVWXYZ
abcdefghijklmnopqrstuvwxyz
1234567890

BASKERVILLE SEMI BOLD

iii

ABCDEFGHIJKLMNOPQRSTUVWXYZ
abcdefghijklmnopqrstuvwxyz
1234567890

*ABCDEFGHIJKLMNOPQRSTUVWXYZ
abcdefghijklmnopqrstuvwxyz
1234567890*

ABCDEFGHIJKLMNOPQRSTUVWXYZ
1234567890

*ABCDEFGHIJKLMNOPQRSTUVWXYZ
1234567890*

ABCDEFGHIJKLMNOPQRSTUVWXYZ
Recut Italic: abcdefghijklmnopqrstuvwxyz

LINOTYPE BASKERVILLE

iii

ABCDEFGHIJKLMNOPQRSTUVWXYZ
abcdefghijklmnopqrstuvwxyz
1234567890
*ABCDEFGHIJKLMNOPQRSTUVWXYZ
abcdefghijklmnopqrstuvwxyz
1234567890*

LINOTYPE BASKERVILLE BOLD

ABCDEFGHIJKLMNOPQRSTUVWXYZ
abcdefghijklmnopqrstuvwxyz
1234567890

ABCDEFGHIJKLMNOPQRSTUVWXYZ
abcdefghijklmnopqrstuvwxyz
1234567890

ATF TYPESETTER BASKERVILLE

ABCDEFGHIJKLMNOPQRSTUVWXYZ
abcdefghijklmnopqrstuvwxyz
1234567890

ATF TYPESETTER BASKERVILLE BOLD

ABCDEFGHIJKLMNOPQRS
abcdefghijklmnopqrstuvwxyz
1234567890

STEMPEL BASKERVILLE MEDIUM

ABCDEFGHIJKLMNOPQRSTU
abcdefghijklmnopqrstuvwxyz
1234567890

ABCDEFGHIJKLMNOPQRSTU
abcdefghijklmnopqrstuvwxyz
1234567890

STEMPEL BASKERVILLE

BASLE ROMAN (HOWARD'S)
Chiswick Press

A design based on the sort of roman used at Basle and in Germany in the first half of the sixteenth century. It was cut by William Howard, a minor founder in Great Queen St. and first used in 1854. It belongs by its weight and distribution of colour to the Venetians rather than the Old Faces. There is a Venetian e and the long s is used. William Morris selected the type for the printing of two of his books in 1889, just before he started his own press. Morris however dropped the long s and had a new e cut. The matrices have now been deposited on permanent loan to the St. Bride Printing Library.

This Small Pica BASLE ROMAN was specially cut for Charles Whittingham in the early nineteenth century by William Howard, who had a Typefoundry in Great Queen Street, London. The Chiswick Press still possess the original punches and matrices, from which this Specimen has been cast.

A B C D E F G H I J K L M N O P Q R S T U V W X Y Z Æ Œ
a b c d e e f g h i j k l m n o p q r s t u v w x y z æ œ ſſ[(?!':;,-.

BASLE ROMAN

BAYER TYPE
Berthold 1935
iv

Designed by Herbert Bayer. A condensed type with short descenders.

HERBERT STEGEMANN GELSENKIRCHEN
Musik-Instrumente jeder Art kauft man am
besten und billigsten nur beim Fachmann
BAYER LIGHT

iv

PRESSEFOTO SCHERL BERLIN LEIPZIG
Wiesbaden pflegt Mode und Gesellschaft
HELSINGBORGS DAGBLAD
Studentkurser i Engelska och Latin
167890
BAYER MEDIUM

iv

STEINGUT IN NEUEN MUSTERN
Kristalle zu ermäßigten Preisen
BAYER BOLD

**BEHRENS
ROMAN**
Klingspor c. 1900
ix

Designed by Peter Behrens. A pen-drawn roman.

ABCDEFGHIJKLMNOPQ
RSTUDWXY3
abcdefghijklmnopqrſßst
uvwxyz
1234567890
ABCDEFGHIJKLMNOPQRSTUDWXY3
abcdefghijklmnopqrſßstuvwxyz
1234567890
BEHRENS

BELINDA
Nacional
ix

The design is based on fifteenth-century Spanish calligraphic writings. Descenders are very short and ascenders high. The terminals of ascenders have fine, curved serifs; and the main strokes are heavy. There are also special decorative initials.

Por el ideal se identifica la desigualdad. Así lo dem
BELINDA

Stanley Morison has called this the first of our modern faces. It was cut by Richard Austin for Bell's British Foundry, and was influenced by Firmin Didot's new roman. We place it here with the eighteenth century types because of its date and because in one way it stands apart from the usual modern face. It has the flat serifs and vertical stress, but the stress is much less abrupt. The serifs are bracketed and sharply cut. There are two **J**'s, one short-ranging, two **K**'s, two **R**'s, one with a curved tail, and two **Q**'s, one with the tail starting inside the counter. The **e** has a large eye, and there are two **t**'s, one modern. The italic is commended for its harmony with the roman, with its wider letters. There are swash varieties of **A, J, N, Q, T** and **V**, and a swash **Y**. See S. Morison's *John Bell* for the interesting history of the type and specimen books. The Monotype Corporation's version dates from 1932.

ABCDEFGHIJKLMNOPQRSTUVWXYZ

abcdefghijklmnopqrstuvwxyz

ABCDEFGHIJKLMNOPQRSTUVWXYZ

abcdefghijklmnopqrstuvwyz

MONOTYPE BELL OR JOHN BELL

iv

Designed by Georg Belwe. The type has old-face qualities, but short ascenders and very short descenders. Serifs are small, bracketed and oblique on the lower case. **A** has a slab serif, the **H, M, N** and **T** are narrow. In **M** the middle strokes stop half-way. **P** and **R** have deep bowls and **U** the lower case design. In the lower case **a** has a large bowl, the **g** a large bowl with the ear pointing north-east and the tail diminutive; **p** and **q** have no foot serifs, **t** is narrow and the bar unbracketed, and **v** is closed at the top. The italic is slightly inclined. On the lower case the serifs are as the roman except **h** and **k**, which have curved terminals. The figures are short-ranging. There are also Medium Bold, Bold and an Inline.

ABCDEFGHIJKLMNOPQRSTUVWXY

abcdefghijklmnopqrſstuvwxyz

1234567890

ABCDEFGHIJKLMNOPQRSTUVWXY

abcdefghijklmnopqrſstuvwxyz

BELWE ROMAN

ix

ABCDEFGHIJKLMNOPQRSTUVWXY

abcdefghijklmnopqrſstuvwxyz

BELWE MEDIUM BOLD

ix

ABCDEFGHIJKLMNOPQRSTUVWXY

abcdefghijklmnopqrſstuvwxyz

1234567890

BELWE BOLD

ix

ABCDEFGHIJKLMNOPQRSTUVWXY

abcdefghijklmnopqrſstuvwxyz

1234567890

BELWE BOLD

ABCDEFGHIJKLMNOPQRSTUVWXY

1234567890

BELWE INLINE

ix

19

BEMBO

Monotype 1929

The first of the Old Faces is a copy of a roman cut by Francesco Griffo for the Venetian printer Aldus Manutius. It was first used in Cardinal Bembo's *De Aetna*, 1495, hence the name of the contemporary version. Although a type cut in the fifteenth century for a Venetian printer we group it with the Old Faces. Stanley Morison has shown that it was the model followed by Garamond and thus the forerunner of the standard European type of the next two centuries. The capitals are shorter than the ascending letters of the lower case, the serifs are slighter than in earlier romans and there are no slab serifs. The serifs on the **T** are divergent. In the lower case the **e** has a horizontal straight to the eye. The **h** has not the curved shank. There is also a TITLING and BEMBO CONDENSED ITALIC (designed by Alfred Fairbank). The bold italic was added in 1959.

ii

ABCDEFGHIJKLMNOPQRSTUVWXYZ
abcdefghijklmnopqrstuvwxyz
1234567890
ABCDEFGHIJKLMNOPQRSTUVWXYZ
abcdefghijklmnopqrstuvwxyz
1234567890

BEMBO

ii

ABCDEFGHIJKLMNOPQRSTUVWXYZ&

abcdefghijklmnopqrstuvwxyz 1234567890

BEMBO CONDENSED ITALIC

ii

ABCDEFGHIJKLMNOPQRSTU
VWXYZ

BEMBO TITLING

ii

ABCDEFGHIJKLMNOPQRSTUVWXYZ
abcdefghijklmnopqrstuvwxyz
1234567890
ABCDEFGHIJKLMNOPQRSTUVWXYZ
abcdefghijklmnopqrstuvwxyz 1234567890

BEMBO BOLD

BERLIN

Intertype (Berlin) 1962

iv

A newspaper type with accentuated centres and serifs, available in two weights.

ABCDEFGHIJKLMNOPQRSTUVWXYZ
abcdefghijklmnopqrstuvwxyz
1234567890
ABCDEFGHIJKLMNOPQRSTUVWXYZ
abcdefghijklmnopqrstuvwxyz
1234567890

BERLIN

iv

ABCDEFGHIJKLMNOPQRSTUVWXYZ
abcdefghijklmnopqrstuvwxyz
1234567890

BERLIN BOLD

Designed by K. E. Forsberg. A roman with the characteristics of an old face. The serifs are inclined and blunt. The **g** has a straight ear. There is also a bold version.

ABCDEFGHIJKLMNOPQRSTUVW XYZÄÖ

abcdefghijklmnopqrstuvwxyzåäö

ABCDEFGHIJKLMNOPQRSTUV WXYZÅÄÖ

abcdefghijklmnopqrstuvwxyzåäö

BERLING

ABCDEFGHIJKLMNOPQRSTUV WXYZÅÄÖ

abcdefghijklmnopqrstuvwxyzåäö

BERLING BOLD

ABCDEFGHIJKLMNOPQRSTUVWXYZ

abcdefghijklmnopqrstuvwxyz

1234567890

ABCDEFGHIJKLMNOPQRSTUVWXYZ

abcdefghijklmnopqrstuvwxyz

1234567890

BERLING MONOTYPE

ABCDEFGHIJKLMNOPQRSTUVWXYZ

abcdefghijklmnopqrstuvwxyz

1234567890

BERLING MONOTYPE SEMI-BOLD

Designed by Albert Augspurg and originally a German type. A set of open capitals, slightly inclined and with hair lines for the thin strokes.

ABCDEFGHIJKLMNOPQRSTU VWXYZÅÄÖ

BERLING KORTVERSALER

ii

ii

ii

ii

21

Berthold and Bauer and Berthold have BERNHARD types on which this face appears to be modelled.

ABCDEFGHIJKLMNOPQRSTUVWXYZ
abcdefghijklmnopqrstuvwxyz
1234567890

BERNARD CONDENSED

Designed by Lucian Bernhard as a text and display type. Among distinguishing marks are the cross-over **W**, the open bowl of the **R** and a tilted **O**.

PHILHARMONISCHES KONZERT
Gold- und Silberscheideanstalt

BERNHARD ANTIQUA

HAMBURGER ILLUSTRIERTE
Typographische Vereinigung

BERNHARD ANTIQUA ITALIC

Gewerbe-Museum in Hamburg

BERNHARD ANTIQUA BOLD CONDENSED

WORMSER ZEITUNG
Handel und Verkehr

BERNHARD ANTIQUA EXTRA BOLD

Hotel zu den Drei Raben

BERNHARD ITALIC EXTRA BOLD

Offenbacher Lederwaren
Letzte Pariser Neuheiten

BERNHARD ITALIC BOLD

Designed by Dennis Morgan. An elongated and condensed fat face based on mid-nineteenth century designs. The Alexander Wilson firm showed a type like this in 1843. Named after the elder Bessemer who had a foundry at Hitchin and later in London. *Cf.* SLIMBLACK.

ABCDEFGIJKLMNOPQRSTUVWXYZ
1234567890 £ÆŒ&

BESSEMER

Designed by Heinrich Jost. **A** has a flat top, projecting to the left, **G** has a spur, and the **W** (lower-case also) no middle serif. The **a** has the two-storeyed design, with a serif terminating the arc, **g** has an open tail, **t** is vertical and has an oblique top, and **y** has a foot serif extending to the right.

There is a light face (which seems to contradict the essence of the design), a medium bold, bold and extra bold; also an open, really a three-dimensional letter.

BETON
Bauer 1931–36; Intertype

ABCDEFGHIJKKLMNOPQRRSTUV
WXYZ
abcdefghijklmnopqrstuvwxyz
1234567890

BETON LIGHT

ABCDEFGHIJKKLMNOPQRRSTUV
WXYZ
abcdefghijklmnopqrstuvwxyz
1234567890

BETON MEDIUM

**ABCDEFGHIJKKLMNOPQRRSTUV
WXYZ
abcdefghijklmnopqrstuvwx**

BETON BOLD

**ABCDEFGHIJKKLMNOPQRRS
TUVWXYZ
abcdefghijklmnopqrstuvwxyz
1234567890**

BETON EXTRA BOLD

**ABCDEFGHIJKKLMNOPQRRSTUVWXYZ
abcdefghijklmnopqrstuvwxyz
1234567890**

BETON MEDIUM CONDENSED

23

ABCDEFGHIJKKLMNOPQRRSTUVW XYZ
abcdefghijklmnopqrstuvwxyz
1234567890

BETON BOLD CONDENSED

ABCDEFGHIJKKLMNOP QRRSTUVWXYZ
12345678

BETON OPEN

The type is similar to RONALDSON OLD STYLE, and was first cut in Scotland about 1863.

A B C D E F G H I J K L M N O P Q R S T U V W
X Y Z & Æ Œ

a b c d e f g h i j k l m n o p q r s t u v w x y z
$1234567890£ $1234567890
æ œ fi fl ff ffi ffl   . , - ' : ; ! ?

ABCDEFGHIJKLMNOPQRSTUVWXYZ&ÆŒ
abcdefghijklmnopqrstuvwxyzææ   fifflff fifl ffl
$1234567890   :;!? $1234567890

BINNY OLD STYLE

The italic cut to accompany POLIPHILUS is based on a formal italic of the Roman calligrapher and printer Lodovico degli Arrighi, called Vicentino. It is named after the Roman printer Antonio Blado, who printed many books in this fount, using it as an individual type and not as a subsidiary to roman. In The Monotype Corporation's version the upper case closely resembles the roman and the inclination is slight. In the lower case the beginning strokes are angular and on the tops of ascenders become inclined serifs. The curves of the **v** and **w** are to be noted.

ABCDEFGHIJKLMNOPQRSTUVWXYZ
abcdefghijklmnopqrstuvwxyz
1234567890   &

BLADO ITALIC

Giambattista Bodoni of Parma was one of the most prolific type designers. In his earlier years he copied Fournier but in his later years carried the modern face to its logical conclusion. His serifs are both flat and unbracketed, the stress is mathematically vertical and the thins are hair lines. Bodoni believed in plenty of white space and therefore descenders are long. The **M** is narrow, in the **Q** the tail at first descends vertically and the **R** has a curled tail. In the lower case the **g** has a small bowl (in The Monotype Corporation's version it is not so small as in the original) and the **w**, in this version, no middle serif. The italic, like all continental modern faces, has roman serifs. The eighteenth century medial **v** and **w** may be noted.

There are two basic models in the modern re-cuttings,

I. American Typefounders by M.F. Benton, from 1907 onwards, possibly antedated by Nebiolo's version; copied by The Monotype Corporation (slightly squarer and heavier); and separately (following more closely, but on body) by Haas 1924–1939 (adopted by the Amsterdam Typefoundry, Stempel, Berthold), who also added an extra-bold with italic, and narrow extra-bold. The Linotype (1914–16), Intertype and Ludlow versions are likewise based on this. J. Wagner made a re-cutting in 1961.

II. Bauer. More delicate than the above re-cutting and not adopted by any other foundry or composing machine manufacturer.

ABCDEFGHIJKLMNOPQRSTUVWXYZ
abcdefghijklmnopqrstuvwxyz
1234567890

ABCDEFGHIJKLMNOPQRSTUVWXYZ
abcdefghijklmnopqrstuvwxyz
1234567890

ABCDEFGHIJKLMNOPQRSTUVWXYZ
abcdefghijklmnopqrstuvwxyz
1234567890

ABCDEFGHIJKLMNOPQRSTUVWXYZ
abcdefghijklmnopqrstuvwxyz
1234567890

MONOTYPE BODONI

ABCDEFGHIJKLMNOPQRSTUVWXYZ
abcdefghijklmnopqrstuvwxyz
1234567890

ABCDEFGHIJKLMNOPQRSTUVWXZ
abcdefghijklmnopqrstuvwxyz

MONOTYPE BODONI HEAVY

ABCDEFGHIJKLMNOPQRSTUVWXYZ
abcdefghijklmnopqrstuvwxyz
1234567980

MONOTYPE BODONI BOLD

iv

25

iv

ABCDEFGHIJKLMNOPQRSTUVWXYZ

abcdefghijklmnopqrstuvwxyz

1234567890

ABCDEFGHIJKLMNOPQRSTUVWXYZ

abcdefghijklmnopqrstuvwxyz

1234567890

MONOTYPE BODONI BOLD CONDENSED

iv

ABCDEFGHIJKLMNOPQRSTUVWXYZ&

abcdefghijklmnopqrstuvwxyz

1234567890

MERGENTHALER LINOTYPE BODONI BOLD CONDENSED

iv

ABCDEFGHIJKLMNOPQRSTUVWXYZ

abcdefghijklmnopqrstuvwxyz

ABCDEFGHIJKLMNOPQRSTUVWXYZ

abcdefghijklmnopqrstuvwxyz

HAAS BODONI LIGHT

iv

ABCDEFGHIJKLMNOPQRSTUVWXYZ

abcdefghijklmnopqrstuvwxyz

ABCDEFGHIJKLMNOPQRSTUVWXYZ

abcdefghijklmnopqrstuvwxyz

HAAS BODONI

iv

ABCDEFGHIJKLMNOPQRSTUVWXYZ

abcdefghijklmnopqrstuvwxyz

ABCDEFGHIJKLMNOPQRSTUVWXYZ

abcdefghijklmnopqrstuvwxyz

HAAS BODONI SEMI BOLD

iv

ABCDEFGHIJKLMNOPQRSTUVWXYZ

abcdefghijklmnopqrstuvwxyz

ABCDEFGHIJKLMNOPQRSTUVWXY

abcdefghijklmnopqrstuvwxyz

HAAS BODONI BOLD

ABCDEFGHIJKLMNOPQRSTUVWXYZ
abcdefghijklmnopqrstuvwxyz

HAAS BODONI BOLD CONDENSED

ABCDEFGHIJKLMNOPQRSTUVWXYZ

abcdefghijklmnopqrstuvwxyz

1234567890

ABCDEFGHIJKLMNOPQRSTUVWXYZ

abcdefghijklmnopqrstuvwxyz

1234567890

ABCDEFGHIJKLMNOPQRSTUVWXYZ

Recut Italic: abcdefghijklmnopqrstuvwxyz

ABCDEFGHIJKLMNOPQRSTUVWXYZ
ABCDEFGHIJKLMNOPQRSTUVWXYZ

MERGENTHALER LINOTYPE BODONI BOOK

ABCDEFGHIJKLMNOPQRSTUVWXYZ

abcdefghijklmnopqrstuvwxyz

1234567890

ABCDEFGHIJKLMNOPQRSTUVWXYZ

abcdefghijklmnopqrstuvwxyz

1234567890

ABCDEFGHIJKLMNOPQRSTUVWXYZ

Recut Italic: abcdefghijklmnopqrstuvwxyz

ABCDEFGHIJKLMNOPQRSTUVWXYZ
ABCDEFGHIJKLMNOPQRSTUVWXYZ

MERGENTHALER LINOTYPE BODONI

ABCDEFGHIJKLMNOPQRSTUVWXYZ

abcdefghijklmnopqrstuvwxyz

1234567890

ABCDEFGHIJKLMNOPQRSTUVWXYZ

abcdefghijklmnopqrstuvwxyz

1234567890

ABCDEFGHIJKLMNOPQRSTUVWXYZ

Recut Italic: abcdefghijklmnopqrstuvwxyz

ABCDEFGHIJKLMNOPQRSTUVWXYZ
ABCDEFGHIJKLMNOPQRSTUVWXYZ

MERGENTHALER LINOTYPE BODONI BOLD

ABCDEFGHIJKLMNOPQRSTUVW
XYZ
abcdefghijklmnopqrstuvwxyz
1234567890
ABCDEFGHIJKLMNOPQRSTUVW
XYZ
abcdefghijklmnopqrstuvvwwxyz
1234567890

BAUER BODONI

ABCDEFGHIJKLMNOPQRSTUVW
XYZ
abcdefghijklmnopqrstuvwxyz
1234567890
ABCDEFGHIJKLMNOPQRSTUV
WXYZ
abcdefghijklmnopqrstuvvww xyz
1234567890

BAUER BODONI BOLD

ABCDEFGHIJKLMNOPQRSTUV
WXYZ
abcdefghijklmnopqrstuvwxyz
1234567890
ABCDEFGHIJKLMNOPQRSTU
VWXYZ
abcdefghijklmnopqrstuvvww
xyz 1234567890

BAUER BODONI EXTRA BOLD

ABCDEFGHIJKLMNOPQRSTUV
WXYZ&!
abcdefghijklmnopqrstuvwxyz
$1234567890

BODONI OPEN

ARCHIVIO

BAUER BODONI OPEN

iv

ABCDEFGHIJKLMNOPQRSTUVWXYZ
abcdefghijklmnopqrstuvwxyz

iv

LANSTON MONOTYPE BODONI BOLD SHADED

New Face in the Bodoni Family 74
Tall Typeface in Narrow Measure

iv

LUDLOW BODONI CAMPANILE

A B C D E F G H I J K L M N O P Q R S T U V
W X Y Z

& $ 1 2 3 4 5 6 7 8 9 0

iv

AMERICAN TYPEFOUNDERS ENGRAVERS' BODONI

ABCDEFGHIJKLMNOPQRSTUVWXYZ
abcdefghijklmnopqrstuvwxyz
1234567890

ABCDEFGHIJKLMNOPQRSTUVWXYZ
abcdefghijklmnopqrstuvwxyz
1234567890

MONOTYPE BODONI ULTRA BOLD

Very like CASLON BOLD FACE OPEN. It may be distinguished by the rounder arc of the lower-case **a**.

ABCDEFGHIJKLMNOPQRSTUVWXY
345   abcdefghijklmnopqrstuvwxyz   6

OUTLINE

BOLOGNA

Stephenson Blake 1946;
American Typefounders

i

A type based on the humanistic scripts of the fifteenth century and therefore resembling TREYFORD and SINIBALDI. Pen-qualities are evident in the serifs and in the gradation of colour in the round letters. The **M** is much splayed. Ascenders and descenders are ample. **v** and **w** have cursive forms.

ABCDEFGHIJKLMNOPQRSTUVWXYZQUQu

abcdefghijklmnopqrst uvwxyz   £&flffhfiffiffl's

1234567890.,-';:?!

BOLOGNA

BOOKMAN or ANTIQUE OLD STYLE

Ludlow 1925;
Mergenthaler Linotype c. 1936;
Monotype

ii

Originally cut as a bold face for Miller & Richard's OLD STYLE. The type has short ascenders and descenders. The upper case has heavy serifs and slight difference of stress. Lower-case serifs are thick and inclined more steeply than in OLD STYLE. The italic is the sloped roman.

ABCDEFGHIJKLMNOPQRSTUVWXYZ

abcdefghijklmnopqrstuvwxyz

1234567890

ABCDEFGHIJKLMNOPQRSTUVWXYZ

abcdefghijklmnopqrstuvwxyz

1234567890

ABCDEFGHIJKLMNOPQRSTUVWXYZ

ABCDEFGHIJKLMNOPQRSTUVWXY

BCDEFGHIJKLMNOPQRSTUVWXYZ

LINOTYPE BOOKMAN

BOUTIQUE

Haas c. 1900

ix

A Victorian design of narrow letters in which many of the capitals descend below the line. Letters are open with many of the strokes not joining.

ABCDEFGHIJKLMNOPQRSTUVWXYZ

abcdefghijklmnopqrstuvwxyz

1234567890

BOUTIQUE

BRAVOUR

Stempel 1912

ix

Designed by M. Jacoby-Boy. A monotone letter with flat serifs except those on the arms of **E, F** and **L**, and those terminating the arc of **C, G**, etc. These are oblique and long. **B, P** and **R** have large bowls. In the **M** the middle strokes descend half-way. Ascenders and descenders are short; the **g** has an open tail. The italic has some cursive capitals, *e.g.* the **H, L, V** and **W** and the serifs of the roman. There is also a bold, which is a heavy display type.

Kunst und Handwerk

BRAVOUR

Designed by Willy Wiegand and cut by Louis Hoell for the Flinsch Typefoundry in one size only (11 pt.), originally for the exclusive use of the Bremer Presse. It has a solid calligraphic quality and is distinguishable by the foot serifs pointing to the right only.
There are also 12 and 16 pt versions which are slightly different.

BREMER
PRESSE
ROMAN
Bauer 1912

i

ABCDEFGHIJKLMNOPQRSTUVWXYZ
abcdefghijklmnopqrstuvwxyz
1234567890

BREMER PRESSE ROMAN

A modified fat face in which the main stroke only is fat, the thins taking over the rest of the letter. The thicks and thins meet at an angle and not in a curve. Several types of the American Typefounders have a similar design. CARLTON is an inline version of this design.

BRISTOL
Amsterdam 1929

BRUXELLES NICE

ix

BRISTOL

ENSURING

ix

CARLTON

Designed by Jan Rambousek. There are a roman and an italic, as well as a bold. Letters are open and have little variations in stress, but in the lower case are somewhat uneven in weight. The tail of the **R** is vertical.

BRNO Z
Grafotechna 1959

ABCDEFGHIJKLMNOPQRSTUVWXYZ
abcdefghikjlmnopqrstuvwxyz
1234567890

iv

ABCDEFGHIJKLMNOPQRSTUVWXYZ
abcdefghijklmnopqrstuvwxyz
1234567890
BRNO Z

ABCDEFGHIJKLMNOPQRSTUVWXYZ
abcdefghikjlmnopqrstuvwxyz
1234567890
BRNO Z BOLD

iv

Designed by Lucien Pissarro for his private press and named after his house in Hammersmith. The capitals are mostly broad and there are slab serifs on the **A** and **M**. The **g** has a large bowl and a squashed tail; the bowl of the **p** is circular and the **t** is narrow.
The type, now in the possession of the Cambridge University Press, was cut in pica only.

BROOK TYPE
Eragny Press 1903

Next as to type. By instinct rather than by conscious thinking it over, I began by getting myself a fount of Roman type. And here what I wanted was letter pure in form; severe, without needless excrescenses; solid without the thickening and thinning of the line, which is the essential fault of the ordinary modern type, and which makes it difficult to read; and not compressed laterally, as all later type has grown to be owing to com-

i

ABCDEFGHIJKLMNOPRSTUVWXYZ QU Qu Æ Œ
abcdefghijklmnopqrstuvwxyz .,;:!?,'—...() æœ
£1234567890 «» àèùéâêîôûëïü ç Ç &

BROOK TYPE

Designed by Sol Hess from the Bruce Foundry's BRUCE OLD STYLE NO. 20 which was first shown in 1869. The type is based on SCOTCH and similar faces.

ABCDEFGHIJKLMNOPQRSTUVWXYZ&ÆŒ
abcdefghijklmnopqrstuvwxyzæœ　fiflffffiffl
$1234567890　.,-'':;!?　$1234567890
ABCDEFGHIJKLMNOPQRSTUVWXYZ&ÆŒ
ABCDEFGHIJKLMNOPQRSTUVWXYZ&ÆŒ
abcdefghijklmnopqrstuvwxyzæœ　fiflffffiffl
$1234567890　:;!?　$1234567890

BRUCE OLD STYLE NO. 31

Designed by Walter Brudi. Serifs are thin and unbracketed. The **M** is splayed and has no top serifs; the italic is only slightly inclined. Figures are ranging.

ABCDEFGHIJKLMNOPQRSTUVWXYZ
abcdefghijklmnopqrstuvwxyz
1234567890
ABCDEFGHIJKLMNOPQRSTUVWXYZ
abcdefghijklmnopqrstuvwxyz
1234567890

BRUDI MEDIAEVAL

BULMER
American Typefounders 1928;
Intertype;
Lanston Monotype;
Monotype

iii

Designed by Morris F. Benton as a replica of a famous type in the history of English printing cut by William Martin about 1790 for William Bulmer of the Shakspeare Press.

The **R** has a curled tail. The **g** has a small bowl with a curved ear and gives the appearance of leaning backwards. **J, K, N, T** and **Y** in the italic are reminiscent of Baskerville, whose pupil Martin was. Figures are ranging.

ABCDEFGHIJKLMNOPQRSTUVWXYZ
abcdefghijklmnopqrstuvwxyz
1234567890
ABCDEFGHIJKLMNOPQRSTUVWXYZ
ABCDEFGHIJKLMNOPQRSTUVWXYZ
abcdefghijklmnopqrstuvwxyz
1234567890

INTERTYPE BULMER

ABCDEFGHIJKLMNOPQRSTUVWXYZ
abcdefghijklmnopqrstuvwxyz
1234567890
ABCDEFGHIJKLMNOPQRSTUVWXYZ
abcdefghijklmnopqrstuvwxyz
1234567890

MONOTYPE BULMER

ABCDEFGHIJKLMNOPQRSTUVWXYZ

abcdefghijklmnopqrstuvwxyz

1234567890

ABCDEFGHIJKLMNOPQRSTUVWXYZ

abcdefghijklmnopqrstuvwxyz

1234567890

AMERICAN TYPEFOUNDERS BULMER

This type face has some resemblance to MEMPHIS. **A** has the slab bar at the top, **G** has a spur, in the **M** the middle strokes stop short of the line, **R** has a curled tail. The lower case has slab serifs at the top and foot, and the **g** has a slab serif at the top and open tail.

ABCDEFGHIJKLMNOPQRSTUVWXYZ

abcdefghijklmnopqrstuvwxyz

1234567890 &£

CAIRO

ABCDEFGHIJKLMNOPQRSTUVWXYZ

abcdefghijklmnopqrstuvwxyz

1234567890 &£

CAIRO BOLD

ABCDEFGHIJKLMNOPQRSTUVWXYZ

abcdefghijklmnopqrstuvwxyz

1234567890

CAIRO HEAVY

ABCDEFGHIJKLMNOPQRSTUVWXYZ

abcdefghijklmnopqrstuvwxyz

1234567890

CAIRO EXTRA BOLD CONDENSED

ABCDEFGHIJKLMNOPQRSTUVWXYZ

abcdefghijklmnopqrstuvwxyz

1234567890

CAIRO BOLD CONDENSED

CALEDONIA

CALEDONIA

Mergenthaler Linotype 1938;
Stempel 1938;
Linotype (Frankfurt) 1939;
Linotype (London)

Designed by W.A. Dwiggins. A modified SCOTCH, which accounts for the name. The stress is vertical and serifs are horizontal but not thin. The G is wide open and the **R** has a curled tail. The **g** has a wide tail and the ear is not curled. The **t** is unbracketed. In the italic **p** and **q** have no foot serifs. In Germany the type is called CORNELIA.

iv

ABCDEFGHIJKLMNOPQRSTUVWXYZ
abcdefghijklmnopqrstuvwxyz
1234567890
ABCDEFGHIJKLMNOPQRSTUVWXYZ
abcdefghijklmnopqrstuvwxyz
1234567890

ABCDEFGHIJKLMNOPQRSTUVWXYZ
abcdefghijklmnopqrstuvwxyz
1234567890
1234567890

ABCDEFGHIJKLMNOPQRSTUVWXYZ
abcdefghijklmnopqrstuvwxyz
1234567890
1234567890
ABCDEFGHIJKLMNOPQRSTUVWXYZ

CALEDONIA

iv

ABCDEFGHIJKLMNOPQRSTUVWXYZ
abcdefghijklmnopqrstuvwxyz
1234567890
ABCDEFGHIJKLMNOPQRSTUVWXYZ
abcdefghijklmnopqrstuvwxyz
1234567890

ABCDEFGHIJKLMNOPQRSTUVWXYZ
abcdefghijklmnopqrstuvwxyz
1234567890
1234567890

ABCDEFGHIJKLMNOPQRSTUVWXYZ
abcdefghijklmnopqrstuvwxyz
1234567890
1234567890
ABCDEFGHIJKLMNOPQRSTUVWXYZ

CALEDONIA BOLD

Designed by Frederic W. Goudy in 1938 for the University of California Press. The type has flat serifs and an italic of slight inclination.

ABCDEFGHIJKLMNOPQRSTUVWXYZ
abcdefghijklmnopqrstuvwxyz
1234567890
ABCDEFGHIJKLMNOPQRSTUVWXYZ
abcdefghijklmnopqrstuvwxyz
1234567890

CALIFORNIAN

Designed by Jan van Krimpen, this italic, based on humanistic penscripts, has, when combined into words, a true hand lettering appeal. There are variations for most upper- and lower-case letters, and ascenders and descenders are ample. Swash letters are very much in evidence. The type complements the same founder's ROMULUS series.

ABCDEFGHIJKLMNOPQRSTUVWXYZÆŒ
abcdefghijklmnopqrstuvwxyzæœç
1234567890&

CANCELLERESCA BASTARDA

Designed by R. Hunter Middleton. A shaded roman and italic with thin serifs, which are inclined in the lower case. The italic has the serifs of the roman. The upper case is similar to NARCISSUS.

ABCDEFGHIJKLMNOPQRSTU
VWXYZ&   1234567890
abcdefghijklmnopqrstuvwxyz

CAMEO

CANDIDA

Ludwig & Mayer 1936
Linotype (Frankfurt)

Designed by J. Erbar. A roman with serifs like an "Egyptian" but thinner. Capitals are wide and the W and w without a middle serif. Lower-case serifs are horizontal and the **a** has a large bowl. ANTIQUA 505 is very similar.

iv

ABCDEFGHIJKLMNOPQRSTUV
WXYZ
abcdefghijklmnopqrstuvwxyz
1234567890

*ABCDEFGHIJKLMNOPQRSTUV
WXYZ
abcdefghijklmnopqrstuvwxyz
1234567890*

CANDIDA

iv

**ABCDEFGHIJKLMNOPQRSTUV
WXYZ
abcdefghijklmnopqrstuvwxyz
1234567890**

CANDIDA SEMI-BOLD

iv

**ABCDEFGHIJKLMNOPQRSTUV
WXYZ
abcdefghijklmnopqrstuvwxyz
1234567890**

***ABCDEFGHIJKLMNOPQRSTU
VWXYZ
abcdefghijklmnopqrstuvwxyz
1234567890***

CANDIDA BOLD

ABCDEFGHIJKLMNOPQRSTUVWXYZ
abcdefghijklmnopqrstuvwxyz
123467890

CANDIDA MEDIUM CONDENSED

ABCDEFGHIJKLMNOPQRSTUVWXYZ
abcdefghijklmnopqrstuvwxyz
1234567890

CANDIDA BOLD CONDENSED

Designed by Karl Erik Forsberg. A set of pen-drawn capitals and ranging numerals with slight serifs. The **O** is nearly square.

ABCDEFGHIJKLMNOPQRST
UVWXYZ

CAROLUS

Designed by Carl Dair. First used by the Canadian printing house of Cape & Co, and designed specially for phototypesetting. There are no italic capitals.

ABCDEFGHIJKLMNOPQRSTUVW
XYZ
abcdefghijklmnopqrstuvwxyz
1234567890
abcdefghijklmnopqrstuvwxyz
1234567890

CARTIER

CASLON ANTIQUE
American Typefounders

Originally cast by Barnhart Brothers & Spindler as FIFTEENTH CENTURY about 1897, although an earlier specimen book with tipped-in pages would suggest 1894–95. An unusual design and oddly named. Some of the lower case letters are condensed, e.g., **a**, **n**, and **u**. The serifs are very blunt.

ii

ABCDEFGHIJKLMNOPQRSTUVWXYZ

&abcdefghijklmnopqrstuvwxyz?

1234567890

ABCDEFGHIJKLMNOPQRSTUVWX
YZ&

abcdefghijklmnopqrstuvwxyz?
1234567890

CASLON ANTIQUE

CASLON OLD FACE
Caslon and other founders

William Caslon started his foundry about the year 1720, but his first roman is not met with before 1725. He modelled his designs on Dutch types of the late seventeenth century, so that his type is classed among the Old Faces rather than with the eighteenth century types. In the upper case the **A** has a hollow in the apex, the **C** has two full serifs or beaks, and the **M** is wide and square. In the lower case the ear of the **g** is thickened at the end; the **s**, upper-case also, is a light letter. In the italic, as in many old-face italics, the capitals are irregular in their inclination; the **A**, **V** and **W** appear to be falling over. Some of the original swash capitals, **Q**, **T**, and **Y** seem to have been abandoned, but the **J** remains.

Matrices based on the original are still in existence at Enschedé, but since its revival the type has been so popular that many foundries have their own versions.

There are also much later-dated adaptations such as Caslon Old Face Heavy, and Old Face Open and an Old Face Open Heavy. The Caslon italic of American Typefounders has additional swash letters. Other series for this typefoundry were redesigned by Frank Bartuska.

Haas base their type on original matrices for roman and italic in small sizes, while the larger sizes were re-cut in 1944. Intertype (F) CASLON BOLD was re-designed and hand-cut in 1960 to match the lighter weight.

ii

ABCDEFGHIJKLMNOPQRSTUVWXYZ

abcdefghijklmnopqrstuvwxy

ABCDEFGHIJKLMNOPQRSTUVWXYZ

abcdedefghiiklmnopqrtuvwxyz

CASLON OLD FACE

ABCDEFGHIJKLMNOPQRSTUVWXYZ

abcdefghijklmnopqrstuvwxyz

1234567890

ABCDEFGHIJKLMNOPQRSTUV

abcdefghijklmnopqrstuvwxyz

HAAS CASLON

38

ABCDEGFKMNPQRTVY

HAAS CASLON SWASH CAPITALS

ABCDEFGHIJKLMNOPQRSTUVWXYZ
abcdefghijklmnopqrstuvwxyz
1234567   1234567890

ABCDEFGHIJKLMNOPQRSTUVWXYZ
abcdefghijklmnopqrstuvwxyz
4567890   1234567890

ii

ii

ABCDEFGHIJKLMNOPQRSTUVWXYZ
ABCDEFGHIJKLMNOPQRSTUVW
DEFGHIJKLMNOPQRSTUVWXYZ

MERGENTHALER LINOTYPE CASLON OLD FACE (1921)

ABCDEFGHIJKLMNOPQRSTUVWXYZ
abcdefghijklmnopqrstuvwxyz
12345678   1234567890

ABCDEFGHIJKLMNOPQRSTUVWXYZ
abcdefghijklmnopqrstuvwxyz
34567890   1234567890

Recut Italic: abcdefghijklmnopqrstuvwxyz

ABCDEFGHIJKLMNOPQRSTUVWXYZ
ABCDEFGHIJKLMNOPQRSTUVWX
CDEFGHIJKLMNOPQRSTUVWXYZ

ii

MERGENTHALER LINOTYPE CASLON NO. 3 (1913)

STRIKING NEW SERIES
suitable for every description
of modern commercial work

DESIGNERS
number increased

ii

CASLON OLD FACE OPEN

CASLON OLD FACE OPEN HEAVY

ABCDEFGHIJKLMNOPQRSTUVWXYZ
abcdefghijklmnopqrstuvwxyz
1234567890 &£

ABCDEFGHIJKLMNOPQRSTUVWXYZ
abcdefghijklmnopqrstuvwxyz
1234567890 &£

ii

CASLON OLD FACE HEAVY

ABCDEFGHIJKLMNOPQRSTUVWXYZ
abcdefghijklmnopqrstuvwxyz
1234567890

ii

CASLON 641

39

CASTELLAR
Monotype 1957

vii

Designed by John Peters. A set of shaded capitals and figures. The serifs are long and thin.

ABCDEFGHIJKL
MNOPQRSTUVX

CENTAUR
Monotype 1929

i

Designed by Bruce Rogers in 1914 as a titling fount only for the Metropolitan Museum of New York, and modelled on Jenson's roman. It is lighter in colour and more modelled than CLOISTER OLD FACE. The italic cut to accompany The Monotype Corporation's version is the ARRIGHI ITALIC shown separately.

ABCDEFGHIJKLMNOPQRSTUVWXYZ
abcdeghijklmnopqrstuvwxyz
1234567890

CENTURY
American Typefounders;

Linotype;

Intertype;

Monotype;

Ludlow

iv

Cut in 1894 by Linn Boyd Benton in collaboration with T.L. De Vinne for the *Century Magazine* to supply a blacker and more readable face than the thin type used previously, and slightly condensed to fit the double-column setting of the magazine. It was first used in 1895.

Morris Fuller Benton designed several versions of this type; and in about 1900 American Typefounders brought out Century Expanded to meet the Typographical Union Standard of the day.

CENTURY NOVA, designed by Charles E. Hughes for American Typefounders in 1966, is a new condensed version of the expanded type.

ABCDEFGHIJKLMNOPQRSTUVW
XYZ
abcdefghijklmnopqrstuvwxyz
1234567890

iv

ABCDEFGHIJKLMNOPQRSTUVW
XYZ
abcdefghijklmnopqrstuvwxyz
1234567890

ABCDEFGHIJKLMNOPQRSTU
VWXYZ
abcdefghijklmnopqrstuvwxyz
1234567890

CENTURY OLD STYLE BOLD

ABCDEFGHIJKLMNOPQRSTUVW
XYZ
abcdefghijklmnopqrstuvwxyz
1234567890

CENTURY EXPANDED

*ABCDEFGHIJKLMNOPQRSTUV
WXYZ
abcdefghijklmnopqrstuvwxyz
1234567890*

CENTURY EXPANDED ITALIC

ABCDEFGHIJKLMNOPQRSTUVW
XYZ
abcdefghijklmnopqrstuvwxyz
1234567890
*ABCDEFGHIJKLMNOPQRSTUV
WXYZ
abcdefghijklmnopqrstuvwxyz
1234567890*

CENTURY SCHOOLBOOK

ABCDEFGHIJKLMNOPQRSTUVWXYZ
abcdefghijklmnopqrstuvwxyz
1234567890
*ABCDEFGHIJKLMNOPQRSTUVWXYZ
abcdefghijklmnopqrstuvwxyz
1234567890*

MONOTYPE CENTURY SCHOOLBOOK

CENTURY

iv

ABCDEFGHIJKLMNOPQRSTUVWXYZ
abcdefghijklmnopqrstuvwxyz
1234567890
ABCDEFGHIJKLMNOPQRSTUVWXYZ
ABCDEFGHIJKLMNOPQRSTUVWXYZ
abcdefghijklmnopqrstuvwxyz
1234567890

INTERTYPE CENTURY SCHOOLBOOK

iv

**ABCDEFGHIJKLMNOPQRSTUVWXYZ
abcdefghijklmnopqrstuvwxyz
1234567890**

INTERTYPE CENTURY SCHOOLBOOK BOLD

iv

**ABCDEFGHIJKLMNOPQRSTUVWXYZ
abcdefghijklmnopqrstuvwxyz
1234567890**

MONOTYPE CENTURY SCHOOLBOOK BOLD

iv

**ABCDEFGHIJKLMNOPQRST
UVWXYZ
abcdefghijklmnopqrstuvwxyz
1234567890**

CENTURY SCHOOLBOOK BOLD

iv

ABCDEFGHIJKLMNOPQRSTUVWXYZ
abcdefghijklmnopqrstuvwxyz
1234567890
ABCDEFGHIJKLMNOPQRSTUVWXYZ
abcdefghijklmnopqrstuvwxyz
1234567890

CENTURY CATALOGUE

iv

ABCDEFGHIJKLMNOPQRSTUVWXYZ
abcdefghijklmnopqrstuvw
12345
ABCDEFGHIJKLMNOPQRSTUVWXYZ
defghijklmnopqrstuvwxyz
67890

ABCDEFGHIJKLMNOPQRSTUVWXYZ

LINOTYPE CENTURY

42

ABCDEFGHIJKLMNOPQRSTUVW
XYZ
abcdefghijklmnopqrstuvwxyz
1234567890

ABCDEFGHIJKLMNOPQRSTU
VWXYZ
abcdefghijklmnopqrstuvwxyz
1234567890

CENTURY BOLD

ABCDEFGHIJKLMNOPQRSTUVWXYZ

abcdefghijklmnopqrstuvwxyz

1234567890

iv

CENTURY BOLD CONDENSED

Designed by Charles Hughes as a variation on CENTURY EXPANDED, with a special emphasis on making the type suitable for printing by different printing processes. The lower case has a larger than normal x-height.

CENTURY
NOVA
American Typefounders 1966

iv

ABCDEFGHIJKLMNOPQRSTUVWXYZ
abcdefghijklmnopqrstuvwxyz
1234567890
ABCDEFGHIJKLMNOPQRSTUVWXYZ
abcdefghijklmnopqrstuvwxyz
1234567890

CENTURY NOVA

Designed by Oldrich Menhart. An angular "uncial" type face of calligraphic quality.

CESKA
UNCIALA
Grafotechna 1945

ix

ABCDEFGHIJKLMNOPQRS
TUVWXYZ
1234567890

CESKA UNCIALA

CHARLESTON
Ludwig & Mayer 1967
ix

Re-designed by Hace Frey as a revival of a Victorian bold angular roman.

ABCDEFGHIJKLMNOPQRSTUVWXYZ
abcdefghijklmnopqrstuvwxyz
1234567890

CHARLESTON

CHATSWORTH
Stephenson Blake 1904

A bold modern face with thick flat serifs almost Egyptian in appearance. Ascenders and descenders are short. The **t** has an oblique top. American Typefounders' KEYSTONE is similar.

iv

FRENCH INVENTION
Newer methods recognized
Papiers Autographiques

CHATSWORTH

CHELTENHAM
Many founders

Originally designed by Bertram G. Goodhue in 1896 for D.B. Updike on the suggestion of a Mr Kimball of the Cheltenham Press of New York. The type was made commercially available by American Typefounders, who produced 18 variations designed by M.F. Benton from 1904–11. The serifs are flat and stubby and although the stress is vertical, it is not abrupt. Descenders are short. The right stem of the **A** projects beyond the left. The **G** has a spur. The **e** is rather small and in the **g** the curve of the tail ends in a thickening and the tail is not closed, in the **r** the thickened ear projects above the top of the letter, the **s** ends in thickenings and the **w** has no middle serif. The italic has the serifs of the roman. The bowls of **e** and **p** are not closed, and **p** and **q** have no foot serifs.

This type became popular and begot a large family, condensed, wide, elongated, bold open, etc. and had several imitators. Among these are WINCHESTER (Stephenson Blake), which may be distinguished by the curl of the ear on the **g** and the serifs of the **s**. The Monotype Corporation's GLOUCESTER has an italic **p** with the normal closed bowl. Intertype CHELTONIAN is another version. Berthold originally called their version SORBONNE (1905).

ii

ABCDEFGHIJKLMNOPQRSTUVWXYZ
abcdefghijklmnopqrstuvwxyz
1234567890

ii

ABCDEFGHIJKLMNOPQRSUVWYZ
abcdefghijklnopqrstuvwxyz
1234567890

CHELTENHAM

ii

ABCDEFGHIJKLMNOPQRSTUVWXYZ
abcdefghijklmnopqrstuvwxyz
1234567890

CHELTENHAM BOLD ITALIC

ABCDEFGHIJKLMNOPQRSTUVWXYZ

abcdefghijklmnopqrstuvwxyz

ii

BERTHOLD CHELTENHAM LIGHT

ABCDEFGHIJKLMNOPQRSTUVWXYZ

abcdefghijklmnopqrstuvwxyz

1234567890

ii

BERTHOLD CHELTENHAM MEDIUM

ABCDEFGHIJKLMNOPQRSTUVWXY

abcdefghijklmnopqrstuvwxyz

ii

BERTHOLD CHELTENHAM BOLD

ABCDEFGHIJKLMNOPQRSTUVWXYZ

abcdefghijklmnopqrstuvwxyz

ii

BERTHOLD CHELTENHAM BOLD CONDENSED

ABCDEFGHIKLMNOPQRST

UVWXY

abcdefghijklmnopqrstuvwxyz

14567890

ii

CHELTENHAM BOLD OUTLINE

ABCDEFGHIJKLMNOPQRSTUVWXYZ

abcdefghijklmnopqrstuvwxyz

1234567890

ABCDEFGHIJKLMNOPQRSTUVWXYZ

abcdefghijklmnopqrstuvwxyz

1234567890

ii

GLOUCESTER OLD STYLE

ABCDEFGHIJKLMNOPQRSTUVWXYZ

abcdefghijklmnopqrstuvwxyz

1234567890

ABCDEFGHIJKLMNOPQRSTUVWXYZ

abcdefghijklmnopqrstuvwxyz

1234567890

ii

GLOUCESTER BOLD

CHELTENHAM

iv

ABCDEFGHIJKLMNOPQRSTUVWXYZ
abcdefghijklmnopqrstuvwxyz
1234567890

GLOUCESTER BOLD CONDENSED

iv

ABCDEFGHIJKLMNOPQRSTUVWXYZ
abcdefghijklmnopqrstuvwxyz
1234567890

GLOUCESTER BOLD EXTRA CONDENSED

iv

ABCDEGHIJKLMNOPQRSTUVWXYZ
abcdefghijklmnopqrstuvwxyz
1234567890

GLOUCESTER BOLD EXTENDED

CHEVALIER

Haas

iv

A set of shaded capitals and figures, modern face or fat face in design. *Cf.* EXCELLENT.

ABCDEFGHIJKLMNOPQRSTUVWXYZ
1234567890

CHEVALIER

CHIC

American Typefounders 1928

ix

Designed by M.F. Benton. Doubly shaded capitals and figures. Each thick stroke is accompanied by two parallel hair lines. The flat serifs are hair lines and they are prolonged on the **C, G** and **S.**

ENCOURAGE

CHIC

CHISEL

Stephenson Blake 1939–56

ix

An inline version of LATIN BOLD CONDENSED, and designed on the suggestion of Robert Harling. There is a double white line, which was originally engraved in Latin type. Earlier experiments with such a method were made at the Cambridge University Press. Enschedé call this type BAVO.

ABCDEFGHIJKLM
NOPQRSTUVWXYZ
abcdefghijklmnopq
rstuvwxyz
1234567890

CHISEL

A roman of even colour, with ranging figures.

ABCDEFGHIJKLMNOPQRSTUVWXYZ
abcdefghijklmnopqrstuvwxyz
1234567890

ABCDEFGHIJKLMNOPQRSTUVWXYZ
abcdefghijklmnopqrstuvwxyz
1234567890

CHISWELL OLD FACE

Designed by Georg Trump. A rectangular letter. TOWER is similar.

ABCDEFGHIJKLMNOPQRSTUVWXYZ
abcdefghijklmnopqrstuvwxyz
1234567890

CITY LIGHT

ABCDEFGHIJKLMNOPQRSTUVWXYZ
abcdefghijklmnopqrstuvwxyz
1234567890

CITY MEDIUM

ABCDEFGHIJKLMNOPQRSTUVWXYZ
abcdefghijklmnopqrstuvwxyz
12345780

CITY BOLD

Designed by R.H. Stevens.

ABCDEFGHIJKLMNOPQRSTUVWXYZ ŒÆ
abcdefghijklmnopqrstuvwxyz
1234567890

CLARENCE CONDENSED

47

CLARENDON
Many founders

Originally put out in 1845 by R. Besley & Co. (the Fann St. Foundry) as a heavy face to accompany an ordinary roman in dictionaries and the like. It became very popular, was soon copied by the other founders and has become a word for a heavy type in the English vocabulary. It is a slab serif type with more differentiation of colour and lighter serifs than in the original model. Some letters follow the roman model, such as the **a**, **e**, **g** and **t**, and the **R** with its curls. This was also the characteristic of the first English "Egyptians". The revived version of the Haas'sche Schriftgiesserei (also cast by Stempel) was designed by Hermann Eidenbenz in 1951–53. Stempel have a revised type of this name designed under the direction of Erich Schulz-Anker. Ludlow introduced a new series in 1966.

v

ABCDEFGHIJKLMNOPQRSTUVWXYZ

abcdefghijklmnopqrstuvwxyz

1234567890

MONOTYPE CLARENDON

v

ABCDEFGHIJKLMNOPQRS

abcdefghijklmnopqrstuvwxy

1234567890

HAAS CLARENDON

v

ABCDEFGHIJKLMNOPQR

abcdefghijklmnopqrstuvwx

HAAS CLARENDON BOLD

v

ABCDEFGHIJKLMNOP
QRSTUVWXYZ
abcdefghijklmnopqrst
uvwxyz
1234567890

CLARENDON BOLD EXTENDED

v

ABCDEFGHIJKLMNOPQRSTUVWXYZ&
abcdefghijklmnopqrstuvwxyz
1234567890

MERGENTHALER LINOTYPE CLARENDON ROMAN

v

ABCDEFGHIJKLMNOPQRSTUVWXYZ&
abcdefghijklmnopqrstuvwxyz
1234567890

MERGENTHALER LINOTYPE CLARENDON BOLD ROMAN

48

ABCDEFGHIJKLMNOPQRS
abcdefghijklmnopqrstuvwxy
1234567890

HAAS LINOTYPE CLARENDON STEMPEL

ABCDEFGHIJKLMNOPQR
abcdefghijklmnopqrstuvwxy
1234567890

CLARENDON SEMI-BOLD

ABCDEFGHIJKLMNOPQRSTUVWXYZ
abcdefghijklmnopqrstuvwxyz
1234567890

CLARENDON CONDENSED

ABCDEFGHIJKL
abcdefghijklmnop
1234567890

CLARENDON EXTRA BOLD EXTENDED

This type was also known as BAUER BASKERVILLE although it has little relation to the real BASKERVILLE. Descenders are very short and the italic has the serifs of the roman.

ABCDEFGHIJKLMNOPQQuRS TUVWXYZ
abcdefghijklmnopqrstuvwxyz
1234567890
ABCDEFGHIJKLMNOPQQuR STUVWXYZ
abcdefghijklmnopqr stuvwxyz
1234567890

CLASSIC

CLARITAS

Monotype;
Linotype (London) 1951

iv

This is the name given to a small (4¾ point) version of the TIMES NEW ROMAN. It is claimed to be the clearest of all small types (hence the name), and is intended for use in newspaper "small" announcements.

COMPANY actively engaged in the manufacture of mining equipment requires additional capital to finance current Government and like contracts. Enquiries from interested companies or individuals.—Box 324.
DIRECTOR of established financially sound firm, dealing retail stationers and stores only, apprehensive about rising cost travelling, seeks confidential discussion

ADELPHI. (Tem. 7611.) To-day, 2.30 & 7.30. ORIGINAL BALLET RUSSE. AURORA'S WEDDING. PRESAGES. PRINCE IGOR.
SADLER'S WELLS. (Ter. 1672.) Evgs., 7. To-night, THE BARBER OF SEVILLE. Wed., IL TROVATORE. Thurs., MARRIAGE OF FIGARO. Fri., SCHOOL FOR FATHERS. Sat., MADAME BUTTERFLY.

ABCDEFGHIJKLMNOPQRSTUVWXYZÆŒ abcdefghijklmnopqrstuvwxyzæœ fiflffffifl 1234567890 ABCDEFGHI
ABCDEFGHIJKLMNOPQRSTUVWXYZÆŒ abcdefghijklmnopqrstuvwxyzæœ fiflffffifl JKLMNOPQRSTU
ABCDEFGHIJKLMNOPQRSTUVWXYZÆŒ abcdefghijklmnopqrstuvwxyzæœ fiflffffifl 1234567890 VWXYZÆŒ

LINOTYPE CLARITAS WITH ITALIC, BOLD AND DROP INITIALS

CLEARFACE

American Typefounders;
Stephenson Blake;
Ludlow 1923;
Mergenthaler Linotype;
Linotype (London);
Monotype;
Lanston Monotype;
Intertype

iii

iii

Designed by M.F. Benton. First produced in 1907 by the American Typefounders and now a stock type of many founders. The letters are rather condensed. Ascenders and descenders are short as in all bold faces. A has a flat top, in M the middle strokes stop short of the line, V and W have apparent serifs owing to the shortening of the thin strokes. In the lower case the thickened terminals sometimes found in modern faces in **a** and **c** are here found also in the **k, s, v, w** and **y**. The italic is regular. **f** ends on the line; **p** and **q** are without foot serifs.

ABCDEFGHIJKLMNOPQRSTUVWXYZ
abcdefghijklmnopqrstuvwxyz
12345 67890

CLEARFACE

ABCDEFGHIJKLMNOPQRSTUVWXYZ
abcdefghijklmnopqrstuvwxyz
123456

CLEARFACE BOLD

CLOISTER OLD STYLE

American Typefounders c. 1897;
Monotype

i

This was among the first of the revived Venetians, apart from the types of the private presses, *e.g.*, William Morris's GOLDEN TYPE. It was designed in the United States by Morris Benton on the model of Jenson's roman. In the upper case note the thickened terminal of the **J**, the slab serifs on the **M**, the two **R**'s, and the parallel serifs on the **T**. In the lower case the **e** has an oblique bar to the eye and the **w** (a letter not in Jenson's fount) has no middle serif. Jenson of course had no italic and the Cloister italic is based on the Old Faces. In the upper case the **A** leans over to the right; on the **M** the slab serifs of the roman are copied. In the lower case the **h** has the curved shank, but curved less than in some early designs. Note the narrow **v** and **w**. There are also a number of swash capitals.

Intertype CLOISTER OLD STYLE has an **e** with a straight bar. American Typefounders had a JENSON after Morris by 1900. There is also a Linotype (London) CLOISTER BOLD.

ABCDEFGHIJKLMNOPQRRSTUVWXYZ
abcdefghijklmnopqrstuvwxyz
ABCDEFGHIJKLMNOPQRSTUVWXYZ
ABCDEFGMNPRTU
abcdefghijklmnqrstuvwxyz

CLOISTER OLD STYLE

i

A B C D E F G H I J K L M N O P Q R R S T U V W X Y Z & Qu
a b c d e f g h i j k l m n o p q r s t u v w x y z
$ 1 2 3 4 5 6 7 8 9 0
A A B B C D D E E F G G H I J K L M M N N O P P Q R R S T
T U V W X Y Y Z & Qu
a b c d e f g h i j k l m n o p q r s t u v v w w x y z
$ 1 2 3 4 5 6 7 8 9 0

CLOISTER BOLD

This type was also known as SONDERDRUCK. The Deberny & Peignot version of which this type appears to be a copy, is called MOREAU-LE-JEUNE, and was also cut around 1912 as GRAVURE by Amsterdam, and these types also have an open version.

The Lanston Monotype COCHIN was first shown 1915, and adapted two years later by Sol Hess, with the bold following in the 1920s. NICOLAS COCHIN, of the same foundry, followed in 1929.

ABCDEFGHIJKLMNOPQRSTU
VWXYZ
abcdefghijklmnopqrstuvwxyz
1234567890

ABCDEFGHIJKLMNOPQRTW
abcdefghijklmnopqrstuvwxyz
1234567

COCHIN LUDWIG & MAYER

ABCDEFGHIJLI
abcdefghijklmnopqx
ABCDEFGHIJKL
abcdefghijklmnopqrstu

GRAVURE

ABCDEFGHIJKLMNOPQRSTUVWXYZ ÆOE
abcdefghijklmnopqrstuvwxyz
1234567890

NICOLAS COCHIN

ABCDEFGHIJKL
MNOPQRSTUVWXYZ
abcdefghijklmnopqrstuvwxyzœæ
1234567890

MOREAU-LE-JEUNE OPEN

51

ABCDEFGHIJKLMNOPQRSTUVWXY
Z & Æ Œ

abcdefghijklmnopqrstuvwxyz

1234567890

ABCDEFGHIJKLMNOPQRSTUV
WXYZ&ÆŒ

abcdefghijklmnopqrstuvwxyz

1234567890

COCHIN

CODEX
Weber 1954–1956

Designed by Georg Trump. A display roman which may be classified as calligraphic. The capitals are freely drawn and most of them very wide. The **M** is splayed. In the lower case the ascenders and descenders are short and the serifs seem to be made with a quill pen. The **g** has an open tail.

ABCDEFGHIJKLMNOPQRS
TUVWXYZ

abcdefghijklmnopqrstuvwxyz

1234567890

EDINBURGH FESTIVAL

CODEX

COLONNA
Monotype 1927

An inline roman, the line passing through all strokes, including the round. The result is that in the round letters parts appear to be cut-off.

ABCDEFGHIJKLMNOPQRSTUVWXYZ

abcdefghijklmnopqrstuvwxyz

1234567890

COLONNA

Designed by Walter H. McKay. A roman which is modern in serif treatment and stress. The **Q** has its tail entirely outside the bowl, the lower case **g** is almost an old face letter. The type is cast in two weights with italics. COLUMBIA BOLD CONDENSED was designed by Jeanette Kosmann-Markus after the sketches of Walter H. McKay. This design is not the earlier (1906) COLUMBIA by Morland.

ABCDEFGHIJKLMNOPQRSTUVW XYZ
abcdefghijklmnopqrstuvwxyz 1234

iv

ABCDEFGHIJKLMNOPQRSTUVW XYZ
abcdefghijklmnopqrstuvwxyz 5678

COLUMBIA

ABCDEFGHIJKLMNOPQRSTUVW YXZ
abcdefghijklmnopqrstuvwxyz 90

iv

ABCDEFGHIJKLMNOPQRSTUVW XYZ
abcdefghijklmnopqrstuvwxyz 123

COLUMBIA BOLD

ABCDEFGHIJKLMNOPQRSTUVXYZÆŒ
abcdefghijklmnopqrstuvwxyz 1234567890£&æœ

iv

COLUMBIA BOLD CONDENSED

ABCDEFGHIJKLMNOPQRSTUVWXYZ
abcdefghijklmnopqrstuvwxyz
1234567890
ABCDEFGHIJKLMNOPQRSTUVWXYZ
abcdefghijklmnopqrstuvwxyz
1234567890
INTERTYPE COLUMBIA

iv

ABCDEFGHIJKLMNOPQRSTUVWXYZ
abcdefghijklmnopqrstuvwxyz
1234567890

INTERTYPE COLUMBIA BOLD

iv

COLUMNA
Bauer 1955

Designed by Max Caflisch. Originally a private type of the Benteli publishing house in Switzerland. Open capitals and ranging figures with very small, thin serifs. There are two **M**'s, one splayed, and two **R**'s, one with an extended tail.

vii

ABCDEFGHIJKLMMNNO
PQRRSTUVWXYZ1234567

COLUMNA

COMPACTES ITALIQUES
Deberny & Peignot

An inclined Egyptian, almost monotone in colour. The main strokes are slightly thicker than the secondary strokes.

v

ABCDEFGHIJKLMNOPQRSTUVWXYZ
abcdefghijklmnopqrstuvwxyz
1234567890

COMPACTES ITALIQUES

CONCORDE
Berthold 1968;
Intertype (Berlin)

Designed by G.G. Lange. A text type of contemporary design following eighteenth-century style.

ii

ABCDEFGHIJKLMNOPQRSTU
abcdefghijklmnopqrstuvwxyzabcd
1234567890

ABCDEFGHIJKLMNOPQRSTU
abcdefghijklmnopqrstuvwxyzabcd
1234567890

CONCORDE

ii

ABCDEFGHIJKLMNOPQRSTU
abcdefghijklmnopqrstuvwxyzabc
1234567890

CONCORDE MEDIUM

A revival of the early English slab serif types, but with greater variation in the weight of the strokes. The original CLARENDON of 1845 is issued as CONSORT BOLD CONDENSED. The italic and the bold are new designs.

CONSORT
Stephenson Blake 1956

ABCDEFGHIJKLMNOPQRSTU
VWXYZÆŒ
abcdefghijklmnopqrstuvwxyz
1234567890

CONSORT LIGHT

ABCDEFGHIJKLMNOPQRSTUV
WXYZÆŒ
abcdefghijklmnopqrstuvwxyz
1234567890
ABCDEFGHIJKLMNOPQRSTUV
WXYZÆŒ
abcdefghijklmnopqrstuvwxyzœœ
1234567890

CONSORT

ABCDEFGHIJKLMNOPQRST
UVWXYZ
abcdefghijklmnopqrstuvwxyz
1234567890

CONSORT BOLD

ABCDEFGHIJKLMNOPQRSTUVWXYZÆŒ
abcdefghijklmnopqrstuvwxyzæœ
1234567890

CONSORT LIGHT CONDENSED

ABCDEFGHIJKLMNOPQRSTUVWXYZ
abcdefghijklmnopqrstuvwxyz
1234567890

CONSORT CONDENSED

ABCDEFGHIJKLMNOPQRSTUVWXYZÆ
abcdefghijklmnopqrstuvwxyz&£
123456789

CONSORT BOLD CONDENSED

v

v

v

v

v

v

CONTACT
American Typefounders 1944

Designed by F. H. Riley. A condensed type with short ascenders and descenders. The italic has the serifs of the roman. IDEAL ROMAN is similar.

v

ABCDEFGHIJKLMNOPQRSTUVWXYZ
abcdefghijklmnopqrstuvwxyz
ABCDEFGHIJKLMNOPQRSTUVWXYZ
abcdefghijklmnopqrstuvwxyz

CONTACT BOLD

CONTURA
Amsterdam 1966

Designed by Dick Dooijes. An outline type with ranging numerals.

ii

ABCDEFGHIJKLMNOPQRSTUVW
XYZ
abcdefghijklmnopqrstuvwxyz
1234567890

CONTURA

COOPER BLACK
American Typefounders;

Designed by Oswald B. Cooper for Barnhart Brothers & Spindler in 1921. An extra bold face based on COOPER OLD STYLE. The serifs are blurred and counters are naturally very small, in the **O** and **Q** they are tilted back. The dot on the **i** and **j** becomes elliptical. The italic is not far from the vertical and has the serifs of the roman. LUDLOW BLACK is very similar. There is also a condensed face and a shaded type called COOPER HILITE.

ix

ABCDEFGHIJKLMNOPQRSTUVWXY
abcdefghijklmnopqrstuvwxyz
£1234567890$

COOPER BLACK

COOPER OLD STYLE
Barnhart Bros. & Spindler 1919–24

Designed by Oswald B. Cooper for Barnhart Brothers & Spindler (1919–24). The design is old face with some calligraphic qualities reminding one of GOUDY. The serifs are unusual with foot serifs being convex. The apex of the **A** bends over to the left. The **Q** has a tail rather like GOUDY and the **R** a turned-up tail. The **f** is unkerned and the **j** has a buttonhook terminal. Descenders are short. The italic has only slight inclination and the final curves of **h**, **k**, **m** and **n** drop below the line. COOPER TOOLED ITALIC has the shading on the left.

iii

ABCDEFGHIJKLMNOPQRSTUV
WXYZ& $
abcdefghijklmnopqrstuvwxyz
1234567890
ABCDEFGHIJKLMNOPQRSTUV
WXYZ& $
abcdefghijklmnopqrstuvwxyz
1234567890

COOPER OLD STYLE

ABCDEFGHIJKLMNOPQRSTU
VWXYZ&
abcdefghijklmnopqrst
uvwxyz
$1234567890£

COOPER TOOLED ITALIC

ABCDEFGHIJKLMNO
PQRSTUVWXYZ
abcdefghijklmnopqrst
uvwxyz
1234567890

COOPER 570

ABCDEFGHIJKLMNOPQR
BDEFGMNPRT
abcdefghijklmnopqrsßtu
vwxyz
1234567890 &£$¢

COOPER 571

ABCDEFGHIJKLMNOPQR
STUVWXYZ
abcdefghijklmnopqrstu
vwxyz
1234567890 &£$¢

COOPER 579

COPPERPLATE GOTHIC
Many founders

The original type (American Typefounders) was designed by Frederic W. Goudy in 1901. Capitals and figures in this titling and card type at first glance have the appearance of a sanserif but there are in fact minute serifs. Capitals are wide and the centre arm of the E is short.

SPARTAN (Monotype and Stephenson Blake), LINING PLATE GOTHIC (Ludlow), PLATE GOTHIC, MIMOSA (Weber and Typoart) and ATALANTE (Nebiolo) are almost identical.

vii
ABCDEFGHIJKLMNOPQRST UVWXYZ&?!
AMERICAN TYPEFOUNDERS COPPERPLATE GOTHIC LIGHT

vii
ABCDEFGHIJKLMNOPQRST UVWXYZ&?!
AMERICAN TYPEFOUNDERS COPPERPLATE GOTHIC HEAVY

vii
ABCDEFGHIJKLMNOPQRS TUVWXYZ&?!
AMERICAN TYPEFOUNDERS COPPERPLATE GOTHIC ITALIC

vii
ABCDEFGHIJKLMNOPQRS TUVWXYZ&?!
AMERICAN TYPEFOUNDERS COPPERPLATE GOTHIC BOLD

vii
ABCDEFGHIJKLMNOPQRSTUVWXY
AMERICAN TYPEFOUNDERS COPPERPLATE GOTHIC LIGHT CONDENSED

vii
ABCDEFGHIJKLMNOPQRSTUVWXY
AMERICAN TYPEFOUNDERS COPPERPLATE GOTHIC HEAVY CONDENSED

vii
ABCDEFGHIJKLMNOP QRSTUVWXYZ&?!
AMERICAN TYPEFOUNDERS COPPERPLATE GOTHIC LIGHT EXTENDED

vii
ABCDEFGHIJKLMNOP QRSTUVWXYZ&?!
AMERICAN TYPEFOUNDERS COPPERPLATE GOTHIC HEAVY EXTENDED

vii
ABCDEFGHIJKLMNOPQRSTU VWXYZ
STEPHENSON BLAKE SPARTAN SHADED

vii
ABCDEFGHIJKLMNOPQRSTUVWXYZ
STEPHENSON BLAKE SPARTAN BOLD CONDENSED

58

ABCDEFGHIJKLMNOPQR
STUVWXYZ

STEPHENSON BLAKE SPARTAN BOLD EXPANDED

ABCDEFGHIJKLMNOPQRST
UVWXYZ

STEPHENSON BLAKE SPARTAN

ABCDEFGHIJKLMNOPQRSTUV
WXYZ
*ABCDEFGHIJKLMNOPQRST
UVWXYZ*

STEPHENSON BLAKE SPARTAN BOLD

**ABCDEFGHIJKLMNOPQRSTUV
WXYZ**

STEPHENSON BLAKE SPARTAN EXTRA BOLD

Designed by George F. Trenholm. A roman with little variation of stress. The **Q** has a tail outside the bowl and the **R** has a curled tail. The italic has short descenders and the serifs of the roman.

CORNELL
Intertype (New York)

ABCDEFGHIJKLMNOPQRSTUVWXYZ
abcdefghijklmnopqrstuvwxyz
1234567890
ABCDEFGHIJKLMNOPQRSTUVWXYZ
ABCDEFGHIJKLMNOPQRSTUVWXYZ
abcdefghijklmnopqrstuvwxyz
1234567890

CORNELL

ABCDEFGHIJKLMNOPQRSTUVWXYZ
abcdefghijklmnopqrstuvwxyz
1234567890

CORNELL BOLD

Designed by C.H. Griffith. A newspaper type, which underwent some adaptation in 1952 to simplify teletypesetting use. Fairly narrow letters with large x-height. The thin strokes and serifs are firm, the counters are open as in **C, G, S, e, s.** ROYAL is very similar.

CORONA
Mergenthaler Linotype 1941;
Linotype (London) 1961

ABCDEFGHIJKLMNOPQRSTUVWXYZ
abcdefghijklmnopqrstuvwxyz
1234567890
ABCDEFGHIJKLMNOPQRSTUVWXYZ
ABCDEFGHIJKLMNOPQRSTUVWXYZ
abcdefghijklmnopqrstuvwxyz
1234567890

CORONA

**ABCDEFGHIJKLMNOPQRSTUVWXYZ
abcdefghijklmnopqrstuvwxyz
12345 67890**

CORONA BOLD

CORONATION
Stephenson Blake c. 1937

A bold and somewhat condensed display roman face, with short descenders. The distinguishing features are the thickened terminals on the **C, E, F, G, T** and **S,** and the similar thickened ends of the arcs of the lower-case **a, e, r** and **s.**

iv

ABCDEFGHIJKLMNOPQRSTUVWXYZ

abcdefghijklmnopqrstuvwxyz

1234567890

CORONATION

CORVINUS
Bauer 1929–34

Designed by Imre Reiner. Ascenders and descenders are short. The condensation of the letters is achieved by flattening the sides of the round letters. Serifs are very thin. **A** and **M** have slab serifs, the **e** has a large eye and the **g** has the ear with link and tail squared up. In the italic the **g** has an unusual vertical shape, and **v** and **w** are cursive forms.

A condensed version of the type is called SKYLINE. EDEN is similar but has heavier square serifs on **E** and **T.** CORONATION is also similar. Lanston Monotype call this type GLAMOUR.

iv

ABCDEFGHIJKLMNOPQRSTUVWXYZ

abcdefghijklmnopqrstuvwxyz

1234567890

AABCDEEFGGHIJKKLMMNNOPQRSTUVW
XYZ

abcdefghijklmnopqrstuvvwwxyz

12345678

CORVINUS LIGHT

ABCDEFGHIJKLMNOPQRSTUVWXYZ

abcdefghijklmnopqrstuvwxyz

1234567

AABCDEEFGGHIJKKLMMNNOPQRSTU
VWXYZ

abcdefghijklmnopqrstuvvwwxyz

CORVINUS MEDIUM

ABCDEFGHIJKLMNOPQRSTUVWX
abcdefghijklmnopqrstuvwxyz
1234567890

CORVINUS BOLD

ABCDEFGHIJKLMNOPQRSTUVWXYZ
abcdefghijklmnopqrstuvwxyz
1234567890

CORVINUS SKYLINE

First cut in 1902 and used by the *Cosmopolitan* magazine. An extra condensed compact roman with a tall lower case.

ABCDEFGHIJKLMNOPQRSTUVWXYZ&ÆŒ
abcdefghijklmnopqrstuvwxyzæœ   fiflffffiffl
1234567890
ABCDEFGHIJKLMNOPQRSTUVWXYZ&ÆŒ
ABCDEFGHIJKLMNOPQRSTUVWXYZ&ÆŒ
abcdefghijklmnopqrstuvwxyzæœ   fiflffffiffl
1234567890

COSMOPOLITAN

Designed by Freeman Craw. The type follows closely the design of the first expanded CLARENDONS, and is one of many revivals and redesigned versions. Note the **G** in both upper and lower case.

ABCDEFGHIJKLMNOPQRSTUVWXYZ&
abcdefghijklmnopqrstuvwxyz
1234567890

CRAW CLARENDON BOOK

ABCDEFGHIJKLMNOPQRST
UVWXYZ&
abcdefghijklmnopqrstuvwxyz
1234567890£

CRAW CLARENDON

ABCDEFGHIJKLMNOPQRSTUVWXYZ
abcdefghijklmnopqrstuvwxyz?
1234567890

CRAW CLARENDON CONDENSED

Designed by Freeman Craw. Letters have considerable breadth and short ascenders and descenders.

ABCDEFGHIJKLMNOP QRSTUVWXYZ abcdefghijklmnopqrstu vwxyz 1234567890
ABCDEFGHIJKLMNOPQRSTUVWXYZ
abcdefghijklmnopqrstuvwxyz   ffffifflfifl
1234567890

CRAW MODERN

iv

ABCDEFGHIJKLMNO PQRSTUVWXYZ abcdefghijklmnopqrs tuvwxyz 1234567890

CRAW MODERN BOLD

Designed by Rémy Peignot. A set of inline capitals with thin, pointed serifs. The double inline strokes are 'bulging.'

ABCDEFGHIJKLMNOPQRS TUVWXYZ 2468

CRISTAL

Named after a group of slightly related types probably commissioned by J. Stearns Cushing, a book printer of Norwood, Massachusetts. The type is monotone in appearance and has small-inclined serifs. Capitals are wide, ascenders and descenders are short. Figures are ranging. CUSHING OLD STYLE bears little relation to this type.

ABCDEFGHIJKLMNOPQRSTUVWXYZ
abcdefghijklmnopqrstuvwxyz
12345
ABCDEFGHIJKLMNOPQRSTUVWXYZ
abcdefghijklmnopqrstuvwxyz

CUSHING

ABCDEFGHIJKLMNOPQRSTUVWXYZ&ŒÆ
abcdefghijklmnopqrstuvwxyzæœ   fiflfffffiffl
1234567890
ABCDEFGHIJKLMNOPQRSTUVWXYZ&ÆŒ

CUSHING MONOTONE

The type was probably commissioned by J. Stearns Cushing (*cf.* CUSHING) from American Typefounders in 1898, with a redesign by F.W. Goudy in 1904. Cushing Antique follows the English Antiques in style. The Ludlow version is more condensed than the original.

ABCDEFGHIJKLMNOPQRSTUVWX
abcdefghijklmnopqrstuvwxyz

CUSHING ANTIQUE

A somewhat condensed type having large bracketed serifs and of fairly uniform weight.

ABCDEFGHIJKLMNOPQRS TUVWXYZ & Æ Œ

abcdefghijklmnopqrstuvwxyz   æ œ fi fl ff ffi ffl

1234567890   1234567890

ABCDEFGHIJKLMNOPQRS TUVWXYZ & Æ Œ

abcdefghijklmnopqrstuvwxyz   æ œ fi fl ff ffi ffl

1234567890

CUSHING OLD STYLE

An inline series of roman capitals. The line passes through the vertical strokes. Serifs are minute. The **M** is slightly splayed. There are also figures. Resembles DELPHIAN.

PÓSITO MARÍT

DALIA

Designed by Giovanni Mardersteig and cut for hand composition by Charles Malin 1947–54. Originally a private press type for the Officina Bodoni at Verona. The capitals are wide and the italic has slight inclination. There is also a titling face.

ABCDEFGHIJKLMNOPQRSTUVWXYZ
ABCDEFGHIJKLMNOPQRSTUVWXYZ
abcdefghijklmnopqrstuvwxyz
ABCDEFGHIJKLMNOPQRSTUVWXYZ
abcdefghijklmnopqrstuvwxyz
1234567890

DANTE

ABCDEFGHIJKLMNOPQRSTUVWXYZ
ABCDEFGHIJKLMNOPQRSTUVWXYZ
abcdefghijklmnopqrstuvwxyz
ABCDEFGHIJKLMNOPQRSTUVWXYZ
abcdefghijklmnopqrstuvwxyz

MONOTYPE DANTE

ii

ABCDEFGHIJKLMNOPQRSTUVWXYZ
1234567890

DANTE TITLING

ii

DAPHNIS
Klingspor 1931

Designed by Walter Tiemann. An outline roman with very small serifs. **E** and **F** are narrow. **M** is splayed. **U** has the lower-case design.

vii

NEUES PAPIER
Leipziger Messe

DAPHNIS

DEAUVILLE
Française 1927

Designed by M. Loewe. A fat face with modifications. The outer curves of the round letters, **D, O, R** and the round lower-case letters are unusual. The **M** has short middle strokes. The arc of the **a** has a thickened terminal, not a blob.

iv

Deauville MODER

DEAUVILLE

DEEPDENE
Lanston Monotype 1929–34

Designed by F.W. Goudy. The italics are narrow in appearance and include several swash characters and have calligraphic quality.

ii

ABCDEFGHIJKLMNOPQRSTUVWXYZ&

abcdefghijklmnopqrstuvwxyz

$1234567890

DEEPDENE 315

ii

ABCDEFGHIJKLMNOPQRSTUVWXYZ&

abcdefghijklmnopqrstuvwxyz

$1234567890

DEEPDENE ITALIC 315

ii

ABCDEFGHIJKLMNOPQRSTUVWXYZ&

abcdefghijklmnopqrstuvwxyz

$1234567890

DEEPDENE BOLD 317

ii

ABCDEFGHIJKLMNOPQRSTUVWXYZ&

DEEPDENE SMALL CAPS 315

Designed by Thomas Maitland Cleland. Based on rubbings of stone-cut capitals seen by the designer in Rome and almost a 'lineale with serifs'.

DELLA ROBBIA
Lanston Monotype 1902

vii

A B C D E F G H I J K L M N O P Q R S T U V W
X Y Z &

a b c d e f g h i j k l m n o p q r s t u v w x y z
fi fl ff ffi ffl
$ 1 2 3 4 5 6 7 8 9 0

DELLA ROBBIA

Designed by Georg Trump. This calligraphic type has capitals in which the tails of **K** and **R** descend below the line. In the slightly inclined lower case the ascenders of **h, l, b** are taller than the capitals. The lower-case **g** has an open tail and the **s** follows the style of German handwriting. DELPHIN II, is a heavier face of much the same design. There are two **z**'s and two **s**'s.

DELPHIN
Weber 1951–55

ix

ABCDEFGHIJKLMNOPQRSTUVWXYZ
abcddefgghijklmnopqrastuvwxyz
1234567890

DELPHIN I

ix

ABCDEFGHIJKLMNOPQRSTUVWXYZ
abcddefgghijklmnopqrastuvwxyz
1234567890

DELPHIN II

Designed by R. Hunter Middleton. Slender inline capitals, the line running through the vertical strokes. Serifs are very small and the variation in the width of the letters follows the model of the Trajan column.

DELPHIAN
OPEN TITLING
Ludlow 1928

vii

ABCDEFGHIJKLMNOPQRSTU
VWXYZ&   1234567890

DELPHIAN TITLING

Designed by P.A. Demeter, and originally a Schriftguss type. Shaded capitals with serifs like lead forms.

DEMETER
Typoart

ix

ABCDEFGHIJKLMNOPQRSTUVWXYZ

DEMETER

DE ROOS

Amsterdam 1947;
Intertype (New York);
American Typefoundry

The roman designed by S.H. De Roos. It is a light face with little variation in colour and somewhat condensed. The serifs are small and oblique on the lower case. The capitals are shorter than the ascenders and narrow, especially **H** and **T**. **U** has the lower-case design. **g** has a large bowl and the **w** no middle serif. The italic has a slight inclination. In the lower case the serifs are as the roman; the **g** has a script form. Numerals are short ranging. There are also in-line capitals.

ii

ABCDEFGHIJKLMNOPQRSTUVWXYZ
abcdefghijklmnopqrstuvwxyz
1234567890
ABCDEFGHIJKLMNOPQRSTUVWXYZ
abcdefghijklmnopqrstuvwxyz

DE ROOS

ii

ABCDEFGHIJKLMNOPQRSTUVWXYZ
abcdefghijklmnopqrstuvwxyz

DE ROOS SEMI-BOLD

ii

ABCDEFGHIJKLMNOPQRSTUVWXYZ
abcdefghijklmnopqrstuvwxyz
1234567890
ABCDEFGHIJ KLMNOPQRSTUVWXYZ
ABCDEFGHIJKLMNOPQRSTUVWXYZ
abcdefghijklmnopqrstuvwxyz
1234567890

INTERTYPE DE ROOS WITH ITALIC AND SMALL CAPS

DEUTSCH RÖMISCH

Weber 1926; Monotype

Designed by F.H.E. Schneidler. Serifs are small. The **A** has a flat apex, and the **M** slab serifs but thin. The **Q** has the tail outside the bowl. In the lower case round letters are condensed. The **f** is narrow, **g** has an oval-like bowl and wide tail. In the italic serifs on ascenders are flat.

ii

ABCDEFGHIJKLMNOPQRSTU
VWXYZ
abcdefghijklmnopqrs
ABCDEFGHIJKLMNOPQRSTU
VWXYZ
abcdefghijklmnopqrs

DEUTSCH RÖMISCH

ii

ABCDEFGHIJKL

DEUTSCH RÖMISCH BOLD

This type named after T.L. De Vinne, was cut for the Central Typefoundry (now American Typefounders) in 1894 by Gustav Schroeder; De Vinne Roman was cut by F.W. Goudy in 1898. Intertype LORIMER was based on a type called ROMAANS by Amsterdam Typefoundry with matrices supplied by Riegerl Weissenborn as an imitation of Schelter & Giesecke's ROMANISCH. Probably the principles of this series were applied in the USA to produce the De Vinne family; in turn this series was soon used as a related bold to all ROMANISCH, ROMISCH and ROMAANS series produced in Europe.

FRENCH OLD STYLE was derived from Gustave Mayeur's ROMAN XVIIe SIECLE of the Elzevier foundry (now Fonderie Typographique Française) and was the basis for the first Schelter & Giesecke re-cutting in 1889.

ABCDEFGHIJKLMNOPQRSTUVWXYZ&
ABCDEFGHIJKLMNOPQRSTUVWXYZ&
abcdefghijklmnopqrstuvwxyz
1234567890

ABCDEFGHIJKLMNOPQRSTUVWXYZ&
abcdefghijklmnopqrstuvwxyz
1234567890

MERGENTHALER LINOTYPE DE VINNE

iv

ABCDEFGHIJKLMN
OPQRSTUVWXYZ&ÆŒ
abcdefghijklmnopqrstuvwxyz
1234567890

ABCDEFGHIJKLMNOPQ
RSTUVWXYZ&
abcdefghijklmnopqrstu
vwxyz 1234567890

DE VINNE NO. 11

ii

ABCDEFGHIJKLMNOPQRSTUVWXYZ
abcdefghijklmnopqrstuvwxyz
12345 67890

DE VINNE CONDENSED

ii

ABCDEFGHIJKLMNO
PQRSTUVWXYZ&ÆŒ
abcdefghijklmnopqrstuvwxyz
1234567890

ABCDEFGHIJKLMNO
PQRSTUVWXYZ&
abcdefghijklmnopqr
stuvwxyz
1234567890

DE VINNE OUTLINE

ii

67

DE VINNE
i

ABCDEFGHIJKLMN
OPQRSTUVWXYZ
abcdefghijklmnopq
rstuvwxyz
£$1234567890
ABCDEFGHIJKLMNOP
QRSTUVWXYZ
abcdefghijklmnopqrstu
vwxyz.
£$1234567890

DE VINNE ORNAMENTAL

DIAMANT Designed by J. Lehmann so shadowed as to produce a three-dimensional lineale.
Schriftguss 1937

vi

UNIVERSUM
DIAMANT

DIAPHANE Inline capitals to accompany MOZART NOIR.
Warnery

iv

KILOMÈTRES
235768

DIAPHANE

Firmin Didot cut the first modern face about 1784. He and other members of the Didot family fixed the standard for book types in France in the nineteenth century. Among the capitals the **H** and **M** are narrower and the **R** has a vertical tail. In the Pierre Didot design the **g** has a contorted shape; The Monotype Corporation's **g** is more normal, but the upper part of the tail is flat. The italic is distinguished from English modern-face italics by the flat serifs on **m**, **n**, **p**, etc. **v** and **w** have eighteenth-century curves. The Monotype Corporation have another version, very similar, called NEO DIDOT. Pierre Didot, elder brother of Firmin, at a later date had his own foundry with types cut by one Vibert. FIRMIN DIDOT of Deberny & Peignot, who hold the original punches, is true to the original, and the Ludwig & Mayer version follows it closely. The FRENCH ROMAN of Typograph also follows this style.

DIDOT

Deberny & Peignot;
Monotype;
Ludwig & Mayer;
Typograph

ABCDEFGHIJKLMNOPQRSTUVWXYZ
abcdefghijklmnopqrstuvwxyz
1234567890
ABCDEFGHIJKLMNOPQRSTUVWXYZ
abcdefghijklmnopqrstuvwxyz
1234567890

FIRMIN DIDOT

iv

ABCDEFGHIJKLMNOPQRSTUV
WXYZ &
abcdefghijklmnopqrstuvwxyz
1 2 3 4 5 6 7 8 9 0

LUDWIG & MAYER FIRMIN DIDOT BOLD

iv

ABCDEFGHIJKLMNOPQRSTUVWXYZ&
abcdefghijklmnopqrstuvwxyz
1234567890
ABCDEFGHIJKLMNOPQRSTUVWXYZ&
abcdefghijklmnopqrstuvwxyz

DIDOT

iv

ABCDEFGHIJKLMNOPQRSTUVWXYZ&
abcdefghijklmnopqrstuvwxyz
1234567890
ABCDEFGHIJKLMNOPQRSTUVWXYZ&
abcdefghijklmnopqrstuvwxyz

NEO DIDOT

iv

ABCDEFGHIJKLMNOPQRSTUVWXYZ&
abcdefghijklmnopqrstuvwxyz
1234567890
ABCDEFGHIJKLMNOPQRSTUVWXYZ&
abcdefghijklmnopqrstuvwxyz

NEO DIDOT (VARIATION)

iv

ABCDEFGHIJKLMNOPQRSTUVWXYZ&
abcdefghijklmnopqrstuvwxyz
1234567890
ABCDEFGHIJKLMNOPQRSTUVWXYZ&
abcdefghijklmnopqrstuvwxyz

PIERRE DIDOT

iv

69

Decorated capitals cut by Pierre Didot l'aîné c. 1820. The main strokes are decorated with a floral pattern, the thins are hair lines and the design modern face. The Didot material was acquired by Enschedé in 1850.

ABCDEHFGIJKLM NOQPRSTUVW XYZ

DIDOT FLORIATED CAPITALS

A new roman designed by Walter Diethelm. Ascenders and descenders are short, serifs are flat. The eye of the **e** is large. The italic is regular and slightly inclined. There are some swash capitals. The serifs on the tops of ascenders are large and inclined.

ABCDEFGHIJKLMNOPQRSTUV
abcdefghijklmnopqrstuvwxyz
1234567890 1234567890
ABCDEFGHIJKLMNOPQRST
abcdefghijklmnopqrstuvwxyz
ABCDEGJKMNPRTV

DIETHELM WITH SWASH CAPITALS

ii

ABCDEFGHIJLMNOPQRSTUV
abcdefghijklmnopqrstuvwxyz

DIETHELM BOLD

Designed by Gudrun Zapf-v.Hesse. A light roman with thin, flat serifs and wide letters in the lower case. The broad, splayed **M** has no top serifs. The tail of the **g** is not closed; **m, n, w** and the round letters are all very wide. The figures are old face. The italic is of slight inclination and the letters much narrower than in the roman.

ABCDEFGHIJKLMNOPQRSTUVW
abcdefghijklmnopqrstuvwxyz
1234567890
ABCDEFGHIJKLMNOPQRSTUVW
abcdefghijklmnopqrstuvwxyz

DIOTIMA

Designed by Lucien Pissarro and cut by E.P. Prince as a private-press-type for the printers in Holland. A calligraphic roman in which several letters have flourished tails and some capitals vertical strokes descending beneath the line. The t has miniscule form, and so has the E.

[Calligraphic specimen:]

¶ Als eerste boek der KUNERA PERS zal eer-
lang verschijnen: ♣ OOSTERSCH. Verzen
naar PERZISCHE en ARABISCHE DICH-
TERS door J. H. LEOPOLD, het vierde boek
voor de Vereeniging der Vijftig.

DISTEL

A face designed to match IBM electric typewriter composition.

ABCDEFGHIJKLMNOPQRSTUVWXYZ
abcdefghijklmnopqrstuvwxyz
1234567890
ABCDEFGHIJKLMNOPQRSTUVWXYZ
abcdefghijklmnopqrstuvwxyz
1234567890

DOCUMENT

Designed by Johannes Schweitzer. A monotone type with some squaring up of letters which leads to a condensed appearance. The e has an unusual vertical terminal and the g a minute ear.

ABCDEFGHIJKLMNOPQRSTUVWXYZ
abcdefghijklmnopqrstuvwxyz
1234567890
ABCDEFGHIJKLMNOPQRSTUVWXYZ
abcdefghijklmnopqrstuvwxyz
1234567890

*ABCDEFGHIJKLMNOPQRSTUVWXYZ
abcdefghijklmnopqrstuvwxyz
1234567890*

DOMINANTE

ABCDEFGHIJKLMNOPQRSTUVWXYZ
abcdefghijklmnopqrstuvwxyz
1234567890
ABCDEFGHIJKLMNOPQRSTUVWXYZ
abcdefghijklmnopqrstuvwxyz
1234567890

DOMINANTE BOLD

DOMINO
Ludwig & Mayer

iv

Designed by Alfred Riedel a fat face roman with short ascenders and descenders. The uprights are concave.

THE PRIMARY FUNCTION
of type is that it shall be read

DOMINO

DOMINUS
Stephenson Blake 1925

ix

A shaded roman with a resemblance to NARCISSUS, but the capitals are narrower. In the **M** the middle strokes stop short of the line. The arcs of **a**, **c** and **r** are terminated in thickenings. The eye of the **e** has an oblique stroke. In all these points the type differs from NARCISSUS. The type is also known as CLEARFACE OPEN or HANDTOOLED.

FORCEFULNESS
news announcem

DOMINUS

DOVES ROMAN
Doves Press 1900

i

The Doves Press was started in 1896 by T.J. Cobden Sanderson and Sir Emery Walker. It was named after an inn in Hammersmith, and possessed only one roman type in one size. This roman, first used in a book in 1900, was based on the favourite model of the early private presses, the type of Nicolas Jenson. It is nearer the original than Morris's GOLDEN TYPE, and is not so black. When the press was closed down the type was thrown into the Thames.

OFFICINA COLUMBARUM excuderunt T. J. Cobden-Sanderson et Emery Walker textum recensu it J. W. Mackail typos composuit J. H. Mason prelum exercuit H. Gage-Cole XIV Kal. Nov. MDCCCC

DOVES ROMAN

DRYNKOV
Grafotechna

ix

Designed by K. Drynkov. A calligraphic roman light in weight.

ABCDEFGHIJK
LMNOPQRSTU
VWXYZ
abcdefghijklmno
pqrstuvwxyz
1234567890

DRYNKOV

Designed by A. Finsterer. Three-dimensional capitals and figures; in design like an Egyptian. DUO SOLID has the face of the letters in black, and DUO OUTLINE in white.

ABCDEFGHIJKLM
NOPQRSTUWXZ
1234567890

DUO OUTLINE

v

ABCDEFGHIJKLM
NOPQRSTUWXZ

DUO SOLID

Designed by Otto Eckmann. A heavy type characterised by flowery characters. There is also a light and a heavy. In concept the type was meant to lean on black letter.

ABCDEFGHIJKLMNOPQRSTUV
WXYZ
abcdefghijklmnopqrsituvwxyz
1234567890

ECKMANN

A shaded roman, in which the shading takes the form of horizontal lines. Such shading always imparts a feeling of movement. Ascenders and descenders are short. The arcs of **a**, **c** and **r** are terminated by blobs.

ABCDEFGHIJKL
MNOPQRSTUV
WXY&Z
Æ Œ
1234567890

ÉCLAIR

EDEN
Ludlow 1934

Designed by R.H. Middleton. An angular type with horizontal serifs and thin upstrokes. There are two weights. Descenders are shorter than ascenders. The lower bowl of the **B** is slightly wider than the upper bowl, and the **R** is also wider at the bottom. The **G** has no spur. It resembles CORVINUS.

iv

ABCDEFGHIJKLMNOPQRSTUVWXYZ&
abcdefghijklmnopqrstuvwxyz 1234567890

EDEN

iv

ABCDEFGHIJKLMNOPQRSTUVWXYZ&
abcdefghijklmnopqrstuvwxyz
1234567890$

EDEN BOLD

EDITOR
Française 1937

Designed by Henri Chaix. A display roman with short ascenders and descenders. The serifs are thin and flat, and the thins are hair lines. In the **M** the middle strokes stop half-way The **g** has an open tail.

ix

Les artistes graphiques
Les artistes graphiques italiens de l'époque présentent leurs

EDITOR

ix

Les artistes graphiques

EDITOR BOLD

EGIPCIA PROGRESO
Gans c. 1923

A monotone type with heavy and oblique serifs in the lower case. Ascenders and descenders are short. *Cf.* PROGRESO.

i

Perfumería Regional BENAMOR 249 586

EGIPCIA PROGRESO

EGIZIANO
Nebiolo 1905

A heavy slab serif type.

v

ABCDEFGHIJKLMNOPQRSTUVWXYZ
abcdefghijklmnopqrstuvxyzw
1234567890

EGIZIANO

74

Designed by Aldo Novarese. Capitals are wide, ascenders and descenders are short. Serifs are flat though there is little variation of stress. The italic has the serifs of the roman.

EGIZIO
Nebiolo 1955–58

ABCDEFGHIJKLMNOPQRST
UVWXYZÇÆŒ&
abcdefghijklmnopqrstuvwxyz
1234567890

*ABCDEFGHIJKLMNOPQRST
UVXYZWÇÆŒ&
abcdefghijklmnopqrstuvxyzw
1234567890*

EGIZIO

iv/v

ABCDEFGHIJKLMNOPQRSTU
VWXYZ
abcdefghijklmnopqrstuvwxyz
1234567890

EGIZIO CONDENSED

iv/v

**ABCDEFGHIJKLMNOPQRS
TUVXYZWÇÆŒ&
abcdefghijklmnopqrstuvwxyz
1234567890**

***ABCDEFGHIJKLMNOPQRS
TUVWXYZÇÆŒ&
abcdefghijklmnopqrstuvwxyz
1234567890***

EGIZIO BOLD

iv/v

A light-faced roman designed by S.H. De Roos. The type has vertical stress, rather thin flat serifs, extending both ways on the top of ascenders. Ascenders are tall and descenders short. The capitals are wide; in **M** the middle strokes stop short of the line. The round **a** has a final top serif, **g** has a large bowl and **t** is tall. Numerals are short ranging. The italic has slight inclination and the serifs of the roman.

iv

ABCDEFGHIJKLMNOPQRSTUVW
XYZ

abcdefghijklmnopqrstuvwxyz 12345

ABCDEFGHIJKLMNOPQRSTUVW
XYZ

abcdefghijklmnopqrstuvwxyz 67890

EGMONT LIGHT

iv

ABCDEFGHIJKLMNOPQRSTUVW
XYZ

abcdefghijklmnopqrstuvwxyz 123

ABCDEFGHIJKLMNOPQRSTUVW
XYZ

abcdefghijklmnopqrstuvwxyz 456

EGMONT

iv

**ABCDEFGHIJKLMNOPQRSTUV
WXYZ**

abcdefghijklmnopqrstuvwxyz 7

EGMONT BOLD

iv

ABCDEFGHIJKLMNOPQRS
TUVWXYZ
1234567890

EGMONT INLINE CAPITALS

ABCDEFGHIJKLMNOPQRSTUVWXYZ
abcdefghijklmnopqrstuvwxyz
1234567890

EGYPTIAN

The condensed type is a revival of a nineteenth-century design. Descenders are very short.

ABCDEFGHIJKLMNOPQRSTUVWXYZ
abcdefghijklmnopqrstuvwxyz
1234567890

EGYPTIAN BOLD CONDENSED

ABCDEFGHIJKLMN
OPQRSTUVWXYZ

EGYPTIAN BOLD EXTENDED

abcdefghijklmnopqrs
tuvwxyz
1234567890

EGYPTIAN BOLD EXTENDED

Originally a nineteenth-century Miller & Richard's design. The type is an extra extended bold design with very pronounced serifs. The open version is a later three-dimension addition to the type range.

ABCDEFGHIJKLMNO
PQRSTUVWXYZ
abcdefghijklmnopqrst
uvwxyz
1234567890

EGYPTIAN EXPANDED

ABCDEFGHI
JKLMNOPQ
RSTUVWXY
ZÆŒ
abcdefghijkl
mnopqrstuvw
xyz
1234567890

EGYPTIAN EXPANDED OPEN

EGYPTIENNES
Française

Distinguishing letters are the upper- and lower-case **J** which end in a round dot.

v

ABCDEFGHIJKLMNOPQRSTUVWXYZÆŒ
abcdefghijklmnopqrstuvwxyzæœ 1234567890

EGYPTIENNES NARROW

v

ABCDEFGHIJKLMNOPQRST
UVWXYZÆŒ
abcdefghijklmnopqrstuvwx
yzæœ 1234567890

EGYPTIENNES BOLD

v

*ABCDEFGHIJKLMNO
PQRSTUVWXYZ
abcdefghijklmnopqrstu
vwxyz 1234567890*

EGYPTIENNE ITALIC

EHMCKE
Bauer

Designed by F. H. Ehmcke in 1908 for the Flinsch Foundry.

ix

ABCDEFGHIJKLMNOPPQ
RSſßTTUVWXYZ
abcdefghijklmnopqrſßstu
vwxyz
1234567890
ABCDEFGHIJKLMNOPQRSſßTTUVW
XYZ
abcdefghijklmnopqrſßstuvwxyz
1234567890

EHMCKE

78

The original types were in the Ehrhardt foundry at Leipzig in the early eighteenth century. The type is another version of JANSON. The upper case **M** is splayed and the **g** has a curved ear. There is also a semi-bold and italic. Special matrices of the Monotype series are available for the composition of the PITMAN INITIAL TEACHING ALPHABET.

ABCDEFGHIJKLMNOPQRSTUVWX

abcdefghijklmnopqrstuvwxyz

12345

ABCDEFGHIJKLMNOPQRSTUVWXYZ
abcdefghijklmnopqrstuvwxyz
1234567890
EHRHARDT

ii

ABCDEFGHIJKLMNOPQRSTUVWXYZ
abcdefghijklmnopqrstuvwxyz
1234567890
EHRHARDT SEMI-BOLD

ii

ABCDEFGHIJKLMNOPQRSTUVWXYZ
abcdefghijklmnopqrstuvwxyz
1234567890

EHRHARDT SEMI-BOLD ITALIC

ii

Designed by W.A. Dwiggins. A book type which is old face in its serif formation and stress. The italic has several swash capitals. There are two sets of figures, non-ranging and ranging.

ELDORADO
Mergenthaler Linotype 1951

ABCDEFGHIJKLMNOPQRSTUVWXYZ

abcdefghijklmnopqrstuvwxyz

1234567890   1234567890

ABCDEFGHIJKLMNOPQRSTUVWXYZ

ABCDEFGHIJKLMNOPQRSTUVWXYZ

abcdefghijklmnopqrstuvwxyz

1234567890   1234567890

ii

ELDORADO

ELECTRA
Nacional

Designed by W.A. Dwiggins. The serifs are flat, but otherwise old face traditions are observed. The letters are so unobtrusive that it is not easy to pick anything out—a compliment to a type. The **Q** has a distinctive tail, the **g** is slightly idiosyncratic. In common with other Linotype faces the **f** is unkerned, and the **t** is unbracketed. The italic is the roman slightly inclined, without any exception. ELECTRA CURSIVE is an alternative italic of orthodox design.

ii

ABCDEFGHIJKLMNOPQRSTUVWXYZ
abcdefghijklmnopqrstuvwxyz
1234567890   1234567890
ABCDEFGHIJKLMNOPQRSTUVWXYZ
ABCDEFGHIJKLMNOPQRSTUVWXYZ
abcdefghijklmnopqrstuvwxyz   abcdefghijklmnopqrstuvwxyz
1234567890   *1234567890*

ELECTRA

ii

ABCDEFGHIJKLMNOPQRSTUVWXYZ
abcdefghijklmnopqrstuvwxyz
1234567890   1234567890
ABCDEFGHIJKLMNOPQRSTUVWXYZ
ABCDEFGHIJKLMNOPQRSTUVWXYZ
abcdefghijklmnopqrstuvwxyz   abcdefghijklmnopqrstuvwxyz
1234567890   1234567890

ELECTRA BOLD

ELIZABETH ROMAN
Bauer 1937

Designed by Miss E. Friedländer, a pupil of Weiss. A roman almost monotone in colour, with small serifs and short descenders. The **E** and **F** are narrow, **J** ranges on the line, **M** has no top serifs as in many contemporary German romans, **U** has the lower-case design and **W**, lower-case also, no middle serif. The **g** has an open tail. Note the serif on the bar of the **t**. Figures are short-ranging. The inclination of the italic is slight; beginning strokes are angular. There is a second series of swash capitals.

ii

ABCDEFGHIJKLMNOPQRSTUVWXYZ
abcdefghijklmnopqrstuvwxyz
1234567890
ABCDEFGHIJKLMNOPQRSTUVWXYZ
abcdefghijkklmnopqrstuvwxyzz
1234567890

CAABDEFGHIJKLMNPRTWZ

ELIZABETH ROMAN

A text roman for phototypesetting and named after the street address of the type founders.

ABCDEFGHIJKLMNOPQRSTUVWXYZ
abcdefghijklmnopqrstuvwxyz
1 2 3 4 5 6 7 8 9 0

ELMORA

iv

ABCDEFGHIJKLMNOPQRSTUVWXYZ
abcdefghijklmnopqrstuvwxyz
1 2 3 4 5 6 7 8 9 0

ELMORA BOLD

iv

A revival of the Victorian condensed and elongated fat faces, a fashion started by SLIMBLACK.

iv

ABCDEFGHIJKLMNOPQRSTUVWXYZ

1234567890

ELONGATED ROMAN

iv

ABCDEFGHIJKLMNOPQRSTUVWXYZ

1234567

ELONGATED ROMAN SHADED

Originally a French type (one version is known as FRENCH OLD STYLE), designed by Théophile Beaudoire in 1858. The upper case is derived from Louis Perrin's LYONS CAPITALS. Note the splayed **M** and the tail of the **R**. The type is somewhat condensed and has short ascenders and descenders. In the **c** and **e** the thickest parts of the curves are very low; the **g** has a steeply inclined tail and there is a tall **t**. The italic has a slight inclination. Linotype (London) OLD STYLE NO. 33 is similar and so is DE VINNE.

ABCDEFGHIJKLMNOPQRSTUVWXYZ&
abcdefghijklmnopqrstuvwxyz
1234567890

ii

ABCDEFGHIJKLMNOPQRSTUVWXYZ&
abcdefghijklmnopqrstuvwxyz

ELZEVIR

81

Sets of quaintly decorated Victorian initials for the Elzevir Press.

ABCDEFG
HIJKLMNO
PQRSTUV

ABCDEFGH
IJKLMNOPQ
RSTUVWYZ

ELZEVIR INITIALS

EMERGO

Enschedé 1948–53

Designed and cut by S.L. Hartz. A light face with little variation in colour, small capitals and serifs, horizontal on the lower case. The **G** has a spur; **H** is wide and has the bar rather high. There are two **R**'s, one with an extended tail. The **g** has a rather wide tail. In the slightly inclined italic capitals are even smaller. In its angularity the type is of the BLADO school. Numerals are non-ranging.

ABCDEFGHIJKLMNOPQRRSTUVWXYZÆŒ&1234567890

ii

ABCDEFGHIJKLMNOPQRSTUVWXYZÆŒ&1234567890

abcdefghijklmnopqrstuvwxyzijæœ1234567890

ABCDEFGHIJKLMNOPQRRSTTUVWXYZÆŒQU

ii

abcdefghijklmnopqrstuvwxyzijæœ&1234567890

& fb ff ffi ffl fh fi fj fk fl Qu

EMERGO

EMERSON

Monotype 1936–39

Designed by Joseph Blumenthal and based on his SPIRAL type, which was cut by Louis Hoell. A type with little differentiation of colour and with blunt, horizontal serifs. The italic has a slight inclination and conforms to the roman, even in the serifs of the lower case. The numerals are non-ranging.

ii

ABCDEFGHIJKLMNOPQRSTUVWXYZ

abcdefghijklmnopqrstuvwxyz

1234567890

EMERSON

ABCDEFGHIJKLMNOPQRSTUVWXYZ EMERSON
abcdefghijklmnopqrstuvwxyz
1234567890
EMERSON ITALIC

ii

A roman following BODONI.

ABCDEFGHIJKLMNOPQRS TUVWXYZ
abcdefghijklmnopqrstuvwxyz
1234567890

EMPIRIANA
Grafotechna 1920

iv

ABCDEFGHIJKLMNOPQRS TUVWXYZ
abcdefghijklmnopqrstuvwxyz
1234567890

EMPIRIANA

ABCDEFGHIJKLMNOPQRS TUVWXYZ
abcdefghijklmnopqrstuvwxyz
1234567890

iv

EMPIRIANA BOLD

ABCDEFGHIJKLMNOPQRS TUVWXYZ   1234567890

iv

EMPIRIANA SHADED

ENDEAVOUR TYPE
Essex House Press 1901

A black face with heavy serifs, designed by C.R. Ashbee, the punches cut by E.P. Prince. This is perhaps the most exotic of the private press types. Few of the letters have a normal design. The bowls of the **B** are divided diagonally. **H** has a very high bar. The **M** has slab serifs and very short middle strokes. **W** has foot serifs and brief middle strokes. In the lower case **e** is a cursive form, **g** has no link and a contorted tail, in the **h**, **m** and **n** the last stroke is curved and descends below the line, **w** has the foot serifs of the capitals. Ascenders and descenders are short. The ampersand is curious. The name is derived from the title of the first book in which the type was used, *An Endeavour towards the Teachings of Ruskin and Morris*. The PRAYER BOOK TYPE of 1903, is the same design in Great Primer.

ix

And his mother said unto him, Upon 13 me be thy curse, my son: only obey my voice, and go fetch me them. And he 14

ENDEAVOUR TYPE

ENGRAVERS' TITLING BOLD
Monotype 1924

A titling type originally cast by American Typefounder's as ENGRAVER'S BOLD, available on Ludlow since 1926, and cast Inland Typefounders as LITHO. Ludlow call their version of 1940 LINING LITHO. In 1914 GNOM, designed by W. Augspurg, was cast by Schelter & Giesecke whose inline version is known as PERKEO or DIAPHANE by Warnery who call the type MOZART. Bauer's NOBLESSE of 1870 is based on the American designs.

iv

ABCDEFGHIJKLMNOPQRSTUVWXYZ
1234567890

ENGRAVERS' TITLING BOLD

ERASMUS
Amsterdam 1923

Designed by S.H. de Roos. Light serifs and short descenders, with many of the serifs shaped as though drawn with a pen. **E** and **F** have centre arms high; the **H** has a high bar and the **U** follows the lower-case design. The **g** has a short tail drawn from right to left; **p** and **q** have oblique foot serifs. The italic has slight inclination and the serifs of the roman.

ix

BORN AT ROTTERDAM
Pension at the Duke of Cleves

ERASMUS

ix

ABCDEFGHIJKLMNOPQRSTUWXZ

abcdefghijklmnopqrstuvwxyzabcdefgir

ERASMUS GRATIUS

ERLER TITLING
Typoart 1953

Designed by Herbert Thannhaeuser. A set of inline capitals with thin serifs and of light weight.

ABCDEFGHIJKLMNOPQRSTUVWXYZ

ix

ERLER TITLING

Designed by Aldo Novarese. Many letters have script quality.

ABCDEFGHIJKLMNOPQRS TUVWXYZ abcdefghijklmnopqrstuvwxyz 1234567890

ESTRO

Another Garamond design due to G.W. Jones, named after the famous family of Paris printers. This roman differs from GRANJON in the greater height of the ascenders and length of the descenders. It is also lighter in colour. Other distinguishing marks are, the **R** which tapers off and descends below the line, and the **g** with a larger bowl.

The italic has less inclination than the Granjon. The **Q** has a tail after the Goudy model. In the lower case the serifs on the tops of ascenders are inclined; the curve of the bowl of the **p** continues beyond the main stroke. The Haas ESTIENNE is an entirely different design.

ABCDEFGHIJKLMNOPQRSTUVWXYZ
abcdefghijklmnopqrstuvwxyz
1234567890
ABCDEFGHIJKLMNOPQRSTUVWXYZ
ABCDEFGHIJKLMNOPQRSTUVWXYZ
abcdefghijklmnopqrstuvwxyz
1234567890

ESTIENNE

Probably a Wagner & Schmidt face of 1902. An elongated and condensed roman with small, pointed serifs. Not to be confused with the Linotype ESTIENNE.

ABCDEFGHIJKLMNOPQRSTUVWXYZ
abcdefghijklmnopqrstuvwxyz
1234567890

ETIENNE

The roman was designed by E. F. Detterer, and the other weights by R. H. Middleton. A faithful copy of the original after Nicolas Jenson, retaining the slab serifs on the **M**. The **Q** has a tail like CLOISTER, while the **W** is like CENTAUR. The lower-case **g** has the appearance of leaning backwards. The italic resembles ARRIGHI, but the capitals are wider. The type's old name is NICOLAS JENSON.

ABCDEFGHIJKLMNOPQRSTUVWXY

EUSEBIUS

ABCDEFGHIJKLMNOPQRSTUVWXYZ

EUSEBIUS BOLD

ABCDEFGHIJKLMNOPQRSTUVW

EUSEBIUS OPEN

EXECUTIVE

Monotype;
Wagner and others 1960

ii

Designed by The Monotype Corporation to provide a printing type compatible with an IBM typewriter face. The alphabet has been divided into four set widths.

ABCDEFGHIJKLMNOPQRSTUVWXYZ

abcdefghijklmnopqrstuvwxyz

1234567890

EXECUTIVE

EXCELSIOR

Mergenthaler Linotype 1931;
Linotype (London);
Linotype (Frankfurt)

iv

Designed by C.H. Griffith. A newspaper type of even colour, and No. 2 of the "Linotype Legibility Group". The roman has horizontal serifs and generally follows the Didone style. The numerals are ranging.

ABCDEFGHIJKLMNOPQRSTUVWXYZ

abcdefghijklmnopqrstuvwxyz

123456789

ABCDEFGHIJKLMNOPQRSTUVWXYZ

ABCDEFGHIJKLMNOPQRSTUVWXYZ

abcdefghijklmnopqrstuvwxyz

234567890

EXCELSIOR

EXPANDED ANTIQUE

Stevens Shanks c. 1880

v

An expanded titling taken over from the foundry of V. & J. Figgins.

ABCDEFGHIJ KLMNOPQRS TUVWXYZ 1234567890£&

EXPANDED ANTIQUE

EXTRA ORNAMENTED 2

Stevens Shanks

ix

A set of inline and ornamented capitals and figures. In plan the letters are English modern face.

ABCDEFGHIJKLMNOPQRST UVWXYZ 1234567890

EXTRA ORNAMENTED No. 2

EXTENDED 3

Stevens Shanks

iv

An expanded type with short ascenders and descenders. Serifs are thin and there are many hair lines. American Typefounders call the type CARD MERCANTILE.

ABCDEFGHIJKLMNOP QRSTUVWXYZ

abcdefghijklmnopqrstuvwxyz

1234567890

EXTENDED No. 3

Designed by Rudolph Ruzicka. There are ranging and non-ranging numerals. The **R** has a curled tail and the **U** follows the lower-case design. The **g** has a large bowl with a minute ear. In the italic **b**, **h**, **m** and **n** the upstrokes take off from the very feet of the downstrokes.

FAIRFIELD
Mergenthaler Linotype
1939–49

iv

ABCDEFGHIJKLMNOPQRSTUVWXYZ
abcdefghijklmnopqrstuvwxyz
1234567890   1234567890
ABCDEFGHIJKLMNOPQRSTUVWXYZ
ABCDEFGHIJKLMNOPQRSTUVWXYZ
abcdefghijklmnopqrstuvwxyz
1234567890   1234567890

FAIRFIELD

ABCDEFGHIJKLMNOPQRSTUVWXYZ
abcdefghijklmnopqrstuvwxyz
1234567890   1234567890
ABCDEFGHIJKLMNOPQRSTUVWXYZ
ABCDEFGHIJKLMNOPQRSTUVWXYZ
abcdefghijklmnopqrstuvwxyz
1234567890   1234567890

FAIRFIELD MEDIUM

iv

Designed by W.A. Dwiggins. A book face with narrow characters and of calligraphic simple design. The **Q** has an unusual angular hooked tail. The italic **y** is almost closed, as are the **v** and **w**.

FALCON
Mergenthaler Linotype 1961

ii

ABCDEFGHIJKLMNOPQRSTUVWXYZ
abcdefghijklmnopqrstuvwxyz
1234567890   1234567890
ABCDEFGHIJKLMNOPQRSTUVWXYZ
ABCDEFGHIJKLMNOPQRSTUVWXYZ
abcdefghijklmnopqrstuvwxyz
1234567890   1234567890

FALCON

A fat face following the traditional English design.

FALSTAFF
Monotype c. 1935

iv

ABCDEFGHIJKLMNOPQRSTUVWXYZ
abcdefghijklmnopqrstuvwxyz
1234567890

ABCDEFGHIJKLMNOPQRSTUVWXYZ
abcdefghijklmnopqrstuvwxyz
1234567890

FALSTAFF

FARMER'S OLD STYLE

Lanston Monotype 1909

ii

One of the first types made available for Monotype machine composition, this face was first cut in 1899 adapted from OLD STYLE NO. 5 of the former A.D. Farmer & Son Foundry, of New York City. The type has not been cut larger than 12 pt.

ABCDEFGHIJKLMNOPQRSTUVWXYZ&ÆŒ

abcdefghijklmnopqrstuvwxyzæœ

1234567890   1234567890

ABCDEFGHIJKLMNOPQRSTUVWXYZ&ÆŒ

ABCDEFGHIJKLMNOPQRSTUVWXYZ&ÆŒ

abcdefghijklmnopqrstuvwxyzæœ

1234567890   1234567890

FARMER'S OLD STYLE

FAUST

Typoart 1959

ix

Designed by Albert Kapr. A roman with many unusual letters. The most conspicuous are the **n**, **m**, and **r**, with inclined top strokes. There is some squaring-up of the round letters. The capitals are wide and lower than the ascenders. There is an italic, slightly inclined.

ABCDEFGHIJKLMNOPQRSTU
VWXYZ&
abcdefghijklmnopqrstuvwxyz?
1234567890

*ABCDEFGHIJKLMNOPQRSTU
VWXYZ&
abcdefghijklmnopqrstuvwxyz?
1234567890*

FAUST

FELIX

Monotype 1934

vii

A titling based on the inscriptional letters designed by Felice Feliciano of Verona in 1463. The manuscript is in the Vatican Library and was reproduced in the Italian periodical *La Bibliofilia* in 1935 and in an edition by Dr Giovanni Mardersteig entitled ALPHABETUM ROMANUM published in 1960 at Verona.

MONOTYPE

FELIX

Many of the old types of the Oxford University Press were bought by John Fell, Bishop of Oxford, about the year 1672, through his agents in Holland. But some of these types, like the one here shown, are probably of French origin. It has recently been established that the larger sizes, formerly thought to be Dutch, were cut at Oxford by Peter Walpergen.

FELL ROMAN
Oxford University Press

ii

The Oxford Printing House holds the oldest punches and matrices surviving in England, material not only treasured but used; types cast therefrom being employed for the composition of books and other printed matter.

ABCDEFGHIJKLMNOPQRSTUVWXYZÆ
ABCDEFGHIJKLMNOPQRSTUVWXYZÆ
abcdefghijklmnopqrstuvwxyzæœ
1234567890
& ff fi fl ffi ffl ſ ſh ſi ſl ſſ ft ffi
FELL ROMAN

A monoline type with short descenders and some terminal flourishes.

FEMINA
Bauer 1927

ix

Forstwirtschaft
Land- und
FEMINA

A condensed reversed slab serif type resembling PLAYBILL but having greater colour contrast. HIDALGO is very similar.

FIGARO
Monotype 1940

v

ABCDEFGHIJKLMNOPQRSTUVWXYZ
abcdefghijklmnopqrstuvwxyz
1234567890
FIGARO

A condensed fat face following the usual English design of the time and taken over from the foundry of V. & J. Figgins.

FIGGINS
CONDENSED
NO. 2
Stevens Shanks c. 1870

iv

ABCDEFGHIJKLMNOPQRSTU
VWXYZÆŒ
abcdefghijklmnopqrstuvwxyz
1224567890

FIGGINS CONDENSED NO. 2

FIGGINS SHADED

Stevens Shanks

iv

Three-dimensional capitals and figures with white faces. In this type there are two distinct designs, 10 and 30 point, first shown by Vincent Figgins in 1815. The 14 and 18 point derive from the foundry of Bessemer and Catherwood and were first shown in their specimen of 1825.

ABCDEFGHIJKLMNOPQRSTUVW
XYZŒÆ&£1234567800

18 POINT FIGGINS SHADED

iv

ABCDEFG

30 POINT FIGGINS SHADED

FIGURA

Klingspor 1955

iv

Designed by Alfred Finsterer. A condensed and elongated fat face, like SLIMBLACK. Ascenders and descenders are very short. The design is Victorian, except perhaps the **t**.

ABCDEFGHIJKLMNOPQRSTUVWXYZ

abcdefghijklmnopqrstuvwxyz

1234567890

FIGURA

FIGURAL

Grafotechna

ii

Designed by Oldrich Menhart. A type leaning somewhat on JENSON but having strong pen characteristics, which become particularly obvious in the italic, where lower-case letters are angular and of varying inclination. In the italic the **R** and **K** have a tail descending below the line, the **U** follows the lower-case design. The swash capitals were added in 1959.

ABCDEFGHIJKLMNOPQRSTUVWXYZ
abcdefghijklmnopqrstuvwxyz
1234567890
ABCDEFGHIJKLMNOPQRSTUVWXYZ
abcdefghijklmnopqrstuvwxyz
1234567890

FIGURAL

viii

ABCDEFGHIJKLMN
OPQRSTUVWXYZ

FIGURAL SWASH CAPS

Designed by John Peters, and presumably intended for newspaper display headings.

632-18 pt

ABCDEFGHIJKLMNOPQRSTUVWXYZ
1234567890

FLEET TITLING

J.M. Fleischman was born in Germany in 1701, but for most of his life he was cutting types for Dutch founders, including the Enschedé firm in their earliest days. All his surviving punches and matrices are now in the possession of the Enschedés. His roman types are rather condensed and of a large x-height. His design is approaching the modern; the stress in some letters is vertical and the serifs are nearer the horizontal. The long arms of the **E** and the squareness of the **M** are to be noted. The **g** is conspicuous with its bulbous ear and rounded link. The italic is moderately inclined, but is somewhat irregular. The modern re-cutting was designed by Georg Belwe for L. Wagner, who spell the name of the type as FLEISCHMANN, following original German style.

ABCDEFGHIJKLMNOPQRSTUVWXYZÆŒ&
ABCDEFGHIJKLMNOPQRSTUVWXYZÆŒ
abcdefghijklmnopqrsſtuvwxyzijæœ1234567890
ct fb ff ffi ffl fh fi fk fl fb fh fi fl ff ß ſſi ſſl ft
ABCDEFGHIJKLMNOPQRSTUVWXYZIJÆŒ&
ABCDJMNPQR
abcdefghijklmnopqrsſtuvvwwxyzijæœ

ENSCHEDE FLEISCHMAN

ABCDEFGHIJKLMNOPQRSTU VWXYZ&
abcdefghijklmnopqrstuvwxyz?
1234567890
ABCDEFGHIJJKLMNOPQQuRSTU VWXYYZ&&
abcdefghbijklmnopqrstuvwxyz?
1234567890

FLEISCHMANN

ABCDEFGHIJKLMNOPQRSTU VWXYZ&
abcdefghijklmnopqrstuvwxyz?
1234567890

FLEISCHMANN BOLD

FLORENCE PRESS TYPE
Chatto & Windus 1908

ix

A roman designed by H.P. Horne, resembling his other romans, MONTALLEGRO and RICCARDI. Serifs are small and inclined on the lower case. The capitals are broader than in Montallegro. **e** has a large bowl with a straight bar. The ampersand has the tall form found in some italics.

'Lear,' although we can hardly imagine they would ever marry, kept single out of a cynical humour or for a broken heart, and not, as we do nowadays, from a spirit of incredulity and preference for the single state. For that matter, if you turn to George Sand's French version of 'As You Like

FLORENCE PRESS TYPE

FLORENZ
L. Wagner 1960

i

Designed by Paul Zimmermann. The type resembles ALDUS. Serifs are very small, the **W** is wide and has no middle serif.

ANTIQUA   FLORENZ

Als der fünfzehnjährige Erhard Ratdolt mit Augsburger Kauffahrern zum erstenmal nach Venedig kam, faßte er eine tiefe Liebe zu dieser Stadt. Im Jahre 1476 zog er als junger Buchdrucker wieder über die Alpen, um sich ganz in Venedig niederzulassen. Dort richtete er mit zwei Deutschen eine Offizin ein, die bald seinen Ruhm über alle Lande tragen sollte.

FLORENZ

FLORIATED CAPITALS
Monotype 1935

ix

Designed by Eric Gill. A set of open capitals with decorative leaf forms.

FLORIATED CAPITALS

FOLKWANG
Klingspor 1954–55

ix

Designed by Hermann Schardt. A somewhat exotic roman in which the lower case is like an upright italic. The serifs at the ends of the arms of **E** and **F** are on the under side only. The **J** has an unusual design. The italic has some characteristics of a script, e.g. in the pen drawn serifs. Numerals are short ranging. The bold differs in many ways from the roman.

ABCDEFGHIJKLMNOPQRSTUV
abcdefghijklmnopqrstuvwxyz
1234567890
ABCDEFGHIJKLMNOPQRST
abcdefghijklmnopqrstuvwxyz

FOLKWANG

ABCDEFGHIJKLMNOPQRST
abcdefghijklmnopqrstuvwxyz

FOLKWANG BOLD

Designed by Giovanni Mardersteig for Collins, the Glasgow publishers and printers in 1936, and based on a type cut by Alexander Wilson of the Glasgow Letter Foundry about 1770. It is a round letter with some affinity to BASKERVILLE. The ascenders are rather short and the capitals modest in height and weight.

FONTANA
Monotype 1961

ABCDEFGHIJKLMNOPQRSTUVWXYZ
abcdefghijklmnopqrstuvwxyz
1234567890
ABCDEFGHIJKLMNOPQRSTUVWXYZ
abcdefghijklmnopqrstuvwxyz
1234567890

FONTANA

Designed by A. Novarese. A set of decorated capitals and figures. All serifs are rounded forms and there are roundels in the centre of the main strokes.

FONTANESI
Nebiolo

ABCDRFGHIJKLMN
OPQTCSUVWXYZ
ÇÆŒ&
1234567890

FONTANESI

Designed by Friedrich Bauer. An inline series of roman capitals. The line passes right through vertical strokes. Serifs are very small. In the **M** the middle strokes stop short of the line. *Cf.* DALIA.

FORTUNA
Trennert 1930

GEISENHEIM

FORTUNA

Designed by K.F. Bauer and Walter Baum. A display roman whose stubby flat serifs give it the appearance of a Clarendon. It is an expanded face and the lower case has very short ascenders and descenders. There are three weights.

iv

ABCDEFGHIJKLMNOPQ
RSTUVWXYZ
abcdefghijklmnopqrstuvw
xyz
1234567

FORTUNE LIGHT

iv

ABCDEFGHIJKLMNOP
QRSTUVWXYZ
abcdefghijklmnopqrstu
vwxyz
1234567890

ABCDEFGHIJKLMNOPQX
abcdefghijklmnopqrstuvwx
1234567890

FORTUNE BOLD

v

ABCDEFGHIJKLMN
OPQRSTUVWXYZ
abcdefghijklmnop
qrstuvwxyz
1234567890

FORTUNE EXTRA BOLD

Designed by Georg Trump. A slab serif type with light (FORUM I) and heavy (FORUM II) **FORUM**
The type is quite different from FORUM CAPITALS. *Weber*

v

ABCDEFGHIJKLMNOPQRSTUVW
XYZ
1234567890

FORUM I

v

ABCDEFGHIJKLMNOP
QRSTUVWXYZ
1243567890

FORUM II

Designed by F.W. Goudy and first shown 1912. The serifs have pen-stroke qualities like other **FORUM**
Goudy designs. The U has the lower-case design and the upper limbs of the Y are curved. **CAPITALS**
Lanston Monotype 1924;
Caslon

vii

ABCDEFGHIJKLMNOPQRS
TUVWXYZ

FORUM CAPITALS

The new roman of the famous Paris founder P.S. Fournier is, apart from the privately owned **FOURNIER**
ROMAINS DU ROI, the first of the "transitional" types. The type is somewhat condensed, though *Monotype 1925*
much less so than others designed by Fournier, such as his POETIQUE. The capitals are tall.
BARBOU is related. There is a short-ranging **J** and an **R** with a curved tail. In the lower
case the **b** has a foot serif which is flat. The italic is notable for its inclined roman serifs on the
m, n, p, z, no doubt designed for the sake of harmony with the roman; nevertheless the Fournier
italic can stand on its own. The curves of the **v, w** and **y** are influenced by contemporary
calligraphy.

iii

ABCDEFGHIJKLMNOPQRSTUVWXYZ
abcdefghijklmnopqrstuvwxyz
1234567890

ABCDEFGHIJKLMNOPQRSTUVWXYZ
abcdefghijklmnopqrstuvwxyz
1234567890

FOURNIER

FOURNIER
Typoart

ix

Designed by P. A. Demeter in 1922.

ABCDEFGHIJKLMNOPQRSTUVWX
DIE SCHRIFT WURDE DIE TRÄGE

FOURNIER

FOURNIER
LE JEUNE
Deberny & Peignot 1913;
Amsterdam

ix

Shaded italic capitals, in which the thick strokes are broken in the middle by the insertion of diamond-shaped ornaments. Based on the decorated letters designed by P.S. Fournier *c.* 1746 and reproduced by Peignot.

FOURNIER LE JEUNE (American Typefounders) is a similar type. It can be distinguished by the thin serifs which curve downwards and end in thickenings.

LETTTERS BULLETIN

DEBERNY & PEIGNOT FOURNIER LE JEUNE

ix

ABCDEFGHI
JKLMNO
PQSTTUVWY

AMSTERDAM FOURNIER LE JEUNE

FRENCH FACE
EXTENDED
Monotype

iv

A modern face with short ascenders and descenders. In spite of its name the design follows English models.

ABCDEFGHIJKLMNOPQRSTUVWXYZ

abcdefghijklmnopqrstuvwxyz

12345

ABCDEFGHIJKLMNOPQRSTUVWXYZ

abcdefghijklmnopqrstuvwxyz

FRENCH FACE EXTENDED

FRENCH
OLD STYLE
Monotype 1908

ii

A type similar to DE VINNE.

ABCDEFGHIJKLMNOPQRSTUVWXYZ

abcdefghijklmnopqrstuvwxyz

1234567890

ABCDEFGHIJKLMNOPQRSTUVWXYZ

abcdefghijklmnopqrstuvwxyz

FRENCH OLD STYLE

ii

ABCDEFGHIJKLMNOPQRSTUVWXYZ

abcdefghijklmnopqrstuvwxyz

1234567890

FRENCH OLD STYLE BOLD

A type similar to ELZEVIR, DE VINNE and OLD STYLE NO. 33.

ABCDEFGHIJKLMNOPQRSTUVWXYZ
abcdefghijklmnopqrstuvwxyz
1234567890
ABCDEFGHIJKLMNOPQRSTUVWXYZ
abcdefghijklmnopqrstuvwxyz

FRENCH ROUND FACE

Designed by Frederick W. Goudy. Almost an italic with swash capitals.

ABCDEFGHIJKLMNOPQRTSUV
WXYZ

abcdefghijklmnopqrstuvwxyz

FRENCHWOOD RONDE

Designed by Lin Yu-Bingnan. A calligraphic type. Bowls of **B**, **P** and **R** do not close in the centre, and in the **g** the tail does not close. In the italic the tail of the **Q** is freely suspended.

ABCDEFGHIJKLMNOPQR
STUVWXYZ
abcdefghijklmnopqrstuvw
xyz

1234567890

ABCDEFGHIJKLMNOPQRST
UVWXYZ
abcdefghijklmnopqrstuvwxyz
1234567890

FREUNDSCHAFT

FRY'S BASKERVILLE
Stephenson Blake

Stephenson Blake give the date as 1768, and the type was perhaps cut by Isaac Moore under the influence of Baskerville. In the **Q** the tail is like BASKERVILLE and the **R** had a straight tail. There are two **w**'s, one with and one without a middle serif.

iii

DETER printed

FRY'S CANON
Kynoch Press

This type, originally from Fry's foundry was cast by Stephenson Blake for Kynoch Press and Curwen Press.

One of the earliest of the Fat Faces, dating from 1808. The design is that of the modern face, with an exaggeration of the contrast between thick and thin strokes. The exaggeration is however less than in the contemporary type THOROWGOOD.

iv

ABCDEFGH
abcdefghijkl
123456789
ABCDEFG
abcdefghijkl
mnopqrstuvw

FRY'S ORNAMENTED
Stephenson Blake

Cut by Richard Austin in 1796. A series of inline capitals in which the centre of the main strokes is further decorated with an oval.

ii

ABCDEFGHIJKLMNOP
QRSTUVWXYZ

A quaintly decorated tooled display face.

GALLIA

Lanston Monotype 1928

ix

ABCDEFGHIJ
KLMNOPQRS
ſSTUVWXYZ
1234567890

GALLIA

A set of inscriptional capitals and ranging figures. The serifs are fairly large and shaped. E and F are narrow; the variation of stress in **O** and **Q** is oblique. **P** has the bowl unclosed. **U** has the lower-case design.

GANTON
Stephenson Blake 1927

vii

CURIOUS EPITAPH

GANTON

Designed by A. Novarese. A type closely following the style of GARAMOND, but in the bold the slight irregularity of the original type is no longer apparent.

GARALDUS
Nebiolo 1956–1960

ii

ABCDEFGHIJKLMNOPQRSTUVXYZWQu
abcdefghijklmnopqrsſtuvxyzwfifflflffiffl
1234567890 1234567890
ABCDEFGHIJKLMNOPQRSTUVXYZÆŒW
abcdefghijklmnopqrstuvxyzæœwfifflflffiffl
1234567890 1234567890

GARALDUS

ABCDEFGHIJKLMNOPQRSTU
VWXYZ   1234567890
abcdefghijklmnopqrstuvwxyz
ABCDEFGHIJKLMNOPQRSTU
VWXYZ   1234567890
abcdefghijklmnopqrstuvwxyz

GARALDUS BOLD

99

GARAMOND or GARAMONT

Many founders

Claude Garamond (1480–1561) based his ROMAIN DE L'UNIVERSITÉ on designs by Aldus Manutius, and first specimens are found in books printed in Paris around 1532. Many of the present-day versions of this type are based on the TYPI ACADEMIAE of Jean Jannon cut in Sedan around 1615. The Imprimerie Nationale in Paris towards the end of the nineteenth century revived the JANNON type of 1641 cut for the then Imprimerie Royale. Ambroise Vollard in 1897 was given permission to use the type for Verlaine's *Paralellement*.

There are the following basic models:

Deberny & Peignot, 1912-28. This design, supervised by Georges and later Charles Peignot —not copied by any other foundry or matrix manufacturer—is based on the original types in the Imprimerie Nationale.

American Typefounders, 1917, designed by M.F. Benton and T.M. Cleland after the original Jannon types. From this source the versions of the Amsterdam Typefoundry, Linotype Garamond No. 3 (1936) and Intertype have been derived.

Lanston Monotype, 1921, designed by F.W. Goudy after Jannon. This version was also adopted by The Monotype Corporation and has not been copied by others. The Monotype Corporation's version follows Jannon in the roman and Granjon in the italic.

Stempel, 1924. This design is based on the Egenolff-Berner sheet, but the characters have been regularised. The design is available on Linotypes.

Mergenthaler Linotype, 1925, issued an adaptation by Joseph Hill. This was also based on the Egenolff-Berner sheet, but considerably bolder and less closely setting than the other Linotype version. This design is no longer available.

Nebiolo's GARALDUS, 1956, designed by Aldo Novarese, is another re-cutting and is shown separately.

Simoncini in Italy—later in co-operation with Ludwig & Mayer, have also issued a Garamond in 1958–61, designed by F. Simoncini and W. Bilz.

Grafotechna introduced a Garamond in 1959 designed by Stanislav Marso.

There are also a number of other adaptations of the American Typefounders' design (based on Jannon). The Ludlow version designed by R. Hunter Middleton in 1930, the Berling version designed by Henri Alm partly based on Granjon designs; and the Typoart version.

ii

ABCDEFGHIJKLMNOPQRSTUVWXYZ
abcdefghijklmnopqrstuvwxyz
1 2 3 4 5   QU & Qu   6 7 8 9 0

ABCDEFGHIJKLMNOPQRSTUVWXYZ
abcdefghijklmnopqrstuvwxyz
1 2 3 4 5   QU & Qu   6 7 8 9 0

DEBERNY & PEIGNOT GARAMONT

ii

ABCDEFGHIJKLMNOPQRSTUVWXYZ
abcdefghijklmnopqrstuvwxyz
123456789   1234567890
ABCDEFGHIJKLMNOPQRSTUVWXYZ
ABCDEFGHIJKLMNOPQRSTUVWXY

ABCDEFGHIJKLMNOPQRSTUVWXYZ
abcdefghijklmnopqrstuvwxyz
1234567890   234567890
BCDEFGHIJKLMNOPQRSTUVWXYZ
Recut Italic: abcdefghijklmnopqrstuvwxyz

LINOTYPE GARAMOND NO. 3

ABCDEFGHIJKLMNOPQRSTUVWXYZ
abcdefghijklmnopqrstuvwxyz
12345678   1234567890
ABCDEFGHIJKLMNOPQRSTUVWXYZ
ABCDEFGHIJKLMNOPQRSTUVWXYZ

ABCDEFGHIJKLMNOPQRSTUVWXYZ
abcdefghijklmnopqrstuvwxyz
34567890   1234567890

ABCDEFGHIJKLMNOPQRSTUVWXYZ
Recut Italic: abcdefghijklmnopqrstuvwxyz

LINOTYPE GARAMOND BOLD NO. 3

ABCDEFGHIJKLMNOPQRSTUVWXYZ
abcdefghijklmnopqrstuvwxyz
1234567890
ABCDEFGHIJKLMNOPQRSTUVWXYZ &&£

ABCDEFGHIJKLMNOPQRSTUVWXYZ
abcdefghijklmnopqrstuvwxyz
1234567890

INTERTYPE GARAMOND

ii

ABCDEFGHIJKLMNOPQRSTUVWXYZ
abcdefghijklmnopqrstuvwxyz 1234567890
ABCDEFGHIJKLMNOPQRSTUVWXYZ
abcdefghijklmnopqrstuvwxyz 1234567890
1234567890 1234567890

INTERTYPE GARAMOND BOLD

ii

ABCDEFGHIJKLMNOPQRSTUVWXYZ
abcdefghijklmnopqrstuvwxyz
1234567890

ABCDEFGHIJKLMNOPQRSTUVWXYZ
abcdefghijklmnopqrstuvwxyz
1234567890

MONOTYPE GARAMOND

ii

101

ABCDEFGHIJKLMNOPQRSTUVWXYZ
abcdefghijklmnopqrstuvwxyz
1234567890
ABCDEFGHIJKLMNOPQRSTUVWXYZ
abcdefghijklmnopqrstuvwxyz
1234567890

MONOTYPE GARAMOND BOLD

ii

ABCDEFGHIJKLMNOPQRS
TUVWXYZ
abcdefghijklmnopqrstuvwxyz
1234567890

ii

ABCDEFGHIJKLMNOPQRS
TUVWXYZ
abcdefghijklmnopqrstuvwxyz
1234567890

GRAFOTECHNA GARAMOND

ii

ABCDEFGHIJKLMNOPQRS
TUVWXYZ
ABCDEFGHIJKLMNOPQRSTUVW
XYZ
1234567890

ABCDEFGHIJKLMNOPQRST
UVWXYZ
1234567890

SIMONCINI GARAMOND

ABCDEFGHIJKLMNOPQRSTUVWXYZ&
abcdefghijklmnopqrstuvwxyz 1234567890$

*ABCDEFGHIJKLMNOPQRSTUV
WXYZ&*
abcdefghijklmnopqrstuvwxyz 1234567890$

ii

A text type derived from a design of the former Genzsch & Heyse Foundry. Tall ascenders characterise this type, which is basically old face, but has ranging figures.

**GENZSCH
ANTIQUA**
Intertype (Berlin)

ii

ABCDEFGHIJKLMNOPQRSTU VWXYZ
abcdefghijklmnopqrstuvwxyz   1234567890
ABCDEFGHIJKLMNOPQRSTUVWXYZ
abcdefghijklmnopqrstuvwxyz   1234567890

ABCDEFGHIJKLMNOPQRSTU VWXYZ
abcdefghijklmnopqrstuvwxyz   1234567890

ii

A roman dating from *c.* 1790, perhaps from the Fry Foundry, but its early history is obscure. The serif formation and differentiation of colour are approaching the modern face. The capitals, in larger sizes, are rather heavy. Descenders are short. The **g** has a curled ear. The italic seems to be an earlier design, a Fry copy of CASLON ITALIC. *Cf.* the slope of the **A**, the swash **J** and **T**.

Linotype GEORGIAN designed by G.W. Jones (and VICTORIAN) are similar to the Stephenson Blake design, but there are a number of small differences, *e.g.* the serif on the lower arc of the **C** and the straight serifs on the arms of the **E**.

GEORGIAN
Stephenson Blake*;

Linotype (London)

ABCDEFGHIJKLMNOPQRSTUVWXYZ
abcdefghijklmnopqrstuvwxyz   123456789
ABCDEFGHIJKLMNOPQRSTUVWXYZ
ABCDEFGHIJKLMNOPQRSTUVWXYZ
abcdefghijklmnopqrstuvwxyz   234567890

iii

Designed by Friedrich Wobst. A fat face italic or script. In the lower case there are not the usual flat serifs, but hooks. The **g** has an open tail. This appears to be a separate face.

Continental Regenmäntel

GLOBUS CURSIVE

Designed by Eric Gill, a rounder form of his PERPETUA. It has the modest capitals, horizontal serifs and slight differentiation of colour of Gill's other romans. The **M** is somewhat splayed. The **g** has a rather large bowl. The **t** is very short. The italic, cut only for the 14 pt. size, is a sloped roman except for the **a** and with it are used the roman capitals, as in the case of JOANNA.

ABCDEFGHIJKLMNOPQuRSTUVWXYZ

abcdefghijklmnopqrstuvwxyz

abcdefghijklmnopqrstuvwxyz

1234567890

GOLDEN COCKEREL TYPE

Designed by William Morris and of importance in the history of modern typography since it began the revolution which has taken place in the design of our type faces. The punches were cut by E.P. Prince and the first book in which it was used was the *Golden Legend*, 1892.

Morris tells us that there was only one source in which to find the model for his first roman, namely, the printers of fifteenth-century Venice and especially Nicolas Jenson. The designer reinforced the type, made it a blacker face than the model and in particular weighted the serifs on the lower case. The **g** is a narrower letter and has an incorrect ear.

American Typefounders made a copy of this type before 1900 and called it NICOLAS JENSON.

All Morris's punches and matrices and some of the types are now in the possession of the Cambridge University Press.

Next as to type. By instinct rather than by conscious thinking it over, I began by getting myself a fount of Roman type. And here what I wanted was letter pure in form; severe, without needless excrescenses; solid without the thickening and thinning of the line, which is the essential fault of the ordinary modern type, and which makes it difficult to read; and not compressed laterally, as all later type has grown to be

ABCDEFGHIJKLMNOPQRSTUVWXYZ

abcdefghijklmnopqrstuvwxyz

1234567890

GOLDEN TYPE

A three-dimensional rather square slab serif type of Victorian style. NUBIAN (not the American Typefounders' version) is very similar.

ABCDEFGHIJKLMNO
PQRSTUVWXYZ
1234567890

GOLDRUSH

Designed by H.R. Möller. Inline fat face capitals and figures. The white line occupies only a small portion of the main strokes. The letters are wide, especially **M** and **W**.

REGATTA is a similar face with horizontal inline. There are two parallel white lines.

MUSEOS **ODAIR**

GOLF REGATTA

Begun, says F.W. Goudy, in 1919. It is a Venetian in some respects, but it was intended as a Bold Face, and has the abbreviated descenders of such faces. The **H** has a high bar and there is the usual Goudy **Q**. In the lower case note the narrow **f** and the position of the dot over the **i** and **j**.

GOUDY ANTIQUE is the name, first applied to Caslon's RATDOLT ROMAN, but it was later applied to design No. 39, cut in 1930 by Goudy himself.

ABCDEFGHIJKLMNOPQRS TUVWXYZ
abcdefghijklmnopqrstuvwxyz

GOUDY ANTIQUE or RATDOLT ROMAN

Designed by Bruce Rogers in collaboration with Sol Hess and based on GOUDY NEWSTYLE of Lanston Monotype, 1920, as a type for the second Lectern Bible.

ABCDEFGHIJKLMNOPQRRSTUVWXYZ
abcdefghijklmnopqrstuvwxyz
1234567890

GOUDY BIBLE

Designed by Morris F. Benton as an adaptation of a basic Goudy design. GOUDY HANDTOOLED is a shaded letter based on this type.

ABCDEFGHIJKLMNOPQRSTUVW XYZ
abcdefghijklmnopqrstuvwxyz
1234567890

GOUDY CATALOGUE

Herds *Judges*

GOUDY HANDTOOLED

GOUDY EXTRA BOLD

Monotype 1926

A type bolder than GOUDY BOLD and approaching COOPER BLACK. The serifs are less blurred. The M is wider than in Cooper. Q has the Goudy tail. The e has an oblique stroke to the eye; in the b the upright tapers to a point below the line. There is no italic.

LUDLOW BLACK, 1924, is a similar design and weight. The e is as in COOPER BLACK, but the w has no middle serif. Intertype RUGGED BLACK, 1929, is again similar, but more condensed.

ix

ABCDEFGHIJKLMNOPQRSTUVWXYZ

abcdefghijklmnopqrstuvwxyz

1234567890

Italic for a Poster Job

LUDLOW BLACK

GOUDY MODERN

Lanston Monotype 1918;
Monotype 1928;
Caslon 1929

The serifs are flat but strong and bracketed; the stress is neither vertical nor abrupt. The capitals are shorter than the ascenders. The shadow version is GOUDY OPEN.

ABCDEFGHIJKLMNOPQRSTUVWXYZ

abcdefghijklmnopqrstuvwxyz

ABCDEFGHIJKLMNOPQRSTUVWX

abcdefghijklmopqrstuvwxyz

ii/iv

GOUDY MODERN

GOUDY OLD STYLE

American
Typefounders 1915–16;
Monotype; Intertype (F)

The capitals were modelled on Renaissance lettering, as F.W. Goudy himself relates. The serifs are small. The lower case is marred, as the designer himself says, by its short descenders. The ear of the g projects upwards. The italic is nearly upright, in fact m and n are upright. Goudy's designs were cut by Robert Wiebking, as indeed most of his work after 1911 until 1926, whereafter Goudy also cut his own types. Several bold versions were designed by Morris F. Benton.

ii

ABCDEFGHIJKLMNOPQRSTUVWXYZ

abcdefghijklmnopqrstuvwxyz

1234567890

ABCDEFGHIJKLMNOPQRSTUVWXYZ

abcdefghijklmnopqrstuvwxyz

ABCDEFGHIJKLMNOPQRSTUVWXYZ

abcdefghijklmnopqrstuvwxyz

GOUDY OLD STYLE

DINERS Engulfed

GOUDY BOLD ITALIC (1919)

Regal Interesting Place

GOUDY EXTRA BOLD (1925)

Designed by F.W. Goudy. A pen-drawn calligraphic roman. Note the slab serifs on the **A**, the open **G** and the pen-drawn **M**. The **a** is one-storeyed, the **g** has an open tail, and the **y** a calligraphic terminal.

GOUDY
THIRTY

ix

Before he died in 1947, Frederic W. Goudy, America's greatest and most prolific type designer, prepared the drawings for a new

GOUDY THIRTY

Designed by Frederic W. Goudy. Serifs on the capitals are unusual. There are a number of swash. Numerals range on the line.

GOUDYTYPE

*American
Typefounders 1916
Lanston Monotype*

i

New Story

GOUDYTYPE

Designed by F.W. Goudy and a revision of the first book face by this designer cut around 1905. FRANCISCAN is similar.

GOUDY
VILLAGE

Lanston Monotype 1936

iv

A B C D E F G H I J K L M N O P Q R S T U V W X Y Z

a b c d e f g h i j k l m n o p q r s t u v w x y z

1 2 3 4 5 6 7 8 9 0
1 2 3 4 5 6 7 8 9 0

A B C D E F G H I J K L M N O P Q R S T U V W X Y Z

a b c d e f g h i j k l m n o p q r s t u v w x y z

1 2 3 4 5 6 7 8 9 0

GOUDY VILLAGE

Designed for Linotype under the supervision of George W. Jones. Although named after another French type designer, Robert Granjon, this roman is the best reproduction of the Garamond type we have. It was based on a sixteenth century Paris book printed in a roman which appears under the name GARAMOND on a specimen sheet of the Egenolff-Berner foundry at Frankfurt, 1592. The capitals are tall in comparison with BEMBO, but sufficiently narrow and light to prevent their being too conspicuous. The middle strokes of the M are slightly overhanging, the bowl of the P is not closed, the R ends in a foot serif on the line. The lower-case Garamond g with a small bowl is well reproduced. The italic is less distinguished than the true old-face italics. The A is rather like CASLON. There is a straight shanked h and a number of swash capitals. The large bowl of the g differentiates this design from the "Garamond," so-called, italics. The Linotype & Machinery bold is also called BERNARD.

ii

ABCDEFGHIJKLMNOPQRSTUVWXYZ
abcdefghijklmnopqrstuvwxyz
1234567890   1234567890
ABCDEFGHIJKLMNOPQRSTUVWXYZ
abcdefghijklmnopqrstuvwxyz
1234567890   1234567890
ABCDEFGHIJ KLMNOPQRSTUVWXYZ

GRANJON

ii

ABCDEFGHIJKLMNOPQRSTUVWXYZ
abcdefghijklmnopqrstuvwxyz
1234567890   1234567890

GRANJON BOLD

Designed by Eugène Grasset. A roman rich in colour, partly derived from script. The blunt serifs are generally on the outside only, *e.g.*, in the F, H, M and P. The M is splayed. In the lower case similar serifs are found at the feet of letters. Note also the feet of v and w in both cases. The italic also has some unusual terminals on the capitals and on the ascender of the lower-case t.

ix

ABCDEFGHIJKLMN
OPQRSTUVWXYZ
abcdefghijklmnopqrstuvw
xyz   1234567890
ABCDEFGHIJKLMNOP
QRSTUVWXYZ
abcdefghijklmnopqrstuvw
xyz   1234567890

GRASSET

Designed by Herbert Thannhaeuser. A double inline roman. The main strokes have two white spaces. The stress is vertical and there is sharp variation of weight. The serifs are hair lines, and the thin strokes in general hair lines.

GRAVIRA

Schelter & Giesecke 1935

ix

A B C D E F G H I J K L M N O P Q R S T U V W X Y Z

GRAVIRA

A shaded bold roman. The serifs are thin and inclined on the lower case. In the lower case the **a** is one-storeyed, **b** has a foot serif and the eye of the **e** has an oblique stroke. The **g**, **v**, **w** and **y** are cursive forms like italic.

GRAVURE

American Typefounders c. 1929

ix

Hosiery

GRAVURE

A type with some calligraphic qualities. The serifs are rather large, especially at the ends of the arms of E, F and L and on S and T. The right-hand stroke of the A and the middle strokes of M and N are pen-drawn and overlap. The serifs on the lower case are concave and descenders are short. The g has a nearly vertical ear and wide tail. The italic is the roman inclined, except for the terminals at the tops of some ascenders, which are pen strokes.

There are also Semi-Bold (Negra), Bold, Ornamented (Adornado) and initials. The ornamented titling fount resembles VESTA, but the serrated edges are on the left of the black strokes. Stevens Shanks call the ornamented version ROSART.

GRECO or BRISTOL

Gans 1925; Stevens Shanks

Que la suprema elegancia se consigue a base de sencillez y de sobriedad es un hecho innegable. En todas las

Que la suprema elegancia se consigue a base de sencillez y de sobriedad es un hecho innegable. En todas las artes

ix

GRECO

Agrupación Deportiva Gans
FUNDACIÓN EGUILAR

Librería y Papelería Oriental
ESTACIÓN DE MADRID

ix

GRECO BOLD

REGLAMENTO DE IMPRESORE

ix

GRECO ADORNADO ROSART*

Designed by William E. Fink. A very condensed elongated type in which the lower case has short ascenders and descenders. Rounded letters are slightly angular, and upstrokes very thin. Serifs are fine. The dots on **r** and **a** are elongated. The bar of the A is rather near the foot line.

GREENWICH

Ludlow 1940

iv

ABCDEFGHIJKLMNOPQRSTUVWXYZ&

abcdefghijklmnopqrstuvwxyz

1234567890

GREENWICH

Originally from the Vincent Figgins foundry, *c.* 1796, and with lower case and figures, as well as 42 pt. capitals added in 1925. A shaded roman with thin, flat serifs. The design is that of a modern face, with short ascenders and descenders.

GRESHAM

Stevens Shanks 1925

iv

ABCDEGHMRS13467

GRESHAM

GRIFFO

Officina Bodini 1928–30

ii

Designed by Giovanni Mardersteig for use in his private press. The design bears resemblance to DANTE and ZENO. Numerals are non-ranging.

ABCDEFGHIJKLMNOPQURRSTUVWXYZ

abcdefghijklmnopqrstuvwxyz

1234567890

ABCDEFGHIJKLMNOPQRRSTUVWXYZ

abcdefghijklmnopqrstuvwxyz

GRIFFO

GWENDOLIN

Monotype
for Gregynog Press 1935

i

Designed by Graily Hewitt and cut by The Monotype Corporation. In general this roman is humanist but reminiscent of the calligrapher in many of the serifs for example on the **E, L** and the feet of **m, n** and **u**. The capitals are mostly wide, especially the splayed **M. U** has the lower-case design. The lower-case **g** has a very broad tail and the **w** a cursive form.

ABCDEFGHIJKLMNOPRSTUVWXYZ

abcdefghijklmnopqrstuvwxyz

1234567890

GWENDOLIN

HAARLEMMER

Monotype c. 1938

ii

Designed by Jan van Krimpen, and commissioned in 1938 by the Vereeniging voor Druk- en Boekkunst. This originally private type was intended for an edition of the *Staten Bijbel* to be printed in small folio format. The type has the qualities of an old face. The serifs on the capitals are thin; on the lower case they are stronger and not quite horizontal. The capitals are wide, especially the **M**. The **g** has a large bowl. The italic is slightly inclined and has angular beginning strokes; the **g** has a calligraphic tail; **v** and **w** have cursive forms. Two styles of figures are provided.

ABCDEFGHIJKLMNOPQRSTUVWXYZÆŒ&

abcdefghijklmnopqrstuvwxyz

ABCDEFGHIJKLMNOPQRSTUVWXYZÆŒ&

abcdefghijklmnopqrstuvwxyz

HAARLEMMER

HADRIANO

Goudy 1918
Lanston Monotype 1929

vii

Designed by F.W. Goudy in 1918 for the Continental Typefounders Association after a Roman inscription seen in the Louvre. The **A** has an extended apex, the **M** is unusually wide and the **Q** has swash form. The serifs, here large, have the usual Goudy pen qualities.

This titling is heavier than FORUM. In 1930 Goudy cut a lower case for Hadriano (which is No. 71 in his *A Half Century of Type Design*).

ABCDEFGHIJKLMNOPQRS
TUVWXYZ&

HADRIANO

ABCDEFGHIJKLMNOP
QRSTUVWXYZ&
1234567890

HADRIANO STONECUT

Designed by Victor Hammer in 1923 for Klingspor together with a set of initials. In 1953 a NEW HAMMER UNCIAL, also known as AMERICAN UNCIAL, was issued, which stems from the new version cut by Nussbaumer in 1945. The characters go back to letter forms practised before black letter or roman were evolved.

ABCDEFGHIJKLMNOPQRSTUVWXYZ
abcdefghijklmnopqrstuvwxyz ch ck ff ß tt
1234567890 1234567890 & et

HAMMER UNCIAL

Serifs are long and thin, and flat. The **g** has an ear like CASLON. Serifs in the italic are those of the roman.

Graphischer Zirkel *Meißner Porzellan*

HÄRTEL

Chemical Industries

iv

HÄRTEL BOLD

Designed by F.W. Kleukens. A roman with moderate variation of stress and very small serifs, flat and bracketed. The round letters, notably the capitals **G**, **O** and **Q**, have a pen-drawn quality. **A** and **H** have high bars. **M** and **U** (with the lower-case design) are narrow letters. The descenders are short. The round lower-case letters are wide.

Das Lob des Buches kann nie ausgefungen werde

Alle Jahrhunderte, alle großen Geifter vereinige

HELGA ANTIQUA

A linear slab serif type.

ABCDEFGHIJKLMN
OPQRSTUVWXYZ
abcdefghijklmnopqrs
tuvwxyz
1234567890

HELLENIC WIDE

A tooling of NEW CASLON and a shaded letter resembling NARCISSUS. It may be distinguished by the more usual **a** and the **g**, on which the ear rises out of the top of the bowl.

Typographic World STEA

HERMES

HEROLD
Berthold 1901

ix

A bold condensed display type with foot serifs pointing right, following end nineteenth-century style.

ABCDEFGHIJKLMNOPQRSTUVWXYZ
abcdefghijklmnopqrstuvwxyz
1234567890

HEROLD

HESS BOLD
Lanston Monotype 1910

ii

Designed by Sol Hess, and not strictly a bold face, though the serifs are drawn to suit a bold type. The design is based on GOUDY LIGHT.

A B C D E F G H I J K L M N O P Q R S T U V W X
Y Z & Æ Œ
a b c d e f g h i j k l m n o p q r s t u v w x y z æ œ
fi fl ff ffi ffl 1 2 3 4 5 6 7 8 9 0

*A B C D E F G H I J K L M N O P Q R S T U V W X
Y Z &
a b c d e f g h i j k l m n o p q r s t u v w x y z
fi fl ff ffi ffl 1 2 3 4 5 6 7 8 9 0*

HESS BOLD

HESS NEOBOLD
Lanston Monotype 1933

ix

Designed by Sol Hess, cast in only one size, and intended as a thin-serifed companion face to light lineales of the period.

ABCDEFGHIJKL
MNOPQRSTUVWX
YZ&
1234567890

HESS NEOBOLD

Designed by Sol Hess to follow JENSON.

A B C D E F G H I J K L M N O P Q R S T U V

W X Y Z & Æ Œ

a b c d e f g h i j k l m n o p q r s t u v w x y z æ

fi fl ff ffi ffl

1 2 3 4 5 6 7 8 9 0

ABCDEFGHIJKLMNOPQRSTUVWXYZ&ÆŒ

abcdefghijklmnopqrstuvwxyzæœ

fiflffffiffl

1234567890

HESS OLD STYLE

Designed by Friedrich Bauer. The serifs are sharp and rather long on the arms of the **E, L, S, Z** and on the **T.** They are similar in the lower case but oblique. The **W** has no middle serif. The **g** has the ear pointing north-east and a wide tail. The italic has the serifs of the roman. The **S** has curled terminals. The **a** is one-storeyed. There is also a Semi-Bold.

Wir fahren nach *Süden* allmählich von der arkadischen

Wir tun noch einen Blick auf die unbedeutenden Reste

HEYSE

Ausstellung von Reiseliteratur

HEYSE SEMI-BOLD

Designed by Stefan Schlesinger. A condensed reversed slab serif type similar to FIGARO and PLAYBILL.

ABCDEFGHIJKLMNOPQRSTUVWXYZ

1234567890

HIDALGO

HIERO RHODE ROMAN
J. Wagner 1945

Designed by Hiero Rhode, with the italic designed by Karl Hans Walter. The type is characterised by concave strokes and the variation in the stress is particularly apparent in the bold. Serifs are only slightly inclined. **E** and **F** have arms which extend over the vertical stroke.

ix

ABCDEFGHIJKLMNOPQRSTUVW
abcdefghijklmnopqrstuvwxyz
1234567890
ABCDEFGHIJKLMNOPQRSTU
VWXYZ
ABCDEFGHIJKLMNOPQRSTU
VWXYZ
abcdefghijklmnopqrstuvwxyz
1234567890

HIERO RHODE ROMAN

ix

ABCDEFGHIJKLMNOPQRSTUV
abcdefghijklmnopqrstuvwxyz

HIERO RHODE ROMAN BOLD

HISPALIS
Nacional

Ascenders are tall and there are two titlings. Upper- and lower-case **V** has a foot serif, and the bowl of the **P** is open.

ix

Nuevas ideas LUISA DE TAPIAS
Palma de Mallorca es

HISPALIS

ix

Ultimas Creaciones DE UNA MA

HISPALIS BOLD

ix

GRACIA Y UN

HISPALIS TITLING

ix

PRIMAVERA

HISPALIS BOLD TITLING

Designed by P.A. Demeter. Shaded roman capitals with thin, flat serifs. There is also a bold and an extended face.

HOLLÄNDISCH

Weber 1922–26

iii

ABCDEFGHIJKLMNOPQRS
TUVWXYZ 1234567890

HOLLÄNDISCH

BOZEN

HOLLÄNDISCH BOLD

SIEG

HOLLÄNDISCH EXTENDED

iii

Designed by S.H. De Roos. A Venetian with short descenders. There are slab serifs on the **A** and **M**. The **U** has the lower-case design. The **g** has a brief open tail. The italic is the roman inclined except for the cursive **v** and **w**. The figures are short-ranging.
There are also a bold, a condensed bold, and special initials.
Intertype called their now obsolete version MEDIAEVAL.

HOLLANDSE
MEDIAEVAL

Amsterdam 1912; Intertype

i

ABCDEFGHIJKLMNOPQRSTUV
abcdefghijklmnopqrstuvwxyz
1234567890

ABCDEFGHIJKLMNOPQRTSUVWXYZ

abcdefghijklmnoprstuvwxyz 1234567890

HOLLANDSE MEDIAEVAL

ABCDEFGHIJKLMNOPQRSTU
abcdefghijklmnopqrstuvwxyz

HOLLANDSE MEDIAEVAL SEMI-BOLD

i

ABCDEFGHIJKLMNOPQRSTUVWXYZ
abcdefghijklmnopqrstuvwxyz

HOLLANDSE MEDIAEVAL SEMI-BOLD CONDENSED

i

ABCDEFGHIJKLMNOPQRSTUVWXYZ

abcdefghijklmnopqrstuvwxyz 1234567890

ABCDEFGHIJKLMNOPQRSTUVWXYZ

abcdefghijklmnopqrstuvwxyz

INTERTYPE MEDIAEVAL

ABCDEFGH

HOLLANDSE MEDIAEVAL INITIALS

ix

HORIZON or
IMPRIMATUR

Bauer 1925;

Intertype (Berlin)

Typograph

iv

Designed by K.F. Bauer and Walter Baum. A narrow roman combining several older alphabets in its design. The letters, with not very pronounced serifs, combine to give an even grey when formed into words. **L, P, E, B** and **S** are very narrow, the ascenders of some lower-case letters are higher than the caps, and the descenders of lower-case letters are short.

ABCDEFGHIJKLMNOPQRSTUVWXYZ
abcdefghijklmnopqrstuvwxyz
123456789
ABCDEFGHIJKLMNOPQRSTUVWX
abcdefghijklmnopqrstuvwxyz
12345678

HORIZON

iv

ABCDEFGHIJKLMNOPQRSTUVWX
YZ
abcdefghijklmnopqrstuvwxyz
123456

HORIZON MEDIUM

iv

**ABCDEFGHIJKLMNOPQRSTUV
WXYZ
abcdefghijklmnopqrstuvwxyz
1234567890**

HORIZON BOLD

iv

**ABCDEFGHIJKLMNOPQRSTUVWXYZ
abcdefghijklmnopqrstuvwxyz
1234567890**

HORIZON BOLD CONDENSED

iv

ABCDEFGHIJKLMNOPQRSTUVWXYZ
abcdefghijklmnopqrstuvwxyz
1234567890
ABCDEFGHIJKLMNOPQRSTUVWXYZ
abcdefghijklmnopqrstuvwxyz
1234567890

INTERTYPE HORIZON

iv

ABCDEFGHIJKLMNOPQRSTUVWXYZ
abcdefghijklmnopqrstuvwxyz
1234567890

INTERTYPE HORIZON BOLD

The type has little differentiation of colour. The capitals are wide. **H** has a high bar. In the lower case serifs are inclined, **e** has an oblique stroke to the eye, **g** has the tail unclosed and the **t** is tall. There is also a heavy face and no italic.

ABCDEFGHIJKLMNOPQRSTUVWXYZ
abcdefghijklmnopqrstuvwxyz
1234567890

ii

HORLEY OLD STYLE

ABCDEFGHIJKLMNOPQRSTUVWXYZ
abcdefghijklmnopqrstuvwxyz
1234567890

ii

HORLEY OLD STYLE BOLD

Designed by Hermann Zapf as a private press type for the Hunt Botanical Library, of Pittsburg, Pennsylvania. A fine calligraphic roman of great clarity. Numerals are non-ranging.

HUNT ROMAN
Stempel 1962

ABCDÉFGHIJKLMÑOPQRSTÜVWXYZÆŒ
abcdefghijklmnopqrstuvwxyz
1234567890

ii

HUNT ROMAN

Designed by Berthold Wolpe. An angular pen-lettered design, with several unusual letters. The right hand serifs of upper- and lower-case **V** and **W** run inwards, the **Y** descends below the line and has a pronounced serif running to the right.

HYPERION
Bauer 1931

ABCDEFGHIJKLMNOPQRSTUVW
XYZ abcdefghijklmnopqrstuvwxyz 123456

ix

HYPERION

A narrow roman with short descenders and comparatively tall ascenders.

IBARRA
Gans

El Congreso de la Federación Gráfica

ii

UNIVERSIDAD DE VALENCIA

Gremio Patronal de Tipógrafos, Cádiz

ECONÓMICO Y FINANCIERO

IBARRA

IBERICA

Nacional 1942

Designed by Carlos Winkow. An open and shaded, that is three-dimensional inclined lineale. Ascenders are tall. The middle and top bar of the A extend to the left.

ix

ABCDEFGHIJKLM NOPQRSTUV WXY&Z

abcdefghijklmnopqrst uvwxyz

1234567890

IBERICA

IDEAL

Intertype; Amsterdam

This type closely follows IONIC and was first used in the Intertype version for *The New York Times*. Haas IDEAL is a condensed fat face and quite different. IDEAL NEWS is called PRESSA on the Continent.

iv

ABCDEFGHIJKLMNOPQRSTUVWXYZ
abcdefghijklmnopqrstuvwxyz
1234567890
ABCDEFGHIJKLMNOPQRSTUVWXYZ
abcdefghijklmnopqrstuvwxyz

AMSTERDAM IDEAL NEWS

iv

ABCDEFGHIJKLMNOPQRSTUVWXYZ
abcdefghijklmnopqrstuvwxyz

AMSTERDAM IDEAL BOLD

iv

ABCDEFGHIJKLMNOPQRSTUVWXYZ
ABCDEFGHIJKLMNOPQRSTUVWXYZ
abcdefghijklmnopqrstuvwxyz
1234567890
ABCDEFGHIJKLMNOPQRSTUVWXYZ
abcdefghijklmnopqrstuvwxyz
1234567890

INTERTYPE IDEAL

ABCDEFGHIJKLMNOPQRSTUVWXYZ

abcdefghijklmnopqrstuvwxyz

1234567890

INTERTYPE IDEAL BOLD

ABCDEFGHIJKLMNOPQRSTUVWXYZ

abcdefghijklmnopqrstuvwxyz

1234567890

ABCDEFGHIJKLMNOPQRSTUVWXYZ

abcdefghijklmnopqrstuvwxyz

1234567890

IDEAL NEWS SPECIAL

ABCDEFGHIJKLMNOPQRSTUVWXYZ

abcdefghijklmnopqrstuvwxyz

1234567890

IDEAL NEWS SPECIAL BOLD

This Haas revival is a condensed semi-bold nineteenth-century design, which is almost a Fat Face. There is the usual long spur to the **G**, curled tail to the **R**, and long serifs in the **E**, **F** and **T**. Ascenders and descenders in the lower case are very short. *Cf.* CONTACT. The present design is cast from 1941 matrices, and the identical type is cast by Stempel, who call it JEANNETTE. The type is quite different from Amsterdam and Intertype IDEAL.

ABCDEFGHIJKLMNOPQRSTUVWXYZ

abcdefghijklmnopqrstuvwxyz

1234567890

IDEAL ROMAN

Designed by Edwin W. Shaar. A newspaper type with very short ascenders and descenders The serifs are slightly inclined and the stress is vertical. The italic has the serifs of the roman, and there is also a bold roman.

ABCDEFGHIJKLMNOPQRSTUVWXYZ

abcdefghijklmnopqrstuvwxyz

1234567890

ABCDEFGHIJKLMNOPQRSTUVWXYZ

ABCDEFGHIJKLMNOPQRSTUVWXYZ

abcdefghijklmnopqrstuvwxyz

1234567890

IMPERIAL

ABCDEFGHIJKLMNOPQRSTUVWXYZ

abcdefghijklmnopqrstuvwxyz

1234567890

IMPERIAL BOLD

Designed by Konrad F. Bauer and Walter Baum as a text type, with affinity to IMPRIMATUR.

ABCDEFGHIJKLMNOPQRSTUV
WXYZ
abcdefghijklmnopqrstuvwxyz
1234567890
*ABCDEFGHIJKLMNOPQRSTUV
WXYZ*
abcdefghijklmnopqrstuvwxyz
1234567890

IMPRESSUM

ii

ABCDEFGHIJKLMNOPQRSTUV
WXYZ
abcdefghijklmnopqrstuvwxyz
1234567890

IMPRESSUM BOLD

IMPRINT
Monotype 1913

A type cut for the periodical of the same name, instigated by Gerald Meynell, J.H. Mason, Ernest Jackson and Edward Johnston. It is modelled on CASLON but has a large x-height. The italic differs much more; the inclination has been regularised and the letters widened. It has lost the character of an independent letter but harmonises better with the roman, which is what printers now desire. There is also Imprint Shadow.

ii

ABCDEFGHIJKLMNOPQRSTUV
WXYZ
abcdefghijklmnopqrstuvwxyz
1234567890
ABCDEFGHIKLMNOPQRSTVYZ
abcdefghijklmnoqrstuvwxyz
1234567890

IMPRINT

ii

ABCDEFGHIJKLMNOPQRSTUVWXYZ
abcdefghijklmnopqrstuvwxyz 1234567890

IMPRINT BOLD (310)

ABCDEFGHIJKLMNOPQRSTUVWXYZ
abcdefghijklmnopqrstuvwxyz 12345
ABCDEFGHIJKLMNOPQRSTUVWXYZ
abcdefghijklmnopqrstuvwxyz 12345

IMPRINT BOLD (410)

ii

ABCDEFGHIJKLMNOPQRSTUV
abcdefghijklmnopqrstuvwxyz

IMPRINT SHADOW

A bold roman with short ascenders and descenders.

ABCDEFGHIJKLMNOPQRSTUVWXYZ

abcdefghijklmnopqrstuvwxyz

1234567890

INDUSTRIE ANTIQUA

INDUSTRIE
ANTIQUA
Wagner;
Linotype (Frankfurt)

iv

The **A** is very narrow, and so are the **M** and **N**. The top serifs of the **T** are pointed outwards. The **G** has a spur and the **R** a curved tail. In the lower case serifs are finer. Ascenders and descenders are comparatively short. Lower-case letters in the italic have very round hair lines.

INGLÉS
Nacional

iv

construída en la terminación de la calle de Alcalá por
SOCIEDAD ESPAÑOLA DE PAVIMENTACIONES
CAPACIDAD CREADORA DE DIVERSOS IDEALES POLÍTICOS
El entendimiento corto y el alma algo pequeña de ciertos
críticos pueden asustar a ingenios por demás eminentes
VIAJE ALREDEDOR DEL MUNDO EN BALANDRO

INGLÉS

Designed by Raffaello Bertieri and based on the roman of Erhard Ratdolt. There are slab serifs on **A**, **M** and **N**. In the **G** the thickest part of the curve is unusually low. The **h** has a curved shank, a form which disappeared with Nicolas Jenson. The italic has swash capitals and a large bowl in the **g**. There are also shaded capitals and a titling.

INKUNABULA
Nebiolo 1911

i

Raffaello dipinse quarantadue Madonne e fra

Prescindendo dalle funzioni strategiche, navali

INKUNABULA

The first IONIC was a bold face cut by Caslon and shown 1842. The original design is similar to Beasley's EXTENDED CLARENDON. It has been revived as a suitable newspaper type. With its strong serifs it has been found to be legible in small sizes (No. 1 in the "Linotype Legibility Group"). It has short ascenders and descenders and considerable differentiation of colour. The eye of the **e** is large.

Linotype IONIC was introduced in 1926 in the *Newark Evening News*, and Intertype later cut their version of IDEAL for the *New York Times*. There is also The Monotype Corporation's version of IONIC.

IONIC
Mergenthaler Linotype 1925;
Linotype (London); Monotype
Simoncini

iv

ABCDEFGHIJKLMNOPQRSTUVWXYZ
abcdefghijklmnopqrstuvwxyz 1234567890
ABCDEFGHIJKLMNOPQRSTUVWXYZ
abcdefghijklmnopqrstuvwxyz 1234567890
ABCDEFGHIJKLMNOPQRSTUVWXYZ

LINOTYPE IONIC

ABCDEFGHIJKLMNOPQRSTUVWXYZ
abcdefghijklmnopqrstuvwxyz 1234567890

LINOTYPE IONIC BOLD

iv

ITALIANA CURSIVA
Gans

A condensed reversed slab serif type with the serifs heavier than the main strokes, and similar to MAGNET.

v

Sindicato Provincial del Metal

ITALIENNE
Française

A revival of an early reversed Egyptian. The founders give the date as 1820. The English founders called the design French Antique and the earliest English fount, according to Mrs. N. Gray's *Nineteenth Century Ornamental Types*, was considerably later than 1820.

v

furieuse tempête dans les mers du sud
IMPRESO COMERCIAL, PUBLICITARIO

ITALIENNE

JANSON
Mergenthaler Linotype 1937;
Stempel;
Linotype (London);
Linotype (Frankfurt);
Lanston Monotype

Another type which has been misnamed. The original dates from about 1690 and was cut by Nicholas Kis, a Hungarian in Amsterdam. The original matrices have survived in Germany and have since 1919 been held by the Stempel foundry. The type was not cut by Anton Janson, a Dutchman who worked at Leipzig. In the upper case the **M** is an easily remembered letter and in the lower case the **g**, which has a curved ear. In general the thin strokes are thinner than in earlier types. In the italic the **m** and **n** are more squared up. Note also the curves of the **v** and **w**. The Linotype version follows the original and was designed under the direction of C.H. Griffith. The Monotype Corporation's EHRHARDT (because the original types were in the Ehrhardt Foundry at Leipzig in the early eighteenth century) is a version of this type. Herman Zapf has redesigned some of the weights and sizes for Stempel, basing his revisions on the original type.

ii

ABCDEFGHIJKLMNOPQRSTUVW
abcdefghijklmnopqrstuvwxyz
1234567890
ABCDEFGHIJKLMNOPQRSTUVWXY
abcdefghijklmnopqrstuvwxyz

STEMPEL JANSON

ABCDEFGHIJKLMNOPQRSTUVWXYZ
abcdefghijklmnopqrstuvwxyz
1234567890   1234567890
ABCDEFGHIJKLMNOPQRSTUVWXYZ
ABCDEFGHIJKLMNOPQRSTUVWXYZ
ABCDEFGHIJKLMNOPQRSTUVWXYZ
abcdefghijklmnopqrstuvwxyz
1234567890   1234567890
ABCDEFGHIJKLMNOPQRSTUVWXYZ
Recut Italic: abcdefghijklmnopqrstuvwxyz

LINOTYPE JANSON

ABCDEFGHIJKLMNOPQRSTUVWXYZ

abcdefghijklmnopqrstuvwxyz

1234567890

ABCDEFGHIJKLMNOPQRSTUVWXYZ

abcdefghijklmnopqrstuvwxyz

1234567890

MERGENTHALER LINOTYPE JANSON

Designed by Jos W. Phinney for American Typefounders (also called NICOLAS JENSON) and a copy of Morris's GOLDEN TYPE.

   The Monotype Corporation's ITALIAN OLD STYLE with which the display sizes of the quite different VERONESE are combined, has a companion bold face. The ITALIAN OLD STYLE of F.W. Goudy is another re-cutting, made for the Lanston Monotype. It has an unusual italic with some swash capitals.

JENSON or ITALIAN OLD STYLE

Stephenson Blake;
Monotype;
Lanston Monotype;
American Typefounders

i

ABCDEFGHIJKLMNOPQRSTUVWX

abcdefghijklmnopqrstuvwxyz

1234567890

ABCDEFGHIJKLMNOPQRSTUVWXYZ

abcdefghijklmnopqrstuvwxyz

1234567890

ITALIAN OLD STYLE

ABCDEFGHIJKLMNOPQRSTUVXYZ

abcdefghijklmnopqrstuvwxy

MERGENTHALER JENSON

i

ABCDEFGHIJKLMNOPQRSTUVWXYZ

abcdefghijklmnopqrstuvwxyz

1234567890

ITALIAN OLD STYLE BOLD

i

A B C D E F G H I J K L M N O P Q R S

T U V W X Y Z

a b c d e f g h i j k l m n o p q r s t u v w x y z

1 2 3 4 5 6 7 8 9 0

JENSON CONDENSED

i

Designed by Rudolf Koch in 1930 for Klingspor, and cut by the artist as a type for the setting of the Bible. The **A** has a wide bar at the top, and the S vertical serifs. Lower-case characters lean on black letter forms.

ĀBCDEFGHIJKLMNOPQRSTUV
WXYZ
abcdefghijklmnopqrſstuvwxyz
1234567890 &

JESSEN

Designed by Eric Gill for Hague & Gill in 1930. A light roman with small horizontal serifs and little differentiation of colour. The type is remarkable for the smallness of the capitals, which do not reach the height of the ascenders, themselves not tall. The bowl of the **g** is rather large. The i talic is the roman inclined except for **a** and **g**. The inclination is very slight. There are no specially cut capitals, but the modest roman capitals are used. This was the practice of Aldus, the first printer to use italic. Eric Gill's *Essay on Typography*, 1931 is printed in Joanna.

ii/iv

as a man who does not know his road can only be on it by accident), so a good clear training in the making of normal letters will enable a man to indulge more efficiently in fancy and impudence.

(Figure 17 : 1, normal sans-serif; 2–5, unseemly abnormalities & exaggerations; 6, normal with serifs; 7, normal bold; 8, overbold and fatuous; 9–13, 15 and 16, seemly 'fancy' varieties of the normal; 14 & 17, R's with normal

HAGUE & GILL JOANNA

ii/iv

ABCDEFGHIJKLMNOPQRSTUVWXYZ
abcdefghijklmnopqrstuvwxyz
1234567890
ABCDEFGHIJKLMNOPQRSTUVWXYZ
abcdefghijklmnopqrstuvwxyz
1234567890

MONOTYPE JOANNA

A bold roman originally cut by the Keystone Type Foundry in 1905. A condensed version was added in 1917.

ABCDEFGHIJKLMNOPQRSTUVWXYZ&ÆŒ
abcdefghijklmnopqrstuvwxyzæœ fiflffffiffl
1234567890

JOHN HANCOCK

iv

ABCDEFGHIJKLMNOPQRSTUVWXYZ
abcdefghijklmnopqrstuvwxyz
1234567890

JOHN HANCOCK CONDENSED

Designed under the direction of Walter Tracy, it was first used by the *Glasgow Herald*. It is not to be confused with Stephenson Blake's JUBILEE, which was designed by Eric Gill. A roman with moderate stress and slightly inclined serifs. Ascenders and descenders are short. There is no middle serif on the **W**. The numerals are ranging. The bold has much greater variation of stress.

ABCDEFGHIJKLMNOPQRSTUVWXYZ

abcdefghijklmnopqrstuvwxyz

1234567890

ABCDEFGHIJKLMNOPQRSTUVWXYZ

ABCDEFGHIJKLMNOPQRSTUVWXYZ

abcdefghijklmnopqrstuvwxyz

1234567890

JUBILEE

ABCDEFGHIJKLMNOPQRSTUVWXYZ

abcdefghijklmnopqrstuvwxyz

12345 67890

JUBILEE BOLD

Designed by S.L. Hartz as a book type. The characters are fairly narrow. The **C** has two serifs, the **U** has arms of equal weight, the **W** is crossed. The **b** has a foot serif, **i** and **j** have diamond dots. The italic is calligraphic in style but fairly upright.

ABCDEFGHIJKLMNOPQRSTUVWXYZ

abcdefghijklmnopqrstuvwxyz

1234567890

ABCDEFGHIJKLMNOPQRSTUVWXYZ

ABCDEFGHIJKLMNOPQRSTUVWXYZ

abcdefghijklmnopqrstuvwxyz

1234567890

JULIANA

Shaded italic capitals and figures, very like Peignot's FOURNIER LE JEUNE. The serifs themselves are ornamented, by which the type may be distinguished. JUNE is rather more ornamented in the serifs than Fournier.

ABCDEFGHIJKLMN
OPQRSTUVWXYZ&

1234567890

JUNE

Inline capitals. The letters are rather wide and have thin bracketed serifs.

ABCDEFGHIJKLMNOPQRSTU
VWXYZ
1234567890

JUNO

KAATSKILL
Lanston Monotype 1929

Designed by F.W. Goudy, originally for an edition of Washington Irving's *Rip van Winkle*. The bowls of the **C**, **D**, **G** and **O** have high arches and similar arches are in the **m** and **n**. The **Q** has the characteristic Goudy tail.

ii

ABCDEFGHIJKLMNOPQRSTUVWXYZ

abcdefghijklmnopqrstuvwxyz

1234567890

KAATSKILL

KALAB
Grafotechna

Designed by Method Kalab. A roman with fine straight serifs and thin hairlines. Figures are ranging.

ii

A B C D E F G H I J K L M N O P Q R S T U V W X Y Z

a b c d e f g h i j k l m n o p q r s t u v w x y z

1 2 3 4 5 6 7 8 9 0

KALAB

KARNAK
Ludlow 1931–42

Designed by R.H. Middleton. **A** has a slab serif, **G** no spur and in **M** the middle strokes stop short of the line. **a** has the lower-case design but no top serif, **g** an open tail and **t** a foot serif on the right only. There is an italic. There are some additional round capitals. There are four weights, and condensed faces, one being called OBELISK.

v

ABCDEFGHIJKLMNOPQRSTUVWX YZ&
abcdefghijklmnopqrstuvwxyz
1234567890

KARNAK LIGHT

v

ABCDEFGHIJKLMNOPQRSTUVW XYZ&
abcdefghijklmnopqrstuvwxyz
1234567890

*ABCDEFGHIJKLMNOPQRSTUVW XYZ&
abcdefghijklmnopqrstuvwxyz
1234567890*

KARNAK INTERMEDIATE

ABCDEFGHIJKLMNOPQRSTUV WXYZ&
abcdefghijklmnopqrstuvwxyz
1234567890

ABCDEFGHIJKLMNOPQRSTUV WXYZ&
abcdefghijklmnopqrstuvwxyz
1234567890

ABCDEFGHIJKLMNOPQRSTUVWXYZ&
abcdefghijklmnopqrstuvwxyz
1234567890

ABCDEFGHIJKLMNOPQRSTUVWXYZ&
abcdefghijklmnopqrstuvwxyz
1234567890

KARNAK

v

v

v

v

Designed by F.W. Goudy for the New York publisher Mitchell Kennerley in 1911 and cut by Robert Wiebking. Short ascenders and descenders. Note the spur on the **G**, the high bar on the **H**, the tail of the **Q** and **R**. The italic is almost upright and has a pen quality common to most of the Goudy italics.

Intertype KENNTONIAN was another version of this type.

KENNERLEY
Lanston Monotype; Caslon 1930

i

BCDEFGHIJKLMNOPQRSTUVW
abcdefghijklmnopqrstuvwxyz
BCDEFGHIJKLMNOPQRSTUVW
abcdefghijklmnopqrstuvwxyz

i

ABCDEFGHIJKLMNOPQRSTU VW
abcdefghijklmnopqrstuvwxyz
123456 7890&£

KEYBOARD
Stephenson Blake 1951

A condensed and elongated slab serif type with thin serifs.

iv

ABCDEFGHIJKLMNOPQRSTUVWXYZ
abcdefghijklmnopqrstuvwxyz
1234567890£

KEYBOARD

iv

ABCDEFGHIJKLMNOPQRSTUVWXYZ
abcdefghijklmnopqrstuvwxyz
1234567890£

KEYBOARD LIGHT

KING'S FOUNT
Vale Press 1903

Another black face with heavy serifs and a number of uncial letters, designed by Charles Ricketts. It was first used in an edition of the King's (James I of Scotland) Quair. In the upper case E has the uncial form and in the lower case **a**, **e**, and **g**. **f**, **r** and **t** have the designs of capitals. An exotic, surpassed only by the ENDEAVOUR and PRAYER BOOK types.

ix

Erectus his sermonibus, consulere pruden-
tiores coepi aetates tabularum, et quaedam
argumenta mihi obscura, simulque causam de-
sidiae praesentis excutere, quum pulcherrimae
artes periissent, inter quas pictura ne mini-

KING'S FOUNT

KINGSTON
Stephenson Blake

A bold roman with rather thick serifs. Thick and thin strokes meet at an angle. The eye of the **e** is almost square. Descenders are short.

iv

ABCDEFGHIJKLMNOPQRSTUV
abcdefghijklmnopqrstuvwxyzæœ

KINGSTON BOLD*

KLANG
Monotype 1955;
Stephenson Blake

Designed by Will Carter. A slightly inclined and slightly shaped sans serif with short ascenders and descenders; Stephenson Blake also have a bold. LYDIAN has some letters that are similar in design.

ix

ABCDEFGHIJKLMNOPQRSTUVWXYZ
abcdefghijklmnopqrstuvwxyz
12345

KLANG

ix

ABCDEFGHIJKLMNOPQRSTUVWXYZ
abcdefghijklmnopqrstuvwxyz
1234567890

STEPHENSON BLAKE KLANG BOLD

Designed by F. W. Kleukens. An angular narrow roman of large x-height.

KLEUKENS
ANTIQUA
Bauer c. 1900

ABCDEFGHIJKLMN OPQRSTUVWXYZ

abcdefghijklmnopq rſsßtuvwxyz

1234567890

KLEUKENS ANTIQUA

Designed by S. Duda, K. Misek and J. Tyfa. A text face in two weights with one italic. There is little variation in stress. The **b** has a pointed spur. The italic has roman serifs and the figures are ranging.

KOLEKTIV
Grafotechna 1952

ABCDEFGHIJKLMNOPQRS TUVWXYZ
abcdefghijklmnopqrstuvwxyz
1234567890
ABCDEFGHIJKLMNOPQRS TUVWXYZ
abcdefghijklmnopqrstuvwxyz
1234567890

KOLEKTIV

ABCDEFGHIJKLMNOPQRS TUVWXYZ
abcdefghijklmnopqrstuvwxyz
1234567890

KOLEKTIV BOLD

KOLONIAL
Woellmer

A heavy display type similar to POST OLD ROMAN. It is somewhat condensed and has short ascenders and descenders. Serifs are thick, blunt and horizontal (except on the **d**). The **K** has a very high waist, the middle strokes of the **M** descend only half-way, the **R** has a tapering tail. The ear of the **g** points north-east. The arches of the **h**, **m** and **n** are splayed. The italic has the serifs of the roman and some swash capitals. There are also a Shaded and an Extended face.

Before World War II the type was also sold as COLUMBIA by the Amsterdam Typefoundry, and is the BUFFALO of the H.C. Hansen Foundry of Boston. It belongs with MORLAND (BLANCHARD of the Inland Type Foundry) to the group of heavy display types of which many American foundries had their own version.

ix

ABCDEFGHIJKLMNO
PQRSTUVWXYZ
abcdefghijklmnopq
rißstuvwxyz
1234567890

KOLONIAL

ix

ABCDEFGHIJKLMNOPQ
RSTUVWXYZ
abcdefghijklmnopqrſßstu
vwxyz
1234567890

KOLONIAL CONDENSED

KOMPAKT
Stempel 1954

Designed by Hermann Zapf. A fat, slightly inclined roman of large x-height and with short descenders and ascenders. The dots on **i** and **j** are diamond-shaped.

ix

ABCDEFGHIJKLM
NOPQRSTUVWXYZ

KOMPAKT

130

abcdefghijklmnopq rst uvwxyz 1234567890

KOMPAKT

Designed by F. H. Schneidler as a bold titling type.

DAS ROSTFREIE UND TAFEL IDEAL = METALL SAUREFESTE FUR KUCHE

KONTRAST

Designed by Albert Augspurg. A monotone display roman. Some of the capitals in design resemble the capitals of SCHWABACHER. The lower case is without serifs and vertical strokes are cut off at an angle. The **e** has an oblique stroke to the eye and the **g** a short open tail. There is also a Bold.

ABCDEF abcdefghch

KRIMHILDE

A narrow roman text and display type designed by Akke Kumlien. There are slab serifs on the ascenders, and also on some lower-case letters like **i, u, n, m,** and **r.** Foot serifs of **d, a,** and **u** point upwards. The tail of the **R** is straight. The italic has calligraphic qualities and is also supplied with swash caps. There are two weights.

ABCDEFGHIJKLMNOPQRST
abcdefghijklmnopqrstuvwxyz
1234567890
ABCDEFGHIJKLMNOPQRSTUVW
abcdefghijklmnopqrstuvwxyz
1234567890

KUMLIEN

ABCDEFGHIJKLMNOPQRS
abcdefghijklmnopqrstuvwxyz
1234567890

KUMLIEN BOLD

Designed by R. Hunter Middleton. An extra condensed bold roman with fine serifs. The dots on **i** and **j** are square.

ABCDEFGHIJKLMNOPQRSTUVWXYZ&
abcdefghijklmnopqrstuvwxyz
1234567890

LAFAYETTE

This type is shown under its original name WELT.
LANDI ECHO, designed by A. Butti, is a slab serif type with inclined inline. LANDI LINEAR, designed by A. Novarese, is an outline type with black horizontal feet and tops of letters.

ABCDEFGHIJK
LMNOPQRST
UVXYZW
1234567890

LANDI LINEAR

ABCDEFGHIJK
LMNOPQRST
UVXYZW
1234567890

LANDI ECHO

A set of roman capitals with very small serifs. Many letters, notably the **A**, **H** and **M** (which is splayed) are very wide.

ABCDEFGHIJKLMNOP
QRSTUVWXYZ
1234567890

LARGO

ABCDEFGHIJKLMNO PQRSTUVWXYZ 1234567890

LARGO BOLD

ABCDEFGHIJKLMNOP QRSTUVWXYZ& 1234567890

vii

LARGO OPEN

The type is characterised by horizontal serifs, cut to a point and connected to the main strokes by a stout triangular piece. Ascenders and descenders are short.

ABCDEFGHIJKLMNOPQRSTUVWXYZ&

abcdefghijklmnopqrstuvwxyz

1234567890

MONOTYPE LATIN ANTIQUE

ix

ABCDEFGHIJKLMNOPQRSTUVWXYZ&

abcdefghijklmnopqrstuvwxyz

1234567890

MONOTYPE LATIN ANTIQUE No. 2

ix

ABCDEFGHIJKLMNOPQRSTUVWXYZ&

abcdefghijklmnopqrstuvwxyz

1234567890

MONOTYPE LATIN ANTIQUE No. 3

ix

ABCDEFGHIJKLMNOPQRSTUVWXYZ&

abcdefghijklmnopqrstuvwxyz

1234567890

MONOTYPE LATIN ANTIQUE No. 4

ix

ABCDEFGHIJKLMNOPQRSTUVWXYZ

abcdefghijklmnopqrstuvwxyz

1234567890

MONOTYPE LATIN CONDENSED

LATIN ANTIQUE
ix

ABCDEFGHIJKL MNOPQRSTUVW XYZ
abcdefghijklmnop qrstuvwxyz

STEPHENSON BLAKE WIDE LATIN

LAUDIAN
Monotype
ii

ABCDEFGHIJKLMNOPQRSTUVWXYZ&ÆŒ
abcdefghijklmnopqrstuvwxyzfifflfffffffflæœ
1234567890
ABCDEFGHIJKLMNOPQRSTUVWXYZÆŒ
ABCDEFGHIJKLMNOPQRSTUVWXYZ&ÆŒ
abcdefghijklmnopqrstuvwxyzfiflfffffffiæœ
1234567890

LAUDIAN OLD STYLE

LAUREATE
Ludlow 1926

A bold display roman.

ABCDEFGHIJKLMNOPQRSTUV WXYZ&
abcdefghijklmnopqrstuvwxyz
1234567890

LAUREATE

LAUREL
Intertype (F) 1960

iv

A roman with the characteristics of a modern face, except for the **g** which resembles the CASLON **g**. The serifs are bracketed.

ABCDEFGHIJKLMNOPQRSTUVWXYZ&
abcdefghijklmnopqrstuvwxyz
1234567890   fi fl ff ffi ffl   1234567890
ABCDEFGHIJKLMNOPQRSTUVWXYZ&
ABCDEFGHIJKLMNOPQRSTUVWXYZ&
abcdefghijklmnopqrstuvwxyz
1234567890   fi fl ff ffi ffl   1234567890

LAUREL

ABCDEFGHIJKLMNOPQRSTUVWXYZ&

abcdefghijklmnopqrstuvwxyz

12345   fi fl ff ffi ffl   67890

ABCDEFGHIJKLMNOPQRSTUVWXYZ&

ABCDEFGHIJKLMNOPQRSTUVWXYZ&

abcdefghijklmnopqrstuvwxyz

12345   fi fl ff ffi ffl   67890

LAUREL BOLD

Adapted from EMERSON for 18-pt settings of Bibles, prayer-books, etc.

ABCDEFGHIJKLMNOPQRSTUVWXYZ

abcdefghijklmnopqrstuvwxyz

1234567890

LECTERN MISSAL

Designed by Dick Dooijes. A book type designed for improved legibility.

ABCDEFGHIJKLMNOPQRSTUVWXYZ
abcdefghijklmnopqrstuvwxyz
1234567890

ABCDEFGHIJKLMNOPQRSTUVWXYZ
abcdefghijklmnopqrstuvwxyz
1234567890

LECTURA

ABCDEFGHIJKLMNOPQRSTUVWXYZ
abcdefghijklmnopqrstuvwxyz

LECTURA BOLD

ABCDEFGHIJKLMNOPQRSTUVWXYZ
abcdefghijklmnopqrstuvwxyz

LECTURA BOLD CONDENSED

ABCDEFGHIJKLMNOPQRSTUVWXYZ
abcdefghijklmnopqr stuvwxyz   1234567890

ABCDEFGHIJKL MNOPQRSTUVWXYZ
abcdefghijklmnopqr stuvwxyz   1234567890

INTERTYPE LECTURA

ABCDEFGHIJKL MNOPQRSTUVWXYZ
abcdefghijklmnopqr stuvwxyz   1234567890

INTERTYPE LECTURA BOLD

LEIPZIG
Typoart 1963

ix

Designed by Albert Kapr and cut by Otto Erler. A text type of large x-height with angular characters.

ABCDEFGHIJKL MNOPQR
STUVWXYZ ÄÖÜ
abcdefghijklmnopqrsßtuvwx
yzäöüchckfift
1234567890
ABCDEFGHIJKLM NOPQRS
TUVWXY Z ÄÖÜ
abcdefghijk lmnopqrstuvwxy
zß&
1234567890

LEIPZIG

LETTRES ORNÉES
Deberny & Peignot

v

Richly decorated, three-dimensional capitals. The founders say from the "fonds de Gillé" and give the date as 1820. The English founder Edmund Fry showed somewhat similar letters in 1824.

LETTRES ORNÉES

LIBERTA
Typoart 1960

ii

Designed by Herbert Thannhaeuser. The **M** is splayed. The **g** has an open tail. The italic is slightly inclined and has roman serifs. The numerals are ranging. The italic has the serifs of the roman. There is a semi-bold.

ABCDEFGHIJKLMNOPQRSTUV
WXYZ&
abcdefghijklmnopqrstuvwxyz?
1234567890
ABCDEFGHIJKLMNOPQRSTUVW
XYZ&
abcdefghijklmnopqrstuvwxyz?
1234567890

LIBERTA

136

ABCDEFGHIJKLMNOPQRST UVWXYZ& abcdefghijklmnopqrstuvwxyz? 1234567890

LIBERTA BOLD

ABCDEFGHIJKLMNOPQRSTUVWXYZ& abcdefghijklmnopqrstuvwxyz? 1234567890

LIBERTA BOLD CONDENSED

This type face, designed by S.H. De Roos, closely follows the pattern of uncial scripts combining the liveliness of a lower case with the emphasis of a capital line. There are two weights.

ABCDEFGHIJKLMNOPQRSTUVWXYZ

LIBRA LIGHT

ABCDEFGHIJKLMNOPQRSTUVWXYZ 1234567890

LIBRA

A newspaper and text type designed for legibility. Angular points are exaggerated to compensate for loss of detail in reproduction.

ABCDEFGHIJKLMNOPQRSTUVWXYZ

abcdefghijklmnopqrstuvwxyz

1234567890

ABCDEFGHIJKLMNOPQRSTUVWXYZ

abcdefghijklmnopqrstuvwxyz

1234567890

ABCDEFGHIJKLMNOPQRSTUVWXYZ

LIFE

ABCDEFGHIJKLMNOPQRSTUVWXYZ

abcdefghijklmnopqrstuvwxyz

1234567890

LIFE BOLD

A condensed fat face of nineteenth-century design. The serifs are very small, but note the beak-like terminations in the **C, E, F, S** and **T**. *Cf.* SLIMBLACK.

ABCDEFGHIJKLMNOPQRSTUVWXYZÆŒ abcdefghijklmnopqrstuvwxyzæœ 1234567890

LILIOM

LILITH
Bauer 1930

Designed by Lucian Bernhard. A shaded fat face italic of a slight inclination. The capitals are further decorated with nodules. The ascending **b**, **h** and **k** are looped; the **l** and **t** have cleft tops.

ix

$$\textit{Famous Pleasure Garden}$$

LILITH

LINOTYPE MODERN
Linotype (London) 1969

Designed by Walter Tracy as a newspaper type and first used by *The Daily Telegraph*. The type was designed to offer compensation for the effects of multiple moulding and high-speed printing on newsprint. Angles of strokes are almost unconnected. Crotches in v-angles of **M** and **W** have been enlarged.

iv

ABCDEFGHIJKLMNOPQRSTUVWXYZ
abcdefghijklmnopqrstuvwxyz
1234567890
ABCDEFGHIJKLMNOPQRSTUVWXYZ
abcdefghijklmnopqrstuvwxyz
1234567890
ABCDEFGHIJKLMNOPQRSTUVWXYZ

LINOTYPE MODERN

iv

ABCDEFGHIJKLMNOPQRSTUVWXYZ
abcdefghijklmnopqrstuvwxyz
1234567890

LINOTYPE MODERN BOLD

LITURGICA
Flinsch

Designed by Willy Wiegand for the *Missale Romanum* of Editio Lacensis, which was set by the Bremer Presse. The punches were cut by Louis Hoell.

ix

In méntibus nostris, quæsumus, Domine, veræ fidei sacramenta Vírgine Deum verum et hominem confirma: ut, qui conceptum de

LITURGICA

LOCARNO or KOCH ANTIQUA
Klingspor 1922

An unusual but popular roman designed by Rudolf Koch. The name is no doubt connected with political events of the year. The vertical strokes taper. Serifs are very small; on the tops of the ascenders they extend both ways. **A** is wide and has a high bar. **C**, **G**, **O** and **Q** are wide and round, while **B**, **E**, **F**, **P**, **R**, **S** and **T** are narrow. **U** has the lower-case design. The **M** is splayed. The lower case has extravagantly tall ascenders. The **a** has a pinched bowl, **e** an oblique bar. In the **g** the link between bowl and tail is omitted and the tail is open. **w** has no middle serif. The figures are short-ranging.
The italic called KOCH CURSIVE, has a shaded upper case. The lower case is the roman inclined except that **p** and **g** are without foot serifs. In spite of all its oddities the type has proved a success, but is no book type. RIVOLI is of very similar design.

ix

ABCDEFGHIJKLMNOPQRSTU
abcdefghijklmnopqrstuvwxyz
1234567890

LOCARNO

ix

ABCDEFGHIJKLMNOPQRSTU
abcdefghijklmnopqrstuvwxyz

LOCARNO BOLD

ABCDEFGHIJJKLMNOPQRSTUVWXYZ

abcdefghijklmnopqrstuvwxyzchckflffifllt

1234567890

ABDEGHKLMRS

LOCARNO ITALIC

A display face designed by M.F. Benton, based on a Bodoni model, but with the peculiarity found in a number of modernistic types of making the thicks and thins meet at an angle. This is especially noticeable in the **O** and **S**. The **g** and **y** have cursive tails. The italic is the roman inclined, except for **a**, which has a flat-foot serif, **v** and **w**. There are three weights, the light having the colour of a normal book type.

Mysterious Flight

Beautiful Drawing

LOUVAINE LIGHT

Simple Design

LOUVAINE MEDIUM

Quaint Styles

LOUVAINE BOLD

A light design by Lucian Bernhard with unusually tall ascenders. The serifs are small and horizontal. All the capitals are wide. In the **M** the middle strokes stop short of the line, **Q** has an extravagant tail and the **W** is unusual. In the **g**, bowl and tail are equal and the ear rises out of the top of the bowl. In **p** and **q** the uprights are extended. The **s** has thickened terminals. The italic is the roman inclined including the **a**, but the **R** tapers.
There are bold, extra-bold and open faces. The extra-bold has an irregular outline. The roman is also known as BERNHARD ROMAN.

ABCDEFGHIJKLMNOPQRSTUVWXYZ

abcdefghijklmnopqrstuvwxyz

1234567890 1234567890

ABCDEFGHIJKLMNOPQRSTUVWXYZ

abcdefghijklmnopqrstuvwxyz

1234567890 1234567890

LUCIAN LIGHT

ABCDEFGHIJKLMNOPQRSTUVWXYZ

abcdefghijklmnopqrstuvwxyz

1234567890

ABCDEFGHIJJKLMNOPQRSTUVWXYZ

abcdefghijklmnopqrstuvwxyz

1234567890

LUCIAN

ABCDEFGHIJKLMNOPQRSTUVWXYZ
abcdefghijklmnopqrstuvwxyz
1234567890
LUCIAN BOLD

ABCDEFGHIJKLMNOPQRSTUVWXYZ
abcdefghijklmnopqrstuvwxyz
1234567890
LUCIAN OPEN

**LUDLOW
BLACK**
Ludlow 1924
iv

Designed by R. Hunter Middleton. The type is similar to COOPER BLACK but the **w** has no middle serif.

ABCDEFGHIJKLMNOPQRSTU
VWXYZ
abcdefghijklmnopqrstuvwxyz
1234567

LUDLOW BLACK

LUNDA
Berling 1941

iv

Designed by K. E. Forsberg. An inclined roman or italic with short ascenders and descenders. The thins are hairlines and the letters have somewhat rigid appearance because of the straight hairlines.

ABCDEFGHIJKLMNOPQRSTUVW
abcdefghijklmnopqrstuvwxyzäöå

LUNDA

LUTETIA
Enschedé 1925;
Monotype 1928

ii

Designed by Jan van Krimpen. The type shares some of the qualities which we have found in a number of contemporary types, small serifs and unobtrusive capitals. The capitals are wide, note especially **E** and **F**. **U** has the lower-case design. In the lower case the **e** has an oblique stroke to the eye, the **g** a large bowl, and the **t** is very short. The figures are old style. In the italic there is a swash series of capitals with prolonged strokes in **A, K, M, N** and **R**. The lower case, very slightly inclined, resembles BLADO in the angularity of the begininng strokes, but the serifs on ascenders are flat. The **g** has a calligraphic form. It is an italic which, again like Blado, will stand on its own. The roman alphabet shown here is the first LUTETIA of 1925 designed 1923–24. With the co-operation of Jan van Krimpen an American printer, Porter Garnett, had it revised in 1928. The present Enschedé Lutetia is of the first form with the exception of the horizontal bar to the **e**, and was adapted by the designer for use on Monotype machines. Lutetia Open was cut about 1930 on the model of hand-tooled capitals which the designer had been using occasionally.

ABCDEFGHIJKLMNOPQ RSTUVWXYZÆŒQU&
abcdefghijklmnopqrsſtuvwxyz
1234567890   1234567890
LUTETIA

$ABCDEFGHIJKLMNOPQRSTUVWXYZÆŒQU\&$

abcdefghijklmnopqrsſtuvwxyz

1234567890   *1234567890*

$\mathcal{ABCDEGHJK\,MNPQRTUY}$

ENSCHEDE LUTETIA ITALIC WITH CAPS AND SWASH CAPS

LUTETIA

ii

Designed by Warren Chappell. A pen-drawn type without serifs with the bars of the **A** and **H**, the arms of **E** and **F** and other strokes being thinner than the main strokes. Ascenders and descenders are short. Numerals are short ranging.

LYDIAN
American Typefounders 1938–46;
Intertype (New York);

ix

ABCDEFGHIJKLMNOPQRSTUVWXYZ

abcdefghijklmnopqrstuvwxyz

1234567890

ABCDEFGHIJKLMNOPQRSTUVWXYZ

abcdefghijklmnopqrstuvwxyz

1234567890

INTERTYPE LYDIAN

ABCDEFGHIJKLMNOPQRSTUVWXYZ

abcdefghijklmnopqrstuvwxyz

1234567890

ABCDEFGHIJKLMNOPQRSTUVWXYZ

abcdefghijklmnopqrstuvwxyz

1234567890

INTERTYPE LYDIAN BOLD

Designed by Louis Perrin about 1846. Serifs are small and bracketed. Letters vary in width, the round letters **C**, **D** and **O** being the wider. The **J** is short ranging, and the tail of the **R** tapers to a point. Perrin's original CARACTÈRES AUGUSTAUX included the lower case and numerals, but the capitals only seem to have been preserved.

LYONS
TITLING
Chiswick Press

TWENTY FOUR POINT LYONS TITLING FOUNDRY CAST IN

LYONS TITLING

Designed by Douglas C. McMurtrie. Shaded capitals with thin, flat serifs. It resembles NARCISSUS and is based on ROSART.

McMURTRIE
TITLE
Condé Nast Press

vii

ABCDEFGHIJKLM

McMURTRIE TITLE

MADISON ANTIQUA

Stempel 1909–19

iv

This type face, originally called AMTS-ANTIQUA, was redesigned in 1965 and is characterised by large x-height and strong serifs.

ABCDEFGHIJKLMNOPQRSTUVWXYZ
abcdefghijklmnopqrstuvwxyz
1234567890
ABCDEFGHIJKLMNOPQRSTUVWX
abcdefghijklmnopqrstuvwxyz
1234567890

MADISON

iv

ABCDEFGHIJKLMNOPQRSTU
abcdefghijklmnopqrstuvwxyz
1234567890

MADISON BOLD

iv

ABCDEFGHIJKLMNOPQRSTUVWXYZ
abcdefghijklmnopqrstuvwxyz
1234567890

MADISON CONDENSED

iv

ABCDEFGHIJKLMNOPQRSTUVWXYZ
abcdefghijklmnopqrstuvwxyz
1234567890

MADISON BOLD CONDENSED

MAGISTER

Nebiolo 1966

ii

Designed by Aldo Novarese as a text type of large x-height.

ABCDEFGHIJKLMNOPQRSTUVX
YZW
abcdefghijklmnopqrstuvxyzw
1234567890
ABCDEFGHIJKLMNOPQRSTUVX
YZW
abcdefghijklmnopqrstuvxyzw
1234567890

MAGISTER

ABCDEFGHIJKLMNOPQRSTUVX YZW
abcdefghijklmnopqrstuvxyzw
1234567890

MAGISTER

ii

MAGISTER BOLD

ABCDEFGHIJK LMNOPQ RSTUVWXYZ &
abcdefghijklmnopqrstuv wxyzß
1234567890

ii

MAGISTER WIDE

A text type having narrow letters.

MAGNA

Typoart 1968

ii

ABCDEFGHIJKLMNOPQRSTUVWXYZ
abcdefghijklmnopqrstuvwxyz ff fi fl ft &
1234567890

ABCDEFGHIJKLMNOPQRSTUVWXYZ
abcdefghijklmnopqrstuvwxyz ff fi fl ft &
1234567890

MAGNA

ABCDEFGHIJKLMNOPQRSTUVWXYZ
abcdefghijklmnopqrstuvwxyz ff fi fl ft &
1234567890

ii

MAGNA BOLD

Designed by Arthur Murawski and based on the nineteenth-century ITALIENNE. A condensed type of heavy colour. The **g** has an open tail and ascenders and descenders are short.

MAGNET

Ludwig & Mayer 1951

v

ABCDEFGHIJKLMNOPQRSTUVWXYZ
abcdefghijklmnopqrstuvwxyz
1234567890

MAGNET

MAJESTIC
Bauer 1926

ix

Designed by R. Gipkens. A fat face with some flourishes and diamond-shaped dots on the **i**.

Eine Schrift von Wirkung

MAJESTIC

MAJESTIC
Mergenthaler Linotype 1953–56

iv

Designed by Jackson Burke. Another of the important newspaper types introduced in the 1950s and 60s, designed for teletypesetter operation.

ABCDEFGHIJKLMNOPQRSTUVWXYZ
abcdefghijklmnopqrstuvwxyz
12345 67890

ABCDEFGHIJKLMNOPQRSTUVWXYZ
abcdefghijklmnopqrstuvwxyz
12345 67890

MAJESTIC

iv

ABCDEFGHIJKLMNOPQRSTUVWXYZ
abcdefghijklmnopqrstuvwxyz
12345 67890

MAJESTIC BOLD

MANILA
Lanston Monotype 1909

iv

A bold text type with heavy serifs.

ABCDEFGHIJKLMNOPQRSTUVWXYZ&ÆŒ
abcdefghijklmnopqrstuvwxyzæœ   fiflffffiffl
1234567890

MANILA

MANUSCRIPT
Grafotechna 1944–50

ix

Designed by Oldrich Menhart. A pen-drawn type closely following the designer's hand-writing. The lower-case italic is similar to that of FIGURAL. The **k** and the **x** in the roman have no right-foot serif, all letters have irregular outlines.

ABCDEFGHIJKLMNOPQRSTUVWXYZ
abcdefghijklmnopqrstuvwxyz
1234567890
ABCDEFGHIJKLMNOPQRSTUVWXYZ
abcdefghijklmnopqrstuvwxyz
1234567890

MANUSCRIPT

Named after the Venetian printer and publisher Aldus Manutius, but by no means a Venetian type! Instead, the design resembles IONIC or even SCHADOW. Unusual is the **r** in the italics which has a rounded foot pointing to the right, and the open design of some swash capital, like **L, N, P**, etc. Ascenders and descenders are short; and there are three weights.

MANUTIUS

L. Wagner

ABCDEFGHIJKLMNOPQRSTUV
abcdefghijklmnopqrstuvwxyz
ABCDEFGHIJKLMNOPRSTUV
abcdefghijklmnopqrstuvwxy
ABCDEFGHIJKLMNOPRS

iv/v

MANUTIUS WITH SWASH CAPITALS

ABCDEFGHIJKLMNOPQRSTUV
abcdefghijklmnopqrstuvwxyz

iv/v

MANUTIUS BOLD

ABCDEFGHIJKLMNOPQRSTUVWXYZ
abcdefghijklmnopqrstuvwxyz

iv/v

MANUTIUS EXTRA BOLD CONDENSED

Designed by Rudolf Koch. A roman with short ascenders and descenders. The serifs are small, but longer at the ends of the arms of **E, F** and **L, M** is rather splayed and is without top serifs, like the **M** in other types designed by Koch. The lower-case **g** has no link and an open tail, again like the **g** in other Koch types. **U** has the lower-case design. In the **W** the middle strokes cross; the lower case **w** has no middle serif. The figures are short-ranging.

MARATHON

Klingspor 1931

ABCDEFGHIJKLMNOPQRSTUV
abcdefghijklmnopqrstuvwxyz
1234567890

ii

MARATHON

A card titling with hair-line serifs. *Cf.* ORLANDO or ENGRAVERS' BODONI.

MARKO

Weber

ABCDEFGHIJKLMNOPQRSTUVWXYZ
1234567890

iv

MARKO

MASTERMAN
Lanston Monotype 1910

iv

A rather legible version of a bold variation of DORIC.

**A B C D E F G H I J K L M N O P Q R S T U V
W X Y Z & Æ Œ**

**a b c d e f g h i j k l m n o p q r s t u v w x y z
æ œ fi fl ff ffi ffl**

1 2 3 4 5 6 7 8 9 0

MASTERMAN

MATHEIS MOBIL
Ludwig & Mayer 1960

ix

Designed by Helmut Matheis. A design of medium weight which is almost without serifs and very nearly monotone. The letters are wide. The **T** has an unusual terminal, found also in the lower-case **r**. There are script qualities in many letters.

ABCDEFGHIJKLMNOPQRSTUVWXYZ

abcdefghijklmnopqrstuvwxyz

1234567890

MATHEIS MOBIL

MATRO NEWS
Matrotype 1968

iv

A newspaper text type designed for legibility and similar to OPTICON.

ABCDEFGHIJKLMNOPQRSTUVWXYZÆŒ
abcdefghijklmnopqrstuvwxyzæœ
1234567890

ABCDEFGHIJKLMNOPQRSTUVWXYZÆŒ
abcdefghijklmnopqrstuvwxyzæœ
1234567890

MATRO NEWS

MATURA
Monotype 1938

ix

Designed by Imre Reiner. A modified bold calligraphic type of sans serif style. It is not quite monotone nor entirely without serifs. A has a slab serif and there are serifs on the **C, N, S, V, W** and **Y**, and also on the lower-case **m** and **n**. The **a** is one-storeyed and the **g** has an open tail. There is also a set of scriptorial caps.

ABCDEFGHIJKLMNOPQRSTUVWXYZ&

abcdefghijklmnopqrstuvwxyz

£1234567890   ÆŒæœ   fifffl

MATURA

ix

ABCDEFGHIJKLMN
OPQRSTUVWXYZ

MATURA SCRIPTORIAL CAPITALS

146

Designed by Georg Trump. A roman with large x-height.

ii

ABCDEFGHIJKLMNOPQRSTU VWXYZ
abcdefghijklmnopqrstuvwxyz
1234567890

MAURITIUS

ii

ABCDEFGHIJKLMNOPQRSTUV WXYZ
abcdefghijklmnopqrstuvwwxyz
1234567890

MAURITIUS ITALIC

ii

ABCDEFGHIJKLMNOPQRSTU VWXYZ
abcdefghijklmnopqrstuvwxyz
1234567890

MAURITIUS BOLD

Designed by Rudolf Koch. A shaded series of capitals with ranging figures. The serifs are thin. The rounded letters, **C**, **O** and **Q**, have the thickest part low down. **M** is splayed and the inner strokes stop short of the line.

ix

MERCHANTS SOCIE

MAXIMILIAN ANTIQUA

A newspaper type for classified advertising.

iv

COMPANY actively engaged in the manufacture of mining equipment requires additional capital to finance current Government and like contracts. Enquiries from interested companies or individuals.— DIRECTOR of established financially sound firm, dealing retail stationers and stores only, apprehensive about rising cost travelling, seeks confiden-

ADELPHI. (Tem. 7611.) To-day, 2.30 & 7.30. ORIGINAL BALLET RUSSE. Aurora's Wedding. Presages. Prince Igor. SADLER'S WELLS. (Ter. 1672.) Evgs., 7. To-night The Barber of Seville. Wed. Il Trovatore. Thurs., Marriage of Figaro. Fri., School for Fathers. Sat., Madame Butterfly.

ABCDEFGHIJKLMNOPQRSTUVWXYZÆŒ abcdefghijklmnopqrstuvwxyzæœ fiflffffifl 1234567890
ABCDEFGHIJKLMNOPQRSTUVWXYZÆŒ abcdefghijklmnopqrstuvwxyzæœ fiflffffifl 1234567890

MAXIMUS

MEIDOORN

Heuvelspers 1927

Designed by S.H. de Roos. **A** and **M** have slab serifs. The **g** has a rather conspicuous tail and **p** and **q** have oblique foot serifs.

Cut by the German punchcutters Wagner & Schmidt in 14 pt only, the type was cast by Amsterdam Typefoundry for the exclusive use of the Heuvelspers. It is now the property of J.F. Duwaer & Zonen of Amsterdam.

i

Aa Bb Cc Dd Ee Ff Gg Hh Ii Jj Kk Ll Mm Nn Oo Pp Qq Rr Ss Tt Uu Vv Ww Xx Yy Zz

MEIDOORN

MEISTER

Typoart c. 1951

Designed by Herbert Thannhaeuser. Serifs are not very pronounced, and most strokes are expanded towards the ends. The **g** has an open tail in both the roman and italic, the **J** descends below the line and the **G** has no spur.

ix

ABCDEFGHIJKLMNOPQRSTUVWX YZ&
abcdefghijklmnopqrſstuvwxyz?
1234567890
ABCDEFGHIJKLMNOPQRSTUVWX YZ&
abcdefghijklmnopqrſstuvwxyz?
1234567890

MEISTER

ix

ABCDEFGHIJKLMNOPQ RSTUVWXYZ

MEISTER INITIALS

ix

ABCDEFGHIJKLMNOPQRSTUVW XYZ&
abcdefghijklmnopqrsſtuvwxyz?
1234567890

MEISTER BOLD

Designed by Hermann Zapf. A rather heavy roman with short ascenders and descenders. The **c** and **g** are rather square. The italic is the roman inclined except for the one-storeyed **a**, the **f** and the **k**.

MELIOR

Stempel 1952;

Linotype (Frankfurt)

iv

ABCDEFGHIJKLMNOPQRSTUVW
abcdefghijklmnopqrstuvwxyz
1234567890

ABCDEFGHIJKLMNOPQRSTUV
abcdefghijklmnopqrstuvwxyz

MELIOR

iv

ABCDEFGHIJKLMNOPQRSTUV
abcdefghijklmnopqrstuvwxyz

MELIOR BOLD

iv

ABCDEFGHIJKLMNOPQRSTUVWX
abcdefghijklmnopqrstuvwxyz

MELIOR BOLD CONDENSED

Designed by Rudolf Weiss. This is the earliest modern revival of the EGYPTIAN. In this design and in those that followed it there is a more thorough adoption of the slab serif, especially in the lower case. **A** has a slab serif; there is also a second **A** with a rounded top. **G** has a spur. In the **M** the middle strokes stop short of the line. In the lower case **a** has the one-storeyed form, with top and foot serifs on the right. **g** has a top serif instead of an ear and an open tail. There are two **f**'s and two **t**'s; in one there is a foot serif extending both ways. The italic is as the roman. There are four weights; and also condensed versions, an open and a three-dimensional letter called LUNA; the two latter designs cast by Stempel only.

MEMPHIS

Stempel 1929;
Mergenthaler Linotype 1935–36;
Linotype (London);
Linotype (Frankfurt)

v

ABCDEFGHIJKLMNOPQRSTUVWXYZ
abcdefghijklmnopqrstuvwxyz
1234567890
AJQ aafgt

ABCDEFGHIJKLMNOPQRSTUVWXYZ
ABCDEFGHIJKLMNOPQRSTUVWXYZ
abcdefghijklmnopqrstuvwxyz
1234567890
AJQ aafgt

ABCDEFGHIJKLMNOPQRSTUVWXYZ

LINOTYPE MEMPHIS LIGHT

v

ABCDEFGHIJKLMNOPQRSTUVWXYZ
abcdefghijklmnopqrstuvwxyz 1234567890
ABCDEFGHIJKLMNOPQRSTUVWX AJQ aafgt
ABCDEFGHIJKLMNOPQRSTUVWXYZ
abcdefghijklmnopqrstuvwxyz 1234567890
CDEFGHIJKLMNOPQRSTUVWXYZ AJQ aafgt

LINOTYPE MEMPHIS MEDIUM

v

ABCDEFGHIJKLMNOPQRSTUVWXYZ
abcdefghijklmnopqrstuvwxyz 1234567890
ABCDEFGHIJKLMNOPQRSTUVWX AJQ aafgt
ABCDEFGHIJKLMNOPQRSTUVWXYZ
abcdefghijklmnopqrstuvwxyz 1234567890
CDEFGHIJKLMNOPQRSTUVWXYZ AJQ aafgt

LINOTYPE MEMPHIS BOLD

v

ABCDEFGHIJKLMNOPQRSTUVWXYZ
abcdefghijklmnopqrstuvw 1234567890
AJQ aafgt
ABCDEFGHIJKLMNOPQRSTUVWXYZ
defghijklmnopqrstuvwxyz 1234567890
AJQ aafgt

LINOTYPE MEMPHIS EXTRA BOLD

v

ABCDEFGHIJKLMNOPQRSTUVWXYZ
abcdefghijklmnopqrstuvwxyz

STEMPEL MEMPHIS UNIVERSAL MEDIUM

v

ABCDEFGHIJKLMNOPQRSTUVWXYZ
abcdefghijklmnopqrstuvwxyz

STEMPEL MEMPHIS UNIVERSAL HEAVY

v

ABCDEFGHIJKLMNOPQRSTUVWXYZ
abcdefghijklmnopqrstuvwxyz

STEMPEL MEMPHIS UNIVERSAL BOLD

v

ABCDEFGHIJKLMNOPQRST

STEMPEL MEMPHIS OPEN

v

ABCDEFGHIJKLMNOP

STEMPEL MEMPHIS LUNA

Designed by Oldrich Menhart. A roman with small serifs, which are horizontal in the lower case, except on the tops of the ascenders. The italic has the serifs of the roman. The round letters and arcs have a certain angularity, and it is this angularity which is the most striking feature of the italic. Originally this type was cut for use in Czechoslovakia.

MENHART

Monotype 1938;
Grafotechna

ii

ABCDEFGHIJKLMNOPQRSTUVWXYZ
abcdefghijklmnopqrstuvwxyz
1234567890
ABCDEFGHIJKLMNOPQRSTUVWXYZ
abcdefghijklmnopqrstuvwxyz
1234567890

MENHART

Designed by O. Menhart. A roman more or less old face in design with the small serifs which are characteristic of contemporary romans. In the upper case **B**, **E**, **F** and **P** are narrow letters, the **M** is slightly splayed and **Q** has its tail outside the bowl. In the **e** the straight to the eye is not quite horizontal. The **g** has a large bowl. The figures range on the line. The italic has a slight inclination. There is also a bold. Different from the Monotype Corporation's MENHART.

MENHART
ROMAN

Bauer 1939

ii

ABCDEFGHIJKLMNOPQRSTUVW
XYZ
abcdefghijklmnopqrstuvwxyz
1234567
ABCDEFGHIJKLMNOPQRSTUVW
XYZ
abcdefghijklmnopqrstuvwxyz
1234567890

MENHART ROMAN

ABCDEFGHIJKLMNOPQRSTUV
WXYZ
abcdefghijklmnopqrstuvwxyz
1234567890

MENHART BOLD

ii

Designed by Hermann Zapf. A newspaper type, modern-face in design like SCOTCH ROMAN. There is also a bold.

ABCDEFGHIJKLMNOPQRSTUVWXYZ

abcdefghijklmnopqrstuvwxyz

67890

ABCDEFGHIJKLMNOPQRSTUVWXYZ

ABCDEFGHIJKLMNOPQRSTUVWXYZ

abcdefghijklmnopqrstuvwxyz

12345

MERGENTHALER

iv

ABCDEFGHIJKLMNOPQRSTUVWXYZ

abcdefghijklmnopqrstuvwxyz

12345

MERGENTHALER BOLD

MERIDIEN

Deberny & Peignot 1957

vii

Designed by A. Frutiger. A classical roman with foot serifs on the **p** and **q**. The **M** is wide and splayed. PRESIDENT is similar.

ABCDEFGHIJKLMN
OPQRSTUVWXYZ
abcdefghijklmnopqrs
tuvwxyz
1234567890

MERIDIEN

MERRY-
MOUNT

Merrymount Press 1894

i

Designed by Bertram G. Goodhue and cut by Woerner of A.D. Farmer & Son. The design is probably influenced by the work of William Morris. The **G** has a small spur, **M** has slab serifs and the tail of the **R** tapers. The **g** has a squat tail and there is a serif on the bar of the **t**.

Et quibus bellum volentibus erat, probare exemplum ac recentis legati animum oppe⁄ riri, cum Agricola, quamquam transvecta

MERRYMOUNT TYPE

152

A text and display type face with heavy serifs and designed for phototypesetting.

ABCDEFGHIJKLMNOPQRSTUVWXYZ
abcdefghijklmnopqrstuvwxyz
1 2 3 4 5 6 7 8 9 0

iv

ABCDEFGHIJKLMNOPQRSTUVWXYZ
abcdefghijklmnopqrstuvwxyz
1 2 3 4 5 6 7 8 9 0

METRION

ABCDEFGHIJKLMNOPQRSTUVWXYZ
abcdefghijklmnopqrstuvwxyz
1 2 3 4 5 6 7 8 9 0

iv

METRION BOLD

Designed by W. Schwerdtner. Vertical strokes are wedge-shaped and thicker at the top. The **g** has an open tail. The light version of the type looses much of the essential character of the design.

ABCDEFGHIJKLMNOPQ

ix

abcdefghijklmnopqrstuvwx

1234567890

METROPOLIS BOLD

ABCDEFGHIJKLMNOP

ix

QRSTUVWXYZ&

£1234567890

METROPOLIS SHADED

MINERVA

Linotype (London) 1954

Designed by Reynolds Stone. The **B, E, F, P** and **R** are narrow letters. The italic has the serifs of the roman. Numerals are both ranging and non-ranging.

ii

ABCDEFGHIJKLMNOPQRSTUVWXYZ
abcdefghijklmnopqrstuvwxyz
1234567890   1234567890

ABCDEFGHIJKLMNOPQRSTUVWXYZ
abcdefghijklmnopqrstuvwxyz
1234567890   1234567890

ii

MINERVA

ABCDEFGHIJKLMNOPQRSTUVWXYZ
abcdefghijklmnopqrstuvwxyz
1234567890   1234567890

ii

MINERVA BOLD

MINISTER

Schriftguss 1929

Designed by M. Fahrenwaldt. Capitals are wide. Serifs on the upper case are shaped and oblique and slightly concave on the lower case. The bowl of the **P** is not closed, the **V** has cursive form. Numerals are short ranging. Decorated initials are called SYMBOL and PROMINENT, and a white on black titling was called KREIS VERSALIEN.

i/ii

ABCDEFGHIJKLMNOPQRSTUVW
XYZ&

abcdefghijklmnopqrstuvwxyz?

1234567890

ABCDEFGHIJKLMNOPQRSTUVW
XYZ&

abcdefghijklmnopqrstuvwxyz?

1234567890

MINISTER

ABCDEFGHIJKLMNOPQRSTUV
WXYZ&
abcdefghijklmnopqrstuvwxyz?
1234567890

MINISTER BOLD

i/ii

ABCDEFGHIJKLMNOPQRS
TUVWXYZ&
abcdefghijklmnopqrstuvwxyz?
1234567890

MINISTER EXTRA BOLD

i/ii

ABCDEFGHIJKLMNOPQRSTUVWXYZ
abcdefghijklmnopqrstuvwxyz?
1234567890

MINISTER BOLD CONDENSED

i/ii

MONTBLANC

KREIS VERSALIEN

ABCDEFG
HIJKLMN
OPQRSTU
VWXY&Z
1234567890

ix

SYMBOL

A type with stubby serifs, oblique on the lower case. Capitals are wide, notably the **N.** Descenders are very short, as indicated by the name. The eye of the **e** has an oblique stroke.

MODERN to meet the needs

FOUNDRY in England

MINSTER LINING OLD STYLE

HIGHEST-CLASS work

MINSTER LINING OLD STYLE BOLD

MODERN

Monotype

A characteristic English face, of which The Monotype Corporation has several versions.

iv

ABCDEFGHIJKLMNOPQRSTUVWXYZ

abcdefghijklmnopqrstuvwxyz

1234567890

ABCDEFGHIJKLMNOPQRSTUVWXYZ

abcdefghijklmnopqrstuvwxyz

MODERN

iv

ABCDEFGHIJKLMNOPQRSTUVWXYZ

abcdefghijklmnopqrstuvwxyz

1234567890

ABCDEFGHIJKLMNOPQRSTUVWXYZ

abcdefghijklmnopqrstuvwxyz

1234567890

MODERN BOLD

iv

ABCDEFGHIJKLMNOPQRSTUVWXYZ

abcdefghijklmnopqrstuvwxyz

1234567890

ABCDEFGHIJKLMNOPQRSTUVWXYZ

abcdefghijklmnopqrstuvwxyz

1234567890

MODERN CONDENSED

iv

ABCDEFGHIJKLMNOPQRSTUVWXYZ

abcdefghijklmnopqrstuvwxyz

1234567890

ABCDEFGHIJKLMNOPQRSTUVWXYZ

abcdefghijklmnopqrstuvwxyz

MODERN WIDE

ABCDEFGHIJKLMNOPQRSTUVWX
YZ
1234567890

MODERN

iv

MODERN BOLD WIDE

ABCDEFGHIJKLMNOPQRSTUVWXYZ

abcdefghijklmnopqrstuvwxyz

fifffffffifflqu& £$12345678

iv

MODERN BOLD CONDENSED

Designed by W.A. Parker. Similar to the same founders' GALLIA, but with an additional decoration of the main strokes.

MODERNISTIC

American Typefounders 1927.

ix

MODERNISTIC

A type with similarity to STEELPLATE.

MODULARIO

Adler Traldi 1965

vii

ABCDEFGHIJKLMNOPQRSTUVWXYZ
1234567890

MODULARIO

Redrawn by S.L. Hartz from a design by the Paris founder Molé. Floral decoration on the open face of three dimensional letters.

MOLE
FOLIATE

Stephenson Blake

iv

MOLÉ FOLIATE

MONA LISA

Ludwig & Mayer 1930

Designed by Albert Auspurg. An inline roman of modern-face design not unlike the same founders' FIRMIN DIDOT. The central arm of the A and other capitals is extended to the left. Ascenders are tall, but descenders are short. The **f** and **t** are unusual in design.

ix

ABCDEFGHIJKLMNOPQRSTUVWXYZ

abcdefghijklmnopqrstuvwxyz

1234567890

MONA LISA

MONASTIC

Ludwig & Mayer

A calligraphic open titling type.

ix

ABCDEFG
HIJKLMN
OPQRSTU
VWXYZ

MONASTIC

MONDIAL

Stempel 1936

Designed by Hans Bohn. A type like CORVINUS, with straight edges to the round letters. The A and M do not have the slab serifs of CORVINUS. The italic is a sloped roman.

iv

ABCDEFGHIJKLMNOPQRSTUVWXYZ

abcdefghijklmnopqrstuvwxyz

ABCDEFGHIJKLMNOPQRSTUVWXYZ

abcdefghijklmnopqrstuvwxyz

MONDIAL

ABCDEFGHIJKLMNOPQRSTUVWXYZ
abcdefghijklmnopqrstuvwxyz
1234567890

MONDIAL SEMI-BOLD

ABCDEFGHIJKLMNOPQRSTU
abcdefghijklmnopqrstuvwxyz

MONDIAL BOLD

ABCDEFGHIJKLMNOPQRSTUVWXYZ
abcdefghijklmnopqrstuvwxyz

MONDIAL BOLD CONDENSED

Designed by Karlgeorg Hoefer as a fat face with almost slab serifs. The type is slightly inclined.

ABCDEFGHIJKLM
NOPQRSTUVWXY
Z
abcdefghijklmnop
qrstuvwxyz
1234567890

MONSOON

Designed by Herbert P. Horne and cut by E.P. Prince. The type has very small serifs, oblique on the lower case. Capitals are rather narrow and the **R** has an extended tail. The **a** has a wide bowl, the **e** a large eye and the **g** a large bowl. The **v** is a wide letter.

virtue and ancient descent, and also of their having inter-
married with imperial blood; inasmuch as Beatrice, sister
of the emperor, Henry II, was wife to Count Bonifazio da
Canossa, then lord of Mantua, of whom was born the
Countess Matilda, a lady of rare and singular prudence and

MONTALLEGRO TYPE

MONTICELLO
Mergenthaler Linotype 1946

Designed by C.H. Griffith and based on RONALDSON ROMAN NO. 1 or OXFORD. The serifs, slightly inclined, have a scooped-out appearance. The lower-case **g** both roman and italic, has an open tail ending in a blob.

iii

ABCDEFGHIJKLMNOPQRSTUVWXYZ

abcdefghijklmnopqrstuvwxyz

1234567890

ABCDEFGHIJKLMNOPQRSTUVWXYZ

ABCDEFGHIJKLMNOPQRSTUVWXYZ

abcdefghijklmnopqrstuvwxyz

1234567890

Recut Italic: abcdefghijklmnopqrstuvwxyz

MONTICELLO

MONUMENT
Grafotechna 1950–52

Designed by Oldrich Menhart. A pen-drawn and calligraphic type with irregular outlines. The bowl of the **P** is open and the **U** is lower case. The descending tail of the **J** is very short.

ix

ABCDEFGHIJKLMNOPQRS

TUVWXYZ

1234567890

MONUMENT

MORLAND
Caslon 1900

Based on BLANCHARD of the Inland Typefoundry. A bold face with uneven outlines, a characteristic visible only in the larger sizes. The serifs are inclined but blurred. The letters are wide. The **H** has a high bar. The **R** is conspicuous with a swollen and extended tail. In the lower case the **a** leans back, **p** and **q** have foot serifs on the outer side only. The italic has the serifs of the roman. In the **M** the middle strokes stop short of the line. The **h** has a curved main stroke; **v** and **w** have initial loops.

One of Goudy's early designs, PABST OLD STYLE, has similar characteristics, and M.F. Benton's ROYCROFT is also similar but narrower.

ix

Latest Estimates *Charming Scenes*

MORLAND

MÖWE
Genzsch & Heyse 1929

Designed by H. Beck. An outline roman in which the open part of each stroke is divided by a second stroke. As a result the counters of **e** and **o** have an unusual appearance.

iv

Moderne Druckarb

MÖWE

MOZART NOIR
Warnery

A set of modern-face capitals in which the thins are hair lines. The letters are of equal width and somewhat extended. An Inline version is called DIAPHANE.

iv

BIEN QUE LES PROCÉD

MOZART NOIR

Designed by W. Schwerdtner. Mainly a display type, if one may judge from its blackness and very short ascenders and descenders. The serifs are very slight and like chisel strokes. The capitals vary in width and in this case among the narrow letters are H and N. M, N and W have no top serifs. *Cf.* the capitals of JOST MEDIAEVAL. a has a large bowl and an unusual finish to the top arc. The g has no link and the tail is open. The i has a dash in place of the dot. The lower-case letters have crushed down serifs. There is also a light face.

MUNDUS

Stempel 1929;

Linotype (Frankfurt)

ix

Ein Werk der Neuzeit

MUNDUS LIGHT

ix

Cerises d'Itxassou

MUNDUS BOLD

Designed by Carlos Winkow. A calligraphic roman. The serifs are steeply inclined and slightly modelled. On some upper case letters there are hooks, and some lower case letters, especially the e, have pen-drawn qualities. The italic has the serifs of the roman, and there is also a bold.

NACIONAL

Nacional 1941

El dibujo de los tipos ofrece mucha dificultad
DISTINCIONES MERECIDAS

ix

La bella historia de las amazonas en Viena
LOS AMANTES DE TERUEL

CLÁSICO NACIONAL I

Penetrando profundamente en la cavidad
REFERENCIA LOCALIZADA

ix

CLÁSICO NACIONAL NEGRO

A type designed by Bernard Naudin with some resemblance in the roman to NICOLAS COCHIN. The serifs are thick, inclined in the lower case. In the capitals the vertical strokes are thickened in the middle. The arm of the L is very wide. The middle strokes of the M stop short of the line. The S ends in a big serif. The ascenders and descenders are ample. Serifs on the tops of ascenders extend both ways. c and e have extended curves; g is a squat letter with a wide tail; s is as in the upper case. There are two sets of figures, one short-ranging. The roman is accompanied by a script, not an italic, based on the designer's own hand. In the upper case many of the serifs have curved ends. G has an odd lower serif. In the H the bar extends to the left. The middle strokes of the M stop half-way. The lower case has pen strokes for serifs. The bowls of a, d, g and o are not closed; g has an open tail drawn from right to left; the curve of the v extends above the letter. A set of open capitals is called NAUDIN CHAMPLEVÉ. This type is not to be confused with Berthold's TRADITION.

NAUDIN or TRADITION

Deberny & Peignot 1911–24;

Stephenson Blake

se présente, comme des 2345
ABCDEFGHIJKLM

ii

Dans mille ans d'ici, il fera verser
des larmes; il sera l'admiration des

TRADITION

ABCDEFGHIJKLMNO
1234567890

ii

CHAMPLEVÉ

161

NEUTRA
Typoart 1968

v

A roman following CLARENDON.

ABCDEFGHIJKLMNOPQR STUVWXYZ
abcdefghijklmnopqrstuvwxyz
1234567890

NEUTRA

NEW CLARENDON
Monotype 1960

v

A text face following English style for these types.

ABCDEFGHIJKLMNOPQRSTUVWXYZ
abcdefghijklmnopqrstuvwxyz
1234567890

NEW CLARENDON

ABCDEFGHIJKLMNOPQRSTUVWXYZ
abcdefghijklmnopqrstuvwxyz
1234567890

NEW CLARENDON BOLD

NEWPORT
American Typefounders c. 1890

ix

A quaint elongated slab serif type which lends to two-colour printing, giving a three-dimensional effect.

ABCDEFGHIJKLMNOP
QRSTUVWXYZ

NEWPORT

ix

ABCDEFGHIJKLMNOP
QRSTUVWXYZ

NEWPORT OUTLINE

NOBLESSE
Bauer c. 1870

iv

A set of modern face capitals and ranging figures with hairline serifs. The thin strokes also are hairline. Ludwig & Mayer's COPPERPLATE and Nebiolo's ORLANDO are very similar and many founders cast such types.

ABCDEFGHIJKLMNOP QRSTUVWXYZ 1234567

NOBLESSE

A text roman with tall ascenders.

A B C D E F G H I J K L M N O P Q R S T U
V W X Y Z

abcdefghijklmnopqrstuvwxyz

1 2 3 4 5 6 7 8 9 0

NORDISCHE ANTIQUA

NORDISCHE ANTIQUA

Genzsch & Heyse;

Linotype (Frankfurt)

ii

A fat face following the original designs of the early nineteenth century. Note the heavy spur on the **G** and the design of the lower-case **g**. See also the blob on the arc of the **c** and other similar letters.

NORMANDE

Haas c. 1875; Berthold 1931

iv

A B C D E F G H I J K L M N O P Q R S T U

abcdefghijklmnopqrstuvwxyz
1234567890

HAAS NORMANDE SEMI-BOLD

A B C D E F G H I J K L M N O P

abcdefghijklmnopqrstu

HAAS NORMANDE

iv

A B C D E F G H I J K L M N O P Q R S T U
V W X Y Z

abcdefghijklmnopqrstuvwxyz
1234567890

A B C D E F G H I J K L M N O P Q R S
T U V W X Y Z

abcdefghijklmnopqrstuvwxyz
1234567890

NORMANDE

iv

A B C D E F G H I J K L M N O P Q R S T U V W X Y Z

abcdefghijklmnopqrstuvwxyz
1234567890

NORMANDE CONDENSED

iv

NORMANDIA

Nebiolo 1946–49

Designed by A. Butti and A. Novarese. A fat face after the Bodoni design. Differing from ULTRA BODONI, this face has thin strokes that curve into the thick strokes. The **b** in the italic has a spur. There is also an outline version.

iv

ABCDEFGHIJKLMNOPQRS
abcdefghijklmnopqrstuvwxyz
1234567890

ABDEFGHIJKLMNOPQ
RSWXYZÇÆŒ&
abcdefghijklmnopqrstuvw
xyzçæœfiflfffffiffl
1234567890

NORMANDIA

iv

ABCDEFGHIJKLMNOPQRSTUVWXYZÇÆŒ&

abcdefghijklmnopqrstuvwxyzçæœfiflfffffiffl

1234567890

NORMANDIA ELONGATED

iv

ABCDEFHIJKLMNOPQR
STUVWXYZÇÆŒ&
abcdefghijklmnopqrstuvwx
yzçæœfiflfffffiffl
1234567890

NORMANDIA OUTLINE

NUBIAN

American Typefounders 1928

Designed by W.T. Sniffin. A fat face of extra weight. The **G** has no spur. In the lower-case ascenders and descenders are extremely short. The tail of the **g** is unfinished. The dot over **i** and **j** is a solid segment. There are none of the globular endings of arcs found in early fat faces.

ix

**Leaving Boston March 11th
on the S.S. San Petro. Will**

NUBIAN*

164

The lower-case letters of this type are based on Spanish uncial forms. Ascenders are high, while the descenders are rather shorter. The capitals follow the style of roman letters and are condensed. The foot of the U is somewhat angular.

Elevando lo pensado
MIENTRAS BUSQUE

NUMANTINA

Designed by Will Carter and David Kindersley. This type face owes much of its character to classical inscriptional letters. Mr Carter writes: "While the ultimate authority is the ancient inscriptional pattern, the special characteristics of the present rendering are manifest in the economic propositions of the shapes and the modified relations of the strokes. Thus, the letters are narrower than the classical forms and their weight heavier."

ABCDEFGHIJKLMNOPQRSTUVWXYZ&ÆŒ

abcdefghijklmnopqrstuvwxyzfiflffffifflæœ

1234567890

ABCDEFGHIJKLMNOPQRSTUVWXYZÆŒ

ABCDEFGHIJKLMNOPQRSTUVWXYZ&ÆŒ

abcdefghijklmnopqrstuvwxyzfiflffffifflæœ

1234567890

OCTAVIAN

Designed by Walter Tiemann. A roman with short ascenders and descenders; in design not unlike CASLON, except for the R with a curled tail and the ear of the g. The numerals range on the line.

ABCDEFGHIJKLMNOPQRS
TUVWXYZ
abcdefghijklmnopqrstuvwxyz
1234567890

OFFIZIN

Designed by Richard McMurtrie. Open and decorated capitals. In the centre of each main stroke is a circle. The serifs are also decorated.

GIGANTIC

OLD DUTCH

An open roman which first appeared in Fry's specimen book of 1788. The design of the letters is like that of FRY'S BASKERVILLE. The Q has a curled tail starting inside the counter.

ABCDFGHIJKLMNOPQRSTUVW
XYZ
1234&

OLD FACE OPEN

OLD STYLE

Many founders

Originally cut by Miller & Richard's employee, Alexander Phemister, and first shown in a specimen of 1860. It was so successful that it was soon copied by all the other founders. Its purpose was to cut a type which would overcome what was regarded as archaic in CASLON. The serifs are slighter and more sharply cut. Stress is vertical, though not abruptly so. Note the curves of **c**, **e** and **p**. Ascenders and descenders are rather short. The eye of the **e** is larger than in Caslon, and the **t** taller. The down stroke of the **g** tail is thickened and steeply inclined. The italic is regularly but steeply inclined.

The adapted Intertype versions of this design was called BOOKFACE, and the Linotype (London) version is BOOKPRINT. The Mergenthaler Linotype versions are OLD STYLE No. 1 and No. 3. There is a Monotype version (Series 2) with a companion bold (Series 544). By a change of seven capitals and small capitals, OLD STYLE No. 1 may be converted to RONALDSON (the characters are **C, E, F, G, L, S, T**).

ii

ABCDEFGHIJKLMNOPQRSTUVWXYZ

abcdefghijklmnopqrstuvwxyz

1234567890

ABCDEFGHIJKLMNOPQRSTUVWXYZ

abcdefghijklmnopqrstuvwxyz

MONOTYPE OLD STYLE

ii

ABCDEFGHIJKLMNOPQRSTUVWXYZ

abcdefghijklmnopqrstuvwxyz

1234567890

MONOTYPE OLD STYLE BOLD

ii

ABCDEFGHIJKLMNOPQRSTUVWXYZ&

ABCDEFGHIJKLMNOPQRSTUVWXYZ&

abcdefghijklmnopqrstuvwxyz

1234567890

ABCDEFGHIJKLMNOPQRSTUVWXYZ&

abcdefghijklmnopqrstuvwxyz

1234567890

MERGENTHALER LINOTYPE OLD STYLE NO. 1

ii

ABCDEFGHIJKLMNOPQRSTUVWXYZ&

ABCDEFGHIJKLMNOPQRSTUVWXYZ&

abcdefghijklmnopqrstuvwxyz

1234567890

ABCDEFGHIJKLMNOPQRSTUVWXYZ&

abcdefghijklmnopqrstuvwxyz

1234567890

MERGENTHALER LINOTYPE OLD STYLE NO. 2

ii

ABCDEGHIJKLMNOPQRSTUVWXYZ

abcdefghijklmnopqrstuvwxyz

1234567890

ABCDEFGHIJKLMNOPQRSTUVWXYZ

abcdefghijklmnopqrstuvwxyz

1234567890

MONOTYPE OLD STYLE BOLD NO. 53

ii

ABCDEFGHIJKLMNOPQRSTUVWXYZ

abcdefghijklmnopqrstuvwxyz

1234567890

MONOTYPE OLD STYLE BOLD NO. 159

ABCDEFGHIJKLMNOPQRSTUVWXYZ
abcdefghijklmnopqrstuvwxyz   1234567890

A ABCDDEEFGHIJKLMMNNOPP
QRRSSTTUVXYZ
abcdefghijklmnopqrstuvwxyz
1234567890

OLD STYLE NO. 5

Designed by Matthew Carter as a newspaper type with large x-height, and believed to have the distinction of being the first copyrighted type in the United States.

ABCDEFGHIJKLMNOPQRSTUVWXYZ&
abcdefghijklmnopqrstuvwxyz
$1234567890

OLYMPIAN

ABCDEFGHIJKLMNOPQRSTUVWXYZ&
abcdefghijklmnopqrstuvwxyz
$1234567890

OLYMPIAN BOLD

A revival of a mid-nineteenth century condensed and elongated fat face. Such a type was shown by the Wilson foundry as early as 1843. Capitals only. VERTICAL is similar but narrower.

ABCDEFGHIJKLMNO

SLIMBLACK

Designed by Gerry Powell. A condensed and elongated fat face in the style of SLIMBLACK. It follows the design of the early fat faces, except for the rather angular **a**.

ABCDEFGHIJKLMNOPQRSTUVWXYZ
abcdefghijklmnopqrstuvwxyz   1234567890

ARSIS

ABCDEFGHIJKLMNOPQRSTUVWXYZ
abcdefghijklmnopqrstuvwxyz   12345

MONOTYPE ONYX

A set of decorated capitals of fat face design. The decoration consists of horizontal lines on the vertical strokes.

ABCDEFGHIJKLMNOP
QRSTUVWXYZ 12345678

OPAL

OPEN ROMAN CAPITALS
Enschedé 1929

Designed by Jan van Krimpen for use with ANTIQUE GREEK or two-line capitals.

ABCDEFGHIJKLMNOPQ RST
UVWXYZ

OPEN ROMAN CAPITALS

OPERA
Sofratype 1960

Designed by Adrien Frutiger. Ascenders and descenders are short, the italic is the roman slightly sloped, except for **a** and an open-tailed **g**. Numerals are ranging.

ABCDEFGHIJKLMNOPQRSTUVWXYZ
abcdefghijklmnopqrstuvwxyz
1234567890
ABCDEFGHIJKLMNOPQRSTUVWXYZ
ABCDEFGHIJKLMNOPQRSTUVWXYZ
abcdefghijklmnopqrstuvwxyz
1234567890
OPERA

ABCDEFGHIJKLMNOPQRSTUVWXYZ
abcdefghijklmnopqrstuvwxyz
1234567890
OPERA BOLD

OPTICON
Mergenthaler Linotype 1935–36

Designed by C.H. Griffith. A newspaper type ranging as No. 3 in the "Linotype Legibility Group", and specially designed to suit newspapers running heavy pictures and a lot of ink.

ABCDEFGHIJKLMNOPQRSTUVWXYZ
abcdefghijklmnopqrstuvwxyz
1234567890
ABCDEFGHIJKLMNOPQRSTUVWXYZ
abcdefghijklmnopqrstuvwxyz
1234567890

OPTICON

ORATOR
Amsterdam 1962

Designed by Leonard H.D. Smit. A bold companion to PROMOTOR, with capitals resembling card types. The type has some similarities to CRAW MODERN, but is more rounded and has less variation in stress between thick and hair-line strokes.

ABCDEFGHIJKLMNOPQ
RSTUVWXYZÆŒ

abcdefghijklmnopqrstu
vwxyz

1234567890£&æœ

ORATOR

These lavishly ornamented letters are in white except for parts of the lower halves, which are in black. The type comes from the foundry of V. and J. Figgins. ROMANTIQUES NO. 1 is identical.

ABCDEFGHIJKLMNOPQRSTUVWXY
1234567890&ÆŒ

ORNAMENTED OUTLINE

Designed by O.H.W. Hadank. A bold copperplate roman in which the black has been replaced by a fine herring-bone inline design. The capitals also have a star in the centre of the down strokes.

ABCDEFGHIJKLMNOPQ
abcdefghijklmnopqrstuvw
1234567890

ORNATA

Designed by Walter Tiemann. A roman with small serifs, slightly oblique on the lower case and with short ascenders and descenders. The **M** is splayed and has no top serifs. In the **W** the middle strokes cross. The swash caps are also called EUPHORION.

ABCDEFGHIJKLMNOPQRSTUV
abcdefghijklmnopqrstuvwxyz
1234567890
ABCDEFGHIJKLMNOPQRSTUV
abcdefghijklmnopqrstuvwxyz

ORPHEUS

ABCDEFGHIJKLMNOPQRST
abcdefghijklmnopqrstuvwxyz

ORPHEUS BOLD

ii

ABCDEFGHIJKLMNOPQRS
TUVWXYZ

EUPHORION

OTTOCENTO

Nebiolo 1930

ix

Shaded capitals in which the left edges of the black strokes are serrated. The letters are wide and the serifs bracketed.

ABCDEFGHIJKLMNOP QRSTUVXYZW 1234567890

OTTOCENTO

OXFORD

American Typefounders

iv

Designed by James Ronaldson and first shown in a specimen book in 1812 by Binny & Ronaldson in Philadelphia, who called it ROMAN No. 1. The type is influenced by the work of Didot. It was used by Updike for the text of his *Printing Types. Cf.* MONTICELLO.

ABCDEFGHIJKLMNOPQRSTUVWXYZ&

abcdefghijklmnopqrstuvwxyz

ABCDEFGHIJKLMNOPQRSTUVWXYZ

1234567890

ABCDEFGHIJKLMNOPQRSTUVWXYZ

abcdefghijklmnopqrstuvwxyz

fifflffiflffl   *fifflffiflffl*

OXFORD

PABST OLD STYLE

Lanston Monotype

ix

Designed by Frederick W. Goudy, but quite unlike PABST ROMAN. Letters have an uneven outline and blurred serifs.

ABCDEFGHIJKLMNOPQRSTUWVX

abcdefghijklmnopqrstuvwxyz

1234567890

PABST OLD STYLE

PABST ROMAN

American Typefounders 1902

ix

Designed by Frederic W. Goudy. Wide letters and somewhat uneven outline characterise this bold type. AVIL was a copy of this type made by the former Inland Typefoundry. Krebs made a copy which was called LATINA.

ABCDEFGHIJKLMNOPQR

klmnopqrstuvwxyz

1234567890

ABCDEFGHIJKLMNOPQR

klmnopqrstuvwxyz

1234567890

PABST ROMAN

Designed by A. Butti under the direction of Raffaello Bertieri. Serifs are small. The **M** is splayed. The **e** has a small eye, the **g** a wide tail and the **y** a flowing tail. The italic has the serifs of the roman.

ABCDEFGHIJKLMNOPQ QuRR
STUVXYWZÇÆŒ&
abcdefghijklmnopqrsſtuvxywzç
1234567890

ABCDEFGHIJKLMNOPQ Qu
RSTUVXYWZÇÆŒ&
abcdefghijklmnopqrstuvxywz
123457890

PAGANINI

ABCDEFGHIJKLMNOPQQuRR
STUVXYWZÇÆŒ&
§ abcdefghijklmnopqrsſtuvxywz çæœ fiflff
1234567890

ABCDEFGHIJKLMNOPQQuR
STUVXYWZÇÆŒ&
abcdefghijklmnopqrstuvyxwz
1234567890

PAGANINI LIGHT

ABCDEFGHIJKLMNOPQQu
RRSTUVXYWZÇÆŒ&
abcdefghijklmnopqrsſtuvxywzç
1234567890

PAGANINI BOLD

ABCDEFGHIJKLMNO
QPRSTUVXYWZÇÆ
1234567890

PAGANINI OPEN

Designed by M. Jacoby-Boy to accompany BRAVOUR.

Denomination   Decorative

PALADIN BOLD CONDENSED   PALADIN SHADED

Designed by Hermann Zapf. A roman with broad letters and strong, inclined serifs. The capitals especially **M** and **W** are wide. The **e** has a large eye, the **g** is wide, and the foot serifs on the final strokes of the **h**, **m** and **n** are on the outside only. Descenders are short. MICHELANGELO and SISTINA are companion titlings.

ABCDEFGHIJKLMNOPQRSTUVW
abcdefghijklmnopqrstuvwxyz
1234567890

ABCDEFGHIJKLMNOPQRSTUVW
abcdefghijklmnopqrstuvwxyz

PALATINO

ABCDEFGHIJKLMNOPQRSTUV
abcdefghijklmnopqrstuvwxyz

PALATINO BOLD

ABCDEFGHIJKLMNOPQRSTUVW
1234567890

MICHELANGELO

ABCDEFGHIJKLMNOPQRSTUV
1234567890

SISTINA

Designed by K. E. Forsberg. A set of double-inline capitals with ranging figures. The thins are hairlines.

PARAD

Berling 1938

ix

ABCDEFGHIJKKLMNOPQRSTUVW XYZÅÄÖ
PARAD

Designed by C.H. Griffith. Very fine up-strokes. The lower case italic **g** has a large bowl and a curiously short tail. The type is a lighter version of EXCELSIOR.

PARAGON

Mergenthaler Linotype 1935; Linotype (London)

iv

ABCDEFGHIJKLMNOPQRSTUVWXYZ
abcdefghijklmnopqrstuvwxyz
1234567890
ABCDEFGHIJKLMNOPQRSTUVWXYZ
abcdefghijklmnopqrstuvwxyz
1234567890
ABCDEFGHIJKLMNOPQRSTUVWXYZ
PARAGON

ABCDEFGHIJKLMNOPQRSTUVWXYZ
abcdefghijklmnopqrstuvwxyz
12345 67890
PARAGON BOLD

iv

Designed by Herbert Thannhaeuser. A heavy type with short descenders and small serifs. **A** has the bar high, the middle strokes of **M** stop short of the line, **R** has a curled tail and **T** is narrow. The **g** has a squashed tail and the **t** is narrow. The italic has slight inclination. The italic **a** has the roman form but serifs are not roman; the **g** has an open tail.

PARCIVAL

Schelter & Giesecke 1930

Eine Type von zeitloser Schönheit ist unsere Parcival-Antiqua. Ihre

ix

Die Parcival-Kursiv zeichnet sich aus durch die freie Bewegung

PARCIVAL

Ihre kraftvolle Schwere und künstlerische Form

ix

PARCIVAL BOLD

Designed by Oldrich Menhart for the printing of the new Czech Constitution. The type was then melted down. It is a calligraphic type of individual angular character.

PARLAMENT

Czech Government Printing Office 1950

ix

KAPITOLA TŘETÍ
přítomna nadpoloviční většina poslancû. Zvolen je ten, pro koho
PARLAMENT

A type with great variation of stress and almost a heavy design. LINING MODERN No. 25 is the same type; but Stephenson Blake's MODERN No. 20 is not the same design and has cupped ends to the **h**, **k**, **n** and **r**.

PARMA

Stevens Shanks c. 1870

ABCDEFGHIJKLMNOPQRSTU?
abcdefghijklmnopqrstuvwxyzææ
£1234567890§
PARMA

iv

PARSONS
American Typefounders 1918

Designed by Will Ransom. A monotone display face with a peculiarity in the serifs. At the tops of the letters the serifs extend to the left only, and at the feet to the right. Some of the capitals have the same design, in a larger size, as the lower-case letters, *e.g.*, the **M, N, P, U, V, W,** and **Y.** There is also a more normal variety of **M** and **N.** There are some additional sorts with extra long ascenders and descenders. The figures are short-ranging. There is no italic and there are two weights. Originally designed for Barnhart Bros. & Spindler.

ix

Printed Things

PARSONS

ix

RESPONSIBLE Big Advertising

PARSONS BOLD

PASTONCHI
Monotype 1927

Designed by F. Pastonchi and E. Cotti. The serifs are small and bracketed.

i

ABCDEFGHIJKLMNOPQRSTUVWXYZ
abcdefghijklmnopqrstuvwxyz
1234567890

ABCDEFGHIJKLMNOPQRSTUVWXYZ
abcdefghijklmnopqrstuvwxyz
1234567890

PASTONCHI

PEARL FOURNIER
Schriftguss 1922
IX

Decorated capitals designed by P.A. Demeter. Many of the strokes assume leaf forms. In Germany the type is called GEPERLTE FOURNIER.

ABCDEFGHIJKLMNOPQRSTUVWXYZ

PEARL FOURNIER

PEGASUS
Monotype c. 1937

Designed by Berthold Wolpe. A somewhat condensed roman designed to complement ALBERTUS.

ii

ABCDEFGHIJKLMNOPQRSTUVWXYZÆŒ&

abcdefghijklmnopqrstuvwxyz

1234567890

PEGASUS

A heavy face with sharply cut serifs, oblique on the lower case, and with vertical stress.

PENTLAND
Miller & Richard 1920

ix

AUSTRALIA TO HONOLU
The quiet cart road leading

PENTLAND

Designed by Alfons Schneider. A roman in five weights. Ascenders are of the same height as the capitals, and descenders are short. Serifs are flat. The capital **G**, like the **g** has a spur, and the lower-case letter an open tail. The **f** curves inward at the top to form a heavy dot.

PERGAMON
L. Wagner 1932; Typoart

iv

ABCDEFGHIJKLMNOPQRSTUVW
XYZ&
abcdefghijklmnopqrstuvwxyz?
1234567890

ABCDEFGHIJKLMNOPQRSTUVW
XYZ&
abcdefghijklmnopqrstuvwxyz?
1234567890

PERGAMON

iv

ABCDEFGHIJKLMNOPQRSTUVW
XYZ&
abcdefghijklmnopqrstuvwxyz?
1234567890

ABCDEFGHIJKLMNOPQRSTUVW
XYZ&
abcdefghijklmnopqrstuvwxyz?
1234567890

PERGAMON BOLD

ABCDEFGHIJKLMNOPQRSTU VWXYZ&
abcdefghijklmnopqrstuvwxyz?
1234567890

ABCDEFGHIJKLMNOPQRSTU VWXYZ&
abcdefghijklmnopqrstuvwxyz?
1234567890

PERGAMON EXTRA BOLD

iv

ABCDEFGHIJKLMNOPQRSTUVWXYZ&
abcdefghijklmnopqrstuvwxyz?
1234567890

PERGAMON BOLD CONDENSED

iv

ABCDEFGHIJKLMNOPQRSTUVWXYZ&
abcdefghijklmnopqrstuvwxyz?
1234567890

PERGAMON BOLD EXTRA CONDENSED

PERIOD OLD STYLE
Intertype

ii

This type is a reproduction of IMPRINT but has a more regular inclination in the italic. Numerals are short ranging. Ascenders and descenders are short.

ABCDEFGHIJKLMNOPQRSTUVWXYZ
abcdefghijklmnopqrstuvwxyz
1234567890

ABCDEFGHIJKLMNOPQRSTUVWXYZ
abcdefghijklmnopqrstuvwxyz
1234567890

ABCDEFGHIJKLMNOPQRSTUVWXYZ &&£

PERIOD OLD STYLE

Designed by Eric Gill, and his most popular roman. First used in a privately printed translation made by Walter Shrewring of *The Passion of Perpetua and Felicity*. The roman was named PERPETUA and the italic, cut later, FELICITY. The serifs are small, sharply cut and horizontal. The stress and gradation of colour are akin to old face. The italic is slightly inclined and is much as the roman. The titling of the same design is widely used. The bold italic was added by The Monotype Corporation in 1959.

Stephenson Blake's foundry type is somewhat different in design.

PERPETUA

Monotype 1925–30 & 1959;

Stephenson Blake

ABCDEFGHIJKLMNOPQRSTUVWXYZ&
abcdefghijklmnopqrstuvwxyz 1234567890

ABCDEFGHIJKLMNOPQRSTUVWXYZ&
abcdefghijklmnopqrstuvwxyz 1234567890

MONOTYPE PERPETUA

ABCDEFGHIJKLMNOPQRSTUVWXYZ?!&ÆŒ£
abccdefghijklmnopqrstuvwxyzfifffflffiflfffiæœ 1234567890

STEPHENSON BLAKE PERPETUA

ABCDEFGHIJKLMNOPQRSTUVWXYZ
abcdefghijklmnopqrstuvwxyz &
1234567890

ABCDEFGHIJKLMNOPQRSTUVWXYZ
abcdefghijklmnopqrstuvwxyz
1234567890

MONOTYPE PERPETUA BOLD

ABCDEFGHIJKLMNOPQRSTU
VWXYZ&
1234567890

MONOTYPE PERPETUA TITLING

ABCDEFGHIJKLMNOPQ
RSTUVWXYZ&

MONOTYPE PERPETUA BOLD TITLING

ABCDEFGHIJKLMNOPQRSTUV
WXYZ&
1234567890

MONOTYPE PERPETUA LIGHT TITLING

177

PHALANX

Genzsch & Heyse 1928

ix

Designed by Hans Möhring. A monotone roman which has thickened terminals rather than serifs. The **e** has a large bowl. The **t** has a thickened terminal to the vertical stroke and a bracketed bar.

Ullsteinbuch

PHALANX

PHARAON

Deberny & Peignot 1933

v

A type with small variation in the weight of the strokes. The **M** has a short middle stroke and the **g** an open tail. The inline version is called PHARAON WHITE.

ABCDEFGHIJKLMNOPQRSTUVW XYZ&

abcdefghijklmnopqrstuvwxyz

1234567890

PHARAON SEMI-BOLD

v

ABCDEFGHIJKLMNOPQRSTU VWXYZ

PHARAON WHITE

PHOEBUS

Deberny & Peignot 1953

ix

Designed by A. Frutiger. Inclined, shaded capitals and figures. Serifs are pointed. The **A** has a rounded apex, and the **V** and **W**, as well as the alternative **M** and **N**, are lower-case in design.

ABCDEFGHIJKLMMNOPQRSTUVW XYZ & 1234567890

PHOEBUS

PIEHLER SCRIPT

Schriftguss

ix

Designed by A. Piehler. Decorated capitals. Both thick and thin strokes are terminated by curled serifs. The bar of the **H**, arms of the **E**, etc., are hair lines and curved. There are also italic capitals.

HEINE BUR

PIEHLER SCRIPT

This type, originally designed by Eric Gill for a book published by the Limited Editions Club of New York, who called this face BUNYAN, is a re-cutting by Linotype. In its general appearance it resembles Gill's JOANNA type. The face is even in colour, and the shading of round characters is vertical. The thick and thin strokes of the letters are not strongly contrasted. Capitals are not as tall as the lower case ascenders. The serifs are bracketed. Distinguishing marks are the equal thickness of the arms of the **U** and the two serifs of the **C**, as well at the flat foot of the **a** and **b**.

ABCDEFGHIJKLMNOPQRSTUVWXYZ

abcdefghijklmnopqrstuvwxyz

1234567890

ABCDEFGHIJKLMNOPQRSTUVWXYZ

ABCDEFGHIJKLMNOPQRSTUVWXYZ

abcdefghijklmnopqrstuvwxyz

1234567890

ABCDEFGHIJKLMNOPQRSTUVWXYZ

PILGRIM

Designed by W.T. Sniffin. A light display face with thin flat serifs and tall ascenders. **M** is slightly splayed. The **e** has an oblique stroke to the eye; **g** has an ear starting from near the top of the bowl; the serifs on **m** and **w** are oblique. The italic is almost a script.

PRINTING IN THE ROMAN LETTER

will follow from the conventions of alphabetical

PIRANESI

ix

A B C D E F G H I J K L M N O P Q R S T U V W X Y Z

a b c d e f g h i j k l m n o p q r s t u v w x y z ct st

1 2 3 4 5 6 7 8 9 0

MODERN Cottage Sold

PIRANESI BOLD

Monotype; Linotype (London);

Stephenson Blake; Intertype

A roman named after the famous Antwerp printer, Christophe Plantin, and designed for The Monotype Corporation by F. H. Pierpont. However, the 16th century type on which it is modelled never seems to have been used by that printer, although it belongs to his generation, being found at Frankfurt and at Basle about 1570. It is a heavy face of large x-height, a pioneer type of the ever-recurring attempt to design founts which would consume less paper. Conspicuous letters are in the upper case the flat-topped **A** and the splayed **M**, and in lower case the **a** with a large bowl and a narrow **t**. The italic is of a regular slope and has very short descenders. There is also a semi-bold face.

ii

ABCDEFGHIJKLMNOPQRSTUV
abcdefghijklmnopqrstuvwxyz
1234567890
ABCDEFGHIJKLMNOPQRSUVX
abcdefghijklmnopqrstuxwxyz
1234567890

MONOTYPE PLANTIN

ii

ABCDEFGHIJKLMNOPQRSTUVWXYZ
abcdefghijklmnopqrstuvwxyz
1234567890
ABCDEFGHIJKLMNOPQRSTUVWXYZ
abcdefghijklmnopqrstuvwxyz
1234567890

PLANTIN LIGHT

ii

**ABCDEFGHIJKLMLOPQRSTU
VWXYZ
abcdefghijklmnopqrstuv**
ABCDEFGHIJKLMNOPQRSTU
abcdefghijklmnopqrstu

MONOTYPE PLANTIN BOLD

ii

**ABCDEFGHIJKLMNOPQRSTUVWXYZ
abcdefghijklmnopqrstuvwxyz
1234567890**

MONOTYPE PLANTIN BOLD CONDENSED

ABCDEFGHIJKLMNOPQRSTUVWXYZ
abcdefghijklmnopqrstuvwxyz
1234567890.

ABCDEFGHIJKLMNOPQRSTUVWXYZ
abcdefghijklmnopqrstuvwxyz
1234597890

STEPHENSON BLAKE PLANTIN

ABCDEFGHIJKLMNOPQRSTUVWXYZ
abcdefghijklmnopqrstuvwxyz   1234567890
ABCDEFGHIJKLMNOPQRSTUVWXYZ
ABCDEFGHIJKLMNOPQRSTUVWXYZ
abcdefghijklmnopqrstuvwxyz   1234567890

LINOTYPE PLANTIN

ABCDEFGHIJKLMNOPQRSTUVWXYZ
abcdefghijklmnopqrstuvwxyz
ABCDEFGHIJKLMNOPQRSTUVWXYZ &&£
ABCDEFGHIJKLMNOPQRSTUVWXYZ
abcdefghijklmnopqrstuvwxyz

INTERTYPE PLANTIN

ABCDEFGHIJKLMNOPQRSTUVWXYZ
abcdefghijklmnopqrstuvwxyz
1234567890

INTERTYPE PLANTIN BOLD

In spite of its name, this type has little connection with PLANTIN, except that it is a heavy face of large x-height. Serifs are very thin on the capitals, and there is abruptness of stress. American Typefounders' NEW CASLON is identical.

ABCDEFGHIJKLMNOPQRSTUV
WXYZ
abcdefghijklmnopqrstuvwxyz
1234567890

ABCDEFGHIJKLMNOPQRSTUV
WXYZ
abcdefghijklmnopqrstuvwxyz
1234567890

PLANTIN OLD STYLE

PLAYBILL
Stephenson Blake 1938

Designed after sketches by Robert Harling. A condensed reversed type face in which the serifs are heavier than the main strokes. It is a revival of a Victorian type. The style was at first called FRENCH ANTIQUE, or sometimes ITALIAN. The Monotype Corporation's FIGARO is a type of this style.

v

ABCDEFGHIJKLMNOPQRSTUVWXYZ

abcdefghijklmnopqrstuvwxyz

1234567890

PLAYBILL

PLYMOUTH
Lanston Monotype 1905–6

A bold display type, also cast in text sizes, and similar to ROYCROFT. E and F have stumpy cross strokes, the M is wide and the italic has swash characters.

ix

**A B C D E F G H I J K L M N O P Q R S T U V
W X Y Z @ Æ Œ**

a b c d e f g h i j k l m n o p q r s t u v w x y z æ œ

$ 1 2 3 4 5 6 7 8 9 0 £

*A B C D E F G H I J K L M N N O P Q R R S T U
U W X Y Z & Æ Œ*

a b c d e f g h i j k l m n o p q r s t u v w x y z œ œ

$ 1 2 3 4 5 6 7 8 9 0 £

PLYMOUTH

POLIPHILUS
Monotype 1923

Before BEMBO was cut The Monotype Corporation had already designed a roman based on another Aldine type, that of the *Hypnerotomachia Poliphili*, 1499, which was in fact Griffo's second version of his roman. The upper case is rather taller than that of Bembo. The curve of the C is less complete and the G has a spur not present in Bembo. The bowl of the P is not closed and there is a second variety of Y with curved upper limbs. In the lower case there are only slight differences. In the w the middle strokes meet at a lower level and the y is narrower. The italic is called BLADO.

ii

ABCDEFGHIJKLMNOPQRSTUVWXYZ

ABCDEFGHIJKLMNOPQRSTUVWXYZ

abcdefghijklmnopqrstuvwxyz

1234567890

POLIPHILUS

Designed by Herbert Post. A book and display type of almost calligraphic quality. Characteristic are the **U**, which is in the style of the lower-case **u**, the bowl of the **G**, which is narrow at the bottom, the top serifs of the **T** which point downward to the left, and the concave strokes of the **A.** The strokes of upper- and lower-case letters are of uneven width. There are two weights and an italic with swash caps.

POST
MEDIAEVAL
Berthold 1951;
Intertype (Frankfurt)

All Tourist Clubs of the United States are private organisations of

ii

Orchestras and Musical Societies give classical concerts in Radioprogrammes

POST MEDIAEVAL

ii

ABCDEFGHIJKLMNOPQRSTUVWXYZ

ii

POST MEDIAEVAL SWASH CAPITALS

The woodcut has become one of the most attractive of the arts

ii

POST MEDIAEVAL MEDIUM

Designed by Herbert Post. A display roman with slight variation of colour. The capitals are almost without serifs and most of them are wide. The lower case has small, strong, horizontal serifs and short descenders. The **e** has an oblique stroke to the eye; **g** has a normal tail but not closed. The figures are short-ranging. There are three weights. The italic is of slight inclination and has the serif formation of the roman.

POST ROMAN
Berthold 1937

ABCDEFGHIJKLMNOPQRSTUVWXYZ
abcdefghijklmnopqrstuvwxyz

ix

POST ROMAN LIGHT

ABCDEFGHIJKLMNOPQRSTUVWX
abcdefghijklmnopqrstuvwxyz
1234567890

ix

POST ROMAN MEDIUM

ABCDEFGHIJKLMNOPQRSTUVWX
abcdefghijklmnopqrstuvwxyz

ix

POST ROMAN BOLD

ABCDEFGHIJKLMNOPQRSTUVWXYZ

ix

POST TITLE LIGHT

ABCDEFGHIJKLMNOPQRSTUVWX

ix

POST TITLE MEDIUM

ABCDEFGHIJKLMNOPQRSTUVWX

ix

POST TITLE BOLD

POSTER BODONI

Mergenthaler Linotype 1929;
Linotype (London)

iv

Designed by C.H. Griffith. A fat face following the general style of fat face romans. *Cf.* ULTRA BODONI.

ABCDEFGHIJKLMNOPQRSTUVWXYZ
abcdefghijklmnopqrstuvw 12345
ABCDEFGHIJKLMNOPQRSTUVWXYZ
defghijklmnopqrstuvwxyz 67890

POSTER BODONI

iv

ABCDEFGHIJKLMNOPQRSTUVWXYZ&
abcdefghijklmnopqrstuvwxyz
1234567890

MERGENTHALER LINOTYPE POSTER BODONI COMPRESSED

POWELL

Ludlow 1925

A heavy roman with rugged outlines and short descenders. The bowls of **B** and **P** are open.

ABCDEFGHIJKLMNOPQRSTUV
abcdefghijklmnopqrstuvwxyz 1234

POWELL

PRACHT

J. Wagner

ix

Designed by Carl Pracht in 1941. A display roman in which the lower case is rather like an upright italic with pen-drawn qualities. The **G** has a long spur and **K** and **R** are unusual. In the italic the capitals have the qualities of a script, while the lower case is the roman inclined. There is a bold and bold condensed.

ABCDEFGHIJKLMNOPQRSTUVW
abcdefghijklmnopqrstuvvxyz
1234567890

ABCDEFGHIJKLMNOPQRST
UVWXYZ
1234567890
abcdefghijklmnopqrstuvvxyz

PRACHT ROMAN

ix

ABCDEFGHIJJKLMNOPQRS
TUVWXYZ

PRACHT CURSIVE INITIALS

ABCDEFGHIJKLMNOPQRSTUV
abcdefghijklmnopqrstuvwxyz

PRACHT BOLD

ABCDEFGHIJKLMNOPQRSTUVWXYZ
abcdefghijklmnopqrstuvwxyz

PRACHT BOLD CONDENSED

A calligraphic roman, light in weight.

ABCDEFGHIJKLMNOPQRSTUV WXYZ
abcdefghijklmnopqrstuvwxyz
1234567890

ABCDEFGHIJKLMNOPQRS TUV WXYZ
abcdefghijklmnopqrstuvwxyz
1234567890

PRAHA

Designed by Vojtech Preissig from 1924–27 for the Government Printing Office in Prague. An angular type with slight inclination in the italic, in which the lower case is even more uneven in outlines than the roman. Numerals are non-ranging. In the roman the **f** does not descend below the line, and in the italic has a pointed descender.

ABCDEFGHIJKLMNOP
abcdefghijkmnopqrstuvwyz
1234567890

ABCDEFGHIJKLMNOPQ
abcdefghijklmnopqrstuvwyz
1234567890

PREISSIG

PRESIDENT
Deberny & Peignot 1954

vii

Designed by A. Frutiger. A set of capitals and ranging figures with very small serifs. Note the wide, splayed **M**.

ABCDEFGHIJKLMNOPQRSTUVWXYZ
12345 &ŒÇ 67890

PRESIDENT

PRIMER
Mergenthaler Linotype 1951

iv

Designed by Rudolph Ruzicka. A newspaper type with short ascenders and descenders. There are ranging and non-ranging numerals.

ABCDEFGHIJKLMNOPQRSTUVWXYZ
abcdefghijklmnopqrstuvwxyz
1234567890
ABCDEFGHIJKLMNOPQRSTUVWXYZ
abcdefghijklmnopqrstuvwxyz
1234567890
ABCDEFGHIJKLMNOPQRSTUVWXYZ
1234567890   *1234567890*

PRIMER

PRIMUS
Berthold 1964

iv

Designed by Friedrich Berthold. A fat face for book and display work.

ABCDEFGHIJKLMNOPQRSTUVWXYZ
abcdefghijklmnopqrstuvwxyz ff fi fl ft &
1234567890

ABCDEFGHIJKLMNOPQRSTUVWXYZ
abcdefghijklmnopqrstuvwxyz ff fi fl ft &
1234567890

PRIMUS

iv

ABCDEFGHIJKLMNOPQRSTUVWXYZ
abcdefghijklmnopqrstuvwxyz ff fi fl ft &
1234567890

PRIMUS BOLD

PRO ARTE
Haas 1954

v

Designed by Max Miedinger. Like FIGARO, etc., this is a revival of a nineteenth-century design. It follows the style of PLAYBILL very closely, but the letters are even more condensed. The tail of the **R** is cut off, and the **Q** is an **O** resting on a flourish.

ABCDEFGHIJKLMNOPQRSTUVWXYZ
1234567890

PRO ARTE

186

Designed by Eugen and Max Lenz. A set of three-dimensional capitals and figures, which are inclined. The heavy black letters are rimmed with a white line.

PROFIL

Haas 1946

v

ABCDEFGHIJKLM
NOPQRSTUVWXYZ
1234567890

PROFIL

A display roman with heavy serifs. They are especially heavy on the arms of the **E** and the terminals of the **S**. Ascenders and descenders are short. The tail of the **g** is not closed. There is also a bold, and a closely similar face called EGIPCIA PROGRESO.

PROGRESO

Gans c. 1923

ix

ix

Ropa Egeo

PROGRESO

Enrejados
MOREDA

PROGRESO BOLD

Designed by Leonard H.D. Smit. An expanded face of medium weight with short ascenders and descenders. The serifs are bracketed, as also is the apex of the **t**.

PROMOTOR

Amsterdam 1960

iv

ABCDEFGHIJKLMNOPQ
RSTUVWXYZÆŒ
abcdefghijklmnopqrstuvw
xyz
1234567890£&æœ

PROMOTOR

A lighter face than SUBIACO. It is based on the roman used at Ulm by Leonhard Holle in an edition of *Ptolemy*, 1482. The punches were cut mechanically. The **U** follows the lower-case design. The **g** has a large bowl and also a large tail, and the **h** has a curved shank. This type is now in the possession of the Cambridge University Press.

PTOLEMY
ROMAN

Ashendene Press 1927

i

QUESTO DANTE FU HONOREVOLE ANTICO

cittadino di Firenze di porta San Piero, & il suo esilio da

PTOLEMY ROMAN

PUBLIC

Grafotechna 1958

Designed by Stanislav Marso. A heavy face with flat serifs and very short ascenders. Round letters are squared-up, e.g., in the **b**, **c**, **e**, **p** and **q**. The **f** has a button-hook terminal. There is also an italic on line composition matrices of the Tos matrix factory.

iv

ABCDEFGHIJKLMNOPQRST UVWXYZ abcdefghijklmnopqrstu vwxyz 1234567890

PUBLIC

iv

ABCDEFGHIJKLMNOPQRSTU VWXYZ abcdefghijklmnopqrstuvwxyz 1234567890

PUBLIC CONDENSED

QUEEN

Klingspor 1954

Designed by Joachim Romann. A set of outline and decorated capitals and ranging figures. The decoration consists of knotted work and is found on the serifs also.

ix

QUEEN

QUIRINUS

Nebiolo 1939

Designed by Alessandro Butti. A display type like CORVINUS. It has the same distinguishing feature of square sides to the normally round letters. But the **M** is square and in the lower case the tops of the ascenders are without serifs. The italic, except for a one-storeyed **a**, is the roman inclined. There are two weights.

iv

ABCDEFGHIJKLMNOPQRSTUVXYWZ abcdefghijklmnopqrstuvxywz 1234567890

QUIRINUS

ABCDEFGHIJKLMNOPQRSTUVXYWZ
abcdefghijklmnopqrstuvxy
1234567890

QUIRINUS ITALIC

ABCDEFGHIJKLMNOPQRSTUVXYWZ
abcdefghijklmnopqrstuvxywz
1234567890

QUIRINUS BOLD

Designed by Adolf Behrmann. A fat face with very small serifs, in which the thins have a moderate weight. Some of the round letters, *e.g.*, **C** and **G**, and the insides of the counters have straight edges. Ascenders are fairly tall and descenders short. There are also capitals shaded horizontally.

RUNDFUNK is the same design with taller capitals and ascenders.

Sidenhuset Eckström
56789

RADIO

Handwerker HOTEL REICHS

RUNDFUNK   RADIO SHADED CAPITALS

A fat face of nineteenth century design and with hair line serifs and very short ascenders and descenders.

ABCDEFGHIJKLMNO
PQRSTUVWXYZ
abcdefghijklmnopqrstu
1234567890
VWXYZ

RAKETE

An extra bold titling fount in which the letters have also been expanded. The negative parts are outlined by fine hair lines and the three-dimensional shading is comparatively thin. Serifs are flat and square-edged. The lower part of **R** and **P** are shorter than the upper parts, while the horizontal strokes in **B**, **E** and **G** are central.

ERZGEBIRGE

RAMONA

RASSE

Ludwig & Mayer 1924

ix

A monotone roman with minute serifs, wide letters and very short ascenders and descenders. The round letters are quite circular.

Grand-Hotel Metro

RASSE

RATIO
ROMAN

Stempel 1923;

Linotype (Frankfurt)

iv

Designed by F.W. Kleukens. A type in the BODONI style. In the **a**, **c** and **e** the terminals are blobs, as in the ear of the **g**. The italic has roman serifs.

ABCDEFGHIJKLMNOPQRSTU
abcdefghijklmnopqrstuvwxyz
1234567890
ABCDEFGHIJKLMNOPQRST
abcdefghijklmnopqrstuvwxyz

RATIO

iv

ABCDEFGHIJKLMNOPQRSTU
abcdefghijklmnopqrstuvwxyz

RATIO BOLD

iv

ABCDEFGHIJKLMNOPQRST
abcdefghijklmnopqrstuvwxy

RATIO EXTRA BOLD

iv

THE VOCAL MUSIC OF BRAHMS

OPEN RATIO TITLING

REGAL

Intertype (New York) 1935;

Intertype (F)

iv

Designed under the direction of H.R. Freund. A newspaper face with short ascenders and descenders. The serifs are less solid than in types like IDEAL; capitals are wide. There is also a bold roman.

ABCDEFGHIJKLMNOPQRSTUVWXYZ
abcdefghijklmnopqrstuvwxyz   1234567890
ABCDEFGHIJKLMNOPQRSTUVWXYZ

ABCDEFGHIJKLMNOPQRSTUVWXYZ
abcdefghijklmnopqrstuvwxyz   1234567890

REGAL

iv

ABCDEFGHIJKLMNOPQRSTUVWXYZ
abcdefghijklmnopqrstuvwxyz   1234567890

REGAL BOLD

A condensed three-dimension titling. The design is an engraved version of this founder's NORMANDE CONDENSED.

ABCDEFGHIJKLMNOPQRSTUVWXYZ
1234567890

REGINA

Designed by Wilhelm Scheffel. A roman of a pronounced pen-drawn quality. The serifs are oblique and on some letters shaped. The upper arm of the **E** and other strokes also are shaped. The **U** has the lower-case design. The **a** is one-storeyed and the eye of the **e** has an oblique stroke. There is also a semi-bold.

REMBRANDT

REMBRANDT

A series of inline roman capitals. Serifs are sharp and bracketed. The bars of the **A**, **H**, and similar strokes are very thin.

BUCKINGHAM

REX

Originally a German roman cut in Leipzig and called UNIVERSITY ROMAN or DRUCKHAUS. It is a heavy face with short ascenders and descenders, modern-face in design, except for the lower case **g**. There are bold and extra bold faces and a condensed bold.

ABCDEFGHIJKLMNOPQRSTUVWX
abcdefghijklmnopqrstuvwxyz
1234567890

RHENANIA

ABCDEFGHIJKLMNOPQRSTU
abcdefghijklmnopqrstuvwxyz

iv

RHENANIA BOLD

ABCDEFGHIJKLMNOPQRST
abcdefghijklmnopqrstuvwx

iv

RHENANIA EXTRA BOLD

ABCDEFGHIJKLMNOPQRSTUVWXYZ
abcdefghijklmnopqrstuvwxyz

iv

RHENANIA BOLD CONDENSED

Designed by Herbert P. Horne. Capitals are made of a uniform width, for instance, the **E** is as broad as the **M**. The **R** has a wide bowl and the tail tapers. The **a** and **e** are broad, and lower-case serifs are small and oblique. Numerals are non-ranging.

Fourteen Point Riccardi together with a selection of the Initial Letters

A private typeface owned by The Medici Society

1 2 3 4 5 6 7 8 9 0 £

RICCARDI

ABCDEKOPRUW

RICCARDI OPEN

ACDEFGINPQSTWV

RICCARDI BOLD

Designed by Richard Gerbig. An open three-dimensional titling in which many of the letters are lineale in design. The bars of **A** and **H** extend to the left of the main strokes.

ABCDEFGHIJKLMNOPQR
STUVWXYZ
1234567890

RICCARDO

Designed by Franz Riedinger. Serifs are strong and bracketed, slightly concave on the lower case. Ascenders and descenders are short. The italic is lightly inclined and has pen strokes in the place of serifs.

Geschwister Bernstein

RIEDINGER MEDIAEVAL ITALIC

Designed by William T. Sniffin. A roman closely resembling Koch's LOCARNO, except that the capitals are shaded like the capitals of the KOCH CURSIV. The serifs at the tops of ascenders are smaller than in LOCARNO. The italic is very close to KOCH CURSIV.

RIVOLI
American Typefounders 1928

ix

MUSIC

Delightful girl entertainer

OLD AUTOMOBILE

Manufacturer displayed relic

RIVOLI

A heavy roman with blurred serifs and short ascenders and descenders. CLAIRE DE LUNE is the inline version. ROYAL LINING is another name for the shaded version of the type.

ROBUR PALE
or
ROYAL LINING

*Deberny & Peignot c. 1912;
Stevens Shanks 1924*

ix

Inventions

ROBUR BLACK

Quotidien

ROBUR BLACK ITALIC

ix

Arts

ROBUR TIGRE

Pianos

CLAIRE DE LUNE

ix

LES CHAMPIONS

CLAIRE DE LUNE ELONGATED

ix

Côte d'Azur Polaires

ROBUR ELONGATED

ix

Récit LETTERS

with advertisers

ix

ROYAL LINING

193

The **A** has a slab serif, the **G** no spur, the **M** is wide, the **Q** has the tail entirely outside the bowl. The **a** is two-storeyed, the **g** has an open tail, and the **t** has a curved foot.
There are four weights, condensed faces, and a SHADOW, which is three-dimensional.

v

ABCDEFGHIJKLMNOPQRSTUVWXYZ
abcdefghijklmnopqrstuvwxyz
1234567890

ROCKWELL LIGHT

v

ABCDEFGHIJKLMNOPQRSTUVWXYZ
abcdefghijklmnopqrstuvwxyz
1234567890

CASTLES and cathedrals of France

ROCKWELL MEDIUM

v

ABCDEFGHIJKLMNOPQRSTUVWXYZ
abcdefghijklmnopqrstuvwxyz
1234567890

ROCKWELL HEAVY

v

ABCDEFGHIJKLMNOPQRSTUVWXYZ
abcdefghijklmnopqrstuvwxyz
1234567890

ROCKWELL BOLD CONDENSED

v

ABCDEFGHIJKLMNOPQRSTUVWXYZ
abcdefghijklmnopqrstuvwxyz
1234567890

ROCKWELL CONDENSED

v

ABCDEFGHIJKLMNOPQRSTUVWXYZ
abcdefghijklmnopqrstuvwxyz
1234567890

ROCKWELL EXTRA BOLD

194

GEOMETRY

ROCKWELL SHADOW

ABCDEFGHIJKLMNOPQRSTUVW
XYZ

abcdefghijklmnopqrstuvwxyz

1234567890

ROCKWELL SHADED

Designed by J. Roesner. A pen-drawn titling.

ABCDEFGHIJKLMNOPQRSTU
VWXYZ

1234567890 &

ROESNER

Designed by Johann Christian Bauer, the founder of the Bauer Typefoundry. Another fat face of the usual early nineteenth-century design. FALSTAFF and RAKETE are similar.

ABCDEFGHIJKLMNOPQRST
UVWXYZ

abcdefghijklmnopqrstuvwxyz
1234567890

ABCDEFGHIJKLMNOPQRS
TUVWXYZ

abcdefghijklmnopqrstuvwxyz
1234567890

ROMAN EXTRA BOLD

195

ROMANA
J. Wagner c. 1904

A display roman of some weight and short ascenders and descenders, and basically a German DE VINNE adaptation. The serif formation is old face. The central arms of **E**, **F** and **H** are above the centre. The final upright in the **G** is tall and the **M** is splayed. There is also a bold.

ii

ABCDEFGHIJKLMNOPQRST UVWXYZ
abcdefghijklmnopqrstuvwxyz
1234567890

ROMANA

ii

ABCDEFGHIJKLMNOPQRS TUVWXYZ
abcdefghijklmnopqrstuvwxyz

ROMANA BOLD

ROMANÉE
Enschedé 1928–1949

Designed by Jan van Krimpen to accompany the only surviving italic of the seventeenth-century Amsterdam founder Christoffel van Dijck. Romanée, named after a wine drunk by the designer at El Vino's in London's Fleet Street, has a considerable resemblance to BEMBO, both in colour and in the modest height of the capitals. The A has a sharper apex and the J a straight tail. There are no italic capitals. The slightly-inclined italic shown here was added twenty-one years after the roman and the designer himself comments that "the distance of twenty years between the coming into existence of the one and the other in a way tells".

ii

ABCDEFGHIJKLMNOPQ RSTUVWXYZ
abcdefghijklmnopqrstuvwxyz
1234567890
abcdefghijklmnopqrstuvwxyz   1234567890

ROMANÉE

ii

ABDEEFGHJJKLMNPQRSTUVWXYZ&

ROMANÉE SWASH CAPS

196

Decorated capitals of Victorian design. In Nos. 1 and 3 the serifs are rounded, in No. 2 the top serifs run to points. In No. 1 the upper halves of letters are white and the lower halves black; in No. 2 the colours are reversed. No. 5 is shaded. ORNAMENTED OUTLINE, which is identical with No. 1 is shown elsewhere.

ABCDEFGHIJKLMNOPQRST
UVWXYZÆŒ
1234567890

ROMANTIQUES No. 2

ABCDEFGHIJKLMNOPQRSTUV
WXYZÆŒ

ROMANTIQUES No. 3

ABCDEFGHIJKLMNOPQ
RSTUVWXYZÆŒ
1234567890

ROMANTIQUES No. 5

Designed by A. Anklam (capitals) and Heinz Koenig (lower case). The type is also known as BRADFORD, HADDONIAN or MCFARLAND.

ABCDEFGHIJKLMN
OPQRSTUVWXYZ
abcdefghijklmnopqrst
uvwxyz
1234567890
ABCDEFGHIJKLMNOP
QRSTUVWXYZ
abcdefghijklmnopqrst
uvwxyz
1234567890

RÖMISCHE ANTIQUA

ROMULUS

Enschedé 1931;
Monotype 1936

Designed by Jan van Krimpen. One of those contemporary romans which cut across the old divisions of type families. In gradation of colour it is akin to the old faces, but the serifs are almost horizontal and the stress nearly vertical. The capitals are unobtrusive and the serifs light. The bowl of the **g** is large. The italic is an interesting experiment in the sloped roman, carried out in every detail with the letters as wide as the roman. The figures are short-ranging. There is also a bold and open versions designed in 1955, and a calligraphic type called CANCELLARESCA BASTARDA shown separately. The type was intended to have a complete range of weights, a related sanserif and Greek. These were cut but do not seem to be generally used.

iii

ABCDEFGHIJKLMNOPQRSTUVWXY

abcdefghijklmnopqrstuvwxyz   Z&

1234567890

ABCDEFGHIJKLMNOPQRSTUVWXY

abcdefghijklmnopqrstuvwxyz   Z&

1234567890

ROMULUS

iii

ABCDEFGHIJKLMNOPQRSTUVWXYZ&

abcdefghijklmnopqrstuvwxyz

1234567890

ROMULUS BOLD

iii

ABCEFGHIJKLMNOPQRSTUVWXYZ

1234567890

ROMULUS OPEN CAPS

RONALDSON OLD STYLE

Monotype 1903;
Linotype (London)

Originally cut in 1884 by the American founders, MacKellar, Smiths & Jordan, and no doubt named after one of the original founders of their house, James Ronaldson, who with Archibald Binny established a typefoundry in Philadelphia in 1796. It is easily distinguished by the beak-like serifs on the capitals and lower case and by the squared-up shoulders of **m** and **n**. In the italic the serifs are more normal and the design becomes very like OLD STYLE. The Monotype Corporation's version has short ascenders and descenders and capitals not rising above the ascenders.

ii

ABCDEFGHIJKLMNOPQRSTUVWXYZ&

abcdefghijklmnopqrstuvwxyz

1234567890

ABCDEFGHIJKLMNOPQRSTUVWXYZ&

abcdefghijklmnopqrstuvwxyz

MONOTYPE RONALDSON OLD STYLE

The original by J.F. Rosart, (1714-77,) a typefounder at Haarlem and later at Brussels. The shaded capitals have since been in the possession of the Enschedé foundry. The type is a series of inline roman capitals almost three-dimensional in appearance. The **Q** has a long descending tail and the **J**, descending below the line, a curled tail. Characters vary in different sizes.

ABCDEFGHIJ KLMNOPQRS TUVWXYZ

ROSART

Designed by Walter Schneider and H. Vollenweider and cut in one size only by the Haas foundry. The lower case is based on 15th century type known as ROTUNDA. The originals are now in the Kunstgewerbemuseum, Zürich.

ABCDEFGHIJKLMNOPQRSTUVWXYZÄÖÜÆ

abcdefghijklmnopqrsßſtuvwxyȝ fffiflftſiſtttäöüæ

1234567890

ROTUNDA

The type was initially designed for use by *The Scotsman*. A newspaper type for classified advertisements and editorials SCOTSMAN ROYAL is based on the standard version of ROYAL. Ascenders and descenders are short and serifs strong, as in other types designed for newspaper work. Very similar to CORONA. Like CLARITAS, MAXIMUS and ADSANS, this type is available in $4\frac{3}{4}$ point.

This example of Intertype's new typeface ROYAL is set in the 9 point size. Royal owes much of its clarity to generous x-height and slightly elongated form. **The bold face** *and complementary italic* are equally successful.

Standard characters

CGKQRW agktw 57   **CGKQRW agktw 57**

ROYAL

ABCDEFGHIJKLMNOPQRSTUVWXYZÆŒ

abcdefghijklmnopqrstuvwxyzæœ

12345 67890

ABCDEFGHIJKLMNOPQRSTUVWXYZÆŒ

abcdefghijklmnopqrstuvwxyzæœ

12345 67890

SCOTSMAN ROYAL

A monoline extra condensed bold roman.

ABCDEFGHIJKLMNOPQRSTUVWXYZ

abcdefghijklmnopqrstuvwxyz

1234567890

RUNIC CONDENSED

A type based on manuscript hands of the Italian fifteenth century. The serifs are shaped, as though made with a pen; many of the round letters also follow the rule of the pen. The **G** has a deep spur and **U** the lower-case design. The **g** has an open tail; **v**, **w** and **y** are cursive forms. It is a black type. The figures are short-ranging. Originally an American type called MOTTO.

Exhibition of Printed Books

RUNNYMEDE

Designed by Paul Hayden-Duensing for his private press. This calligraphic titling lacks a cross-bar in the **A**, and has unparallel left-hand strokes in the **M**.

ABCDEFGHIJKLMNOPQURSTUVWXYZ

RUSTICA

Designed by Jan Tschichold and jointly developed by Linotype, Monotype and Stempel, in response to a common need of German master printers for a type face to be made in identical form for mechanical composition by linecasting and single-type methods, and also for hand composition in foundry type.

The sources for the design are to be found on a specimen sheet of the Frankfurt type-founder, Konrad Berner, who married the widow of another typefounder, Jacques Sabon—hence the name of the face. The roman is based on a fount engraved by Garamond and the italic on a fount by Granjon, but Tschichold has introduced many refinements to make these models suitable for the typographic needs of today and for the varying requirements of the three manufacturing companies.

ABCDEFGHIJKLMNOPQRSTUVWXYZ

abcdefghijklmnopqrstuvwxyz

1234567890

ABCDEFGHIJKLMNOPQRSTUVWXYZ

abcdefghijklmnopqrstuvwxyz

1234567890

SABON

ABCDEFGHIJKLMNOPQRSTUVWXYZ

abcdefghijklmnopqrstuvwxyz

1234567890

SABON BOLD

Designed by H. Maehler. A close-set linear extra bold face with moderate variation in colour.

ABCDEFGHIJKLMNOPQ
abcdefghijklmnopqrstuv
1234567890

SALUT

Designed by Hermann Zapf. Decorated capitals of fat face design. The decoration is based on leaf forms. There is also a set of ranging figures (FESTIVAL NUMERALS).

ABCDEFGHIJKLMNOPQR

SAPPHIRE

1234567890

FESTIVAL NUMERALS

Designed by Jan Tschichold. An italic with considerable variation of stress and short ascenders and descenders. It is without serifs but there are thickened terminals of the arcs of c, s and similar letters. The eye of the e and the bowls are not quite closed. ZEUSS is somewhat similar.

Eigenart voll Vornehmheit und Eleganz zutage, die sie weit erhebt über alles Hergebrachte und Alltägliche. Wer eindrucksvoll und doch voll Milde

SASKIA •

The **A** has no top serif, **J** has a round loop, **R** a slightly curved tail and the **W** no middle serif. The **a** is two-storeyed, **b** has no foot serif, **g** has the open tail of the continental versions and **t** a curved terminal. There is an italic, a light face and a bold.

ABCDEFGHIJKLMNOPQRSTUVXYZ
abcdefghijklmnopqrstuvwxyz
1234567890£

SCARAB LIGHT

ABCDEFGHIJKLMNOPQRSTUVWXYZ
abcdefghijklmnopqrstuvwxyz
1234567890
ABCDEFGHIJKLMNOPQRSTUVWXYZ
abcdefghijklmnopqrstuvwxyz
1234567890£

SCARAB

Designed by Georg Trump. An angular type with horizontal serifs. The **g** has flourished but open tail.

v

ABCDEFGHIJKLMNOPQRSTUVW
XYZ
abcdefghijklmnopqrstuvwxyz
1234567890

SCHADOW LIGHT

v

ABCDEFGHIJKLMNOPQRSTU
VWXYZ
abcdefghijklmnopqrstuvwxyz
1234567890
*ABCDEFGHIJKLMNOPQRSTU
VXYZ*
abcdefghijklmnopqrstuvwxyz
1234567890

SCHADOW WERK

v

**ABCDEFGHIJKLMNOPQRS
TUVWXYZ**
abcdefghijklmnopqrstuvwxy
1234567890

SCHADOW BOLD

v

**ABCDEFGHIJKLMNOPQRST
UVWXYZ**
abcdefghijklmnopqrstuvwxy
1234567890

SCHADOW EXTRA BOLD

v

ABCDEFGHIJKLMNOPQRSTUVWXYZ
abcdefghijklmnopqrstuvwxyz
1234567890

SCHADOW BOLD CONDENSED

Designed by F.H.E. Schneidler. Similar to MENHART but with less variation of stress. The **M** is splayed and without top serifs. The **Q** has a brief tail outside the bowl and does not descend below the line. Numerals range. SCHNEIDLER INITIALS have pointed and very small serifs. **B, E, F, P** and **R** are narrow letters. The **M** is wide and splayed, and the **U** of lower-case design. AMALTHEA (1957) is an italic companion design.

ABCDEFGHIJKLMNOPQRSTUVWXYZ

vii

abcdefghijklmnopqrstuvwxyz

12345678

SCHNEIDLER OLD STYLE

ABCDEFGHIJKLMNOPQR

vii

SCHNEIDLER INITIALS

Designed by Albert Auspurg. A heavy shaded italic. The shading is horizontal. The capitals are of the swash variety and the serifs thin.

SCHÖNBRUNN
Krebs 1928

Bremer Ratskeller

ix

SCHÖNBRUNN

An important type and a revival of some ninety years ago of a series of types which appear in the specimens of William Miller, of Edinburgh, for 1813. The type in its original may be the work of Richard Austin. It was for a time perhaps the most favoured of English faces in use for literary texts, because it avoids some of the extremes. The letters are sturdy and the serifs bracketed.

SCOTCH
ROMAN

Miller & Richard;

Linotype (London);

Mergenthaler Linotype;

Monotype; Intertype

    Monotype SCOTCH ROMAN (46) was cut in 1907, and (137) in 1920 for R. & R. Clark, the printers, as an accurate re-cutting of the Miller & Richard type (though the 14 pt size is not strictly derived from the original). There are variations in the design of different sizes.

ABCDEFGHIJKLMNOPQRSTUVWXYZ

iv

abcdefghijklmnopqrstuvwxyz

1234567890

ABCDEFGHIJKLMNOPQRSTUVWXYZ

abcdefghijklmnopqrstuvwxyz

1234567890

MONOTYPE SCOTCH ROMAN

ABCDEFGHIJKLMNOPQRSTUVWXYZ&

iv

ABCDEFGHIJKLMNOPQRSTUVWXYZ&

abcdefghijklmnopqrstuvwxyz

1234567890

ABCDEFGHIJKLMNOPQRSTUVWXYZ&

abcdefghijklmnopqrstuvwxyz

1234567890

MERGENTHALER LINOTYPE SCOTCH NO. 2 ROMAN

SCROLL SHADED

Stevens Shanks

ix

Three-dimensional, decorated capitals from the foundry of V. & J. Figgins. The style was originated around 1815 by Figgins as an ORNAMENTED ETRUSCAN.

ABCDEFGHIJKLMNOPQR
STUVWXYZÆŒ&

SCROLL SHADED

SELECT or ALBERT

Berling;
Amsterdam c. 1936

iv

Designed by Albert Augspurg. Shaded capitals, the shading being horizontal. The graduation of stress is abrupt and the serifs thin.

ABCDEFGHIJKLMNOPQRS
TUVWXYZ
1234567890

SELECT

SERIE 16

Deberny & Peignot;
Linotype (London);
Mergenthaler Linotype

iv

A modern face with rather short ascenders and descenders. The **Q** has the tail entirely outside the bowl. The italic, as frequently in French types, has the serifs of the roman. The Linotype version is called No. 61.

ABCDEFGHIJKLMNOPQRSTUVWXYZ
abcdefghijklmnopqrstuvwxyz
1234567890
ABCDEFGHIJKLMNOPQRSTUVWXYZ
abcdefghijklmnopqrstuvwxyz
1234567890

SERIE 16

SERIE 18

Deberny & Peignot

iv

A roman with considerable variation of stress. Serifs are small and slightly inclined. There are both ranging and non-ranging figures. The italic has some of the qualities of a script, as in the upper arms of the **E** and **F**, and in the **R**. Linotype called their version TRANSIT, which was also known as BASKERVILLE OLD STYLE, and is no longer available.

ABCDEFGHIJKLMNOPQRSTUVWXYZ
abcdefghijklmnopqrstuvwxyz
1234567890 & 1234567890
ABCDEFGHIJKLMNOPQRSTUVWXYZ
abcdefghijklmnopqrstuvwxyz
1234567890 & 1234567890

SERIE 18

Designed by Adrian Frutiger. A type based on the geometric linear forms of UNIVERS to which slab serifs have been added.

SERIFA

Bauer 1967

v

ABCDEFGHIJKLMNOPQRSTUV
WXYZ
abcdefghijklmnopqrstuvwxyz
1234567890

SERIFA LIGHT

v

ABCDEFGHIJKLMNOPQRSTUV
WXYZ
abcdefghijklmnopqrstuvwxyz
1234567890

SERIFA MEDIUM

Designed by Karl Michel. A shaded roman, the shading being horizontal.

SHADED
ROMAN

Klingspor 1919

ii

History of Scot

SHADED ROMAN

Designed by Georg Belwe, a display face of rich colour, even in the lightest weight. The serifs are strong and stubby in the lower case. The **A** has a slab serif and the **R** a wide, shallow bowl. In the **M** the middle strokes stop short of the line. The descenders are very short. The italic has a moderate inclination. The middle strokes of the **M** are curved. The **y** is a script form. There is also a bold, an extra bold, and condensed faces.

SHAKESPEARE

MEDIAEVAL

Schelter & Giesecke 1927–29

MINERALOGIA E GEOLO

ix

Carta della provincia di Per

Editore Ferdinando Dalmo Mi

SHAKESPEARE MEDIAEVAL

DAMPFSCHIFF-VERKE

ix

Jahresausstellung in Barcel

Conférence internationale 1

SHAKESPEARE MEDIAEVAL BOLD

Publication du Gouvern

ix

SHAKESPEARE MEDIAEVAL EXTRA BOLD CONDENSED

Designed by Paul Hayden-Duensing for his private press after a set of very rough punches acquired by the designer in Italy from which after much work castable matrices were produced. Some letters were added by engraving new punches.

ABCDEFGHIJKLMNOPQuRSTUVVXYZ

abcdefghijklmnopqrstuvvxyz

⸿ æ&t āđēęĩñóp̄q̄q̄p̄īū✠

XVITH CENTURY ROMAN

Designed by Walter Höhnisch. A condensed roman with most of the characteristics of a modern face. Some of the serifs, *e.g.*, on the **E** and **S**, are heavier. The **M** is splayed. The ascenders and descenders are short. The thickened terminals of arcs are blobs and the **g** has an open tail. There is also a Bold face. In Germany the founders call the type SCHLANKE.

iv

ABCDEFGHIJKLMNOPQRSTUVWXYZ

abcdefghijklmnopqrstuvwxyz

1234567890

ABCDEFGHIJKLMNOPQRSTUVWXYZ

abcdefghijklmnopqrstuvwxyz

1234567890

SLENDER

iv

ABCDEFGHIJKLMNOPQRSTUVWXYZ

abcdefghijklmnopqrstuvwxyz

1234567890

SLENDER SEMIBOLD

iv

ABCDEFGHIJKLMNOPQRSTUVWXYZ

abcdefghijklmnopqrstuvwxyz

1234567890

SLENDER BOLD

Designed by G. Zapf-v. Hesse. A set of outline capitals with hair-line serifs.

ABCDEFGHIJKLMNOPQRSTUVWXYZ

SMARAGD

Designed by G.G. Lange. An uncial type. *Cf.* AMERICAN UNCIAL and LIBRA. There is one case only, some letters resembling those of the upper case and others those of the lower case.

ABCDEFGHIJKLMNOPQRSTUVWXYZ
1234567890

SOLEMNIS

Designed by Eric Gill. A roman with slight variation of stress and horizontal serifs. There are two **M**'s, one slightly splayed, and the other with the middle strokes descending half-way. The lower case **g** has a resemblance to that letter in Gill's PERPETUA. There is no italic and the numerals are short ranging.

MUCH DIFFERENT, AND THE CHANGES
worse than the garden of one hundred years

SOLUS

A condensed fat face with short ascenders and descenders. The **a** and **r**, but not the **s**, have the bulbous terminations frequent in fat faces. The **f** has a button-hook top and the **g** an open tail.

HOCHSCHULEN

Königsberg

SPARTA

SPECTRUM

Enschedé 1952;
Monotype 1955
ii

Designed by Jan van Krimpen. A roman in the Aldine tradition. The **W** is composed of two **V**'s and comparatively narrow. The italic is based on the calligraphy of Arrighi.

ABCDEFGHIJKLMNOPQRSTUVWXYZ
abcdefghijklmnopqrstuvwxyz
1234567890 1234567890

As Frederic Warde aptly put it, 'as long as we work with the arbitrary signs of the alphabet, we shall be dependent on the past and—like

ABCDEFGHIJKLMNOPQRSTUVWXYZ

abcdefghijklmnopqrstuvwxyz

1234567890 1234567890

SPECTRUM

SPHINX

Deberny & Peignot 1925

A fat face in which the thin strokes are not hair lines. In the lower case the terminations of the arcs of **a, c** and **r** are not quite circular. The **g** has an open tail. In the italic lower case the serifs are blunted.

There is also a condensed face and a set of inline capitals. There are also special modernistic borders for this fount.

iv

ABCDEFGHJKLMNOPQRSTUVXYZ

SPHINX

VIGNETTES

iv

SPHINX INLINE CAPITALS

SPIRE

Lanston Monotype 1938

Designed by Sol Hess as an extra condensed fat face.

ix

AABCDEFGHIJKKLMMNNOPQRRSTUUV
WWXYZ&
$1234567890ᶜ

SPIRE

Designed by Sol Hess and based on STYMIE EXTRABOLD.

SQUAREFACE
Lanston Monotype 1939

Designed by Sol Hess and based on STYMIE EXTRABOLD.

SQUAREFACE
Lanston Monotype 1939

v

A A B C D E F G H I J K L M N O P Q R S T U
V W X Y Z &

a a b c d e f g h i j k l m n o p q r s t u v w
x y z

1234567890

SQUAREFACE

A heavy display italic, in which the serifs are merely thickenings of the ends of strokes. The capitals are of the swash variety. Ascenders and descenders are extremely short.

STABIL
Woellmer 1926

ix

Gewerbe und Hand

STABIL

Designed by E. Grundeis. A has a rounded top, and the bars of **A** and **H**, arms of **E** and similar strokes are extended beyond the main strokes. **M**, **U** and **W** follow lower-case design. Short serifs are cut off obliquely.

STADION
Schriftguss 1929

ix

Kunstausstellung München
Heinrich Zille und sein Werk

STADION

A fat face with tall capitals and ascenders, in which the thins have a certain weight. The capitals are rather narrow, but the lower-case letters are wide. The **g** has a curled ear on top of the bowl. The **t** has its top cut off obliquely.

STAFETTE
Woellmer 1930

iv

Moderne Handarbeit

STAFETTE

STAR NEWS
Star Parts 1962

A newspaper type designed for printing on rough papers and for teletypesetter work. The 8 and 9 pt are cut to the same alphabet length.

ii

ABCDEFGHIJKLMNOPQRSTUVWXYZ

abcdefghijklmnopqrstuvwxyz fiflffffiffl

1234567890

STAR NEWS

ii

ABCDEFGHIJKLMNOPQRSTUVWXYZ

abcdefghijklmnopqrstuvwxyz

1234567890

STAR NEWS BOLD

STEEL
Klingspor 1939

Designed by Rudolf Koch (capitals derived from his OFFENBACH) and Hans Kuehne (lower case). A pen-drawn roman called STAHL in Germany. It is without serifs but not monotone. The capitals vary in width as in the other Koch romans. The **M** is splayed and the **U** has the lower-case design. In the lower case descenders are very short. The **g** has an open tail. The most striking characteristic is the pen-drawn quality of the letters.

ix

ABCDEFGHIJKLMNOPQRSTU

abcdefghijklmnopqrstuvwxyz

1234567890

ABCDEFGHIJKLMNOPQRSTU

abcdefghijklmnopqrstuvwxyz

STEEL

ix

ABCDEFGHIJKLMNOPQRST

abcdefghijklmnopqrstuvwxyz

STEEL BOLD

ix

ChineseporcelainandV

STEEL BOLD CONDENSED

STEELPLATE GOTHIC BOLD
American Typefounders

Capitals with minute serifs. Wide letters of Victorian design. The face was designed to complement Frederic Goudy's COPPERPLATE GOTHIC. *Cf.* PLATE GOTHIC.

vii

FINE QUALITY CON

STEELPLATE GOTHIC BOLD

Designed by R. Hunter Middleton. A set of bold capitals with stubby serifs and with white gaps between some strokes. The round letters have a break in the top and another at the foot. American Typefounders' STENCIL is similar.

STENCIL
Ludlow 1938

iv

MODERN 896

STENCIL

A condensed and elongated fat face. *Cf.* ONYX and SLIMBLACK. Another nineteenth century revival. In Germany the type is called STEPHANIE.

STEPHANA or STEPHANIE
Bauer c. 1870

iv

ABCDEFGHIJKLMNOPQRSTUVWXYZ

abcdefghijklmnopqrstuvwxyz

1234567890

STEPHANA

Designed by Morris F. Benton with later additions by Sol Hess for Lanston Monotype and Garry Powell for American Typefounders. **A** has a slab serif, **G** has a spur, the middle strokes of **M** stop short of the line. The **a** is two-storeyed—but the one-storeyed **a** is also supplied, **g** has an open tail and **t** a foot serif to the right only. The italic has the one-storeyed **a**. In other respects it conforms to the roman. There are four weights, and a compressed. STYMIE ANTIQUE SHADED does not really belong in this group.

STYMIE
American Typefounders 1931;

Lanston Monotype

v

ABCDEFGHIJKLMNOPQRSTUV WXYZ&
abcdefghijklmnopqrstuvwxyz
1234567890
ABCDEFGHIJKLMNOPQRSTUV WXYZ&
abcdeffghijklmnopqrrstuvwxyz
1234567890

STYMIE MEDIUM

AAABCDEFGHIJKLMNOPQRRSTU VWXYZ&
aabcdeffghijklmnopqrs
ABCDEFGHIJKLMNOPQRSTUV WXYZ&
abcdeffghijklmnopqrstuvwxyz
1234567890

STYMIE LIGHT

v

ABCDEFGHIJKLMNOPQRRSTU
VWXYZ&$$

abcdefghijklmnopqrstuvwxyz
1234567890

ABCDEFGHIJKLMNOPQRSTUV
WXYZ&$

abcdeffghijklmnopqrrstuvwxyz
1234567890

STYMIE BOLD

v

ABCDEFGHIJKLMNOPQRSTUV
WXYZ&$$

abcdefghijklmnopqrstuvwxyz
1234567890

STYMIE BLACK

v

ABCDEFGHIJKLMNOPQRSTU
VWXYZ&$

abcdefghijklmnopqrstuvwxyz
1234567890

STYMIE ANTIQUE SHADED

Designed for C.H.St.J. Hornby after the first roman used in Italy about 1464 by Sweynheym and Pannartz at Subiaco. The punches were cut by E.P. Prince. It is a black face with small serifs and capitals much less conspicuous than is usual with early romans. E and F are narrow. G has a large terminal. In H the right-hand vertical stroke is short. The middle stroke of N reaches neither top nor foot of the uprights. M is splayed and has no middle serifs. W also has no middle serif. In the lower case the g is a straighter letter than the original; h has the curved shank common in early romans; i has an accent for the dot. This face is now in the possession of the Cambridge University Press.

i

Conrad Sweynheym and Arnold Pannartz
introduced printing into Italy, setting up a
press at Subiaco in 1465. Their type, though

SUBIACO

A text type.

ABCDEFGHIJKLMNOPQRSTUVWXYZ&ÆŒ

abcdefghijklmnopqrstuvwxyzæœ   fiflffffiffl

1234567890

ABCDEFGHIJKLMNOPQRSTUVWXYZ&ÆŒ

ABCDEFGHIJKLMNOPQRSTUVWXYZ&ÆŒ

abcdefghijklmnopqrstuvwxyzæœ   fiflffffiffl

1234567890

SUBURBAN FRENCH

Designed by Franz Deixler. A heavy display italic with blunt serifs. Some of the capitals resemble those of the traditional German gothic types.

𝕮tadion in 𝕭erlin

SUGGESTION

A condensed type face with short ascenders and descenders. The dots on **i** and the German *Umlaut*-vowels are square. Many letters are very similar to Ludwig & Mayer's TEMPO, but the **A** has no slab serif and the arcs of **a** and **r** are curved down. SUPERBA ILLUSTRA is a three-dimensional type. There is also a bold version. Berling's SMALFET EGYPTIENNE is another very similar type.

ABCDEFGHIJKLMNOPQRSTUVWXYZ

abcdefghijklmnopqrstuvwxyz

1234567890

SUPERBA CONDENSED

ABCDEFGHIJKLMNOPQRSTU

abcdefghijklmnopqrstuvwxyz

SUPERBA BOLD

ABCDEFGHIJKLMNOPQRSTU

1234567890

SUPERBA ILLUSTRA

TALLONE

Alberto Tallone 1952

Designed by Alberto Tallone for his private press. A text face of even colour with fine serifs. The downward serifs of the **T** point outwards, the **b** has no lower serif. The tail of the **g** in the italic is open and flourished, the lower-case **k** has a bowl. Old style numerals.

ii

A Womans face with natures owne hand painted,
Haste thou the Master Mistris of my passion,
A womans gentle hart but not acquainted
With shifting change as is false womens fashion,

Fra le molte e molte centinaia, ch' io ho visto
e catalogato nella mia Bibliografia manzoniana,
dovrei forse risalire alla prima del Ferrario, per
trovare il quasi perfetto accordo testo-stampa.

TALLONE

TALLONE MAX FACTOR

Lanston Monotype 1959
ii

Designed by Alberto Tallone for the use of a cosmetics manufacturer. Descenders and ascenders are tall. Figures are cut ranging and non-ranging. The **T** has a bowl-shaped wide top. Serifs are fine.

ABCDEFGHIJKLMNOPQRSTUVWXYZ

abcdefghijklmnopqrstuvwxyz

1234567890   1234567890

ABCDEFGHIJKLMNOPQRSTUVWXYZ

abcdefghijklmnopqrstuvwxyz

1234567890   1234567890

TALLONE MAX FACTOR

TEA CHEST

Stephenson Blake 1939

A set of bold, condensed capitals with stubby serifs and with white gaps in some strokes, that is to say a stencil letter. The round letters have a break in the top and another at the foot. The **T** has two breaks in the top. **W** has two breaks between thick and thin strokes. There are also figures. Ludlow STENCIL is similar but not condensed.

ix

ABCDEFGHIJKLMN
OPQRSTUVWXYZ
1234567890

TEA CHEST

A slab serif type with some gradation of colour. The **A** has a top serif pointing to the left only, **G** has a spur and the **b** has no foot serif.

ABCDEFGHIJKLMNOPQRSTUV
WXYZ&
abcdefghijklmnopqrstuvwxyz?
1234567890

*ABCDEFGHIJKLMNOPQRSTUV
WXYZ&
abcdefghijklmnopqrstuvwxyz?
1234567890*

TECHNOTYP

**ABCDEFGHIJKLMNOPQRSTU
VWXYZ&
abcdefghijklmnopqrstuvwxyz?
1234567890**

TECHNOTYP MEDIUM

**ABCDEFGHIJKLMNOPQRSTUVWXYZ&
abcdefghijklmnopqrstuvwxyz?
1234567890**

TECHNOTYP MEDIUM CONDENSED

**ABCDEFGHIJKLMNOPQRST
UVWXYZ&
abcdefghijklmnopqrstuvwxyz?
1234567890**

TECHNOTYP BOLD

TECHNOTYP

v

ABCDEFGHIJKLMNOPQRSTUVWXYZ&
abcdefghijklmnopqrstuvwxyz?
1234567890

TECHNOTYP BOLD CONDENSED

v

ABCDEFGHIJKLMNOPQRST
UVWXYZ&
abcdefghijklmnopqrstuvwxyz?
1234567890

TECHNOTYP EXTRA BOLD

TEIMER

Grafotechna

iv

Designed by S. Teimer. A roman with italic, ranging and non-ranging figures. Weight of characters is even, and serifs are straight.

ABCDEFGHIJKLMNOP
QRSTUVWXYZ
abcdefghijklmnopqrstu
vwxyz
1234567890 1234567890
ABCDEFGHIJKLMNOP
QRSTUVWXYZ
abcdefghijklmnopqrstu
vwxyz
1234567890 1234567890

TEIMER

TEMPO

Ludwig & Mayer

v

A condensed Egyptian. The A has a slab serif. The lower-case **a** is two-storeyed and the **g** has an open tail. The arc of the **r** is a circle, an unusual form in an Egyptian. This type should not be confused with Ludlow's TEMPO, a sans serif.

PRIMARY FUNCTION is that it shall be

TEMPO

216

A newspaper type like IDEAL and IONIC, with stubby serifs, little variation of stress and long ascenders.

TEXTYPE

Mergenthaler Linotype 1929

iv

ABCDEFGHIJKLMNOPQRSTUVWXYZ

abcdefghijklmnopqrstuvwxyz

1234567890

ABCDEFGHIJKLMNOPQRSTUVWXYZ

ABCDEFGHIJKLMNOPQRSTUVWXYZ

abcdefghijklmnopqrstuvwxyz

1234567890

TEXTYPE

Designed by Herbert Thannhaeuser. A type of linear appearance but with minute serifs which in some letters are simple thickenings of strokes. There is slight variation of stress. The **a** is one-storeyed and the **e** has a large eye.

THANN-
HAEUSER

Schriftguss 1929

vii

ABCDEFGHIJKLMNOPQRSTUVWX
YZ&
abcdefghijklmnopqrstuvwxyz?
1234567890

ABCDEFGHIJKLMNOPQRSTUVW X
YZ&
abcdefghijklmnopqrstuvwxyz?
1234567890

THANNHAEUSER

ACBCDEFGHIJKLMNOPQRSTUV
WXYZ&
abcdefghijklmnopqrstuvwxyz?
1234567890

vii

THANNHAEUSER BOLD

A B C D E F G H I J K L
M N O P Q R S T U
W X Y Z

ix

THANNHAEUSER INITIALS

THOMAS TYPE

Typoart 1956

Designed by F. Thomas. Among the capitals are a round-topped **A** and a round **E**. In the lower case there are the rudiments of serifs and some modelled strokes.

ix

ABCDEFGHIJKLMNOPQRSTUVWXYZ

abcdefghijklmnopqrstuvwxyz

THOMAS TYPE

THORNE SHADED

Stephenson Blake 1938–48

One of the earliest three-dimensional letters, dating from about 1820. The greatly modified design is based on the contemporary fat face capitals, but with thicker serifs. The proportions of the larger sizes are different.

v

ABCDEFGHIJKLMNOPQ
RSTUVWXYZ
1234567890

THORNE SHADED

THOROWGOOD

Stephenson Blake

Cut by the English type-founder Robert Thorne, predecessor of William Thorowgood, and first shown in his specimen books in the early nineteenth century. The larger series probably derived from the Thorne Foundry, but the smaller 12 pt and the 18 pt (shown here) did not appear until 1836. The fat face has been revived in roman (1953) and italic. **S** and **C** appear to be smaller than other capitals. Most serifs are flat and thin horizontals. In the italic the main strokes of **h**, **k**, **m**, **n** and **r** are curved inwards at the foot.

iv

ABCDEFGHIJKLMNOPQRSTUV
WXYZ
abcdefghijklmnopqrstuvxwyz
1234567890£

ABCDEFGHIJKLMNOPQRSTU
VWXYZ
abcdefghijklmnopqrstuvwxyz
1234567890£

THOROWGOOD

218

A German modern face designed by Walter Tiemann, said to be after DIDOT. It is a heavy face with short descenders, perhaps intended for display. The serifs are brief hair lines. The arms of E and F also are hair lines. The J has a button-hook termination, the M is slightly splayed and the W (lower-case also) has no middle serif. The b has a rudimentary foot serif. In the italic the Q has a tail like GOUDY. Y is a swash letter. In the lower case the serifs are inclined like FOURNIER, and the curves of v and w also resemble FOURNIER.

TIEMANN
Klingspor 1923

ABCDEFGHIJKLMNOPQRS

abcdefghijklmnopqrstuvwxyz

1234567890

ABCDEFGHIJKLMNOPQRST

abcdefghijklmnopqrstuvwxyz

TIEMANN

Care is an enemy to life

iv

Hermann und Dorot

iv

NARCISS

Designed by Walter Tiemann. A calligraphic italic, cast as WREN by Pavyers & Bullens.

TIEMANN
MEDIAEVAL
Klingspor 1909

ix

ABCDEFGGHIJKLLM

MNNOPQRSSTUVWX

YZ

TIEMANN MEDIAEVAL

TIMES NEW ROMAN

Monotype 1932;

Linotype (London) 1932;

Mergenthaler Linotype 1935;

Linotype (Frankfurt);

Intertype 1954;

Intertype (F) 1955;

Ludlow;

Stephenson Blake 1955

Commissioned by *The Times*, 1931, the design was supervised by Stanley Morison. A newspaper type with short ascenders and descenders. Serifs are small and sharply cut. It is a rather black type, in comparison for instance with the previous TIMES roman. The capitals, being no higher than the short ascenders, are small, and unobtrusive. On the lower case the serifs are oblique and the stress is neither abrupt nor vertical. The thickest parts of **c** and **e** are very low down. The **g** has a wide tail. The italic is regular, of a moderate inclination, and has the serifs of the roman. The figures are ranging, but non-ranging figures are also available.

A modified version, with longer descenders, for book work, is available. There are also Titlings in two weights and a Condensed Titling. The special small design to this type is called CLARITAS, and is shown separately. For German setting special light capitals are available. TIMES HEVER TITLING presumaby named after Lord Astor of Hever, is not really similar to the TIMES NEW ROMAN series.

ii

ABCDEFGHIJKLMNOPQRSTUVWXYZ

abcdefghijklmnopqrstuvwxyz

1234567890

ABCDEFGHIJKLMNOPQRSTUVWXYZ

abcdefghijklmnopqrstuvwxyz

1234567890

TIMES NEW ROMAN

ii

ABCDEFGHIJKLMNOPQRSTUVWXYZ

abcdefghijklmnopqrstuvwxyz

1234567890

ABCDEFGHIJKLMNOPQRSTUVWXYZ

abcdefghijklmnopqrstuvwxyz

1234567890

TIMES BOLD

ii

ABCDEFGHIJKLMNOPQRSTUVWXYZ

abcdefghijklmnopqrstuvwxyz

1234567890

TIMES SEMI-BOLD

ii

ABCDEFGHIJKLMNOPQRSTUVWXYZ

abcdefghijklmnopqrstuvwxyz

1234567890

ABCDEFGHIJKLMNOPQRSTUVWXYZ

abcdefghijklmnopqrstuvwxyz

1234567890

TIMES WIDE

ABCDEFGHIJKLMNOPQRSTUVWXYZ

1234567890

TIMES TITLING

ABCDEFGHIJKLMNOPQRSTUVWXYZ

1234567890

TIMES BOLD TITLING

ABCDEGHJKMNOPQRSTUVWXYZ

1234567890

TIMES EXTENDED TITLING

ABCDEFGHIJKLMNOPQRSTUVWXYZ

1234567890

TIMES HEVER TITLING

ABCDEFGHIJKLMNOPQRS
TUVWXYZ&
abcdefghijklmnopqrstuvw
xyz
1234567890

TIMES NEW ROMAN HEAVY

Shaded capitals based on COPPERPLATE ROMAN and originally a type of the Inland Typefoundry. The letters are wide and the shading horizontal. ENGRAVERS' SHADED (Stephenson Blake and American Typefounders), designed by Morris F. Benton, is very similar in treatment. The type is also known as AZURE. Bauer called their version EXCELLENT.

TITLE SHADED
LITHO
American Typefounders

ABCDEFGHIJKLMNO
PQRSTUVWXYZ
1234

EXCELLENT

TORINO
Nebiolo c. 1908

A somewhat condensed roman with abrupt variation of colour. Hair lines are frequent. The tail of the **g** is not closed. The type is also known as ROMANO MODERNO.

iv

ABCDEFGHIJKLMNOPQRST
UVWXYZ
abcdefghijklmnopqrstuvwxyz
1234567890

*ABCDEFGHIJKLMNOPQRS
TUVWXYZ
abcdefghijklmnopqrstuvwxyz
1234567890*

TORINO

TOTFALUSI
Magyar 1956

Designed by Antal Thalwieser and Wenzel Wendler.

ii

ABCDEFGHIJKLMNOPQRSTUVWXYZ
ÁÉÍÓÚÖÜŐŰÄ
abcdefghijklmnopqrstuvwxyzáéíóúöüőűäàßfffiflft
1234567890

*ABCDEFGHIJKLMNOPQRSTUVWXYZ
ÁÉÍÓÚÖÜŐŰÄĖ
abcdefghijklmnopqrstuvwxyzáéíóúöüőűäëàèßfffiflft
1234567890*

TOTFALUSI

ii

ABCDEFGHIJKLM
NOPQRSTUVWXYZ

TOTFALUSI

TOWER
American Typefounders 1934

Designed by Morris F. Benton. The type is completely monotone in colour. The top serif on the **A** points to the left only.

v

ALL KNIGHTS OF THE MID
After an apprenticeship

TOWER

A set of capitals and figures with hair-line serifs. Almost a fat face and following English models; *e.g.* note the spurred **G**. *Cf.* the same founder's NORMANDE. Not to be confused with the type also known as NAUDIN or TRADITION.

ABCDEFGHIJKLMNOPQRSTU

TRADITION

The serifs are small and descenders short. The **J** ends on the line, in the **M** the middle stroke stops half-way, **Q** has an unusual tail and **R** tapers to a point. The **f** is narrow, the ear of the **g** projects north-east.

USE OF THE CAMERA

About five hundred years ago experiments for photo etching were made in Lille.

TRAJAN

Designed by Albert Auspurg. Shaded roman capitals. Presumably the name derives from the lettering on the Trajan column, but that model is not closely followed. The arms of **E** and **F** and the bar of the **H** are high. The **M** is splayed.

ESCUELA DE NAVEGA

TRAJAN INITIALS

Designed by Warren Chappell. The **B**, **E**, **F** and **P** are narrow, the **M** has no top serifs. The **U** has the lower-case design. In the lower-case descenders are short and serifs slightly inclined. The **g** has a small tail compared with the bowl; **t** has a serif at the end of the bar. Numerals are short ranging.

ABCDEFGHIJKLM

A Series of Sixteen Promenade Concerts in the Open

Stangjärnshammåre

TRAJANUS

Kortvågssändare

TRAJANUS BOLD

Designed by John Peters and made originally for the British Railways Board.

ABDEGHJKMNQRSTUVWXYZ
abcdefghijklmnopqrstuvwxyz
1234567890

TRAVELLER

Designed by G.F. Trenholm. A swash calligraphic titling.

TRENHOLM INITIALS

Designed by G.F. Trenholm. The **C** and **G** are wide letters and the **H** rather narrow. The **M** is slightly splayed. In the lower case serifs are inclined on the ascenders as well as on **m**, **n**, etc. The **g** has a sharp-angled link and a straight ear. The italic has a slight inclination. The capitals are swash letters. In the lower case serifs have been eliminated. Numerals are short ranging. There is also a bold.

ABCDEFGHIJKLMNOPQRSTU
VWXYZ&

a b c d e f g h i j k l m n o p q r s t u v w x y z
1 2 3 4 5 6 7 8 9 0

A B C D E F G H I J K L M N O P Q R
S T U V W X Y Z &

a b c d e f g h i j k l m n o p q r s t u v w x y z fi fl
1 2 3 4 5 6 7 8 9 0

TRENHOLM OLD STYLE

Designed by Friedrich Bauer. A display roman with thin bracketed serifs and short ascenders and descenders. There are slab serifs on the **A** and **M**. On the lower case the serifs are horizontal. The distinguishing feature is the squared-up shoulders of the **h**, **m** and **n**. The **g** has the ear on the top and the tail not completed. The italic is a sloped roman. There are also some swash capitals and there are three weights.

Im achtzehnten Jahrhundert wurde die Freiheit

ix

TRENNERT

Neuestes Krematorium in Frankfurt

ix

TRENNERT ITALIC WITH SWASH CAPITALS

den meisten Fällen den Irrweg gegangen, die

ix

TRENNERT SEMI-BOLD

Nordlandreise mit dem modernen Flugzeug

ix

Seit etwa 70 Jahren stellt man die Frage

TRENNERT BOLD

Akademie für Sozial= und Handelswissenschaft in Berlin

ix

HAMBURGS STELLUNG IM HANDEL

TRENNERT BOLD CONDENSED

Designed by Graily Hewitt in accordance with principles laid down in his tract *The Pen and Type Design*. It has therefore the qualities of a script. Serifs are very small, there is little differentiation of colour and the capitals are toned down. **A** has a high bar and the apex extends to the left. **G** has a long terminal, **M** is slightly splayed and **U** has the lower-case design. In the lower case ascenders are shorter than descenders. **v** and **w** are given cursive forms and **y** a vertical stroke. The italic is slightly inclined—seven degrees we are told—and differs from the roman in the one-storeyed **a** and the feet of **m**, **n**, etc. The matrices were cut by The Monotype Corporation.

ABCDEFGHIJKLMNOPQRSTUVWXYZ

ix

abcdefghijklmnopqrstuvwxyyz

fifflffffiffl ft & 1234567890

ABCDEFGHIJKLMNOPQRSTUVWXYZ

abcdefghijklmnopqrstuvwxyyz

fiflffffiffl ft gg & 1234567890

TREYFORD

Designed by Oldrich Menhart. A calligraphic text type of good readability even in the small sizes. It is a bold face of italic inclination and angular character. The lower case **k** is unusual as the swash centre does not link up with the main stroke. The **J** descends below the line but depart in form from conventional characters, ending in a slightly inclined node below the line.

A B C D E F G H I J K L M N O P Q R S T U V W X Y Z

ix

1 2 3 4 5 6 7 8 9 0

a b c d e f g h i j k l m n o p q r s t u v w x y z

TRIGA

Morris's second type was based on early German fifteenth century founts, though not a direct copy of any one of them. It is a round Gothic with leanings toward roman, the design the Germans have called GOTICO ANTIQUA, antiqua being German for roman. Many of the letters are those of a bold roman. In the lower case there are no foot serifs to **m**, **n**, **p**, etc. The **g** has an open tail; **v** and **w** have curved forms. The TROY TYPE also was copied by the American Typefounders. They called it SATANICK. Morris's third type, the CHAUCER, 1893, was a smaller size of the Troy, pica instead of great primer. TROY and CHAUCER are now in the possession of the Cambridge University Press.

ix

ABCDEFGHIJKLMNOPQRSTUV
WXYZ &
abcdefghijklmnopqrstuvwxyz
æ œ fi ff fl ffi ffl   1234567890

TROY TYPE

Designed by Georg Trump. The **E** has a short upper arm, and the **M** is splayed. In the lower case ascenders and descenders are short; the **w** has no serifs. The italic is the sloped roman except for the one-storeyed **a**, the **e** and **f**. There are special capitals and alternative lower case. TRUMP GRAVUR is a three-dimensional companion type.

ii

ABCDEFGHIJKLMNOPQRSTUVW
XYZ
abcdefghijklmnopqrstuvwxyz
1234567890 1234567890

ABCDEFGHIJKLMNOPQRSTUVW
XYZ
abcdefghijklmnopqrstuvwxyz
1234567890 1234567890
ABCDEGJMNPRTVW aekmntvwz

TRUMP MEDIAEVAL

ii

**ABCDEFGHIJKLMNOPQRSTUVW
XYZ
abcdefghijklmnopqrstuvwxyz
1234567890 1234567890**

TRUMP MEDIAEVAL BOLD

ABCDEFGHIJKLMNOPQRST UVWXYZ
abcdefghijklmnopqrstuvwxy
1234567890 1234567890

TRUMP MEDIAEVAL EXTRA BOLD

ii

ABCDEFGHIJKLMNOPQRSTUVWXYZ
abcdefghijklmnopqrstuvwxyz
1234567890 1234567890
ABCDEFGHIJKLMNOPQRSTU VWXYZ
abcdefghijklmnopqrstuvwxyz
1234567890 1234567890

ii

ii

TRUMP MEDIAEVAL BOLD CONDENSED

ABCDEFGHIJKLMNOPQRS TUVWXYZ 1234567890

ii

TRUMP GRAVUR

Designed by Helmut Tschörtner. Serifs are small. The U follows the lower-case design, and the w has no middle serif. The italic is slightly inclined and has the serifs of the roman. Numerals are ranging and non-ranging.

ii

ABCDEFGHIJKLMNOPQRSTUV WXYZ&
abcdefghijklmnopqrstuvwxyz?
1234567890
ABCDEFGHIJKLMNOPQRSTUVW XYZ&
abcdefghijklmnopqrstuvwxyz?
1234567890

TSCHÖRTNER

TYFA
Grafotechna 1959

Designed by Josef Tyfa. Serifs are flat and unbracketed. The **t** is unbracketed and the **w** has no middle serif. Numerals are non-ranging.

iv

ABCDEFGHIJKLMNOPQRSTU
VWXYZ
abcdefghijklmnopqrstuvwxyz
1234567890
ABCDEFGHIJKLMNOPQRSTU
VWXYZ
abcdefghijklmnopqrstuvwxyz
1234567890

TYFA

TYPO ROMAN
American Typefounders c. 1920

Capitals and ascenders are tall, descenders long. The **M** is splayed and the middle strokes stop short of the line. The **W** has no serif in the short middle stroke. The **g** is a script form with a large tail. There is also a shaded version.

iv

The Susquehanna Literary and Musical Society
Recital of Shakespearean Songs

TYPO ROMAN

ULTRA BODONI
American Typefounders 1928;
Monotype

A fat face in which the thick strokes do not curve into the thin but meet them at an angle. Thus the counters in **B, D, O, P, Q** and **R** are bounded by straight lines.

iv

ABCDEFGHIJKLMNOPQ
RSTUVWXYZ
abcdefghijklmnopqrs

MONOTYPE ULTRA BODONI

ABCDEFGHIJKLMNOPQR STUVWXYZ abcdefghijklmnopqrstuvw xyz

MONOTYPE ULTRA BODONI

Designed by Oldrich Menhart. A pen-drawn uncial with an unusual **A**, and the **G** following the style of ordinary romans.

ABCDEFGHIJKLMNOPQRST UVWXYZ 1234567890

UNCIALA

The oldest of the English decorated types, which belonged about 1700 to the Grover Foundry and has descended to the present owners *via* Fry's and the Fann Street Foundry. It is an italic with swash capitals and open letters which are decorated with pearls or unions.

ABCDEFGHIJKLMNOPQRSTUVWXYZ abcdefghijklmnopqrstuvwxyz

UNION PEARL

Designed by Charles Ricketts and named after his house. The type has heavy serifs and the blackness of GOLDEN TYPE. Capitals are wide. The **G** has a long spur. The **g** has the bowl larger than the tail and an ear pointing north-east. The **t** is very short.
AVON, designed by Ricketts for a Shakespeare edition is a small pica of the same design.

Trimalchio autem miti ad nos vultu respexit; et, Vinum, in-
quit, si non placet, mutabo: vos illud, oportet, bonum faciatis.
Deorum beneficio non emo, sed nunc, quidquid ad salivam facit,
in suburbano nascitur meo, quod ego adhuc non novi. Dicitur
confine esse Tarracinensibus et Tarentinis. Nunc conjungere

VALE

VAN DIJCK
ROMAN
Monotype 1935

Designed with the assistance of Jan van Krimpen and based on the roman of Christoffel van Dijck, the leading founder in Amsterdam in the middle of the seventeenth century. It closely resembles CASLON, which is not surprising since Caslon took Van Dijck as his model, especially in his italic. One size of the original Van Dijck italic still survives in the Enschedé foundry. A few small points by which the type can be distinguished from Caslon are: the ear of the **g** is straighter in Van Dijck. In the italic the bar in the **J** is higher up in Caslon and there is no foot serif on the right limb of the **N**. The type bears some resemblance to the larger FELL ROMAN.

ii

ABCDEFGHIJKLMNOPQRSTUVWXYZ
abcdefghijklmnopqrstuvwxyz
1234567890
ABCDEFGHIJKLMNOPQRSTUVWXYZ
abcdefghijklmnopqrstuvwxyz
1234567890

VAN DIJCK

ii

ABCDEFGHIJKLMNOPQRSTUVWXYZÆ
abcdefghijklmnopqrsſtuv-vw-wxyzijæœ&
as ch ct ff ffi ffl fi fl fr is ll qꝫ ſt ſch ſh ſi ſl ſp ſſ ß ſſi ſſl ſt ſz us

ENSCHEDÉ VAN DIJCK ITALIC

VENDÔME
Olive 1952; Bauer 1962

Designed by François Ganeau and related to 17th century French types. The width of the letters varies greatly, but they are of even weight. The foot serifs of lower case letters are generally shorter on the right, and the thin vertical strokes of the capitals are tapered either toward the top or the bottom of the letter. The curve of the **e** is accentuated toward the left, and the **b** has no horizontal foot serif, but instead a tapered vertical touching the base of the, line.

ii

ABCDEFGHIJKLMNOPQRSTUVX
abcdefghijklmnopqrstuvwxyzabcdeg
1234567890
ABCDEFGHIJKLMNOPQRSTUVWZ
abcdefghijklmnopqrstuvwxyzabcdefgho
1234567890

VENDÔME

ABCDEFGHIJKLMNOPQRSTUI
abcdefghijklmnopqrstuvwxyzab
1234567890

ABCDEFGHIJKLMNOPQRSTUVWXYZ
abcdefghijklmnopqrstuvwxyzabcdefgh
1234567890

VENDÔME BOLD

ABCDEFGHIJKLMNOPQRSTUVWXYZABCDEFGHIJKLMNOPQRM

abcdefghijklmnopqrstuvwxyzabcdefghijklmnopqrstuvwxyz

1234567890

VENDÔME CONDENSED

ABCDEFGHIJKLMNOPQRX
abcdefghijklmnopqrstuvxyz
1234567890

VENDÔME EXTRA BOLD

Originally cut by E.P. Prince for George W. Jones at the Sign of the Dolphin. An italic was designed by F.W. Goudy in 1925. The original type had slab serifs on the **M**. The hyphen is oblique and the full-stop diamond shaped. The italic has angular beginning strokes.

ABCDEFGHIJKLMNOPQRSTUVWXYZ
abcdefghijklmnopqrstuvwxy
ABCDEFGHIJKLMNOPQRSTUVWXYZ
abcdefghijklmnopqrstuvwxyz

VENEZIA

i

VENEZIANA
Grafotechna 1920

A calligraphic roman with tall ascenders.

ii

ABCDEFGHIJKLMNOPQRSTUV
WXYZ
abcdefghijklmnopqrstuvwxyz
1234567890
ABCDEFGHIJKLMNOPQRSTUV
WXYZ
abcdefghijklmnopqrstuvwxyz
1234567890

VENEZIANA

ii

ABCDEFGHIJKLMNOPQRST
UVWXYZ
abcdefghijklmnopqrstuvwxyz
1234567890

VENEZIANA BOLD

VERDI
Bauer c. 1851

Designed by J.C. Bauer, although the present type, re-issued in 1957, is modified. The shading in letters like the **A**, **E**, **H**, **P**, etc. completely fills the letters.

v

ABCDEFGHIJKLMNOP
QRSTUVWXYZ
1234567890

VERDI

Descenders are short, and the ear of the **g** is quite unorthodox. The italic is moderately inclined and has the serif formation of the roman, except the **A** where the serif is projected to the left, and the curved **V** and **W**. The **p** and **q** are without foot serifs.

American Typefounders' VERONA is quite different.

VERONA IS LACLEDE OLD STYLE and was bought in 1920 by Barnhart Brothers & Spindler from the Laclede Typefoundry of St Louis; it was rechristened MUNDER and supplied with a bold and an italic cut by Robert Wiebking.

VERONA
Stephenson Blake 1923

ABCDEFGHIJKLMNOPQRSTUVWXYZ
abcdefghijklmnopqrstuvwxyz
1234567890

ABCDEFGHIJKLMNOPQRST UVWXYZ
abcdefghijklmnopqrstuvwxyz
1234567890

VERONA

i

ABCDEFGHIJKLMNOPQRSTUVWXYZ
abcdefghijklmnopqrstuvwxyz

ABCDEFGHIJKLMNOPQRSTUVWXYZ
abcdefghijklmnopqrstuvwxyz

VERONA BOLD

i

ABCDEFGHIJKLMNOPQRSTUVWXYZ
abcdefghijklmnopqrstuvwxyz

VERONA BOLD CONDENSED

i

ABCDEFGHIJKLMNOPQRSTUVWXYZ
abcdefghijklmnopqrstuvwxyz

VERONA EXTRA BOLD

i

A heavy face with short ascenders and descenders. The thick slab serifs and monotone colour of this type give it almost the appearance of an Egyptian. **R** tapers to a point. Note the short tail of the **y**; the ampersand also has a short tail. The italic has the serifs of the roman.

VERONESE
Monotype

ABCDEFGHIJKLMNOPQRSTUVWXYZ&
abcdefghijklmnopqrstuvwxyz

VERONESE

v

VERTICAL
Haas 1955

A condensed and elongated fat face, a re-cutting of a nineteenth-century design. Capitals only. *Cf.* SLIMBLACK

A somewhat heavier face similiar to this one in ROMAN EXTRA BOLD CONDENSED of the former A.D. Farmer & Son Typefoundry.

iv

ABCDEFGHIJKLMNOPQRSTUVWXYZ
THE QUICK BROWN FOX

VERTICAL

VESTA
Berthold 1926

Designed by Albert Augspurg. A shaded titling. Black strokes have a serrated edge on the right side.

iv

GEWERBE-MUSEUM IN BREMEN
29 DEUTSCHE KUNST 56

VESTA

VICTORIA
Adler Traldi 1966

A modern line composition type designed for improved photographic reproducibility.

iv

ABCDEFGHIJKLMNOPQRST
abcdefghijklmnopqrstuvwxyz
1234567890

ABCDEFGHIJKLMNOPQRST
abcdefghijklmnopqrstuvwxyz
1234567890

VICTORIA

iv

ABCDEFGHIJKLMNOPQRST
abcdefghijklmnopqrstuvwxyz
1234567890

ABCDEFGHIJKLMNOPQRST
abcdefghijklmnopqrstuvwxyz
1234567890

VICTORIA BOLD

VICTORIA ITALIC
Ludlow 1927

A titling with fine serifs.

vii

ABCDEFGHIJKLMNOPQRSTUVWXYZ

1234567890

VICTORIA ITALIC

A titling in the SCOTCH style.

ABCDEFGHIJKLMNOPQRSTUVWXYZ
1234567890
VICTORIA TITLING

ABCDEFGHIJKLMNOPQRSTUVWXYZ
1234567890
VICTORIA TITLING CONDENSED

iv

ABCDEGHIJKMNOPQRSTUVWXYZ
1234567890
VICTORIA TITLING BOLD

iv

ABCDEFGHIJKLMNOPQRSTUVWXYZ
1234567890
VICTORIA TITLING BOLD CONDENSED

iv

Designed by Oldrich Menhart. An angular text type.

Á B C D E F G H I J K L
M N O P Q R Š Ů T W V Y
Z X & Æ Œ
a b c ď e f g h i j k l
m n o p q ř s ť ů v w x
ý z ff fi fl ß § æ œ
1 2 3 4 5 6 7 8 9 0
Á B C D E F G H I J K L M N O P Q
R Š T Ů V W Y Z X & Æ Œ
a b c d e f g h i j k l m n o p q r š ť
ů v w ý z x œ œ
1 2 3 4 5 6 7 8 9 0
VICTORY

WALBAUM

Berthold; Monotype 1934;

Linotype (Frankfort) 1960

J.E. Walbaum (1768–1839) was a founder at Goslar and at Weimar. His modern face was cut in the early years of the nineteenth century. The original matrices are still extant in Germany in the Berthold foundry, which acquired them in 1919. The type was introduced into England by the Curwen Press in 1925. Walbaum followed Didot rather than Bodoni. His capitals are noticeably wider than Bodoni's; the **J** is short ranging. The **b** has no foot serif and the **t** is unbracketed. There are two sets of figures, old face and modern. In the italic there are the flat roman serifs of all continental modern faces. There are no foot serifs to **p** and **q**; **v** and **w** are of normal design and have not the eighteenth-century curves of BODONI. The Berthold and Linotype versions shown here are not cast from Walbaum's original matrices.

iv

ABCDEFGHIJKLMNOPQRSTUVWXYZ
abcdefghijklmnopqrstuvwxyz
1234567890
ABCDEFGHIJKLMNOPQRSTUVWXY
abcdefghijklmnopqrstuvwxyz

BERTHOLD WALBAUM

iv

ABCDEFGHIJKLMNOPQRSTUVWXYZ
abcdefghijklmnopqrstuvwxy

BERTHOLD WALBAUM MEDIUM

WALLAU

Klingspor 1925–30

Designed by Rudolf Koch. The capitals are roman and appear to be quill-drawn. They are without serifs except for a slab serif on the **A**. The lower case is black letter in design.

ix

ABCDEFGHIJKLMNOPQRSTUVWXYZ

abcdefghijklmnopqrstuvwxyz

1234567890

WALLAU

ix

ABCDEFGHIJKLMNOPQRSTU

abcdefghijklmnopqrstuvwxyz

WALLAU BOLD

WAVERLEY

Intertype (New York) 1941

The type has the vertical stress and flat serifs of a modern face, but the gradation of colour is not abrupt and the serifs are strong. **M** is a wide letter and **R** has a curled tail. The **g** has an ear like CASLON and the bar of the **t** is unbracketed. The italic has the serifs of the roman; **p** and **q** are without foot serifs. The figures are short-ranging. It is very similar to WALBAUM.

iv

ABCDEFGHIJKLMNOPQRSTUVWXYZ
ABCDEFGHIJKLMNOPQRSTUVWXYZ
abcdefghijklmnopqrstuvwxyz
1234567890

WAVERLEY

Designed by Emil Rudolf Weiss. The **B** is narrow and **H** wide. **M** has no top serifs. **U** has the lower-case design. In the lower case **a** has the upper story wide open, **f** is unkerned and **w** has no middle serif. Decenders are rather short. The italic (1931) is of the BLADO school, of very slight inclination and with angular beginning strokes. Most of the capitals are swash varieties. The **g** has an open tail drawn from right to left; **p** and **q** have no foot serifs and the uprights ascend well above the bowls. This roman shares the contemporary affection for very small serifs.

WEISS
ROMAN

Bauer 1926;

Intertype (New York);

Intertype (Berlin)

ii

ABCDEFGHIJKLMNOPQQuRSTUV
WXYZ
abcdefghijklmnopqrstuvwxyz
1234567890
ABCDEFGHIJKLMNOPQRSTUVWXYZ
abcdefghijklmnopqrstuvwxyz e m n t
1234567890
AABCDEFGHIJJKLMNOPQuQRST
UVVWWXYYZ

WEISS ROMAN

ii

ABCDEFGHIJKLMNOPQQuRSTUV
WXYZ
abcdefghijklmnopqrstuvwxyz
1234567890

WEISS ROMAN BOLD

ii

ABCDEFGHIJKLMNOPQQuRSTU
VWXYZ
abcdefghijklmnopqrstuvwxyz
1234567890

WEISS ROMAN EXTRA BOLD

ii

ABCDEFGHIJKLMNOPQRST
UVWXYZ   1234567890

WEISS INITIALS SERIES I

237

AABCDEFGGHIJKLMNOPQ
RSTUVWXYZ 1234567890

ii

AABCDEFGGHIJKLMNOP
QRSTUVWXYZ 123456789

ii

ABCDEFGHIJKLMNOPQRS
TUVWXYZ 1234567890

ii

ABCDEFGHIJKLMNOPQRSTUVWXYZ

abcdefghijklmnopqrstuvwxyz

1234567890

ABCDEFGHIJ KLMNOPQRSTUVWXYZ

ABCDEFGHIJKLMNOPQRSTUVWXYZ

abcdefghijklmnopqrstuvwxyz

1234567890

**WEISS
RUNDGOTISCH**
Bauer 1936

Designed by E.R. Weiss. A calligraphic type following the German style of the period and leaning on black letter, but also on Italian and Spanish manuscript writing. Descenders are very short.

ix

ABCDEFGHIJKLMNOPQRST
UVWXYZ

abcdefghijklmnopqrstuvwryz

1234567890

Designed by Hans Wagner. The **G** has a wide horizontal serif. The **M** is splayed. The **t** is flat across the top and has a curved terminal. Nebiolo's inline version LANDI ECHO is a titling with short-ranging figures and the outline version LANDI LINEAR has black horizontal feet and tops of letters. The type is also known as LUXOR. Nebiolo call it LANDI, Fonderie Française RAMSES and Amsterdam Typefoundry ATLAS.

WELT

Ludwig & Mayer 1931;

Nebiolo; Française;

Amsterdam;

Linotype (Frankfurt)

ABCDEFGHIJKLMNOPQRSTUVWXYZ
abcdefghijklmnopqrstuvwxyz
1234567890

ABCDEFGHIJKLMNOPQRSTUVWXYZÇ
abcdefghijklmnopqrstuvwxyzçœæ

WELT LIGHT

ABCDEFGHIJKLMNOPQRSTUVWXYZ
abcdefghijklmnopqrstuvwxyzçæœ
ABCDEFGHIJKLMNOPQRSTUVWXYZ
abcdefghijklmnopqrstuvwxyzçœæ

WELT MEDIUM

ABCDEFGHIJKLMNOPQRSTUVWXYZ
abcdefghijklmnopqrstuvwxyz

WELT BOLD

THE PRIMARY FUNCTION
of type is that it shall be

WELT EXTRA BOLD

ABCDEFGHIJKLMNOPQRSTUVWXYZÇÆŒ&
abcdefghijklmnopqrstuvwxyzçæœ
1234567890

WELT CONDENSED

239

WERBEDRUCK

J. Wagner

A display roman (originally cut by Norddeutsche Schriftgiesserei in 1930), as one may infer from its weight and shortness of ascenders and descenders.

The design is close to NEW CASLON, but the figures are short ranging.

ii

ABCDEFGHIJKLMNOPQ RSTUVWXYZ
abcdefghijklmnopqrstuvwxyz
1234567890

WERBEDRUCK

ii

ABCDEFGHIJKLMNOPQR
abcdefghijklmnopqrstuvwxyz

WERBEDRUCK BOLD

WESTMINSTER OLD STYLE or **DELLA ROBBIA**

American Typefounders 1903;

Stephenson Blake 1907;

Deberny & Peignot 1911

Lanston Monotype;

Amsterdam

vii

Designed by T.M. Cleland. It is a roman of light colour and monotone. The serifs are small and inclined on the lower case. The bowls of **B**, **P** and **R** are not closed. **H** is wide and has a high bar. **M** is splayed and the middle strokes descend half-way. **W** is very wide. The **e** is Venetian; **g** has a large bowl and the tail not closed. Descenders are short and the figures modern.

The Monotype Corporation's CANTERBURY (1915) based on M.F. Benton's Della Robbia Light (1903) is a closely similar design. It may be distinguished by the straight tail of the **R**.

Amsterdam call the type FIRENZE.

ABCDEFGHIJKLMNOPQRSTUVWXYZ
abcdefghijklmnopqrstuvwxyz
1234567890

WESTMINSTER OLD STYLE

WHITEFRIARS BOLD

Chiswick Press

ix

Formerly a roman of the Whitefriars Foundry.

ABCDEFGHIJKLMNOPQR
abcdefghijklmnopqrstuvwxy!
1234567890£

WHITEFRIARS BOLD

Designed by Morris F. Benton, and originally called BENTON. Serifs are not quite horizontal and the stress not quite vertical. The **G** is like CASLON.

RINGLET Photographs

WHITEHALL

Designed by Morris F. Benton and originally called BOLD ANTIQUE. A bold type with slab serifs.

ABCDEFGHIJKLMNOPQRS TUVWXYZ abcdefghijklmnopqrstuvwxyz 1234567890

WHITIN BLACK

ABCDEFGHIJKLMNOPQRSTUVW XYZ abcdefghijklmnopqrstuvwxyz 1234567890

WHITIN BLACK CONDENSED

Designed under the direction of Edwin W. Shaar. A newspaper type. Stephenson Blake's WINDSOR is quite different.

ABCDEFGHIJKLMNOPQRSTUVWXYZ
abcdefghijklmnopqrstuvwxyz
1234567890

WINDSOR

ABCDEFGHIJKLMNOPQRSTUVWXYZ
abcdefghijklmnopqrstuvwxyz
1234567890

WINDSOR BOLD

241

WINDSOR
Stephenson Blake c. 1905

A display type of a rich colour, even in the light face. There are many odd forms in both cases. Some of the capitals, E, F, G, T and S, have beak-like serifs. M has small slab serifs. P and R have large bowls. U has a horse-shoe shape. The lower case has oblique serifs and very short descenders. a has a large bowl, e an oblique stroke to the eye, the squat g has the ear at the top, the last limbs of m and n are splayed, and s has serifs like the upper case. The italic (in the medium weight) is regular and has the serifs of the roman. There are three weights of the roman, also a condensed, elongated and outline. Intertype WINDSOR is a newspaper type.

ix

ABCDEFGHIJKLMNOPQ
RST
abcdefghijklmnopqrstuvwxyz
123
WINDSOR

ix

ABCDEFGHIJKLMNOPQRST
abcdefghijklmnopqrstuvwxyz&
WINDSOR CONDENSED

ix

ABCDEFGHIJKLMNOPQRSTUVWX
YZ
abcdefghijklmnopqrstuvwxyz
1234567890
WINDSOR BOLD

ix

ABCDEFGHIJKLMNOPQRSTUVWXYZ
abcdefghijklmnopqrstuvwxyz
WINDSOR ELONGATED

ix

ABCDEFGHIJKLMNOPQRSTUVWXYZ
abcdefghijklmnopqrstuvwxyz
WINDSOR OUTLINE

WOLFRAM
Ludwig & Mayer 1930

Designed by Hans Wagner. A heavy, upright italic. All the serifs are rounded. Some capitals are of the swash variety. There is considerable variation of colour.

ix

Mauxion Schokol
WOLFRAM

Designed by Lucian Zabel. A roman with slight variation of stress and small, horizontal and stubby serifs. The **E, F, L** and **T** are narrow letters. **E** and **F** have the centre arms above the middle. **M** has no top serifs. In the lower case descenders are short. The **e** has a large eye and the **g** an open tail. Some vertical strokes are thickened towards the top; this feature is more evident in the bold face. There is no italic.

ZABEL
ROMAN
Woellmer 1928–30

ix

SCHRIFTGIESSEREI

ZABEL ROMAN

ix

Die Bilderschrift ist ein Element, und zwar das wichtigste, aus dem sich die Schrift entwickelt hat. Es gibt aber noch andere Anfänge der Schrift DIESE ANFÄNGE DER SCHRIFT FINDET MAN BEI ALLEN VÖLKERN

ZABEL ROMAN BOLD

Designed by Giovanni Mardersteig. Based on the early Italian romans. The punches were cut by Charles Malin.

ZENO
Officina Bodoni 1937

ii

ABCDEFGHIJKLMNOPQURRSTUVWXYZ

ABCDEFGHIJKLMNOPQURRSTUVWXYZ

abccdefghijklmmnopqrrstuvwxyz

1234567890

ZENO

Designed by Michael Harvey. An accentuated outline titling, giving a somewhat three-dimensional effect.

ZEPHYR
Ludlow 1964

ix

ABCDEFGHIJKLMNOPQRST

UVWXYZ&

1234567890

ix

ZEPHYR

Designed by S.H. Roos. A roman based on JENSON. The **E, G** and **L** have the large serifs found in several De Roos types. The **U** has the lower-case design. The **g** has a large bowl and narrow tail. The **t** has a serif at the end of the bar.

The matrices were cut by Wagner & Schmidt and the type was cast by Amsterdam Typefoundry.

ZILVER TYPE
Zilverdistel Pers 1915

YZATEN DIEN EERSTEN AVOND NA,
dat wij aan land waren gekomen tot laat in den
tuin van mijn broeder, ik heb nog nimmer zulk
een schoonen maanlichten avond weêr gezien,

i

ZILVER

LINEALES

THE EARLIEST "SANS SERIFS" appear in the specimen books of Vincent Figgins, of 1830 and Thorowgood, of 1832. The earliest is the type shown by W. Caslon IV in 1816 and called Egyptian, although it is a lineale. Blake and Stephenson in 1833 called their version Sans Surryphs. Thorowgood called the type Grotesque and the American name Gothic was often used. Figgin's name Sans Serif describes the important characteristic. The type was monotone and the capitals were of equal width. The early designs were heavy and it was some years before lighter faces were cut and even longer before a lower case was cut. The Caslon Doric appears in a number of weights in their specimen book of 1854 and there was already an Outline Doric. With some slight exceptions, no great change took place in the design until the German founders in this century reformed the type by varying the width of the letters and by replacing some of the square ends by tapering strokes. The specimen books of many founders show Dorics, Gothics and Grotesques. "Lineales" is the description applied by Maximilien Vox to types without serifs. In some cases, the distinction between a calligraphic roman and a modified lineale approaching a roman of calligraphic style is hard to draw.

Designed by A.M. Cassandre. A titling in which the letters are partly black and partly white.

ACIER NOIR
Deberny & Peignot 1936

iv

SOUVERAINES

CONCERNANT TOUT LE MONDE MÉDICAL

ACIER NOIR

Designed by Freeman Craw. This type was designed by cutting the letter images out and thus has some wood-cut character. Numerous alternative characters are provided, and in the lower case some characters have slight inclination. Several lower-case characters may be turned upside down without losing alignment, to obtain additional alternative character images.

ADLIB
American 1961

iv

ABCDEEFGHIJKLMNNOOPQRRSSTTUV

WXYZ

aabccdeeffgghijkllmmnoopqrrssttuvwxyz

12345678900

ADLIB

ADONIS
EXTENDED
Stephenson Blake 1962

vi

Designed by André Bretton on the basis of the same founder's SPARTAN, but entirely without serifs. An expanded type of medium weight with a sloped version. The **M** is square. The **g** has an open tail. There are ranging figures.

ABCDEFGHIJKLMNOP
QRSTUVWXYZ
abcdefghijklmnopqrstu
vwxyzæœ
1234567890

ABCDEFGHIJKLMNOPQ
RSTUVWXYZ
abcoefghijklmnopqrstuvw
xyzæœ
1234567890

ADONIS EXTENDED

ADSANS
Linotype (London) 1959

vi

A newspaper type for classified advertising in 4¾ pt only and first used in the London *Evening News*.

CLERK Reqd for cost office, preferably with some experience, age 21 to 26 years.—Apply Employment Department, FIRTH-VICKERS STAINLESS STEELS LTD., Weedon st., Tinsley. **COPY TYPIST** Reqd by small tool manufacturers, aged 25-30 years; experience in office routine an advantage.—Apply in own writing to Cintride Ltd., Grange Lane Works, Sheffield, 5.

ADELPHI. Tem 7611 7.30 Wed & Sat. 2.30. Van Johnson, Maureen Hartley. **THE MUSIC MAN.** London's happiest musical with the show-stopping 76 Trombones. **ALDWYCH.** Tem 6404. (7.30 Mat W & S 2.30). Royal Shakespeare Co. in **THE CHERRY ORCHARD** (until Jan 6 then Jan 15/17). Peggy Ashcroft, John Gielgud. Also **THE HOLLOW CROWN** (Feb 1-3). As You Like It Joins rep Jan 10.

ABCDEFGHIJKLMNOPQRSTUVWXYZÆŒ abcdefghijklmnopqrstuvwxyzæœ fiflffflffl 1234567890
ABCDEFGHIJKLMNOPQRSTUVWXYZÆŒ abcdefghijklmnopqrstuvwxyzæœ fiflffflffl 1234567890

ADSANS and ADSANS BOLD

ADVERTISE
MENT
GROTESQUE
Haas 1945–46

vi

A bold and rather condensed type. In the lower case ascenders and descenders are abbreviated. In the **G** there is a spur as in nineteenth century designs. COMMERCIAL GROTESQUE is the same design in a lighter weight with less abbreviated ascenders and descenders. NARROW GROTESQUE is the condensed face dating back to *c.*1865.

ABCDEFGHIJKLMNOPQRSTUVWXYZ
abcdefghijklmnopqrstuvwxyz

ADVERTISEMENT GROTESQUE

AGENCY
GOTHIC
American 1933

vi

Designed by Morris F. Benton. Lineale capitals and figures in which the normally round strokes are made straight, *e.g.* **C** and **O** are rectangular. There are two **M**'s one with an unusual middle stroke, the **A** has also two versions.

A A B C D E F G H I J K L M M N O P Q R S
T U V W X Y Z & 1 2 3 4 5 6 7 8 9 0

AGENCY GOTHIC

Designed by Carlos Winkow. An inline three-dimensional titling. **A**, **M** and **N** have rounded tops.

ABCDEFGHIJKLMNOPQRSTUVWXYZ

ALCÁZAR

Designed by M.F. Benton. A narrow bold type following nineteenth-century style.

ABCDEFGHIJKLMNOPQRSTUVWXYZ

abcdefghijklmnopqrstuvwxyz

1234567890

ALTERNATE GOTHIC

An inclined lineale titling which is not monotone. The round letters have considerable variation of colour and look like pen-drawn letters. These initials are also intended for use with the lower case of BURGUND.

THERMOS

AMBASSADOR

Originally issued by Wagner & Schmidt in 1914, when it was called GROTESK V and later KRUPP HALLO. This is one of the most widely distributed type faces, and appears in the catalogues (either following or copying the original design) of many Dutch, Spanish, German, French and Italian type-founders. Amsterdam call the type ANNONCE. John called their version KOLOSS, Wagner EDEL GROTESQUE EXTRA BOLD WIDE, Weber PROGRESS and Weisert FAVORIT. ANTIQUES DOUBLES LARGES of Deberny & Peignot is identical. Nebiolo called the type CAIROLI. Ludwig & Mayer now call the type HALLO and added an italic in 1959.

ABCDEFGHIJKLMNO
PQRSTUVWXYZÆŒ
abcdefghijklmnopqr
stuvwxyz
1234567890£&æœ

ANNONCE GROTESQUE

ABCDEFGHIJKLMNOPQRSTUVW
XYZ
abcdefghijklmnopqrstuvwxyz
1234567890

HALLO ITALIC

247

A condensed lineale of nineteenth-century design. The **Q** has a curiously wedge-shaped tail. Ascenders are short.

ABCDEFGHIJKLMNOPQRSTUVWXYZÆŒ
abcdefghijklmnopqrstuvwxyzæœ
1234567890

ANTIQUE BOLD CONDENSED

Designed by Roger Excoffon. Ascenders and descenders are short. The extra bold and ultra bold are known as COMPACT and NORD respectively.

ABCDEFGHIJKLMNOPQRSTUVWX
abcdefghijklmnopqrstuvwxyz
1234567890

ABCDEFGHIJKLMNOPQRSTUVWXY
abcdefghijklmnopqrstuvwxyz
1234567890

ANTIQUE OLIVE

vi

ABCDEFGHJKLMNOPQRSTUWXY
abcdefghijklmnopqrstuvwxyz
1234567890

ANTIQUE OLIVE MEDIUM

vi

ABCDEFGHIJKLMNOPQRSTUVWXYZ
abcdefghijklmnopqrstuvwxyz
1234567890

ANTIQUE OLIVE CONDENSED

ABCDEFGHIKLMNOPQRS
abcdefghiklmnopqrstv
1234567890

ANTIQUE OLIVE WIDE

ABCDEFGHIJKLMNOPQRSTUVWXYZ
abcdefghijklmnopqrstuvwxyz
1234567890

ANTIQUE OLIVE CONDENSED BOLD

ABCDEFGHJKLMNOPQRSTUVW
abcdefghijklmnopqrstuvwx
1234567890

ANTIQUE OLIVE BOLD

ABCDEFGHKLMNOPQRSTU
abcdefghjlmnopqrstuvz
1234567890

ANTIQUE OLIVE COMPACT

ABCDEFGHIKMNORX
abcdefghijklmnost
1234567890

ABCDEFGHILMNOPRST
abcdefghijklmnoprstz
1234567890

NORD

ASTUR
Nacional

A three-dimensional type with an informal effect. The letters are somewhat shaded and angular.. Most strokes overlap. In some of the rounded letters the curves are broken.

ix

ABCDEFGHIJKL
MNOPQRSTU
VWXY&Z
abcdefghijklmnopq
rstuvwxyz
1234567890

ASTUR

ATLANTIS
Weber

A lineale following German style. The position of the bar in **A** and the one-storeyed **a** are characteristic features.

vi

ABCDEFGHIJKLMNOPQRSTUVWXYZ
abcdefghijklmnopqrstuvwxyz

ATLANTIS GROTESQUE

vi

ABCDEFGHIJKLMNOPQRSTUVWXYZ
abcdefghijklmnopqrstuvwxyz

ATLANTIS GROTESQUE MEDIUM

vi

ABCDEFGHIJKLMNOPQRSTUVWXYZ
abcdefghijklmnopqrstuvwxyz

ATLANTIS GROTESQUE BOLD

Designed by K.H. Schaefer. A shaded lineale with five parallel shading lines. Schriftguss called the type FATIMA and were the original founders.

ATLAS

Designed by M.R. Kaufmann. Freely drawn characters and figures are slightly inclined. Counters and bowls are not completely closed. The bars of **A** and **H** and the arms of **E** and **F** protrude to the left. *Cf.* CARTOON.

ABCDEFGHIJKLMNOPQRSTUVWXYZ
1234567890

BALLOON

ABCDEFGHIJKLMNOPQRSTUV
WXYZ

BALLOON EXTRA BOLD

Designed by Roger Excoffon. A lineale titling with figures, which is not monotone. Letters are slightly inclined. Some vertical strokes extend above the general level. There are no lower case letters and the strokes are often cut at uneven angles at the ends. The **C** has a short down stroke at the top right. Most letters consist basically of individual heavy strokes arranged next to each other.

ABCDEFGHIJKLMNOPQRSTUVXYZ
1234567890

BANCO

A titling which in the main alphabet is very wide, but for about half the letters a second version is shown which is very narrow. Some letters resemble VOGUE (Stephenson Blake).

AA B CC DD EE FF G HH I J K LL M
NN O PP Q RR SS TT UU V W X Y Z
Æ Œ &
1234567890

BANJO

BANK GOTHIC

American

vi

Probably designed by M.F. Benton. Capitals in which the normally round letters are squared, *e.g.* the **C**, **G**, **O**, **P**, **Q**, **R** and **U**. COMMERCE GOTHIC is a Ludlow version.

ABCDEFGHIJKLMNOPQRSTUVWXYZ&
1234567890
BANK GOTHIC LIGHT

vi

ABCDEFGHIJKLMNOPQRSTUVWXYZ&
1234567890
BANK GOTHIC MEDIUM

vi

ABCDEFGHIJKLMNOPQRSTUVWXYZ&
1234567890
BANK GOTHIC BOLD

vi

ABCDEFGHIJKLMNOPQRSTUVWXYZ&
1234567890
BANK GOTHIC CONDENSED MEDIUM

vi

ABCDEFGHIJKLMNOPQRSTUVWXYZ&
1234567890
BANK GOTHIC CONDENSED LIGHT

BASALT

Genzsch & Heyse 1927

ix

Designed by W. Ege. Bold capitals which have some relatively thin strokes, *e.g.* the arm of the **E**. The type was redesigned in 1934.

ENMITGLIED
BASALT

BASUTO

Stephenson Blake 1927

ix

An extra bold titling distinguished by the shape of the counters. In the **O** the counter is an inclined oval; in the **P** and **R** they have the shape of a **D**.

ABCDEFGHIJKLMNOPQRSTU VWXYZ1234?
BASUTO

BELL GOTHIC

Mergenthaler Linotype c. 1938; Intertype 1958; Linotype; Monotype

vi

A type designed initially by the Bell Telephone Company's typographer and Mergenthaler Linotype for use in directories and due to its slender design very space saving. The weight of the line is moderate and uniform.

ABCDEFGHIJKLMNOPQRSTUVWXYZ   ABCDEFGHIJKLMNOPQRSTUVWXYZ
abcdefghijklmnopqrstuvwxyz   abcdefghijklmnopqrstuvwxyz
Æ fi ff fi fl ffi ffl Œ   Æ fi ff fl ffi ffl Œ
1234567890   1234567890

BELL GOTHIC and GOTHIC BOLD

BERNHARD FASHION

American 1929; Intertype

vi

Designed by Lucian Bernhard. An extra light type. The bars of **A** and **H** and the arms of **E** and **F** protrude to the left. Ascenders are tall and the **a** is one-storeyed.

A A A B C D E E E F G H I J K L M N N O P
Q R S S S T U V W X Y Z &
a b c d e f g h i j k l m n o p q r s t u v w x y z
1 2 3 4 5 6 7 8 9 0
BERNHARD FASHION

252

Designed by Lucian Bernhard. The arms of **E** and **F** and the bar of **H** are low. **M** is splayed and pointed (but not in the light face). The tail of the **Q** is external to the bowl. **a** is two-storeyed and **g** has an open tail. There are four weights, with italics to the two lightest.

ABCDEFGHIJKLMNOPQRSTUVW
XYZ abcdefghijklmnopqrstuvwxyz
1234567890

vi

BERNHARD GOTHIC LIGHT

ABCDEFGHIJKLMNOPQRSTUVW
XYZ abcdefghijklmnopqrstuvwxyz
1234567890

vi

ABCDEFGHIJKLMNOPQRSTUV
WXYZ abcdefghijklmnopqrstuvwxyz
1234567890

BERNHARD GOTHIC MEDIUM

ABCDEFGHIJKLMNOPQRSTUVWXYZ
abcdefghijklmnopqrstuvwxyz
1234567890

vi

BERNHARD GOTHIC MEDIUM CONDENSED

ABCDEFGHIJKLMNOPQRSTUVW
XYZ abcdefghijklmnopqrstuvwxyz
1234567890

vi

BERNHARD GOTHIC HEAVY

ABCDEEFGHIJKKLMNOPQRST
UVWXYZ
abcdefghijklmnopqrstuvwxyz
1234567890

vi

BERNHARD GOTHIC EXTRA HEAVY

253

BERTHOLD GROTESQUE

Berthold 1928;
Intertype (Berlin)

A true lineale of the usual continental design. There are five weights, two of them with italics. The ascender of the **t** is pointed, and the bottom curve of the **G** is broken. PLASTICA is a shaded titling fount based on this type. NOBEL is very similar.

vi

ABCDEFGHIJKLMNOPQRSTUVWXYZ
abcdefghijklmnopqrstuvwxyz

ABCDEFGHIJKLMNOPQRSTUVWXYZ
abcdefghijklmnopqrstuvwxyz

BERTHOLD GROTESQUE LIGHT

vi

ABCDEFGHIJKLMNOPQRSTUVWXYZ
abcdefghijklmnopqrstuvwxyz 1234567890

ABCDEFGHIJKLMNOPQRSTUVWXYZ
abcdefghijklmnopqrstuvwxyz

BERTHOLD GROTESQUE

vi

ABCDEFGHIJKLMNOPQRSTUVWXYZ
abcdefghijklmnopqrstuvwxyz

BERTHOLD GROTESQUE CONDENSED

vi

ABCDEFGHIJKLMNOPQRSTUVWXYZ
abcdefghijklmnopqrstuvwxyz

BERTHOLD GROTESQUE BOLD CONDENSED

vi

ABCDEFGHIJKLMNOPQRSTUVWXYZ
abcdefghijklmnopqrstuvwxyz

BERTHOLD GROTESQUE MEDIUM

vi

ABCDEFGHIJKLMNOPQRSTUVWXY
abcdefghijklmnopqrstuvwxyz

BERTHOLD GROTESQUE BOLD

BIFUR

Deberny & Peignot 1929

Designed by A.M. Cassandre. A lineale in which about half of each letter is omitted. The **A** has no bar, **E** has arms only, **G** is represented by the lower half only and **N** has the middle stroke only. A shaded background helps the eye to the recognition of the whole letter. This daring innovation was applied to an upper case only. It has been called a stencil letter.

vi

DANGER

BIFUR

254

Designed by J. Binder. A condensed and elongated type face with very short ascenders and descenders. *Cf.* PLACARD.

ABCDEFGHIJKLMNOPQRSTUVWXYZ

abcdefghijklmnopqrstuvwxyz

1234567890

BINDER STYLE

ABCDEFGHIJKLMNOPQRSTUVWXYZ

abcdefghijklmnopqrstuvwxyz

1234567890

BINDER STYLE BOLD

vi

Designed by J. Trochut Blanchard as a lineale with vertical stress and rounded letters.

BISONTE
Iranzo 1940–48
vi

Alegría de Viena - CONDESTABLE

BISONTE

Alegría de Viena - CONDESTABLE

BISONTE ITALIC

vi

Alegría de Viena-CONDESTABLE

BISONTE BOLD

vi

Designed by H. Hoffmann and setting a style-trend which was soon followed by others. Woellmer called their version HERMES. A bold sans of the usual German pattern. Ascenders and descenders are much abbreviated. There is also a condensed face.

BLOCK
Berthold 1908

ABCDEFGHIJKLMNOPQRSTUVW

abcdefghijklmnopqrstuvwxyz

1234567890

BLOCK

vi

ABCDEFGHIJKLMNOPQRSTUVWXYZ

abcdefghijklmnopqrstuvwxyz

BLOCK CONDENSED

vi

trische Personen- und Transportw
KIELER ELEKTROMOBIL-WERKE

HERMES GROTESQUE SEMI-BOLD

vi

DRESDEN Genf

HERMES GROTESQUE SHADED

vi

BOUL MICH
American c. 1928
vi

An inline titling version of this founder's BROADWAY and different from BROADWAY ENGRAVED.

SEASON
BOUL MICH

BOWERY
Bruce c. 1890
vi

A rounded three-dimensional and bold type, also known as ROUND SHADED.

ABCDEFGHIJKLMNOPQRSTUVWXYZ
BOWERY

BRAGGA DOCIO
Monotype 1930

vi

Designed by W.A. Woolley. A heavy type face with a resemblance to FUTURA BLACK by the omission of thin strokes. But the letters are wider and the main strokes thicker; ascenders and descenders are shorter. The **G** has a spur; the **J** tapers to a point on the line. In the lower case **c** and **s** with their blobs approach more closely to the usual fat face design.

ABCDEFGHIJKLMNOPQRSTUVW
XYZ
abcdefghijklmnopqrstuvwxyz
1234567890
BRAGGADOCIO

BRITANNIC
Stephenson Blake

vi

A type like ROTHBURY, combining the qualities of a fat face. The thins have a considerable weight. The **G** has a spur and the **Q** a curled tail. The lower case follows the usual English design, as in the **a**, **e**, **g** and **t**. Ascenders are short. The thins are thicker than in ROTHBURY.

ABCDEFGHIJKLM NOPQRSTUV
WXYZ !?
abcdefghijklmno pqrstuvwxyz
1234
BRITANNIC

BROADWAY
American 1929;
Lanston Monotype 1928–29

vi

The American Typefounders type, designed by M.F. Benton, has a condensed version. A type combining characteristics of fat face and lineale. In most of the letters only the main stroke is fat, the thins taking over the rest of the letter. Thins and thicks meet at an angle and not in a curve.

A B C D E F G HIJKLMNO P QR ſ S ſſ
T U V W X Y Z & ! ?
a b c d e f g h i j k l m n o p q r s ſ t u v w
x y z
1 2 3 4 5 6 7 8 9 0
BROADWAY

ABCDEFGHIJKLMNOPQ

RƒSƒƒTUVWXYZ&!?

1234567890

BROADWAY INLINE

Designed by Rudolf Koch. In some points it resembles the designer's LOCARNO, *e.g.* in the varying width of the capitals. **G** has no terminal bar. **J** is short and has a wide loop. **M** is slightly splayed. The arms of **E**, **F** and **L** and the top of the **T** are sheared off obliquely. **U** has the lower-case design. The **a**, **e** and **g** have the same design in the normalised version as in LOCARNO. **t** has a curved terminal. The Klingspor versions, which are the original, are no longer cast.

There are four weights (the heaviest being modified considerably) italics or sloped romans, condensed faces and an inline, which is also called ZEPPELIN.

ABCDEFGHIJKLMNOPQRSTUV

abcdefghijklmnopqrstuvwxyz

ABCDEFGHIJKLMNOPQRSTUVWX

CABLE LIGHT

ABCDEFGHIJKLMNOPQRSTUV

abcdefghijklmnopqrstuvwxyz

CABLE MEDIUM

ABCDEFGHIJKLMNOPQRSTU

abcdefghijklmnopqrstuvwxyz

ABCDEFGHIJKLMNOPQRSTUV

abcdefghijklmnopqrstuvwxyz

CABLE BOLD

ABCDEFGHIJKLMNOPQRSTU

abcdefghijklmnopqrstuvwxy

CABLE HEAVY

ABCDEFGHIJKLMNOPQRSTU
abcdefghijklmnopqrstuvwxyz

CABLE CONDENSED

ABCDEFGHIJKLMNOPQRSTUVWXYZ
abcdefghijklmnopqrstuvwxyz

CABLE BOLD CONDENSED

LOPQRS

CABLE INITIALS

Romeo and Juliet
LORD BYRON

ZEPPELIN

Designed by Roger Excoffon. Decorated and three-dimensional capitals. The letters are formed from shaped material.

ABCDEFGHIJLMNOPQRSTU
VWXYZABCDEFGHIJKLMNO

CALYPSO

Designed by Bronislav Maly. A text lineale in which vertical stokes expand at the feet.

AÁBCCČDDĎEÉĚFGHIÍJKLMNNÑOÓPQRRŘSSŠTŤU
ÚŮVWXYÝZŽÆŒ
aábcčddďeéěfghiíjklmnňoópqrřsšttťuůvw
xyýzžæœ
1234567890

CANTORIA

Designed by K.H. Schaefer. The shading of this lineale consists simply of an additional stroke on the outside of the main strokes.

BELVEDERE

CAPITOL

Designed by H.A. Trafton. A series of freely-drawn capitals and figures. There is little variation in colour and serifs are almost entirely lacking. The bars of the **A** and **H**, and the centre arm of the **E** protrude. The bowls of **B** and **R** are not closed. The capitals of STUDIO are similar. There are two weights. In Germany the type is called FRESKO.

CARTOON or
FRESKO
Bauer 1936

ix

ABCDEFGHIJKLMNOPQRST
UVWXYZ 1234567890

CARTOON

ABCDEFGHIJKLMNOPQRST
UVWXYZ 1234567890

CARTOON BOLD

ix

Designed by Roger Excoffon as a lineale with stressed down strokes.

CHAMBORD
Olive 1945–51

vi

ABCDEFGHIJKLMNOPQRSTUVWXYZ
abcdefghijklmnopqrstuvwxyz
1234567890

CHAMBORD MEDIUM

ABCDEFGHIJKLMNOPQRSTUVWYZ
abcdefghijklmnopqrstuvwxyz
1234567890

ABCDEFGHIJKLMNOPQRSTUVWXYZ
abcdefghijklmnopqrstuvwxyz
1234567890

CHAMBORD SEMI-BOLD

vi

ABCDEFGHIKLMNOPQRSTUW
abcdefghijklmnopqrstuvwxyz
1234567890

CHAMBORD BOLD

vi

ABCDEFGHIJKLMNOPQRSTUVWXYZ
abcdefghijklmnopqrstuvwxyz 1234567890

CHAMBORD CONDENSED

vi

An angular type without a lower case.

ABCDEFGHIJKLMNOPQRSTUVWXYZ&
1234567890

CHAMFER GOTHIC

Designed by W.F. Kemper. A type in which the strokes vary in weight. The U is like the lower case; the ends of many letters are cut at a single angle. VIDEO ROMA has some similarity.

ABCDEFGHIJKLMNOPQRSTUV
WXYZ
abcdefghijklmnopqrstuvwxyz
1234567890
ABCDEFGHIJKLMNOPQRSTUV
WXYZ
abcdefghijklmnopqrstuvwxyz
1234567890

COLONIA

ABCDEFGHIJKLMNOPQRST
UVWXYZ
abcdefghijklmnopqrstuvwxyz
1234567890

COLONIA BOLD

Capitals in which the normally round letters are squared. BANK GOTHIC is similar.

ABCDEFGHIJKLMNOPQRSTUVWXYZ&
1234567890

COMMERCE GOTHIC LIGHT

ABCDEFGHIJKLMNOPQRSTUVWXYZ&   1234567890

COMMERCE GOTHIC LIGHT CONDENSED

ABCDEFGHIJKLMNOPQRSTUVWXYZ&
1234567890

COMMERCE GOTHIC MEDIUM

ABCDEFGHIJKLMNOPQRSTUVWXYZ&   1234567890

COMMERCE GOTHIC MEDIUM CONDENSED

A bold rather condensed lineale. COMMERCIALE COMPACTE is a companion type for larger sizes.

COMMERCIAL
GROTESQUE
Haas 1945–46
vi

ABCDEFGHIJKLMNOPQRSTUVWXYZ
abcdefghijklmnopqrstuvwxyz
1234567890

COMMERCIAL GROTESQUE

ABCDEFGHIJKLMNOPQRSTUVWXYZ
abcdefghijklmnopqrstuvwxyz

vi

COMMERCIAL GROTESQUE BOLD

A condensed extra bold variation of the same founder's COMMERCIAL GROTESQUE BOLD.

COMMERCIALE
COMPACTE
Haas 1966
vi

Modelle der diesjährigen Winter-Damenmode
Einladung zur Ausstellung der schönsten

COMMERCIALE COMPACTE

A rimmed fat lineale. Bauer call their version ASTORIA.

COMSTOCK
American c. 1880
vi

ABCDEFGHIJKLMNOPQR
STUVWXYZ&
abcdefghijklmnopqrstuvw
xyz
1234567890

COMSTOCK

A condensed inclined type. Ascenders and descenders are very short. The lower case is not entirely without serifs, the **m, n** and **u** having foot serifs.

CONDENSA
Monotype
vi

ABCDEFGHIJKLMNOPQRSTUVWXYZ&
abcdefghijklmnopqrstuvwxyz

CONDENSA

261

CONDENSED GOTHIC OUTLINE
Ludlow 1953

vi

Designed by R. Hunter Middleton. An outline lineale following the nineteenth-century model.

ABCDEFGHIJKLMNOPQRSTUVWXYZ&
abcdefghijklmnopqrstuvwxyz
1234567890

CONDENSED GOTHIC OUTLINE

CONTACT
Ludwig & Mayer 1968

ix

Designed by Imre Reiner.   A bold slightly inclined brush script.   There are a few slight serifs and some vertical strokes are curved. In the lower case ascenders and descenders are very short. The **a** and **y** have italic forms. There are two weights.

A B C D E F G H I J K L M
N O P Q R S T U V W X Y Z
a b c d e f g h i j k l m n o p q r
s t u v w x y z æ œ ff fi ffi fl ffl
1 2 3 4 5 6 7 8 9 0

CONTACT

CYCLONE
Fanfare Press

vi

Designed by W. Ingram. An inclined and condensed titling. The tail of the **Q** is short and entirely outside the bowl. The **G** has a pointed spur, and the vertical strokes in straight letters are inclined at the foot and top.

ABCDEFGHIJKLMNOPQRSTUVWXYZ
1234567890

CYCLONE

DELIA
Simoncini 1962

vi

Designed by Francesco Simoncini. A newspaper type for classified advertisements almost linear in style but with expanding feet. The characters avoid parallel lines, there is variation of stress, normally straight lines are slightly curved, and especially in the lower case there are gaps between the strokes. All this is designed to prevent any filling in on newsprint.

ABCDEFGHIJKLMNOPQRSTUVWXYZ abcdefghijklmnopqrstuvwxyz 1234567890

ABCDEFGHIJKLMNOPQRSTUVWXYZ abcdefghijklmnopqrstuvwxyz 1234567890

DELIA

DIGI GROTESK
Hell 1968

vi

A lineale specially designed for cathode ray tube phototypesetting and based on German lineals. VIDEO TECHNICA is similar.

ABCDEFGHIJKLMNOPQRSTUVWXYZ
abcdefghijklmnopqrstuvwxyz
1234567890

DIGI GROTESK

ABCDEFGHIJKLMNOPQRSTUVW XYZ
1234567890

DIGI GROTESK BOLD

A stencil type following the DIN German industrial standard lettering style used by engineers and drawing offices.

ABCDEFGHIJKLMNOPQRSTUVW
abcdefghijklmnopqrstuvwxyz
1234567890

DIN

Designed by Max Salzmann. A heavy type with considerable variation in colour. The bars of **A** and **H** are triangular pieces. The lower-case letters are very wide and descenders very short. The **j**, **p** and **q** are cut off obliquely at the feet. There is also a decorated face, called ZIERDOLMEN.

Aus römischen Sagen   MAINZER JAHRBUCH

DOLMEN

GUNTHER

ZIERDOLMEN

Designed by Pete Dom. A lineale which is almost monotone and has letters freely or casually drawn. Vertical strokes are irregular ending at different heights, and some are slightly shaped. There is some variation of stress in the rounded letters. Lanston Monotype's FLASH is similar and was designed by Edwin W. Sharr in 1939.

Amsterdam call the type POLKA.

DOM CASUAL   abcdefghijklmnopqrstuvw

DOM CASUAL

ABCDEFGHIJKLMNOPQRSTUVWXYZTT
abcdefghijklmnopqrstuvwxyz 12345678

DOM DIAGONAL

ALL KNIGHTS OF THE MIDDLE AG
After an apprenticeship as page and

DOM BOLD

DORIC 1 ITALIC
Stephenson Blake

One of the late nineteenth-century designs from Germany cut by John in Hambury in 1892. Amsterdam call the type OLD GOTHIC BOLD and Fonderie Typographique Française call it WASHINGTON.

vi

ABCDEFGHIJKLMNOPQRSTU

VWXYZÆŒ

abcdefghijklmnopqrstuvwxyz

1234567890

DORIC No. 1 ITALIC

DORIC 12
Stephenson Blake

One of the early sans serif designs from Caslon. It has the two English characteristics of a uniform width of capitals and a nearer approach to contemporary romans in the lower case. Note the wide **E** and **R**, and the design of the **a** and **g**. Intertype DORIC (1962) is a quite different type design and is duplexed with ROYAL under which heading it is shown.

vi

MANCHESTER HO
Distinguished Master

DORIC 12

DRESCHER INITIALS
Schriftguss 1927

Designed by A. Drescher. An open lineale titling with letters of equal width. The **M** is square.

UNIVERSUM

vi

DRESCHER INITIALS

DUPLEX
Typoart 1930

Designed by Arno Drescher. A titling type with fine incline and heavy centre strokes.

vi

ABCDEFGHIJKLMNOPQRSTUVWXYZAMW
DIE SCHRIFT WURDE DIE TRÄGERIN DES

DUPLEX

Designed by K. Sommer. Vertical strokes are thickened slightly where normally serifs would be found. Some of the capitals are unequal across the top. MOTOR is a partially shaded version of this type.

DYNAMO
Ludwig & Mayer 1930

ix

ABCDEFGHIJKLMNO PORSTUVWXYZ 1234567890

DYNAMO

ABCDEFGHIJKLMNO PORSTUVWXYZ 1234567890

ix

MOTOR

A type face designed to meet the needs of magnetic character recognition in automatic cheque and document reading equipment. MOORE COMPUTER complements the numerals.

E 13 B
Monotype and others

ix

1234567890

E 13 B

Designed by Peter Bell. A three-dimensional lineale with open letters.

ECHO
Stephenson Blake 1956

vi

ABCDEFGHIJKLMN OPQRSTUVWXYZ abcdefghijklmnop qrstuvwxyz 1234567890

ECHO

Originally issued by Wagner & Schmidt around 1914 as WOTAN, and taken on by many German typefounders. Wagner have combined their LESSING, WOTAN and REICHSGROTESK under this name. The extra bold wide is ANNONCE GROTESQUE. Several versions were added to the original type faces.

vi

ABCDEFGHIJKLMNOPQ
RSTUVWXZ
1234567890
abcdefghijklmnopqrstuvwz

EDEL GROTESQUE LIGHT EXTENDED or GROTESQUE LIGHT

vi

ABCDEFGHIJKLMNOPQRSTUVW
abcdefghijklmnopqrstuvwxyz

EDEL GROTESQUE LIGHT or WOTAN LIGHT

vi

ABCDEFGHIJKLMNOPQRSTUVW
abcdefghijklmnopqrstuvwxyz
1234567890

EDEL GROTESQUE MEDIUM or WOTAN MEDIUM

vi

ABCDEFGHIJKLMNOPQRSTU
abcdefghijklmnopqrstuvwxyz

WOTAN BOLD

vi

ABCDEFGHIJKLMNOP
QRSTUVWXYZ
abcdefghijklmnopqrstuvz

EDEL GROTESQUE BOLD EXTENDED or LESSING GROTESQUE BOLD

vi

ABCDEFGHIJKLMNOPQRSTUVWXYZ
abcdefghijklmnopqrstuvwxyz

EDEL GROTESQUE BOLD CONDENSED or WOTAN BOLD CONDENSED

266

Designed by Carlos Winkow. A sans serif following Continental models. In the **A** and **E** the bars protude to the left, and the **M** is splayed. The **a** is one storeyed. There is a semi-bold and a bold, and in these the bar of the **A** becomes a triangle. There are condensed faces for two weights and also an inline version.

Demostraciones científicas sobre gases metaloides
PROPIAS TRIBULACIONES

ELECTRA FINA

vi

El doctor Merino en la Cátedra de Alta Cultura
CAMINO INADECUADO

ELECTRA SEMINEGRA

vi

Deliciosa e inconfundiblemente encantadora
CONOCIMIENTO GENERAL

ELECTRA NEGRA

vi

Dieron la vuelta al mundo montados en bicicleta
MARAVILLOSO PANORAMA

ELECTRA CURSIVA

vi

Conferencia del doctor Rodrigáñez sobre los valores nutritivos de la miel
ARQUITECTURA ARABE EN LA PENINSULA

ELECTRA ESTRECHA FINA

vi

Recepción en honor de los Miembros del Congreso Internacional
GRAN CONCIERTO DE MUSICA CLASICA

ELECTRA ESTRECHA NEGRA

vi

ABCDEFGHIJKLMNOPQRSTUVWXYZ

ELECTRA CLARA

vi

Designed by Hans Möhring. The **G** is wide, the **M** square with the middle strokes stopping short of the line. **E** and especially **T** are narrow. The lower case follows the usual continental model. There are many pointed terminations of vertical strokes. There are three weights and an inline. Stephenson Blake's GUILDFORD SANS is identical.

vi

Neue Rundschau

ELEGANT GROTESQUE LIGHT

vi

ABCDEFGHIJKLM NOPQRSTU VWXYZ
abcdefghijklmnopqrstuvwxyz
1234567890

ELEGANT GROTESQUE

vi

Ein kurzer Rückblick mag über die Verwendung der Elektrizität in der Medizin

ELEGANT GROTESQUE   MEDIUM BOLD

vi

A B C D E F G H I J K L M N O P Q R S T U V W X Y Z &

ELEGANT GROTESQUE INLINE

vi

SPORTKLUB

ELEGANT GROTESQUE BOLD

A condensed titling. The top of the **A** is rounded, and the horizontal strokes of **A**, **E**, **H** and **R** are central.

vi

ABCDEFGHIJKLMNOPQRSTUVWXYZ
1234567890

IRIS

Letters have very slight inclination, originally designed as a photolettering style by Studio Hollenstein of Paris. The type supplements the large display sizes of the photolettering design.

vi

ABCDEFGHIJKLMNOPQRSTUVWXYZ ÄÖÜ ÆOE
abcdefghijklmnopqrstuvwxyz
§& 1234567890 ß

ERAS

Designed by J. Erbar. One of the first and most popular of the new sans. **A** has a low bar. **E**, **F**, **L** and especially **T** are narrow. The tail of the **Q** is a short horizontal stroke. The **a** is one-storeyed, **g** has an open tail, and **t** has the top cut off at any angle.

There are four weights, with italic and condensed faces. The bold face has also an inline called PHOSPHOR. A set of capitals, white on black, is called LUCINA and an open version LUMINA. There are four weights of ERBAR CONDENSED on Mergenthaler Linotype and two weights on Linotype (London).

ERBAR
Ludwig & Mayer 1922–30 & 1960;

Linotype (Frankfurt);

Mergenthaler Linotype 1933–37;

Linotype (London);

Typograph

ABCDEFGHIJKLMNOPQRSTUVWXYZ

abcdefghijklmnopqrstuvwxyz

1234567890

ERBAR BOOK (LUDWIG & MAYER)

ABCDEFGHIJKLMNOPQRSTUVWXYZ
12345 abcdefghijklmnopqrstuvwxyz 67890

When it is considered that it was the intention to make the book one of practical instruction, and that it was written with the hope that it might be placed in the hands of each printer's boy on entering the business, I trust this sin of inelegance may [from Savage's Dictionary

LINOTYPE ERBAR BOLD

vi

ABCDEFGHIJKLMNOPQRSTUVWXYZ
12345 abcdefghijklmnopqrstuvwxyz 67890

MERGENTHALER LINOTYPE ERBAR MEDIUM CONDENSED

vi

ABCDEFGHIJKLMNOPQRSTUVWXYZ
12345 abcdefghijklmnopqrstuvwxyz 67890

ABCDEFGHIJKLMNOPQRSTUVWXYZ

When it is considered that it was the intention to make the book one of practical instruction, and that it was written with the hope that it might be placed in the hands of each printer's boy on entering the business, I trust this sin of inelegance may be pardoned. No one but [from Savage's Dictionary

LINOTYPE ERBAR LIGHT CONDENSED

vi

ABCDEFGHIJKLMNOPQRSTUVWXYZ
12345 abcdefghijklmnopqrstuvwxyz 67890

ABCDEFGHIJKLMNOPQRSTUVWXYZ

When it is considered that it was the intention to make the book one of practical instruction, and that it was written with the hope that it might be placed in the hands of each printer's boy on entering the business, I trust this sin of inelegance may be pardoned. No one but [from Savage's Dictionary

LINOTYPE ERBAR BOLD CONDENSED

vi

THE PRIMARY FUNCTION of type is

ERBAR LIGHT

vi

THE PRIMARY FUNCTION of type is that it shall be read, and the first considera-

vi

THE PRIMARY FUNCTION of type is that it

ERBAR

THE PRIMARY FUNCTION of type is

ERBAR MEDIUM

THE PRIMARY FUNCTION of type is that it shall be read, and the first

THE PRIMARY FUNCTION of type

ERBAR BOLD

THE PRIMARY FUNCTION of type is that it shall be read,

ERBAR CONDENSED

THE PRIMARY FUNCTION of type is that it shall

ERBAR MEDIUM CONDENSED

JAHRESBERICHT

LUCINA

FERD

LUMINA

ABCDEFGHIJKLMNOPQRST UVWXYZ 1234567890

LUX

ABCDEFGHIJKLMNOPQRS TUVWXYZ 1234567890

PHOSPHOR

Designed by A. Novarese. A new series to complement the same founder's MICROGRAMMA titling types by offering a lower case. Letters are square-shaped, and have some pen-drawn characteristics. There are several weights in preparation.

EUROSTILE

Nebiolo 1962

vi

ABCDEFGHIJKLMNOPQRSTUVXY
ZW

abcdefghijklmnopqrstuvxyzw

1234567890

EUROSTILE

vi

ABCDEFGHIJKLMNOPQRSTUVXYZW

abcdefghijklmnopqrstuvxyzw

1234567890

EUROSTILE CONDENSED

vi

ABCDEFGHIJKLMNOPQ
RSTUVXYZW

abcdefghijklmnopqrstuvx
yzw

1234567890

EUROSTILE EXTENDED

vi

ABCDEFGHIJKLMNO
PQRSTUVXYZW

abcdefghijklmnopqrstu
vxyzw

1234567890

EUROSTILE BOLD EXTENDED

vi

EUROSTILE

ABCDEFGHIJKLMNOPQRSTUVXYZW

abcdefghijklmnopqrstuvxyzw

1234567890

EUROSTILE BOLD CONDENSED

vi

ABCDEFGHIJKLMNOPQRSTUVXYZW

abcdefghijklmnopqrstuvxyzw

1234567890

EUROSTILE COMPACT

vi

ABCDEFGHIJKLMNOPQRSTUV
XYZW

abcdefghijklmnopqrstuvxyzw

1234567890

EUROSTILE BOLD

Designed by Louis Oppenheim. An extra bold lineale of unusual angular design.

FANFARE
Berthold 1927

ix

Lehrbuch für Gartenbau

FANFARE

FEDER
GROTESK
Ludwig & Mayer 1910

vi

Designed by J. Erbar. A bold sans serif italic, which is not monotone. The arms of **E** and **F**, etc., are comparatively light. The tops of the short ascenders are cut off obliquely.

ABCDEFGHIJKLM
NOPQRSTUVWXYZ
1234567890
abcdefghijklmnopqr
ſßstuvwxyz

ix

Frühjahrsmod

FEDER ITALIC

Designed by Phillip Boydell and his associates of the London Press Exchange for Festival advertising and to commemorate the Festival of Britain. Based upon condensed sans italic capitals it has a three-dimensional form making it suitable for use in exhibition display typography. Capitals and numerals only.

ABCDEFGHIJKLMNOPQRST
UVWXYZ
1234567890

FESTIVAL

Designed by Marcel Jacno. Sans serif capitals and figures. The face of the letters is in white and they are three-dimensional. They are placed on a criblé ground.

ABCDEFGHIJKLM
NOPQRSTUVXYZ

FILM

Designed by Hans Möhring. Light sans serif capitals, which are not monotone. Upstrokes, arms, etc., are half the weight of the downstrokes. In the **M** the middle strokes stop short of the line.

ABCDEFGHIJKLMNOPQRSTUVW
1234567890

FLORIDA

Designed by Imre Reiner. A three-dimensional angular titling in which the faces of letters are horizontally shaded.

ABCDEFGHIJKLMNOPQRS
TUVWXYZ
1234567890

FLORIDE

Designed by Konrad F. Bauer and Walter Baum. Fonderie Typographique Francaise call this type CARAVELLE. A sans serif following nineteenth century models, e.g., the **G** and **M**. There are 17 versions of the basic design.

vi

ABCDEFGHIJKLMNOPQRSTUVO
abcdefghijklmnopqrstuvwxyzabcdel
1234567890

ABCDEFGHIJKLMNOPQRSTUVX
abcdefghijklmnopqrstuvwxyzabcdz
1234567890

FOLIO LIGHT

vi

ABCDEFGHIJKLMNOPQRSTUYZ
abcdefghijklmnopqrstuvwxyzabcde
1234567890

FOLIO MEDIUM

vi

ABCDEFGHIJKLMNOPQRSW
abcdefghijklmnopqrstuvxyz
1234567890

ABCDEFGHIJKLMNOPQRSZ
abcdefghijklmnopqrstuwyr
1234567890

FOLIO MEDIUM EXTENDED

vi

ABCDEFGHIJKLMNOPQRSTW
abcdefghijklmnopqrstuvwj
1234567890

FOLIO EXTRA BOLD

vi

ABCDEFGHIJKLMNOPQRSTUVWXYZABCDEFGH
abcdefghijklmnopqrstuvwxyzabcdefghijklmj
1234567890

FOLIO BOLD CONDENSED

Designed under the direction of Aldo Novarese, by a team of designers including Franco Grignani, Giancarlo Iliprandi, Bruno Munari, Ilio Negri, Till Neuburg, Luigi Oriani and Pino Tovaglia. A "waisted" type with strokes of characters slightly thickened towards their ends to provide for improved readability in continuous texts and better reproducibility.

FORMA

Nebiolo 1966–70

vi

ABCDEFGHIJKLMNOPQRSTUVX
abcdefghijklmnopqrstuvxyzw
1234567890

ABCDEFGHIJKLMNOPQRSTUVX
abcdefghijklmnopqrstuvxyzw
1234567890

FORMA

ABCDEFGHIJKLMNOPQRSTUVX
abcdefghijklmnopqrstuvxyzw
1234567890

vi

FORMA BOLD

ABCDEFGHIJKLMNOPQRSTUV
abcdefghijklmnopqrstuvwxyz
XYZ 1234567890

vi

FORMA CONTORNATA

Designed by Morris F. Benton. A heavy sans serif after the English models. Note the **G**, upper and lower case, and the square **M**. Ludlow's version is somewhat taller.

FRANKLIN
GOTHIC

*American Typefounders
1903–12;.
Lanston Monotype;
Ludlow; Intertype*

ABCDEFGHIJKLMNOPQRSTUVWXYZ
abcdefghijklmnopqrstuvwxyz
1234567890

vi

FRANKLIN GOTHIC EXTRA CONDENSED

ABCDEFGHIJKLMNOPQRSTUVWXYZ
abcdefghijklmnopqrstuvwxyz
1234567890

vi

FRANKLIN GOTHIC CONDENSED

ABCDEFGHIJKLMNOPQRSTU
VWXYZ
abcdefghijklmnopqrstuvwxyz
1234567890

ABCDEFGHIJKLMNOPQRSTU
VWXYZ
abcdefghijklmnopqrstuvwxyz
1234567890

FRANKLIN GOTHIC

vi

ABCDEFGHIJKLMNOPQR
STUVWXYZ
abcdefghijklmnopqrstuv
wxyz 1234567890

FRANKLIN GOTHIC WIDE

vi

ABCDEFGHIJKLMNOPQRSTUVW
XYZ 1234567890
abcdefghijklmnopqrstuvwxyz

FRANKLIN GOTHIC CONDENSED ITALIC

FUNDAMENTAL

L. Wagner 1938

Designed by Arno Drescher. A sans serif with short descenders, in four weights and two condensed versions. The **b** has a spur at the foot; dots on letters like **i** and the German *Umlaut*-vowels are square. In the bold versions the curved strokes are narrow where they meet vertical strokes. The type is like SUPER GROTESQUE, but the **M** in the latter is splayed.

vi

Elektrische Geräte im Kraftfahrzeug

FUNDAMENTAL LIGHT ITALIC

vi

des Magnetismus und der Elektrizität

FUNDAMENTAL LIGHT CONDENSED

vi

Kapazität einer Sammlerbatterie

FUNDAMENTAL MEDIUM

276

Laden der Sammler mit der Lichtmaschine

FUNDAMENTAL BOLD CONDENSED

Unterbrecher und Kondensator

FUNDAMENTAL BOLD

Primär- und Sekundär-Stromkreise

FUNDAMENTAL EXTRA BOLD CONDENSED

Designed by Paul Renner. One of the popular German sans. The **M** is splayed, the **Q** has a straight tail starting inside the bowl, the **T** is narrow but less so than in Erbar. The **a** is one-storeyed, **g** has the usual open tail, **t** is square across the top, and **u** has the design of the upper case. There are six weights, a condensed in three weights, and an inline. Deberny & Peignot also issue this type and call it EUROPE. SPARTAN (American Typefounders and Mergenthaler Linotype) is rather similar to this German design, although also similar to ERBAR. FUTURA BOOK—not shown here—is also on German Linotype (Frankfurt).

FUTURA BLACK differs considerably from the main series. By the omission of the thin strokes many of the letters are formed of three and others of two detached parts. The lower-case **r** for example consists of a thick vertical stroke and a detached blob. It resembles a stencil type.

Intertype and Intertype (Fotosetter) FUTURA EXTRA BOLD were designed (roman) by Edwin W. Shaar in 1952 and (italic) by Edwin W. Shaar and Tommy Thompson in 1955.

ABCDEFGHIJKLMNOPQRSTUVWXYZ
abcdefghijklmnopqrstuvwxyz
1234567890

FUTURA LIGHT

ABCDEFGHIJKLMNOPQRSTUVWXYZ
abcdefghijklmnopqrstuvwxyz
1234567890

FUTURA LIGHT OBLIQUE

ABCDEFGHIJKLMNOPQRSTUVWXYZ
abcdefghijklmnopqrstuvwxyz
1234567890

FUTURA LIGHT CONDENSED

FUTURA
Bauer 1927–30;
Intertype; Typograph
vi

ABCDEFGHIJKLMNOPQRSTUVWXYZ
abcdefghijklmnopqrstuvwxyz
1234567890

INTERTYPE FUTURA EXTRA BOLD CONDENSED OBLIQUE

vi

ABCDEFGHIJKLMNOPQRSTUVWXYZ
abcdefghijklmnopqrstuvwxyz
1234567890

ABCDEFGHIJKLMNOPQRSTUVWXYZ
abcdefghijklmnopqrstuvwxyz
1234567890

INTERTYPE FUTURA EXTRA BOLD WITH OBLIQUE

vi

ABCDEFGHIJKLMNOPQRSTUVWXYZ
abcdefghijklmnopqrstuvwxyz
123456789

FUTURA DISPLAY

vi

ABCDEFGHIJKLMNOPQRSTU
VWXYZ
abcdefghijklmnopqrstuvwxyz
1234567890

FUTURA BLACK

vi

ABCDEFGHIJKLMNOPQRSTUVW
XYZ
1234567890

FUTURA INLINE

ABCDEFGHIJKLMNOPQRSTUVWXYZ

abcdefghijklmnopqrstuvwxyz

1234567890

ABCDEFGHIJKLMNOPQRSTUVWXYZ

abcdefghijklmnopqrstuvwxyz

1234567890

FUTURA BOOK

ABCDEFGHIJKLMNOPQRSTUVWXYZ
abcdefghijklmnopqrstuvwxyz
1234567890

ABCDEFGHIJKLMNOPQRSTUVWXYZ
abcdefghijklmnopqrstuvwxyz
1234567890

FUTURA BOOK WITH OBLIQUE

ABCDEFGHIJKLMNOPQRSTUVWXYZ
abcdefghijklmnopqrstuvwxyz
1234567890

FUTURA BOOK BOLD

ABCDEFGHIJKLMNOPQRSTUVWXYZ

abcdefghijklmnopqrstuvwxyz

1234567890

ABCDEFGHIJKLMNOPQRSTUVWXYZ

abcdefghijklmnopqrstuvwxyz

1234567890

FUTURA MEDIUM

ABCDEFGHIJKLMNOPQRSTUVWXYZ
abcdefghijklmnopqrstuvwxyz
1234567890

FUTURA MEDIUM CONDENSED

ABCDEFGHIJKLMNOPQRSTUVW
XYZ
abcdefghijklmnopqrstuvwxyz

FUTURA SEMI-BOLD

ABCDEFGHIJKLMNOPQRSTUV
WXYZ
abcdefghijklmnopqrstuvwxyz
1234567890

ABCDEFGHIJKLMNOPQRSTUV
WXYZ
abcdefghijklmnopqrstuvwxyz
1234567890

FUTURA BOLD AND FUTURA BOLD OBLIQUE

ABCDEFGHIJKLMNOPQRSTUVWXYZ
abcdefghijklmnopqrstuvwxyz
1234567890

FUTURA BOLD CONDENSED

ABCDEFGHIJKLMNOPQRSTUVWXYZ
abcdefghijklmnopqrstuvwxyz
1234567890

INTERTYPE FUTURA EXTRA BOLD CONDENSED

A newspaper type of large x-height.

ABCDEFGHIJKLMNOPQRSTUVWXYZ
abcdefghijklmnopqrstuvwxyz
1234567890

ABCDEFGHIJKLMNOPQRSTUVWXYZ
abcdefghijklmnopqrstuvwxyz
1234567890

GALAXY

vi

ABCDEFGHIJKLMNOPQRSTUVWXYZ
abcdefghijklmnopqrstuvwxyz
1234567890

GALAXY BOLD

Designed by Eric Gill. It owes something to the letters designed by Edward Johnston for the Underground Railways in 1918. In some ways it is closer in design to the original sans serifs than the modern German versions. There is a more uniform width of the capitals and the only points are at the feet of **V** and **W**. The final stroke in the **G** is shorter than in the German versions. The **M** is square and the middle strokes descend half-way. In the lower case the **a**, **g** and **t** follow the normal roman designs, but there are alternative sorts.

There are four weights, italic (with a one-storeyed **a**), a condensed and a GILL SHADOW, a three-dimensional letter. GILL CAMEO and KAYO are shown separately.

ABCDEFGHIJKLMNOPQRSTUVWXYZ
abcdefghijklmnopqrstuvwxyz
1234567890

vi

ABCDEFGHIJKLMNOPQRSTUVWXYZ
abcdefghijklmnopqrstuvwxyz
1234567890

GILL SANS LIGHT

ABCDEFGHIJKLMNOPQRSTUVWXYZ
abcdefghijklmnopqrstuvwxyz
1234567890

vi

ABCDEFGHIJKLMNOPQRSTUVWXYZ
abcdefghijklmnopqrstuvwxyz
1234567890

GILL SANS

ABCDEFGHIJKLMNOPQRSTUVWXYZ
1234567890

vi

GILL SANS MEDIUM

281

ABCDEFGHIJKLMNOPQRSTUVWXYZ

abcdefghijklmnopqrstuvwxyz

1234567890

vi

GILL SANS MEDIUM CONDENSED

vi

ABCDEFGHIJKLMNOPQRSTUVWXYZ

abcdefghijklmnopqrstuvwxyz

1234567890

ABCDEFGHIJKLMNOPQRSTUVWXYZ

abcdefghijklmnopqrstuvwxyz

1234567890

GILL SANS BOLD

vi

ABCDEFGHIJKLMNOPQRSTUVWXYZ

abcdefghijklmnopqrstuvwxyz

1234567890

GILL BOLD CONDENSED

vi

ABCDEFGHIJKLMNOPQRSTUVWXYZ

abcdefghijklmnopqrstuvwxyz

1234567890

GILL BOLD EXTRA CONDENSED

vi

ABCDEFGHIJKLMNOPQRSTUVWXYZ

abcdefghijklmnopqrstuvwxyz

1234567890

GILL EXTRA BOLD

vi

ABCDEFGHIJKLMNOPQRSTUVWXYZ

abcdefghijklmnopqrstuvwxyz

1234567890

GILL KAYO or SANS ULTRABOLD

THE MANY TYPES 12

GILL CAMEO

THE MANY TYPES 123

vi

GILL CAMEO RULED

VISIT CORNWALL

vi

GILL SHADOW TITLING

VISIT CORNWALL

vi

GILL SHADOW No. 1

ABCDEFGHIJKLMNOPQRSTU
VWXYZ

vi

abcdefghijklmnopqrstuvwxyz

vi

1234567890

vi

GILL SANS SHADOW LINE

First cut around 1906. There are condensed and extra condensed versions. The **E, F** and **H** have high cross-bars, and **V** and **W** in capitals and lower case have an angular finish to the stems of the caps.

ABCDEFGHIJKLMNOPQRS
TUVWXYZ&

vi

abcdefghijklmnopqrstuv
wxyz

1234567890

GLOBE GOTHIC

ABCDEFGHIJKLMNOPQRSTUVWXYZ

vi

abcdefghijklmnopqrstuvwxyz

1234567890

GLOBE GOTHIC CONDENSED

GOTHIC No. 13
Linotype (New York) 1912

vi

A traditional American condensed gothic or lineale.

ABCDEFGHIJKLMNOPQRSTUVWXYZ&
abcdefghijklmnopqrstuvwxyz
1234567890

GOTHIC NO. 13

GOTHIC CONDENSED No. 25
Linotype (London) 1956

vi

A sans serif after the English models, as in the spur of the **G** and the regularity in the width of the capitals.

ABCDEFGHIJKLMNOPQRSTUVWXYZ
abcdefghijklmnopqrstuvwxyz
1234567890

GOTHIC CONDENSED No. 25

GOTHIC OUTLINE NO. 61
American Typefounders c. 1890

vi

A set of outline sans serif capitals of nineteenth-century design. Note the **G** and **R**. The type was originally introduced by another American foundry around 1890.

BRAZIL AND OTHER COUNTRIES WERE SENDING TO PORTUGAL

GOTHIC OUTLINE NO. 61

GOUDY SANSERIF
Lanston Monotype 1930–31

vi

Designed by F.W. Goudy in 1925, with the bold originally called GOUDY GOTHIC and first shown in 1922. Some capitals are scriptorial.

AAABCDEFGHIJKLMNOPQRRSSTTUVWXYZ
aabcdeefghijklmnopqrstuvwxyz fiflffffiffl&
$1234567890

GOUDY SANSERIF

vi

AAABCDEFGHIJKLMNNOPQRRSSTTUVWXYZ
aabcdeefghijklmnopqrstuvwxyz fiflffffiffl&
$1234567890

GOUDY SANSERIF BOLD

The M is like GILL and the tail of the **Q** like FUTURA. The lower case follows the German model, except the **t** with a curved foot. The dot is diamond-shaped. There are four weights, with italic, a condensed face, an inline, white on black called CAMEO, and a GRANBY SHADOW, a three-dimensional letter.

ABCDEFGHIJKLMNOPQRSTUV
WXYZÆ
abcdefghijklmnopqrstuvwxyz
123456780

ABCDEFGHIJKLMNOPQRSTUVWXYZ
abcdefghijklmnopqrstuvwxyz
12345

GRANBY

ABCDEFGHIJKLMNOPQRSTUVWXYZ
abcdefghijklmnopqrstuvwxyz

ABCDEFGHIJKLMNOPQRSTUVWXYZ
abcdefghijklmnopqrstuvwxyz

GRANBY LIGHT

ABCDEFGHIJKLMNOPQRSTUVWXYZÆŒ
abcdefghijklmnopqrstuvwxyzæœ
1234567890

GRANBY LIGHT CONDENSED

ABCDEFGHIJKLMNOPQRSTUVWXYZÆŒ
abcdefghijklmnopqrstuvwxyzæœ
123456

GRANBY CONDENSED

ABCDEFGHIJKLMNOPQRSTUVWXYZ
abcdefghijklmnopqrstuvwxyz
123456

GRANBY BOLD CONDENSED

vi

vi

vi

vi

vi

285

ABCDEFGHIJKLMNOPQRSTUVWX
YZ&
abcdefghijklmnopqrstuvwxyz
£1234567890

GRANBY BOLD

vi

ABCDEFGHIJKLMNOPQRSTUVWX
YZÆŒ
abcdefghijklmnopqrstuvwxyzæœ
1234567890

GRANBY EXTRA BOLD

vi

ABCDEFGHIJKLMNOPQRSTU
VWXYZÆŒ
abcdefghijklmnopqrstuvwxyz
1234567890

GRANBY ELEPHANT

vi

ABCDEFGHIJKLMNOPQRST
UVWXYZ
£1234567890

GRANBY SHADOW

vi

ABCDEFGHIJKLMNOPQRSTUVWXYZ
abcdefghijklmnopqrstuvwxyzæœ
1234567890

GRANBY INLINE

vi

GRANBY CAMEO

Cut after original designs by Hermann Eidenbenz. A set of open, three-dimensional and condensed sans serif capitals and figures. The design is derived from a nineteenth-century model.

ABCDEFGHIJKLMNOPQRSTUVWXYZ
1234567890

GRAPHIQUE

A sans serif with thick and thin strokes. The thicks and thins meet at an angle and not in a curve. There is an additional oddity of a partial inline. Capitals and figures only.

ABDEGHJKMNPQRSTUVWXYZ
1234567890

GROCK

A modified light sans serif not unlike VOGUE and with tall ascenders. The Z has a bar at x-height level.

ABCDEFGHIJKLMNOPQRSTUVWXYZ

bdfhkl∫βt   Switzerland

GROTESKPFEILER

One of the early sans serifs, that of Thorowgood, 1832, was called GROTESQUE, and the name is still in use for sans serif types based on nineteenth-century models. The capitals are of equal width, the G has a spur and the M is square. The lower case follows the usual design of contemporary English romans, as in the a, e, g and t. The Monotype Corporation's HEADLINE BOLD closely follows Stephenson Blake's GROTESQUE NO. 9.

ABCDEFGHIJKLMNOPQRSTUVWXYZ
abcdefghijklmnopqrstuvwxyz

MONOTYPE GROTESQUE No. 1 BOLD

ABCDEFGHIJKLMNOPQRSTUV
WXYZ

GROTESQUE No. 3

ABCDEFGHIJKLMNOPQRSTUVWXYZ

abcdefghijklmnopqrstuvwxyz

MONOTYPE GROTESQUE CONDENSED No. 4

ABCDEFGHIJKLMNOPQRSTUV
WXYZÆŒ&
abcdefghijklmnopqrstuvwxyzæ
œ£1234567890

GROTESQUE No. 8

vi

ABCDEFGHIJKLMNOPQRSTUVWXYZ
abcdefghijklmnopqrstuvwxyz
1234567890
ABCDEFGHIJKLMNOPQRSTUVWXYZ
abcdefghijklmnopqrstuvwxyz
1234567890

GROTESQUE NO. 9 (MONOTYPE HEADLINE BOLD)

vi

ABCDEFGHIJKLMNOPQRST
UVWXYZ
abcdefghijklmnoqrstuvwxyz
1234567890

GROTESQUE No. 10

vi

ABCDEFGHIJKLMNOPQRSTUV
WXYZ
1234567890

GROTESQUE No. 12

vi

ABCDEFGHIJKLMNOPQRSTUVWXYZÆ
Œ abcdefghijklmnopqrstuvwxyzæœ&
£1234567890

GROTESQUE No. 18

ABCDEFGHIJKLMNOPQRSTUVWXYZ
abcdefghijklmnopqrstuvwxyz
1234567890

GROTESQUE CONDENSED No. 33

ABCDEFGHIJKLMNO
PQRSTUVWXYZ
abcdefghijklmnopq
rstuvwxyzæœ
£&1234567890

GROTESQUE No. 66

ABCDEFGHIJKLMNOPQRSTUVWXYZÆŒ
abcdefghijklmnopqrstuvwxyzæœ&
£1234567890

GROTESQUE No. 77 '

ABCDEFGHIJKLMNOPQRSTUVWXYZ
abcdefghijklmnopqrstuvwxyz
1234567890
ABCDEFGHIJKLMNOPQRSTUVWXYZ
abcdefghijklmnopqrstuvwxyz
1234567890

GROTESQUE LIGHT No. 12 6

ABCDEFGHIJKLMNOPQRSTUVWXYZ
abcdefghijklmnopqrstuvwxyz
1234567890

GROTESQUE BOLD EXTENDED No. 150

ABCDEFGHIJKLMNOPQRSTUVWXYZ
abcdefghijklmnopqrstuvwxyz
1234567890

vi

GROTESQUE BOLD EXTENDED No. 150

vi

ABCDEFGHIJKLMNOPQRSTUVWXYZ
abcdefghijklmnopqrstuvwxyz
1234567890

ABCDEFGHIJKLMNOPQRSTUVWXYZ
abcdefghijklmnopqrstuvwxyz
1234567890

GROTESQUE No. 215

vi

ABCDEFGHIJKLMNOPQRSTUVWXYZ
abcdefghijklmnopqrstuvwxyz
1234567890

GROTESQUE BOLD No. 216

vi

ABCDEFGHIJKLMNOPQRSTUVWXYZ
abcdefghijklmnopqrstuvwxyz
1234567890

GROTESQUE CONDENSED No. 318

vi

ABCDEFGHIJKLMNOPQRSTUVWXYZ
abcdefghijklmnopqrstuvwxyz
1234567890

vi

ABCDEFGHIJKLMNOPQRSTUVWXYZ
abcdefghijklmnopqrstuvwxyz
1234567890

ABCDEFGHIJKLMNOPQRSTUVWXYZ
abcdefghijklmnopqrstuvwxyz
1234567890

GROTESQUE BOLD CONDENSED

ABCDEFGHIJKLMNOPQRSTUVWXYZ
1234567890

GROTESQUE BOLD CONDENSED TITLING

A condensed considerably elongated titling.

ABCDEFGHIJKLMNOP
QRSTUVWXYZ12345

GROTESQUE CONDENSED TITLING

A condensed lineale with short descenders.

ABCDEFGHIJKLMNOPQRSTUVWXYZ
abcdefghijklmnopqrstuvwxyz
1234567890

HANSEATIC

ABCDEFGHIJKLMNOPQRSTUVWXYZ
abcdefghijklmnopqrstuvwxyz
1234567890

HANSEATIC BOLD

A condensed and elongated sans serif, with short ascenders and descenders. The bars of **A**, **E**, **F** and **H**, and some of the up-strokes are thin. There is also a bold.

ABCDEFGHIJKLMNOPQRSTUVXYWZ
abcdefghijklmnopqrstuvyxwz
1234567890

HASTILE

ABCDEFGHIJKLMNOPQRSTUVXYWZ
abcdefghijklmnopqrstuvxywz
1234567890

HASTILE BOLD

HELION

Schriftguss 1935; Française 1935

Designed by Arno Drescher. Three-dimensional sans serif capitals, similar to FILM but on a white ground. The shading does not give a true three-dimensional effect and is very wide. In France the type is called HELIOS.

vi

ABCDEFGHIJKLMNOPQRSTUVWXYZ

HELION

HELVETICA

Haas 1957; Stempel; Linotype
(Frankfurt, London & New
York); Typograph

Designed by M. Miedinger. A traditional following the nineteenth-century style. The **a** has a curved spur and the tail of the **Q** is oblique. The type was formerly called NEUE HAAS GROTESK.

vi

ABCDEFGHIJKLMNOPQRSTUVWXYZ
abcdefghijklmnopqrstuvwxyz
£1234567890

ABCDEFGHIJKLMNOPQRSTUVWXYZ
abcdefghijklmnopqrstuvwxyz
£1234567890

HELVETICA LIGHT

vi

ABCDEFGHIJKLMNOPQRSTUVWXYZ&
abcdefghijklmnopqrstuvwxyz
1234567890

ABCDEFGHIJKLMNOPQRSTUVWXYZ&
abcdefghijklmnopqrstuvwxyz
1234567890

MERGENTHALER LINOTYPE HELVETICA LIGHT

vi

ABCDEFGHIJKLMNOPQRSTUVWXYZ
abcdefghijklmnopqrstuvwxyz
1234567890

ABCDEFGHIJKLMNOPQRSTUVWXYZ
abcdefghijklmnopqrstuvwxyz
1234567890

HELVETICA

292

ABCDEFGHIJKLMNOPQRSTUVWXYZ
abcdefghijklmnopqrstuvwxyz
£1234567890

HELVETICA CONDENSED

ABCDEFGHIJKLMNOPQRSTUVWXYZ&
abcdefghijklmnopqrstuvwxyz
1234567890

ABCDEFGHIJKLMNOPQRSTUVWXYZ&
abcdefghijklmnopqrstuvwxyz
1234567890

MERGENTHALER LINOTYPE HELVETICA

ABCDEFGHIJKLMNOPQRSTUV
abcdefghijklmnopqrstuvwxyz
£1234567890

HELVETICA EXTENDED

ABCDEFGHIJKLMNOPQRSTUVWXYZ
abcdefghijklmnopqrstuvwxyz
1234567890

ABCDEFGHIJKLMNOPQRSTUVWXYZ
abcdefghijklmnopqrstuvwxyz
1234567890

HELVETICA MEDIUM

ABCDEFGHIJKLMNOPQRSTUVWXYZ&
abcdefghijklmnopqrstuvwxyz
1234567890

ABCDEFGHIJKLMNOPQRSTUVWXYZ&
abcdefghijklmnopqrstuvwxyz
1234567890

MERGENTHALER LINOTYPE HELVETICA BOLD

ABCDEFGHIJKLMNOPQRSTUVWXYZ

abcdefghijklmnopqrstuvwxyz

1234567890

HELVETICA BOLD

ABCDEFGHIJKLMNOPQRSTUVWXYZ

abcdefghijklmnopqrstuvwxyz

1234567890

ABCDEFGHIJKLMNOPQRSTUVWXYZ

abcdefghijklmnopqrstuvwxyz

1234567890

HELVETICA EXTRA BOLD

ABCDEFGHIJKLMNOPQRSTUVWXYZ

abcdefghijklmnopqrstuvwxyz

1234567890

HELVETICA BOLD CONDENSED

ABCDEFGHIJKLMNOPQRSTUVWXYZ

abcdefghijklmnopqrstuvwxyz

1234567890

HELVETICA COMPACT

ABCDEFGHIJKLMNOPQRSTUVWXYZ

abcdefghijklmnopqrstuvwxyz

1234567890

MERGENTHALER LINOTYPE HELVETICA EXTRA COMPRESSED

ABCDEFGHIJKLMNOPQRSTUVWXYZ

abcdefghijklmnopqrstuvwxyz

1234567890

MERGENTHALER LINOTYPE HELVETICA ULTRA COMPRESSED

Designed by Werner Rebhuhn in 1955 for Genzsch & Heyse. A heavy type with letters drawn casually. There is some variation of stress in the rounded, somewhat angular letters.

HOBBY

Berthold

ix

Die Wahl der richtigen Schrift

ABCDEFGHIJKLMNOPQRSTUVWXYZ

abcdefghijklmnopqrstuvwxyz

1234567890

HOBBY

Designed by Morris F. Benton. Vertical strokes and bars are curved, and there is some variation of stress. Descenders have been eliminated.

HOBO

American Typefounders 1910;
Intertype

ix

ABCDEFGHIJKLMNOPQRSTUV WXYZ

abcdefghijklmnopqrstuvwxyz

1234567890

HOBO

Designed by Max Miedinger. A heavy titling with almost square letters.

HORIZONTAL

Haas 1964

vi

ABCDEFGHIJKLMN OPQRSTUVWXYZ 1234567890

HORIZONTAL

Designed and cut in wood by A. van der Vossen. A heavy almost monotone lineale with very short ascenders and descenders. The chief characteristic is the squaring off of the curves in the lower case which is almost uncial.

HOUTSNEE-
LETTER

Enschedé 1927

ix

ABCDEFGHIJKLMNOPQRSTUVWXYZ abcdefghijklmnopqrstuvwxyz

HOUTSNEELETTER

HUXLEY VERTICAL
American Typefounders 1935

vi

Designed by Walter Huxley. The bars of the **A**, **B**, **E**, **F**, etc., are low and project to the left. **A**, **M** and **N** have each two sorts, one with a rounded top. There is also a second, rounded **W**.

HUXLEY VERTICAL

HUXLEY VERTICAL

LE DE FRANCE
Française 1960–61; Typograph

vi

Designed by E. Crous-Vidal. A lineale type but by no means monotone. In the bold face there is much variation of colour. In the semi-bold there are two capital **O**'s, one with vertical and one oblique stress. The **M** is splayed.

ABCDEFGHIJKLMNOPQRSTUVWXY

abcdefghijklmnopqrstuvwxyz

1234567890

ILE DE FRANCE

vi

ABCDEFGHIJKLMNOPQRSTUVW

abcdefghijklmnopqrstuvwxyz

1234567890

ILE DE FRANCE BOLD

vi

ABCDEFGHIJKLMNOPQRSTU
VWXYZ

abcdefghijklmnopqrstuvwxyz

1234567890

ILE DE FRANCE EXTRA BOLD

ILERDA or CHAMPS-ELYSÉES
Nacional 1954; Française 1956

vi

Designed by E. Crous-Vidal. A condensed slightly inclined lineale in the Continental style. The **A** has a rounded top, the **E** a low bar, and the lower case **t** an unusually low cross bar.

La vanidad, el orgullo, la soberbia y otras pasiones ciegan la inteligencia humana

LA EDUCACION DE LA VOLUNTAD

ILERDA

Designed by Geoffrey Lee. An extra bold type.

ABCDEFGHIJKLMNPOQRSTUVWX YZ J abcdefghijklmnopqrstuvwxyz r 1234567890&£$

IMPACT

Designed by G. Collette and J. Dufour. An extra bold stylized lineale.

Steam Traction NEIGHBOURS

INDEPENDANT

A rounded titling type with a horizontal straight white line running at half height through all characters. The type can also be used in two-colours using upper and lower halves to print in different colours.

ABCDEFGHIJKLMNOPQRSTUVW

INTERPOL

Designed by Rea Irvin and made by Lanston Monotype for the American magazine. Some letters of POST ROMAN are similar, but this type was designed for straight setting and no letter-spacing or fitting is being done in the columns of the *New Yorker*, thus retaining the informal character.

ABCDEFGHIJKLMNOPQRSTUVWXYZ

1234567890 &

IRVIN

Designed by Marcel Jacno. A lineale which is not monotone. The capitals **A**, **M**, **N** and **U** have the lower-case design; the **A** is one-storeyed.

a B C Ç D E F G

JACNO

A condensed titling with alternative rounded characters.

ABCDEFGHIJKLMNOPQRSTUVWXYZ KRSWM 1234567890

JEFFERSON GOTHIC

JIM CROW
American Typefounders c. 1890

vi

One of the quaint types of the period, a shaded three-dimensional and angular titling. Originally cast by the Dickinson Type Foundry, of Boston.

ABCDEFGHIJKLMNOPQR
STUVWXYZ
1234567890

JIM CROW

JOCUNDA
Monotype 1933

vi

Designed by Stanley Baxter. A type in which the bars of **A** and **H**, the centre arms of **E** and **F** protrude to the left, and these strokes are shaped. The tails of **K** and **R** and the top of **T** also are shaped.

ABCDEFGHIJKLMNOPQRSTUV
WXYZ

JOCUNDA

JOHNSTON'S RAILWAY TYPE or UNDERGROUND
London Transport (1918)

iv

Designed by Edward Johnston for the London Underground Railways. It is the first of the twentieth-century sans serifs. The proportions of the letters are based on old face and not on the designs of the nineteenth century. Eric Gill based some of his GILL SANS on this type, it is said.

ABCDEFGHIJKLMNOP
QRSTUVWXYZ
abcdefghijklmnopqrst
uvwxyz
1234567890&£

JOHNSTON'S RAILWAY TYPE

KAMENE
Grafotechna 1956

vi

Designed by Stanislav Marso.

ABCDEFGHIJKLMNOPQRSTUVWXYZ
abcdefghijklmnopqrstuvwxyz
1234567890

KAMENE

vi

ABCDEFGHIJKLMNOPQRSTUVWXYZ
abcdefghijklmnopqrstuvwxyz
1234567890

KAMENE BOLD

Designed by M. Dovey. A modified lineale type. The bars of the **A** and **H** are triangular pieces. The distinguishing feature is that in both upper and lower case the round letters are flat across the top.

KINO
Monotype 1930

ix

ABCDEFGHIJKLMNOPQRSTUVWXYZ

abcdefghijklmnopqrstuvwxyz

1234567890

KINO

Designed by J. Erbar. An extra bold type face which is not monotone and thus suggests a fat face. It needs only the addition of thin serifs to become a type like NUBIAN.

KOLOSS
Ludwig & Mayer 1923

vi

The best publicity

COMES FROM THE

KOLOSS

Sans serif bold capitals with horizontal shading. The **A**, **M** and **N** have rounded tops. Nebiolo's FREGIA MECANO is similar.

KOMBINETTE
Ludwig & Mayer 1932

vi

ABCDEF

KOMBINETTE

The **G** has a spur. The lower case follows the usual German model, with a one-storeyed **a**. The **t** has the top cut obliquely and a curved tail. There are four weights, with oblique faces, several extended faces, a condensed and an inline. Only caps in small sizes are now cast by Typoart.

KORALLE
Schelter & Giesecke 1913

vi

ABCDEFGHIJKLMNOPQRSTUVWXYZ
ABCDEFGHIJKLMNOPQRSTUVWXYZ

KORALLE LIGHT

ABCDEFGHIJKLMNOPQRSTUVWXYZ
ABCDEFGHIJKLMNOPQRSTUVWXYZ

vi

KORALLE LIGHT EXTENDED

ABCDEFGHIJKLMNOPQRSTUVWXYZ
ABCDEFGHIJKLMNOPQRSTUVWXYZ

vi

KORALLE EXTENDED

vi

KORALLE BOLD INLINE

The tail of the **J** descends below the line, the **M** is splayed and the **Q** has a short tail outside the bowl. Alternative **A, M, N, V** and **W** have flattened vertical strokes. The lower case follows the usual German model. The ascenders are rather taller than in most sans. There are three weights and a bold condensed. Originally cut by Wagner & Schmidt, and called POLAR by John in 1930 and also sold by Weber (RUND GROTESK), Berling (SAXO) and Iranzo (PREDILECTA), and under other names.

vi

ABCDEFGHIJKLMNOPQRSTUVWXYZ

abcdefghijklmnopqrstuvwxyz

KRISTALL GROTESQUE

vi

ABCDEFGHIJKLMNOPQRSTUVWXYZABCDEFGHIJKLMNOPQRSTUVWX

abcdefghijklmnopqrstuvwxyzabcdefghijklmnopqrstuvwxyzabcdefghijklmnopqrstuvwxyz

KRISTALL BOOK

vi

ABCDEFGHIJKLMNOPQRSTUVWXYZ

abcdefghijklmnopqrstuvwxyz

1234567890

ABCDEFGHIJKLMNOPQRSTUVWXYZ

abcdefghijklmnopqrstuvwxyz

KRISTALL GROTESQUE BOLD

vi

ABCDEFGHIJKLMNOPQRSTUVWXYZ

abcdefghijklmnoprqstuvwxyz

KRISTALL GROTESQUE BOLD CONDENSED

vi

ABCDEFGHIJKLMNOPQRSTUV

abcdefghijklmnopqrstuvwxyz

KRISTALL GROTESQUE EXTRA BOLD

vi

ABCDEFGHIJKLMNOPQRSTUVWXYZ

abcdefghijklmnopqrstuvwxyz

KRISTALL GROTESQUE EXTRA BOLD CONDENSED

vi

ABCDEFGHIJKLMNOPQRSTUVZ

KRISTALL BOOK INLINE

A three-dimensional lineale titling. The shadow is deeper and the letters are narrower than in HELION.

KUPFERBERG

LEUCHT
GROTESK
Schriftguss 1932

vi

LEUCHT GROTESK

A light lineale following American style.

ABCDEFGHIJKLMNOPQRSTUVWXYZ&
abcdefghijklmnopqrstuvwxyz
1234567890

LIGHTLINE
GOTHIC
American Typefounders

vi

LIGHTLINE GOTHIC

Designed by Umberto Fenocchio.

ABCDEFGHIJKLMNOPQRSTUVY
XWZ&GR
abcdefghijklmnopqrstuvwxyza
1234567890

LINEA
Cooperativa 1966–69

iv

LINEA

ABCDEFGHIJKLMNOPQRSTUV
WXYZ&GR
abcdefghijklmnopqrstuvwxyza
1234567890

iv

LINEA BOLD

ABCDEFGHIJKLMNOPQRSTUVWXYZ&GR
abcdefghijklmnopqrstuvwxyza
1234567890

vi

LINEA BOLD CONDENSED

ABCDEFGHIJKLMNOPQRSTUVWXYZ&
abcdefghijklmnopqrstuvwxyza
1234567890

LINEA EXTRA BOLD CONDENSED

A grotesque following the English model.

vi

ABCDEFGHIJKLMNOPQRSTUVWXYZ&ÆŒ
abcdefghijklmnopqrstuvwxyzæœ
1234567890
LINING GOTHIC TEXT

vi

ABCDEFGHIJKLMNOPQRSTUVWXYZ&
1234567890
LINING GOTHIC COMPRESSED CAPITALS

vi

A B C D E F G H I J K L M N O P Q R S T U V W X Y
Z & Æ Œ
a b c d e f g h i j k l m n o p q r s t u v w x y z æ œ
fi fl ff ffi ffl
1 2 3 4 5 6 7 8 9 0 £
LINING GOTHIC

vi

A B C D E F G H I J K L M N O P Q R S T U V W
X Y Z & Æ Œ
a b c d e f g h i j k l m n o p q r s t u v w x y z æ œ
fi fl ff ffi ffl
1 2 3 4 5 6 7 8 9 0 £
LINING GOTHIC BOLD

vi

A B C D E F G H I J K L M N O P Q R S T U V
W X Y Z & Æ Œ
a b c d e f g h i j k l m n o p q r s t u v w x y z æ œ
fi fl ff ffi ffl
1 2 3 4 5 6 7 8 9 0 £
LINING GOTHIC CONDENSED BOLD

vi

A B C D E F G H I J K L M N O P Q R S T U V W X Y Z
a b c d e f g h i j k l m n o p q r s t u v w x y z
1 2 3 4 5 6 7 8 9 0 &
LINING GOTHIC CONDENSED EXTRA BOLD

vi

ABCDEFGHIJKLMNOPQRSTUVWXYZ&ÆŒ
abcdefghijklmnopqrstuvwxyzæœ fiflffffiffl
1234567890
LINING GOTHIC BOLD EXPANDED

An English lineale with an expanding tail to the **Q**. For body sizes there is also a titling.
"Lining" means that the face is cast on standard line.

ABCDEFGHIJKLMNOPQRSTUV WXYZÆŒ
abcdefghijklmnopqrstuvwxyz
1234567890£&œæ

LINING SANS SERIF 25

A heavy type of even colour. The ends of all strokes are rounded. The dot on the **i** is an oval.
There is also an inline version.

Hilario WATER

MAMMOTH BLACK

MAMMOTH INLINE

Designed by Stanislav Marso.

ABCDEFGHIJKLMNOPQRS TUVWXYZ
abcdefghijklmnopqrstuvwxyz
1234567890

MARSO GROTESQUE

vi

ABCDEFGHIJKLMNOPQRS TUVWXYZ
abcdefghijklmnopqrstuvwxyz
1234567890

MARSO GROTESQUE BOLD

vi

ABCDEFGHIJKLMNOPQRS TUVWXYZ
abcdefghijklmnopqrstuvwxyz
1234567890

MARSO GROTESQUE EXTRA BOLD

Designed by Dick Dooijes. The **R** has a straight tail, and the tail of the **Q** is oblique and is outside the bowl only.

vi

ABCDEFGHIJKLMNOPQRSTUV
WXYZÆŒ
abcdefghijklmnopqrstuvwxyz
1234567890£&æœ

MERCATOR LIGHT

vi

ABCDEFGHIJKLMNOPQRSTUV
WXYZ
abcdefghijklmnopqrstuvwxyz
1234567890£&æœ

*ABCDEFGHIJKLMNOPQRSTU
VWXYZÆŒ
abcdefghijklmnopqrstuvwxyz
1234567890£&æœ*

MERCATOR

vi

ABCDEFGHIJKLMNOPQRSTUVWXYZ
abcdefghijklmnopqrstuvwxyz
1234567890

MERCATOR CONDENSED LIGHT

vi

**ABCDEFGHIJKLMNOPQRSTU
VWXYZÆŒ
abcdefghijklmnopqrstuvwxyz
1234567890£&æœ**

MERCATOR BOLD

ABCDEFGHIJKLMNOPQRS TUVWXYZÆŒ

abcdefghijklmnopqrstuvwxyz

1234567890£&æœ

MERCATOR BOLD ITALIC

ABCDEFGHIJKLMNOPQRSTUVWXYZ

abcdefghijklmnopqrstuvwxyz

1234567890

vi

MERCATOR BOLD CONDENSED ITALIC

Designed by Imre Reiner. A bold type which is not monotone and thus suggests a fat face. It is like KOLOSS, but is less bold and the thins are tapered.

ABCDEFGHIJKLMNOPQRST
abcdefghijklmnopqrstuvwxyz
1234567889

vi

MERIDIAN

Designed by Albert Auspurg. This sans has several peculiarities. The bars of the A and H, the centre arms of E and F are diamond-shaped. The tails of the K and R descend below the line. The e has an oblique stroke to the eye. There are three weights, the bold being capitals only, and an inline.

Euler & Hotz   LONDON

ix

MESSE GROTESK

PAPIERFABRIK

ix

MESSE GROTESK INLINE

305

METRO

Mergenthaler Linotype 1929–30;
Linotype (London)

Designed by W.A. Dwiggins. In the No. 1 series the **M** is straight-sided and **N, W, V** are un-pointed; in the No. 2 series the letters are splayed and pointed. The alternative characters convert No. 2 into No. 1. The **Q** has the tail attached to the left corner of the bowl. The lower case follows the Continental design. The **t** has a curved foot. The three weights are called METROLITE, METROMEDIUM and METROBLACK, and there is also a very light METROTHIN of the Mergenthaler Linotype.

vi

ABCDEFGHIJKLMNOPQRSTUVWXYZ AGJMNVWW

abcdefghijklmnopqrstuvwxyz agvwe

1234567890

METROTHIN No. 2

vi

ABCDEFGHIJKLMNOPQRSTUVWXYZ AGJMNVWW

abcdefghijklmnopqrstuvwxyz agvwe

1234567890

ABCDEFGHIJKLMNOPQRSTUVWXYZ AGJMNVWW

abcdefghijklmnopqrstuvwxyz agvwe

1234567890

METROMEDIUM No. 2

vi

ABCDEFGHIJKLMNOPQRSTUVWXYZ AGJMNVWW

abcdefghijklmnopqrstuvwxyz agvwe

123456789

ABCDEFGHIJKLMNOPQRSTUVWXYZ

abcdefghijklmnopqrstuvwxyz

234567890

METROLITE No. 2

vi

ABCDEFGHIJKLMNOPQRSTUVWXYZ

abcdefghijklmnopqrstuvwx

12345

METROBLACK

vi

ABCDEFGHIJKLMNOPQRSTUVWXYZ AGJMNVW

abcdefghijklmnopqrstuvwxyz agvwe

123456789

ABCDEFGHIJKLMNOPQRSTUVWXYZ AGJMNVW

abcdefghijklmnopqrstuvwxyz agvwe

234567890

METROBLACK No. 2

METROPOL

Nebiolo 1967

Designed by Aldo Novarese. A condensed extra bold type.

vi

ABCDEFGHIJKLMNOPQRSTUVXYZW

abcdefghijklmnopqrstuvxyzw

1234567890

METROPOL

Designed by A. Butti and A. Novarese. An angular titling face with no lower case. Basically these letters consist of squares with rounded corners. **M** and **N** have wide flattened strokes at the top and bottom. EUROSTYLE is similar and has a lower case.

ABCDEFGHIJKLMNOPQRSTUVXY
WZÆŒ&
1234567890

MICROGRAMMA CONDENSED

vi

ABCDEFGHIJKLMNOPQ
RSTUVXYWZÇÆŒ&
1234567890

MICROGRAMMA

vi

ABCDEFGHIJKLM
NOPQRSTUVXYZ
1234567890

MICROGRAMMA EXTENDED

vi

ABCDEFGHIJKLMNOP
QRSTUVWXYZÆŒ&
1234567890

MICROGRAMMA BOLD

vi

ABCDEFGHIJKL
MNOPQRSTUV
XYWZÇÆŒ&
1234567890

MICROGRAMMA BOLD EXTENDED

vi

MODERNIQUE
American Typefounders 1928

Designed by M.F. Benton. A type very like MERIDIEN, that is a mixture of lineale and fat face; the thick strokes are heavier than in Meridien. In place of the dot on **i** and **j** there is a solid segment.

vi

A B C D E F G H I J K L M N O P
Q R S T U V W X Y Z &
a b c d e f g h i j k l m n
o p q r s t u v w x y z
1 2 3 4 5 6 7 8 9 0

MODERNIQUE

MONTAN
Stempel 1954

Designed by A.M. Schildbach. A bold, condensed titling. In the **M** the centre arms stop short of the line.

vi

ABCDEFGHIJKLMNOPQRSTUVW
1234567890

MONTAN

MONUMENT
Genzsch & Heyse 1924

Designed by Heinrich Schmidt, and now incorporated in the REFORM or INFORMATION family of types. A lineale type of nineteenth-century design. The capitals are of equal width and the **M** square. In the lower case the **a** is two-storeyed and the **t** is rounded at the base.
There are three weights and also extended faces.

vi

Constantin ROSENHEIM

MONUMENT LIGHT

vi

Liedertafel

MONUMENT LIGHT EXTENDED

vi

Hansestädte

MONUMENT SEMI-BOLD

vi

Reisebild BREM

MONUMENT MEDIUM BOLD EXTENDED

vi

Holland MARN

MONUMENT BOLD EXTENDED

Designed by Martin Kausche. A set of bold sans serif capitals and figures of irregular design. The **C**, **D** and **Q** are like lower-case letters. The **M** is wide and splayed. The **W** equally wide. In some ways the design is like that of uncials.

ABCDEFGHIJKLMNOPQRSTUVWXYZ
1234567890

MOSAIK

A nineteenth-century design of tall, condensed letters with two-storeyed **a** and square dots on **i** and **j**. The **G** has a spur. ANTIQUES BOLD CONDENSED of Fonderie Typographique Française is identical. The type is also known as ADVERTISEMENT GROTESQUE CONDENSED.

ABCDEFGHIJKLMNOPQRSTUVWXYZ
abcdefghijklmnopqrstvwxyz
1234567890

NARROW GROTESQUE

Designed by G. de Milano. A modified lineale titling. The **A** has a rounded apex. **E**, **M**, **N** and **U** have lower-case design. NEON OMBRATA is a three-dimensional version.

ABCDEFGHIJKLMNOPQRSTUVWXYZ
1234567890

NEON BOLD

vi

ABCDEFGHIJKLMNOPQRSTUVWXYZ
1234567890

NEON

vi

ABCDEFGHIJKLMNOPQRSTUU
WXYZÇÆŒ&
1234567890

NEON OMBRATA

NEON
Weber 1936

Designed by W. Schaefer. A three-dimensional lineale titling. The face of the letters is thin and the shadow is deep. The bar of the A is low and in the M the middle stroke stops short of the line.

vi

ABCDEFGHIJKLMNOPQRSTUV
WXYZ
1234567890

NEON

NEULAND
Klingspor 1923

Designed by Rudolf Koch. Bold sans serif capitals, with some modifications. There is some angularity about the round letters, especially the C and G. Many strokes are cut off obliquely, as the centre arm of the E, the S, top of the T and the U. The M is splayed. Some vertical strokes are slightly concave. Monotype OTHELLO is an imitation of this design. This type is said to have been designed as cut, the shapes of individual letters therefore vary considerably from one size to another.

ix

ABCDEFGHIJKLMN
OPQRSTUVWXYZ
1234567890

NEULAND

NEW AURORA GROTESQUE
Weber 1966

A type face identical with NORMAL GROTESQUE but with ("new") bold condensed and extra bold condensed added later.

vi

ABCDEFGHIJKLMNOPQRSTUVWXYZ
abcdefghijklmnopqrstuvwxyz
1234567890

NEW AURORA GROTESQUE BOLD CONDENSED

vi

ABCDEFGHIJKLMNOPQRSTUVWXYZ
abcdefghijklmnopqrstuvwxyz
1234567890

NEW AURORA GROTESQUE EXTRA BOLD CONDENSED

310

The light faces were designed by Morris F. Benton for American Typefounders, but the new companion bold faces for Intertype were designed under the direction of H.R. Freund and are generally narrower than the original. New additional weights were added 1958–66, including designs by Frank Bartuska for American Typefounders.

ABCDEFGHIJKLMNOPQRSTUVWXYZ
abcdefghijklmnopqrstuvwxyz
1234567890

vi

NEWS GOTHIC

ABCDEFGHIJKLMNOPQRSTUVWXYZ
abcdefghijklmnopqrstuvwxyz
1234567890

vi

NEWS GOTHIC CONDENSED

ABCDEFGHIJKLMNOPQRSTUVWXYZ
abcdefghijklmnopqrstuvwxyz
1234567890

vi

NEWS GOTHIC EXTRA CONDENSED

ABCDEFGHIJKLMNOPQRSTUVWX
YZ abcdefghijklmnopqrstuvwxyz
1234567890

vi

NEWS GOTHIC BOLD

ABCDEFGHIJKLMNOPQRSTUVWXYZ
abcdefghijklmnopqrstuvwxyz
1234567890

vi

INTERTYPE NEWS GOTHIC CONDENSED

ABCDEFGHIJKLMNOPQRSTUVWXYZ
abcdefghijklmnopqrstuvwxyz
1234567890

vi

INTERTYPE NEWS GOTHIC BOLD CONDENSED

ABCDEFGHIJKLMNOPQRSTUVWXYZ
abcdefghijklmnopqrstuvwxyz
1234567890

INTERTYPE NEWS GOTHIC

vi

ABCDEFGHIJKLMNOPQRSTUVWXYZ
abcdefghijklmnopqrstuvwxyz
1234567890

INTERTYPE NEWS GOTHIC BOLD

vi

ABCDEFGHIJKLMNOPQRSTUVWXYZ
abcdefghijklmnopqrstuvwxyz
1234567890

INTERTYPE NEWS GOTHIC EXTENDED

vi

ABCDEFGHIJKLMNOPQRSTUVWXYZ
abcdefghijklmnopqrstuvwxyz
1234567890

INTERTYPE NEWS GOTHIC BOLD EXTENDED

NOBEL GROTESQUE
Amsterdam 1929–31; Intertype

A lineale after the Continental model, with some vertical strokes pointed. There are two M's, one square with the middle strokes ending half-way, and the other splayed. The **T** is narrowed. The **a** is one-storeyed and **g** has an open tail. The **t** has a curved terminal. There are three weights, with italics, a condensed medium and an inline.

vi

ABCDEFGHIJKLMNOPQRSTUVWXYZ
abcdefghijklmnopqrstuvwxyz
1234567890

ABCDEFGHIJKLMNOPQRSTUVWXY
abcdefghijklmnopqrstuvwxyz

NOBEL

312

ABCDEFGHIJKLMNOPQRSTUVWXYZ

abcdefghijklmnopqrstuvwxyz

vi

ABCDEFGHIJKLMNOPQRSTUVWXYZ

abcdefghijklmnopqrstuvwxyz

NOBEL LIGHT

ABCDEFGHIJKLMNOPQRSTUVWXY

vi

abcdefghijklmnopqrstuvwxyz

NOBEL BOLD

ABCDEFGHIJKLMNOPQRSTUVWXYZ

vi

abcdefghijklmnopqrstuvwxyz

NOBEL NARROW

ABCDEFGHIJKLMNOPQRSTUVWXYZ

vi

abcdefghijklmnopqrstuvwxyz

NOBEL NARROW BOLD

A B C D E F G H I J K L M M N

vi

O P Q R S T U V W X Y Z &

1 2 3 4 5 6 7 8 9 0

NOBEL INLINE CAPITALS

Based on AKZIDENZ GROTESK or STANDARD and modified by Edmund Thiele. The Berthold type of this name is different. In design this lineale is like English nineteenth-century models, *e.g.* the capitals are square and the **G** has a spur. But the lower-case **g** is of the German variety.
NORMAL GROTESQUE REGULAR was added in 1943. In the Linotype version the design of some of the letters has been modified.

vi

ABCDEFGHIJKLMNOPQRSTUVW
abcdefghijklmnopqrstuvwxyz

NORMAL GROTESQUE

vi

ABCDEFGHIJKLMNOPQRSTUV
abcdefghijklmnopqrstuvwxyz
1234567890

NORMAL GROTESQUE MEDIUM

vi

ABCDEFGHIJKLMNOPQRS
abcdefghijklmnopqrstuvwxy

NORMAL GROTESQUE BOLD

vi

ABCDEFGHIJKLMNOPQ
abcdefghijklmnopqrstuvw

NORMAL GROTESQUE LIGHT EXTENDED

vi

ABCDEFGHIJKLMNOP
abcdefghijklmnopqrstuv

NORMAL GROTESQUE MEDIUM EXTENDED

vi

ABCDEFGHIJKLMNO
abcdefghijklmnopqr

NORMAL GROTESQUE BOLD EXTENDED

vi

ABCDEFGHIJKLMNOPQRSTUVWXYZ
abcdefghijklmnopqrstuvwxyz
1234567890

NORMAL GROTESQUE REGULAR LIGHT

314

Designed by Morris F. Benton. A fat lineale face somewhat similar to KOLOSS but the arms of E and F are triangular pieces. Many of the vertical strokes are cut off obliquely.

NOVEL
GOTHIC
*American
Typefounders 1928*

vi

A B C D E F G H I J K L M N O P

Q R S T U V W X Y Z &

NOVEL GOTHIC

A lineale designed to meet optical character recognition criteria as defined by the US Bureau of Standards for business machine input and output printing.

OCR–A
American Typefounders 1968

ix

ABCDEFGHIJKLM NOPQRSTUVWXYZ

0123456789

OCR–A

Designed by Adrian Frutiger. In 1961 a technical committee was established by the European Computer Manufacturers Association (ECMA) to recommend standards for character recognition systems. The committee recommended two fount designs: the one to satisfy immediate requirements and the other (OCR—B) to "permit and encourage the widest possible use of optical character recognition by the use of character shapes which are as distinguishable as possible without undue sacrifice of their acceptability by the public as a general-purpose type fount".

The ECMA standard defines three sizes of letters (and envisages a fourth), but only sizes 1 and 2 are for normal printing purposes. If combined in a matrix-case arrangement for composition with some other fount, the OCR—B characters must be 10 to the inch.

OCR—B
Monotype 1968

vi

ABCDEFGHIJKLMNOPQRSTUVWXYZ

1234567890

OCR—B

Designed by Rudolf Koch. A set of capitals without serifs but not monotone. They have the appearance of having been drawn with a quill pen. The ends of arms and verticals are cut off obliquely. The capitals are intended for use with a gothic lower case. However, STEEL provides a roman lower case.

OFFENBACH
Klingspor c. 1935

ix

ABCDEFGHIKLMNOPQRSTUVWXYZ

aabcdefghijklmnopqrſstuvwxyzzchckßtz&

+1234567890

OFFENBACH

Designed by F.W. Kleukens. A fat face in which the serifs have almost disappeared; there is just a slight thickening at the ends of strokes. The thins have a considerable weight. The dot over the i is oblong.

OMEGA
Stempel 1926

ix

Süddeutschland

REFORMATION

OMEGA

ONDINA
Schriftguss 1935

Designed by K. Kranke. Shaded and inclined roman capitals.

DIPLOMA

ONDINA

OPTIMA
Stempel 1958; Linotype (Frankfurt) 1960

Designed by Hermann Zapf. A stressed sans serif with strokes thickened towards the end. The **M** is slightly splayed and the **g** has the Venetian form. This is a modified sans serif, intended as a text type. Like KLANG, which it does not, however, resemble, it can be described as either a calligraphic roman or a modified sans serif.

vi

ABCDEFGHIJKLMNOPQRSTUVW
abcdefghijklmnopqrstuvwxyz
1234567890
ABCDEFGHIJKLMNOPQRSTUVWXY
abcdefghijklmnopqrstuvwxyz
1234567890

OPTIMA

vi

ABCDEFGHIJKLMNOPQRSTUVW
abcdefghijklmnopqrstuvwxyz
1234567890

OPTIMA BOLD

vi

ABCDEFGHIJKLMNOPQRSTUVWXYZ&
abcdefghijklmnopqrstuvwxyz
1234567890

ABCDEFGHIJKLMNOPQRSTUVWXYZ&
abcdefghijklmnopqrstuvwxyz
1234567890

LINOTYPE (FRANKFURT) OPTIMA

vi

ABCDEFGHIJKLMNOPQRSTUVWXYZ&
abcdefghijklmnopqrstuvwxyz
1234567890

MERGENTHALER LINOTYPE OPTIMA MEDIUM

vi

ABCDEFGHIJKLMNOPQRSTUVWXYZ&
abcdefghijklmnopqrstuvwxyz
1234567890

LINOTYPE (FRANKFURT) OPTIMA BOLD

vi

ABCDEFGHIJKLMNOPQRSTUVWXYZ&
abcdefghijklmnopqrstuvwxyz
1234567890

MERGENTHALER LINOTYPE OPTIMA BLACK

An angular type in which curves are almost eliminated. **C, G, O**, etc., have straight sides. **A** has a flat top, **M, N** and **W** are like the lower-case letters. The **g** has an open tail.

The Monotype Corporation's OTHELLO, an imitation of NEULAND, is a set of capitals differing from the normal in some angular letters, *e.g.* the **G**. The **M** is slightly splayed. There is also OTHELLO SHADOW.

ix

ABCDEFGHIJKLMNOPQRSTUVW
XYZ&
abcdefghijklmnopqrstuv
1234567890

AMERICAN TYPEFOUNDERS OTHELLO

ix

ABCDEFGHIJKLMNOPQRSTUVWXYZ
1234567890

MONOTYPE OTHELLO

ix

ABCDEFGHIJKLMN

MONOTYPE OTHELLO SHADOW

Designed by W. Brudi. A three-dimensional open lineale titling, with somewhat condensed letters.

ORBIS
Stempel 1953

vi

ABCDEFGHIJKLMNOPQRSTUVWXYZ
1234567890

ORBIS

Designed by Hans Bohn. A three-dimensional lineale titling. **A** and **M** have flat tops. **K** and **R** have vertical tails. There are additional rounded-top **A** and **M**, and a round-based **W**.

ORPLID
Klingspor 1929

vi

ABCDEFGHIJKLMNOPQRSTUVWXYZ
1234567890

ORPLID

Designed by E. Crous-Vidal. A modified inclined lineale titling with a shaded version called FLASH (quite different from the Monotype Corporation's type of the same name). Letters have a calligraphic quality, and upward and horizontal strokes extend towards the ends. The **G** has a slight spur, and the cross-bar of the **T** gives the impression of being slightly curved. The tail of the **Q** is a wedge cutting through the foot of the bowl.

PARIS
Française 1953

ix

ABCDEFGHIJKLMNOPQRSTUV
WXYZÆŒ1234567890

PARIS LIGHT

317

ABCDEFGHIJKLMNOPQRSTU
VWXYZÆŒ 1234567890

ABCDEFGHIJKLMN
OOPQRSTUVWXYZ
ÆŒ1234567890

ABCDEFGHIJKLM
NOOPQRSTUVWX
1234567890

PARISIAN
American Typefounders 1928;
Intertype (New York)

Designed by M.F. Benton. The type is not monotone, but has abrupt variation of colour. The thins occupy much of the letter. There are two **E**'s and two **M**'s, one with short middle strokes. In the lower case the ascenders are tall. The lower-case **r** has a bowl. The **t** is a cross with an oblique top. Intertype's version is considerably modified.

IMPORTED GOWNS
Enthusiastic Buyer Rewarded

PASCAL
Amsterdam 1960

Designed by José Mendoza y Almeida. A type face with some variation in colour and of considerable weight. The **M** is somewhat splayed; the **g** has an open tail. Ascenders and descenders are short and the figures ranging. ILE DE FRANCE of Fonderie Typographique Française is similar; and also has a bold.

ABCDEFGHIJKLMNOPQRSTUV
WXYZÆŒ

abcdefghijklmnopqrstuvwxyz
1234567890£&æœ

Designed by A.M. Cassandre. A lineale in which the lower-case letters with the exception of **b**, **d** and **f**, are small capitals. It is an attempt to revive the original form of the roman alphabet. In the **h** the left-hand vertical is taller than the right. There are three weights and a titling.
Central Typefoundry had a type not unlike this one, which was called QUAINT GOTHIC.

PEIGNOT
Deberny & Peignot 1937

vi

ABCDEFGHIJKLMNOPQRSTUVWXYZ
abcdefghijklmnopqrstuvwxyz
1234567890 1234567890

PEIGNOT LIGHT

ABCDEFGHIJKLMNOPQRSTUVWXYZ
abcdefghijklmnopqrstuvwxyz
1234567890

PEIGNOT

ABCDEFGHIJKLMNOPQRSTUV
WXYZ
abcdefghijklmnopqrstuvwxyz
1234567890 1234567890

PEIGNOT BOLD

A B C D E F G H I J K L M N O P Q R S T U V
W X Y Z Œ &
1 2 3 4 5 6 7 8 9 0

INITIALS PEIGNOT ETROIT

Designed by Robert Foster. An angular titling with an unusual **E**. The tail of the **R** extends and is bent at a right angle.

PERICLES
American Typefounders 1934

vi

A B C D E Ƹ F G H I J K L M N O P Ǫ
W X Y Z & Ꞧ R S T U V
1 2 3 4 5 6 7 8 9 0

PERICLES

319

PERMANENT

Ludwig & Mayer 1962;
Simoncini

vi

Designed by Karlgeorg Hoefer.

ABCDEFGHIJKLMNOPQRSTUVWXYZ

abcdefghijklmnopqrstuvwxyz

1234567890

ABCDEFGHIJKLMNOPQRSTUVWXYZ
abcdefghijklmnopqrstuvwxyz
1234567890

ABCDEFGHIJKLMNOPQRSTUVWXYZ
abcdefghijklmnopqrstuvwxyz
1234567890

PERMANENT

vi

ABCDEFGHIJKLMNOPQRSTUVW
XYZ
abcdefghijklmnopqrstuvwxyz
1234567890

ABCDEFGHIJKLMNOPQRSTUVWXYZ
abcdefghijklmnopqrstuvwxyz
1234567890

PERMANENT MEDIUM

vi

ABCDEFGHIJKLMNOPQRSTUVWXYZ
abcdefghijklmnopqrstuvwxyz
1234567890

PERMANENT CONDENSED

vi

ABCDEFGHIJKLMNOPQRSTUVWXYZ
abcdefghijklmnopqrstuvwxyz
1234567890

PERMANENT BOLD CONDENSED

vi

ABCDEFGHIJKLMNOPQRSTUVW
XYZ
abcdefghijklmnopqrstuvwxyz
1234567890

PERMANENT BOLD

ABCDEFGHIJKLMNOPQRSTUVWX YZ abcdefghijklmnopqrstuvwxyz 1234567890

PERMANENT ULTRA BOLD COMPRESSED

Designed by M.F. Benton. A condensed type with rounded tops to **A** and **M**, and rounded base to the **W**. The bar of the **A** and arms of the **E** and **F** overlap to the left. The **g** has an open tail and **t** is a plain cross.
SHADOW is an open, three-dimensional set of capitals based on this design.

ABCDEFGHIJKLM NOPQRSTUVWXYZ &
abcdefghijklmnopqrstuvwxyz
1234567890

PHENIX

A condensed lineale with very short ascenders and descenders. The **M** is slightly splayed. The **g** has an open tail and the **t** is a cross.

ABCDEFGHIJKLMNOPQRSTUVWXYZ
abcdefghijklmnopqrstuvwxyz
1234567890

PLACARD BOLD CONDENSED

ABCDEFGHIJKLMNOPQRSTUVWXYZ
abcdefghijklmnopqrstuvwxyz
1234567890

PLACARD LIGHT EXTRA CONDENSED

ABCDEFGHIJKLMNOPQRSTUVWXYZ
abcdefghijklmnopqrstuvwxyz
1234567890

PLACARD CONDENSED

321

PLASTICA
Berthold

A three-dimensional version of BERTHOLD GROTESQUE without lower case. The plastic effect of this face is enhanced by the shading, which is done in perspective. UMBRA (Ludlow) is very similar and was designed by R. H. Middleton in 1935.

vi

FINE OLD TABLE WIN

PLASTICA

vi

ABCDEFGHIJKLMNOPQRSTUV
1234567890

UMBRA

OST MARCATO
Berthold 1963

Designed by Herbert Post. A bold display type having wood-cut qualities, with short ascenders and descenders.

vi

ABCDEFGHIJKLMNOPQRSTUVWXYZ
abcdefghijklmnopqrstuvwxyz

PRAZKE KAMENE
Grafotechna 1958
vi

Designed by Stanislav Marso. A condensed and elongated sans serif of medium weight.

ABCDEFGHIJKLMNOPQRSTUVWXYZ
abcdefghijklmnopqrstuvwxyz
1234567890

PRAZKE KAMENE

PRISMA
Klingspor 1931

An inline version of Rudolf Koch's CABLE. The shading is made by three parallel white lines. Capitals and ranging figures only.

vi

ABCDEFGHIJKLMNO
PQRSTUVWXYZ
1234567890

PRISMA

PSSITT
Française 1953

Designed by René Ponot. A lineale with some variation of colour. Note the lower-case **g** with a straight ear pointing north-east.

ix

ABCDEFGHIJKLMNOPQRSTUVWXYZÆŒ
abcdefghijklmnopqrstuvwxyzæœ

PSSITT

322

Designed by R.H. Middleton. The type is not monotone, and is somewhat condensed. The **G** has no spur and the **M** is square. The lower-case **g** has an open tail. The heavy version is like BRITANNIC or ROTHBURY.

Advertising Increases

ABCDEFGHIJKLMNOPQRSTUVWXYZ&
abcdefghijklmnopqrstuvwxyz
1234567890$

RADIANT MEDIUM

More Composition

RADIANT BOLD

Installed the Ludlow System

ABCDEFGHIJKLMNOPQRSTUVWXYZ&
abcdefghijklmnopqrstuvwxyz
1234567890$

RADIANT BOLD CONDENSED

Greater Appeal with Strong Dignity

RADIANT BOLD EXTRA CONDENSED

Big Machinery Ad

RADIANT HEAVY

vi

vi

vi

vi

vi

vi

Designed by G. da Milano. A condensed lineale titling which is negative on a square mesh background.

FREGIO RAZIONALE

FREGIO RAZIONALE

ABCDEFGHIJKLMNOPQRSTUVXYZW
[1234567890]

RAZIONALE

vi

vi

Designed by R.H. Middleton (except the earliest versions). A lineale type following the English design with several weights and with extended and condensed versions of both roman and italic. RECORD GOTHIC OFFSET is a mirror type.

vi

ABCDEFGHIJKLMNOPQRSTUVWXYZ&
abcdefghijklmnopqrstuvwxyz
1234567890$

RECORD GOTHIC

vi

ABCDEFGHIJKLMNOPQRSTUVWXYZ&
abcdefghijklmnopqrstuvwxyz
1234567890$

RECORD GOTHIC CONDENSED

vi

ABCDEFGHIJKLMNOPQRSTUVWXYZ&
abcdefghijklmnopqrstuvwxyz
1234567890$

ABCDEFGHIJKLMNOPQRSTUVWXYZ&
abcdefghijklmnopqrstuvwxyz
1234567890$

RECORD GOTHIC EXTRA CONDENSED

vi

ABCDEFGHIJKLMNOPQRSTUVWXYZ&
abcdefghijklmnopqrstuvwxyz
1234567890$

RECORD GOTHIC THINLINE CONDENSED

vi

ABCDEFGHIJKLMNOPQRSTUVWXYZ
abcdefgghijklmnopqrstuvwxyz
11234567890$

RECORD GOTHIC LIGHT MEDIUM EXTENDED

ABCDEFGHIJKLMNOPQRSTUVW
XYZ&
abcdefghijklmnopqrstuvwxyz
1234567890$

*ABCDEFGHIJKLMNOPQRSTUV
WXYZ&
abcdefghijklmnopqrstuv
wxyz
1234567890$*

RECORD GOTHIC EXTENDED

ABCDEFGHIJKLMNOPQRSTUV
WXYZ&
abcdefghijklmnopqrstuvwxyz
1234567890$

RECORD GOTHIC MEDIUM EXTENDED

**ABCDEFGHIJKLMNOPQRSTUVWXYZ&
abcdefghijklmnopqrstuvwxyz
1234567890$**

*ABCDEFGHIJKLMNOPQRSTUVWXYZ&
abcdefghijklmnopqrstuvwxyz
1234567890$*

RECORD GOTHIC BOLD

**ABCDEFGHIJKLMNOPQRSTU
VWXYZ&
abcdefghijklmnopqrstuvwxyz
1234567890$**

RECORD GOTHIC BOLD MEDIUM EXTENDED

vi

vi

vi

ABCDEFGHIJKLMNOPQRST
UVWXYZ&
abcdefghijklmnopqrstuvw
xyz
1234567890$

RECORD GOTHIC BOLD EXTENDED

vi

ABCDEFGHIJKLMNOPQRSTUVW
XYZ&
abcdefghijklmnopqrstuvwxyz
1234567890$

RECORD GOTHIC BOLD MEDIUM EXTENDED

vi

ABCDEFGHIJKLMNOPQRSTUVWXYZ
abcdefghijklmnopqrstuvwxyz
1234567890

RECORD GOTHIC BOLD CONDENSED

vi

ABCDEFGHIJKLMNOPQRSTUVWXY
abcdefghijklmnopqrstuvwxyz
Z1234567890

RECORD GOTHIC HEAVY CONDENSED

RECTA
Nebiolo 1958–61

Designed by Aldo Novarese. The **a** has a roman design and the **g** an open tail. There are ranging figures.

vi

ABCDEFGHIJKLMNOPQRSTUVXYZW
abcdefghijklmnopqrstuvxyzw
1234567890

RECTA LIGHT

vi

ABCDEFGHIJKLMNOPQRSTUVXYZW
abcdefghijklmnopqrstuvxyzw
1234567890

RECTA LIGHT CONDENSED

ABCDEFGHIJKLMNOPQRSTUVXYZW

abcdefghijklmnopqrstuvxyzw

1234567890

ABCDEFGHIJKLMNOPQRSTUVXYZW

abcdefghijklmnopqrstuvxyzw

1234567890

RECTA

A B C D E F G H I J K L M N O P Q R S T U
V W X Y Z

a b c d e f g h i j k l m n o p q r s t u v w x y z

1 2 3 4 5 6 7 8 9 0

RECTA MEDIUM CONDENSED

ABCDEFGHIJKLMNOPQRSTUVXYZW

abcdefghijklmnopqrstuvxyzw

1234567890

RECTA EXTRA CONDENSED

**ABCDEFGHIJKLMNOPQRSTU
V W X Y Z**

abcdefghijklmnopqrstuvwxyz

1234567890

*ABCDEFGHIJKLMNOPQRSTU
V W X Y Z*

abcdefghijklmnopqrstuvwxyz

1234567890

RECTA BOLD

ABCDEFGHIJKLMNOPQRSTU
VWXYZ
abcdefghijklmnopqrstuvwxyz
1234567890

*ABCDEFGHIJKLMNOPQRSTU
VWXYZ*
abcdefghijklmnopqrstuvwxyz
1234567890

RECTA CONDENSED BOLD

vi

**ABCDEFGHIJKLMNOPQRSTUVX
YZW
1234567890**

*ABCDEFGHIJKLMNOPQRSTUVX
YZW
1234567890*

RECTA CONDENSED BOLD

**REFORM
GROTESQUE and
INFORMATION**
Stempel

The **A** has a low bar, **E** and **F** are wide, **M** is square and **R** has a wide and short bowl. There is a slight variation of colour in the lower case—but not in the light face. The design was modernised in the 1930s. Klingspor called the type INFORMATION.

INFORMATION EXTRA BOLD WIDE was designed by F.K. Sallway in 1958 for Klingspor and taken over by Stempel, and in Germany called BREITE FETTE INFORMATION. Some of the MONUMENT types now also appear under this name.

vi

ABCDEFGHIJKLMNOPQRS
abcdefghijklmnopqrstuvz1234

REFORM GROTESQUE

vi

ABCDEFGHIJKLMNOPQRST
abcdefghijklmnopqrstuvwxyz

INFORMATION MEDIUM

ABCDEFGHIJKLMNOPQRSTUVW

REFORM
GROTESQUE

abcdefghijklmnopqrstuvwxyz

vi

INFORMATION MEDIUM

ABCDEFGHIJKLMN

vi

abcdefghijklmnopqrst

INFORMATION LIGHT EXTENDED

ABCDEFGHIJKLM

vi

abcdefghijklmnopqr

INFORMATION BOLD EXTENDED

ABCDEFGHIJKLMNOPQR

vi

abcdefghijklmnopqrstuvw

ABCDEFGHIJKLMNOPQRSTUVW

abcdefghijklmnopqrstuvwxyz

INFORMATION BOLD

ABCDEFGHIJKLMNOPQRSTUVWXYZ

vi

abcdefghijklmnopqrstuvwxyz

INFORMATION MEDIUM CONDENSED

ABCDEFGHIJKLMNOPQRSTUVWXYZ

vi

abcdefghijklmnopqrstuvwxyz

INFORMATION BOLD CONDENSED

ABCDEFGHIJKLMNOPQRSTUVWXYZ

vi

abcdefghijklmnopqrstuvwxyz

INFORMATION EXTRA BOLD CONDENSED

DEFGHIJKLMNOPQRSTUVWXY
abcdefghijklmnopqrstuvw
1234567

ABCDEFGHIJKLMNOPQRSTUVW

REFORM GROTESQUE LIGHT

vi

ABCDEFGHIJKLMNOPQRS
abcdefghijklmnopqr
1234567

ABCDEFGHIJKLMNOPQRS
defghijklmnopqrst
1234567

REFORM GROTESQUE BOLD

vi

ABCDEFGHIJKLMNOPQR
bcdefghijklmno
12345678

REFORM GROTESQUE EXTRA BOLD

vi

ABCDEFGHIJKLMNOPQRSTUVWXYZ
abcdefghijklmnopqrstuvwxyz

REFORM GROTESQUE EXTRA BOLD CONDENSED

vi

ABCDEFGHIJKLM
abcdefghijklmnop
1234567890

INFORMATION EXTRA BOLD WIDE

Designed by Zoltan Nagy as a display titling of calligraphic character. The **g** is curious.

ABCDEFGHIJKLM NOPQRSTUVWXYZ
fghijklmnopqrstuvwxyz

REKLAM

Designed by H. Brünnel. A mixture of fat face and lineale type. The letters where there would be normally hair lines there are complete breaks in the strokes. The **M** is splayed. Ascenders and descenders are very small, the **g** having an abbreviated tail. *Cf.* BASALT.

ABCDEFGHIJKLMNOPQRSTUVXZ
abcdefghijklmncpqrstuvxywz

RESOLUT

A German lineale. The bar of the **A** is low. The **G** has no spur. The **M** is pointed and the middle strokes stop short of the line. The **T** is narrow. The lower-case **a** is two-storeyed, the **g** has an open tail and the **t** is a plain cross. There are three weights.

Der Architekt und die moderne Baukunst **Erzeugnisse der optischen Industrie**

RYTHMUS   RHYTHMUS MEDIUM

Synthetic Fibres and Plastics

RYTHMUS BOLD

vi·

Designed by A. Novarese. The bars and some upstrokes are thinner than the main strokes.

ABCDEFGHIJKLMNOPQRSTUVXYZ
abcdefghijklmnopqrstuvxywz

RITMO

Originally designed by Matthews of the Inland Typefoundry around 1906 and cast by Caslon. A bold lineale which is not monotone, resembling KOLOSS and BRITANNIC.

MONMOUTH JOURNAL
Newport Parish Magazine
Christmas Reading
182nd Special Number

ROTHBURY

ROYAL GOTHIC

Stevens Shanks

vi

An extra bold type face with some variation of colour. The **g** has an open tail and the ascender of the **t** is not shorter than that of other letters with ascenders. The **G** has a spur on the foot of the line.

ABCDEFGHIJKLMNOPQRSTUVWXYZÆŒ
abcdefghijklmnopqrstuvwxyzæoe&$
1234657890

ABCDEFGHIJKLMNOPQRSTUVWXYZ
abcdefghijklmnoqrpstuvwxzæ
1234567890

ROYAL GOTHIC

SAMSON

Ludlow 1940

ix

Designed by R.H. Middleton. A heavy type face in which there is some gradation of colour.

ABCDEFGHIJKLMNOPQRST
UVWXYZ&
abcdefghijklmnopqrs
tuvwxyz

SAMSON

NARROW SANS ITALIC

Stephenson Blake

vi

This condensed and inclined sans serif follows the usual English nineteenth century model. *Cf.* NARROW GROTESQUE.

ABCDEFGHIJKLMNOPQRSTUVWXYZ
abcdefghijklmnopqrstuvwxyz
1234567890

SANS ITALIC NARROW

SANS SERIF CONDENSED

Stephenson Blake

vi

These designs are lighter versions of the same founders' GROTESQUE types.

ABCDEFGHIJKLMNOPQRSTUVWXYZ
abcdefghijklmnopqrstuvwxyz
1234567890

CONDENSED SANS SERIF No. 5

vi

ABCDEFGHIJKLMNOPQRSTUVWXYZ
abcdefghijklmnopqrstuvwxyz

CONDENSED SANS SERIF No. 7

A sans serif based on the GILL SANS family and practically identical, but with a straight tail to the **R**.

ABCDEFGHIJKLMNOPQRSTUVWXYZ

abcdefghijklmnopqrstuvwxyz

1234567890 &£

SANS SERIF No. 2

ABCDEFGHIJKLMNOPQRSTUVWXYZ

abcdefghijklmnopqrstuvwxyz

1234567890 &£

SANS SERIF No. 2 BOLD

A three-dimensional lineale titling. This is the type first shown by Thorowgood in 1839 as SANS SURRYPHS SHADED and forerunner of the English "sans serifs". Several founders had this type around the middle of the nineteenth century. The letters are of equal width, the **G** has a spur and the **M** is square.

ABCDEFGHIJKLMN
OPQRSTUVWXYZ
ÆŒ&£
1234567890

SANS SERIF SHADED

Designed by K.H. Schaefer. A heavy modified lineale titling on shaded ground. There are a few small serifs as on the **E** and **R**.

SCHAEFER VERSALIEN

Designed by Walter Diethelm. A three-dimensional condensed grotesque, with fine white inline.

ABCDEFGHIJKLMNOPQRS
TUVWXYZ
1234567890

SCULPTURA

A lineale following the Continental model. It may be distinguished by the vertical strokes in the **a** and **d**, which do not descend below the bowls. The **t** is a vertical with a bar on the right only.

vi

ABCDEFGHIJKLMNOPQRSTUVWXYZ
abcdefghijklmnopqrstuvwxyz
1234567890

ABCDEFGHIJKLMNOPQRSTUVWXYZ
abcdefghijklmnopqrstuvwxyz
1234567890

SEMPLICITÀ LIGHT

vi

ABCDEFGHIJKLMNOPQRSTUVWXYZ
abcdefghijklmnopqrstuvwxyz
1234567890

ABCDEFGHIJKLMNOPQRSTUVWXYZ
abcdefghijklmnopqrstuvwxyz
1234567890

SEMPLICITÀ

vi

ABCDEFGHIJKLMNOPQRSTUVWXYZ
abcdefghijklmnopqrstuvwxyz
1234567890

SEMPLICITÀ BOLD

vi

ABCDEFGHIJKLMNOPQRSTUVWXYZ
abcdefghijklmnopqrstuvwxyz
1234567890

SEMPLICITÀ CONDENSED

vi

ABCDEFGHIJKLMNOPQRS
TUVWXYZ
1234567890

SEMPLICITÀ OMBRA

334

Designed by George Trump. A highly condensed type. The **Q** has the tail separate from the bowl. The **T** is particularly narrow. In the lower case ascenders and descenders are short. There are two **g**'s.

ABCDEFGHIJKLMNOPQRSTUVWXYZ
abcdefghijklmnopqrstuvwxyz
1234567890

SIGNUM

Designed by S.H. de Roos and based on the same founder's LIBRA as a lineale which incorporates a number of uncial forms, for example, the **a**, **d** and **e**. Some of the letters have the upper-case design. Ascenders are short.

art must not be a superficial talent
but must begin farther back in man

SIMPLEX

die kraft reichtümer zu schaffen, ist
wichtiger, als der reichtum selbst

SIMPLEX SEMI-BOLD

Designed by H. Sinkwitz. A lineale titling of calligraphic appearance.

ABCDEFGHIJKLMN
OPQRSTUVWXYZ
1234567890 &

SINKWITZ-VERSALIEN

The most widely used lineale in the USA and copied from FUTURA. The **t** is designed like a cross. **A** and **V** are flattened at top or bottom respectively; the **g** has an open tail. Two versions of the **a** are supplied. There are several weights. The Lanston Monotype version is called TWENTIETH CENTURY and was designed by Sol Hess.

ABCDEFGHIJKLMNOPQRSTUVWXYZ
abcdefghijklmnopqrstuvwxyz
1234567890

MERGENTHALER LINOTYPE SPARTAN LIGHT

ABCDEFGHIJKLMNOPQRSTUVWXYZ
abcdefghijklmnopqrstuvwxyz
1234567890
ABCDEFGHIJKLMNOPQRSTUVWXYZ
abcdefghijklmnopqrstuvwxyz
1234567890

ABCDEFGHIJKLMNOPQRSTUVWXYZ

MERGENTHALER LINOTYPE SPARTAN BOOK

ABCDEFGHIJKLMNOPQRSTUVWXYZ

abcdefghijklmnopqrstuvwxyz

1234567890

MERGENTHALER LINOTYPE SPARTAN BOOK CONDENSED

vi

ABCDEFGHIJKLMNOPQRSTUVWXYZ

abcdefghijklmnopqrstuvwxyz

1234567890

ABCDEFGHIJKLMNOPQRSTUVWXYZ

abcdefghijklmnopqrstuvwxyz

1234567890

MERGENTHALER LINOTYPE SPARTAN MEDIUM

vi

ABCDEFGHIJKLMNOPQRSTUVWXYZ

abcdefghijklmnopqrstuvwxyz

1234567890

MERGENTHALER LINOTYPE SPARTAN MEDIUM CONDENSED

vi

ABCDEFGHIJKLMNOPQRSTUVWXYZ

abcdefghijklmnopqrstuvwxyz

1234567

ABCDEFGHIJKLMNOPQRSTUVWXYZ

abcdefghijklmnopqrstuvwxyz

4567890

MERGENTHALER LINOTYPE SPARTAN BOLD

vi

ABCDEFGHIJKLMNOPQRSTUVWXYZ

abcdefghijklmnopqrstuvwxyz

1234567890

ABCDEFGHIJKLMNOPQRSTUVWXYZ

abcdefghijklmnopqrstuvwxyz

1234567890

MERGENTHALER LINOTYPE SPARTAN BOLD CONDENSED

vi

ABCDEFGHIJKLMNOPQRSTUVWXYZ

abcdefghijklmnopqrstuvwxyz

1234567890

ABCDEFGHIJKLMNOPQRSTUVWXYZ

abcdefghijklmnopqrstuvwxyz

1234567890

MERGENTHALER LINOTYPE SPARTAN HEAVY

ABCDEFGHIJKLMNOPQRSTUVWXYZ
abcdefghijklmnopqrstuvw
1234567
ABCDEFGHIJKLMNOPQRSTUVWXYZ
defghijklmnopqrstuvwxyz
4567890

MERGENTHALER LINOTYPE SPARTAN BLACK

ABCDEFGHIJKLMNOPQRSTUVWXYZ
abcdefghijklmnopqrstuvwxyz
1234567890

MERGENTHALER LINOTYPE SPARTAN HEAVY CONDENSED

ABCDEFGHIJKLMNOPQRSTUVWXYZ
abcdefghijklmnopqrstuvwxyz
1234567890
ABCDEFGHIJKLMNOPQRSTUVWXYZ
abcdefghijklmnopqrstuvwxyz
1234567890

MERGENTHALER LINOTYPE SPARTAN BLACK CONDENSED

ABCDEFGHIJKLMNOPQRSTUVWXYZ
abcdefghijklmnopqrstuv
12345
ABCDEFGHIJKLMNOPQRSTUVWXYZ
fghijklmnopqrstuvwxyz
67890

MERGENTHALER LINOTYPE SPARTAN EXTRA BLACK

ABCDEFGHIJKLMNOPQRSTUVWXYZ
abcdefghijklmnopqrstuvwxyz
1234567890

MERGENTHALER LINOTYPE SPARTAN EXTRA BLACK CONDENSED

ABCDEFGHIJKLMNOPQR
STUVWYXZ
abcdefghijklmnopqrstuv
wxyz 1234567890&$

LANSTON MONOTYPE 20th CENTURY ULTRABOLD EXTENDED

ABCDEFGHIJKLMNOPQRSTUV
WXYZ

SPARTAN OUTLINE

Designed by R.H. Middleton. A square lineale following the nineteenth-century model.

ABCDEFGHIJKLMNOPQRST UVWXYZ&
abcdefghijklmnopqrstuvwxyz
1234567890$

SQUARE GOTHIC

A Continental lineale in four weights. The **G** has a spur, the **A** is flattened at the top. The **a,** in some weights, has a curved flat serif at the bottom, and the **g** has an open tail, the **y** a flattened tail. Also called AKZIDENZ GROTESK, this is one of the types so frequently used in Swiss typography of the 1950's and followed in the U.S.A. and Germany.

STANDARD MEDIUM CONDENSED was first shown in Berthold's 1896 specimen. The extra bold extended and condensed were added in 1956 and 1957. Book weights were added in 1970. Intertype ALTERNATE GOTHIC is very much like the medium condensed of this type. STANDARD GOTHIC is a newspaper type for classified advertisements.

vi

ABCDEFGHIJKLMNOPQRSTUVWXYZ
abcdefghijklmnopqrstuvwxyz

STANDARD LIGHT

vi

ABCDEFGHIJKLMNOPQRSTUVWXYZ
abcdefghijklmnopqrstuvwxyz

STANDARD LIGHT CONDENSED

vi

ABCDEFGHIJKLMNOPQRSTUV
abcdefghijklmnopqrstuvwxyz

STANDARD EXTRA LIGHT EXTENDED

vi

ABCDEFGHIJKLMNOPQRSTU
abcdefghijklmnopqrstuvwxyz

STANDARD LIGHT EXTENDED

vi

ABCDEFGHIJKLMNOPQRSTUVWXYZ
abcdefghijklmnopqrstuvwxyz
1234567890

STANDARD

vi

ABCDEFGHIJKLMNOPQRS
abcdefghijklmnopqrstuvwxyz

STANDARD EXTENDED

ABCDEFGHIJKLMNOPQRSTUVWXYZ
abcdefghijklmnopqrstuvwxyz vi

STANDARD CONDENSED

ABCDEFGHIJKLMNOPQRSTUVW vi
abcdefghijklmnopqrstuvwxyz
1234

ABCDEFGHIJKLMNOPRSTUVWXZ
abcdefghijklmnopqrstuvwxyz
5890

STANDARD BOOK

ABCDEFGHIJKLMNOPQRSTUVWXYZ vi
abcdefghijklmnopqrstuvwxyz

STANDARD MEDIUM

ABCDEFGHIJKLMNOPQRSTUVWXYZ vi
abcdefghijklmnopqrstuvwxyz
1234567890

STANDARD MEDIUM CONDENSED

ABCDEFGHIJKLMNOPQRSTUVW vi
XYZ
abcdefghijklmnopqrstuvwxyz
1234567890

ABCDEFGHIJKLMNOPQRSTUVWXYZ vi
abcdefghijklmnopqrstuvwxyz
1234567890

STANDARD BOOK MEDIUM

ABCDEFGHIJKLMNOPQRSTUVWX vi
abcdefghijklmnopqrstuvwxyz

STANDARD BOLD

ABCDEFGHIJKLMNOPQRSTUVWXYZ
abcdefghijklmnopqrstuvwxyz

STANDARD BOLD CONDENSED

vi

ABCDEFGHIJKLMNOPQRSTUVWXYZ
abcdefghijklmnopqrstuvwxyz
1234567890

STANDARD EXTRA BOLD CONDENSED

vi

ABCDEFGHIJKLMNOPQRSTUVWXYZ
abcdefghijklmnopqrstuvwxyz
1234567

STANDARD COMPACT

vi

ABCDEFGHIJKLMNOPQRSTUV WXYZ
abcdefghijklmnopqrstuvwxyz
1234567890

STANDARD GOTHIC EXTRA BOLD EXTENDED

STEINSCHRIFT
Haas c. 1860

A revival of an early lineale. A condensed design, following nineteenth-century models. The **G** has a long spur, the **M** is square, **R** has a curved tail. The narrow **T** is unlike the usual letter of that period.

vi

ABCDEFGHIJKLMNOPQRSTUVWXYZ
abcdefghijklmnopqrstuvwxyz
1234567890

STEINSCHRIFT

STELLAR
Ludlow 1929

Designed by R.H. Middleton. The type is not quite monotone. The main strokes are thickened towards the ends. The bars of the **A** and **H**, and the arms of **E** and **F** are comparatively thin. The feet of the **A**, **M** and **R** are cut off obliquely.

vi

RENDERS THE LUDLOW
system particularly worthy of the

STELLAR

FEW PARTICULAR POIN
ints of utility and adaptability

STELLAR BOLD

Designed by C.W. Pischiner. The **M** and round capitals are wide. **E**, **F** and **T** are narrow, **J** is short-ranging. The **a** is one-storeyed; **g** has the usual continental open tail. There are four weights. NEUZEIT BOOK was added in 1959.

ABCDEFGHIJKLMNOPQRSTUVWXY

abcdefghijklmnopqrstuvwxyz

ABCDEFGHIJKLMNOPQRSTUVWXYZ

abcdefghijklmnopqrstuvwxyz

STEMPEL SANS LIGHT

ABCDEFGHIJKLMNOPQRSTUVW

abcdefghijklmnopqrstuvwxyz

1234567890

STEMPEL SANS MEDIUM

vi

ABCDEFGHIJKLMNOPQRSTUVW

$XYZ£

abcdefghijklmnopqrstuvwxyz

1234567890

STEMPEL SANS BOLD

vi

ABCDEFGHIJKLMNOPQRSTUVWXYZ

abcdefghijklmnopqrstuvwxyz

STEMPEL SANS MEDIUM CONDENSED

vi

ABCDEFGHIJKLMNOPQRSTUVWXYZ

abcdefghijklmnopqrstuvwxyz

STEMPEL SANS SEMI-BOLD CONDENSED

vi

ABCDEFGHIJKLMNOPQRSTUVWXYZ

abcdefghijklmnopqrstuvwxyz

$1234567890£

NEUZEIT BOOK

vi

STEMPEL SANS
or NEUZEIT
GROTESQUE
vi

ABCDEFGHIJKLMNOPQRSTUVW
abcdefghijklmnopqrstuvwxyz
1234567890

NEUZEIT BOOK-S

vi

ABCDEFGHIJKLMNOPQRSTUVWXYZ
abcdefghijklmnopqrstuvwxyz

$1234567890£

NEUZEIT BOOK BOLD

STEREO
Ludwig & Mayer 1968

A three-dimensional lineale of stencil design.

vi

ABCDEFGHIJKLM
NOPQRSTUVWXYZ
1234567890

STEREO

STOP
Nebiolo 1970

Designed by Aldo Novarese. A bold lineale based on computer printout and neon-lighting lettering somewhat in the again fashionable style of the 1930s. Several letters have unusual shape, such as the A which follows the Greek A, the Q and 9 are almost identical.

vi

ABCDEFGHIJKLMNOPQ
RSTUVWXYZ
1234567890%

STOP

STRIDON
Warnery 1952

An inclined upper case and short-ranging figures. Three-dimensional.

vi

ABCDEFGHIJK
LMNOPQR

STRIDON

Designed by A. Overbeek. One of those almost monotone types with freely drawn letters which seem to be based on "print script" writing as taught in schools. *Cf.* CARTOON. Ascenders and descenders are short and serifs are almost non-existent. The **a** is one-storeyed, the eye of the **e** has an oblique stroke and the **g** an open tail. The bold is also called FLAMBARD.

ABCDEFGHIJKLMNOPQRSTUVW XYZ
abcdefghijklmnopqrstuvwxyz
1234567890

STUDIO

ABCDEFGHIJKLMNOPQRSTUVW
abcdefghijklmnopqrstuvwxyz

STUDIO BOLD

A heavy lineale which is not monotone and thus has the effect of a fat face. It has some resemblance to the same founders' ULTRA MODERN, but the counters are much smaller. Ascenders and the feet of **p** and **q** are cut off obliquely. There is an italic, which has swash capitals.

Unique and Popular Designs

Attention Compelling Designs

STYGIAN BLACK

Designed by Arno Drescher. The **M** is square and the middle strokes stop short of the line. The **a** is one-storeyed, **g** has an open tail and the **t** is curved at the foot.

    There are four weights and a book face, as well as similar types called SUPREMO, shaded capitals called SUPER REFLEX, others shaded obliquely called SUPER ELEKTRIK.

ABCDEFGHIJKLMNOPQRSTUVWXYZ&
abcdefghijklmnopqrstuvwxyz?
1234567890

ABCDEFGHIJKLMNOPQRSTUV WXYZ
abcdefghijklmnopqrstuvwxyz&
1234567890

SUPER LIGHT

ABCDEFGHIJKLMNOPQRSTUVWXYZ&
abcdefghijklmnopqrstuvwxyz?
1234567890

*ABCDEFGHIJKLMNOPQRSTU
VWXYZ
abcdefghijklmnopqrstuvwxyz&
1234567890*

SUPER

ABCDEFGHIJKLMNOPQRSTUVWXYZ&
abcdefghijklmnopqrstuvwxyz?
1234567890

SUPER CONDENSED

**ABCDEFGHIJKLMNOPQRSTUV
WXYZ&
abcdefghijklmnopqrstuvwxyz?
1234567890**

SUPER GROTESQUE BOLD

**ABCDEFGHIJKLMNOPQRSTUVWXYZ&
abcdefghijklmnopqrstuvwxyz?
1234567890**

SUPER BOLD CONDENSED

**ABCDEFGHIJKLMNOPQRSTU
VWXYZ&
abcdefghijklmnopqrstuvwxyz?
1234567890**

SUPER GROTESQUE EXTRA BOLD

ABCDEFGHIJKLMNOPQRS
TUVWXYZ
abcdefghijklmnopqrstuvw
xyz&
1234567890

SUPER EXTRA BOLD ITALIC

ABCDEFGHIJKLMNOPQRSTUVWXYZ&
abcdefghijklmnopqrstuvwxyz?
1234567890

SUPER GROTESQUE EXTRA BOLD CONDENSED

ABCDEFGHIJKLMNOPQRSTUVWXYZ
abcdefghijklmnopqrstuvwxyz
1234567890

SUPER GROTESQUE BOOK LIGHT

ABCDEFGHIJKLMNOPQRSTUVWXYZ
abcdefghijklmnopqrstuvwxyz
1234567890

SUPER GROTESQUE BOOK BOLD

ABCDEFGHIJKLMNOPQRSTUVWXYZ
abcdefghijklmnopqrstuvwxyz
1234567890

SUPER GROTESQUE BOOK LIGHT ITALIC

KEDİ PENCESİ

SUPER ELEKTRIK

ESCURSIONE

SUPER REFLEX

SYNTAX
Stempel 1969

Designed by Hand Eduard Meyer, and leaning on Renaissance minuscule writing, while capitals follow the roman "lapidar" style. All terminal strokes are cut off at right angle.

vi

ABCDEFGHIJKLMMNOPQRSTUVWXYZ
abcdefghijklmnopqrstuvwxyz
1234567890

SYNTAX

vi

ABCDEFGHIJKLMMNOPQRSTUVWXY
abcdefghijklmnopqrstuvwxyz
1234567890

SYNTAX BOLD

TEMPO
Ludlow 1930–42

Designed by R.H. Middleton. A sans serif after the continental model. The **B, E, F, P, R** and **T** are narrow letters. The **M** is splayed. The lower-case **g** has an open tail and the **t** is a vertical stroke with a bar. The italic acquires some foot serifs on the **a, d, h, m,** etc. There are five weights, condensed faces, and also a heavy inline. Additional weights were added in 1961.

vi

ABCDEFGHIJKLMNOPQRSTUVWXYZ&
abcdefghijklmnopqrstuvwxyz
1234567890

ABCDEFGHIJKLMNOPQRSTUVWXYZ&
abcdefghijklmnopqrstuvwxyz
1234567890

TEMPO LIGHT

vi

ABCDEFGHIJKLMNOPQRSTUVWXYZ&
abcdefghijklmnopqrstuvwxyz
1234567890

ABCDEFGHIJKLMNOPQRSTUVWXYZ&
abcdefghijklmnopqrstuvwxyz
1234567890

TEMPO MEDIUM

346

ABCDEFGHIJKLMNOPQRSTUVWXY
Z&
abcdefghijklmnopqrstuvwxyz
1234567890

ABCDEFGHIJKLMNOPQRSTUVWXYZ
abcdefghijklmnopqrstuvwxyz
1234567890

TEMPO BOLD

ABCDEFGHIJKLMNOPQRSTUVWXYZ&
abcdefghijklmnopqrstuvwxyz
1234567890

TEMPO BOLD CONDENSED

ABCDEFGHIJKLMNOPQRSTUVW
XYZ&
abcdefghijklmnopqrstuvwxyz
1234567890

TEMPO HEAVY

ABCDEFGHIJKLMNOPQRSTUVWXYZ&
abcdefghijklmnopqrstuvwxyz
1234567890

TEMPO HEAVY CONDENSED

ABCDEFGHIJKLMNOPQRSTUV
WXYZ&
abcdefghijklmnopqrstuvwxyz
12345678

TEMPO EXTRA HEAVY

ABCDEFGHIJKLMNOPQ RSTUVWXYZ& abcdefghijklmnopqrstuv wxyz 1234567890

TEMPO BOLD EXTENDED

ABCDEFGHIJKLMNOP QRSTUVWXYZ& abcdefghijklmnopqrst uvwxyz 1234567890

TEMPO BLACK EXTENDED ITALIC

ABCDEFGHIJK LMNOPQRSTU VWXYZ 1234567890

TEMPO INLINE

TIMES GOTHIC

Intertype (New York) 1960

A type face specially designed for classified advertising, and first used by the *New York Times*. The type face is cut in one size only, and joins the ranks of such specialised types as ADSANS, etc.

ABCDEFGHIJKLMNOPQRSTUVWXYZ
abcdefghijklmnopqrstuvwxyz
1234567890

TIMES GOTHIC

ABCDEFGHIJKLMNOPQRSTUVWXYZ
abcdefghijklmnopqrstuvwxyz
1234567890

TIMES GOTHIC BOLD

Designed by Paul Renner and based on his FUTURA. It is a condensed type in which the normally round letters acquire straight sides. The capitals **A**, **E**, **M** and **W** appear in two forms, the second designs being rounded.

AABCDEEFGHIJKKLMMNNOPQRSTUVWWXYZ
abcdefghijklmnopqrstuvwxyz
1234567890

ABCDEFGHIJKLMNOPQRSTUVWXYZ
abcdefghijklmnopqrstuvwxyz
1234567890

TOPIC MEDIUM

AABCDEEFGHIJKKLMMNNOPQRSTUVW
WXYZ
abcdefghijklmnopqrstuvwxyz
1234

ABCDEFGHIJKLMNOPQRSTUVWXYZ
abcdefghijklmnopqrstuvwxyz
1234567890

TOPIC BOLD

Designed by A.M. Cassandre, in collaboration with Charles Peignot, following the style of the PEIGNOT face of the same founders, but eight of the lower-case letters have been modified to give them the more traditional appearance of the standard lower-case alphabets.

HER Bord ÉDITEUR

TOURAINE

Touraine MIN

TOURAINE BOLD

TOURIST GOTHIC

Lanston Monotype 1909

vi

Designed by Sol Hess, with an italic added in 1938. A bold type of even weight.

AABCCDEEEFFGGHIJJHKLMMMMN OPQRRSSTUV
WWHXYYZ&ÆŒ£$
abcdefghijklmnopqrstuvwxyzæœ
1234567890

ABCDEFGHIJKLMNOPQRSTUVWXYZ&
abcdefghijklmnopqrstuvwxyz
1234567890

TOURIST GOTHIC

TRADE GOTHIC

*Mergenthaler
Linotype 1948-60;
Linotype (London)*

vi

Designed by Jackson Burke. A lineale type with short ascenders and descenders. The design is nineteenth century, except for the **g**. There are also bold, condensed, and extra condensed faces. Linotype (London) issue the condensed forms.

ABCDEFGHIJKLMNOPQRSTUVWXYZ
abcdefghijklmnopqrstuvwxyz
1234567890

TRADE GOTHIC

ABCDEFGHIJKLMNOPQRSTUVWXYZ&
abcdefghijklmnopqrstuvwxyz
1234567890

ABCDEFGHIJKLMNOPQRSTUVWXYZ&
abcdefghijklmnopqrstuvwxyz
1234567890

TRADE GOTHIC LIGHT

vi

ABCDEFGHIJKLMNOPQRSTUVWXYZ
abcdefghijklmnopqrstuvwxyz
1234567890

TRADE GOTHIC CONDENSED (No. 18)

vi

ABCDEFGHIJKLMNOPQRSTUVWXYZ
abcdefghijklmnopqrstuvwxyz
1234567890

TRADE GOTHIC EXTRA CONDENSED (No. 17)

vi

ABCDEFGHIJKLMNOPQRSTUVWXYZ
abcdefghijklmnopqrstuvwxyz
1234567890

TRADE GOTHIC BOLD EXTRA CONDENSED (No. 19)

vi

ABCDEFGHIJKLMNOPQRSTUVWXYZ
abcdefghijklmnopqrstuvwxyz
1234567890

TRADE GOTHIC EXTENDED

ABCDEFGHIJKLMNOPQRSTUVWXYZ
abcdefghijklmnopqrstuvwxyz

1234567890

TRADE GOTHIC ITALIC BOLD

ABCDEFGHIJKLMNOPQRSTUVWXYZ
abcdefghijklmnopqrstuvwxyz

1234567890

TRADE GOTHIC BOLD NO. 2

vi

ABCDEFGHIJKLMNOPQRSTUVWXYZ
abcdefghijklmnopqrstuvwxyz
1234567890

ABCDEFGHIJKLMNOPQRSTUVWXYZ
abcdefghijklmnopqrstuvwxyz
1234567890

TRADE GOTHIC BOLD

vi

ABCDEFGHIJKLMNOPQRSTUVWXYZ
abcdefghijklmnopqrstuvwxyz
1234567890

TRADE GOTHIC BOLD CONDENSED (No. 20)

vi

ABCDEFGHIJKLMNOPQRSTUVWXYZ
abcdefghijklmnopqrstuvwxyz
1234567890

TRADE GOTHIC EXTENDED BOLD

vi

Designed by J. Tschichold. A heavy stencil type. Most of the letters are in two and some in three parts. The arms of the E and F are separate triangular pieces. The r consists of a fat vertical stroke and a separate circle. The t is a vertical rounded at the foot with the remains of a bar on the right.

TRANSITO
Amsterdam 1931

The Local Government Examiner
DISTINGUISHED ELOCUTIONIST 3

TRANSITO

vi

Designed by H.R. Möller. The thin strokes, hair lines, occupy one half of most of the letters in the same manner as in BROADWAY. The M is pointed and splayed. Capitals and figures only. TRIO B is a shaded version and TRIO C an inline version, with three white lines.

TRIO
Schriftguss 1937

ABCDEFGHIJKLMNOPQRSTUVWXYZ

TRIO A

vi

ABCDEFGHIJKLM

TRIO B

NOPQRSTUVWXYZ

TRIO C

**ULTRA
MODERN**
Ludlow 1928

Designed by Douglas C. McMurtrie. Vertical strokes are slightly concave. The arms of **E** and **F** are shaped. The **R** has a curled tail. The counters of some of the round letters have straight edges, *e.g.* in the **G**, **O** and **Q**, and the lower-case **a**, **e**, **o**, etc.

INQUIRIES conducted

ULTRA MODERN

**UMKEHR
SCHRIFT**
Wagner 1930

A type based on German Standard DIN 1451 engineering lettering. There is also a light and a condensed version.

UTSRQPONMLKJIHGFEDCBA
VWXYZ
ß zyxwvutsrqponmlkjihgfedcba
0987654321

UMKEHRSCHRIFT

UNIVERS
Deberny & Peignot 1957;
American Typefounders 1961;
Monotype 1961;
Matrotype 1967;
Photon

Designed by Adrian Frutiger. A new lineale of individual style incorporating characteristics of weights, but unfortunately several of the versions now available are slightly varied so that they are not always truly compatible. This is different from SABON, the other purpose-designed UNIVERSAL foundry, machine composition and phototypesetting type of the 1960s.

Univers   *Univers*

UNIVERS 45   UNIVERS 46

ABCDEFGHIJKLMNOPQRSTUVWXYZ
abcdefghijklmnopqrstuvwxyz
1234567890

UNIVERS 47

ABCDEFGHIJKLMNOPQRSTUVWXYZ
abcdefghijklmnopqrstuvwxyz
1234567890

UNIVERS 48

ABCDEFGHIJKLMNOPQRSTUVWXYZ
abcdefghijklmnopqrstuvwxyz
1234567890

UNIVERS LIGHT EXTRA CONDENSED

Univers

UNIVERS 53

vi

ABCDEFGHIJKLMNOPQRSTUVW XYZ

abcdefghijklmnopqrstuvwxyz

1234567890

UNIVERS 55

ABCDEFGHIJKLMNOPQRSTUV 12345 WXYZ 67890

abcdefghijklmnopqrstuvwxyz

vi

UNIVERS 56

ABCDEFGHIJKLMNOPQRSTUVWXYZ

abcdefghijklmnopqrstuvwxyz

1234567890

vi

UNIVERS 57

ABCDEFGHIJKLMNOPQRSTUVWXYZ

abcdefghijklmnopqrstuvwxyz

1234567890

vi

UNIVERS 58

Univers

UNIVERS 59

Univers

UNIVERS 63

vi

ABCDEFGHIJKLMNOPQRSTU VWXYZ

abcdefghijklmnopqrstuvwxyz

1234567890

vi

UNIVERS 65

ABCDEFGHIJKLMNOPQRSTU
VWXYZ
abcdefghijklmnopqrstuvwxyz
1234567890

UNIVERS 66

vi

ABCDEFGHIJKLMNOPQRSTUVWXYZ
abcdefghijklmnopqrstuvwxyz
1234567890

UNIVERS 67

vi

ABCDEFGHIJKLMNOPQRSTUVWXYZ
abcdefghijklmnopqrstuvwxyz
1234567890

UNIVERS 68

vi

ABCDEFGHIJKLMNOPQRSTUVWXYZ
abcdefghijklmnopqrstuvwxyz
1234567890

UNIVERS MEDIUM EXTRA CONDENSED

Univers

UNIVERS 73

vi

ABCDEFGHIJKLMNOPQRST
UVWXYZ
abcdefghijklmnopqrstuvwxyz
1234567890

UNIVERS 75

vi

ABCDEFGHIJKLMNOPQRST
UVWXYZ
abcdefghijklmnopqrstuvwxyz
1234567890

UNIVERS 76

Univers

UNIVERS 83

A lineale following German design of the period.

ABCDEFGHIJKLMNOPQRS
TUVWXYZ
abcdefghijklmnopqrstuvwxyz
1234567890

ABCDEFGHIJKLMNOPQRS
TUVWXYZ
abcdefghijklmnopqrstuvwxyz
1234567890

UNIVERSAL

ABCDEFGHIJKLMNOPQRS
TUVWXYZ
abcdefghijklmnopqrstuvwxyz
1234567890

UNIVERSAL BOLD

ABCDEFGHIJKLMNOPQRS
TUVWXYZ
abcdefghijklmnopqrstuvwxyz
1234567890

UNIVERSAL EXTRA BOLD

ABCDEFGHIJKLMNOPQRS
TUVWXYZ
abcdefghijklmnopqrstuvwxyz
1234567890

UNIVERSAL EXTRA BOLD ITALIC

355

ABCDEFGHIJKLMNOPQRSTUVWXYZ
abcdefghijklmnopqrstuvwxyz
1234567890

UNIVERSAL EXTRA BOLD CONDENSED

VALIANT
Lanston Monotype 1941
vi

Designed by Edwin W. Shaar as an angular bold display type.

ABCDEFGHIJKLMNOPQRSTUVWXYZ&

aabcdefgghijkklmnopqrstuvwxyz

1234567890

VALIANT

VEGA
Grafotechna 1965
vi

An angular lineale with variation in stress between down and up strokes.

ABCDEFGHIJKLMNOPQRS
TUVWXYZ
abcdefghijklmnopqrstuvwxyz
1234567890

VEGA

vi

ABCDEFGHIJKLMNOPQRS
TUVWXYZ
abcdefghijklmnopqrstuvwxyz
1234567890

VEGA BOLD

VENUS
Bauer 1907–27

Originally a Wagner & Schmidt design, and some weights sold to several founders. A lineale which looks, in the upper case, like a revival of a nineteenth-century type. Capitals are of equal width. The **M** is square. The **a** is two-storeyed, the **g** has an open tail and the **t** a curved terminal.

vi

ABCDEFGHIJKLMNOPQRSTUVW
XYZ
abcdefghijklmnopqrstuvwxyz
1234567890

VENUS LIGHT

356

ABCDEFGHIJKLMNOPQRSTUVWXYZ
abcdefghijklmnop qrstuvwxyz
1234567890

VENUS LIGHT

ABCDEFGHIJKLMNOPQRSTUVWXYZ
abcdefghijklmnopqrstuvwxyz
1234567890

VENUS LIGHT CONDENSED

ABCDEFGHIJKLMNOPQRSTUVW
XYZ
abcdefghijklmnopqrstuvwxyz
1234567890

ABCDEFGHIJKLMNOPQRSTUVWXYZ
abcdefghijklmnopqrstuvwxyz
1234567890

VENUS MEDIUM

ABCDEFGHIJKLMNOPQRSTUV
abcdefghijklmnopqrstuvwxyz
1234567890

ABCDEFGHIJKLMNOPQRST
abcdefghijklmnopqrstuvwxyz
1234567890

VENUS BOLD

ABCDEFGHIJKLMNOPV
abcdefghijklmnopqrstuv
1234567890

VENUS BOLD EXTENDED

ABCDEFGHIJKLMNOPQR STUVWXYZ abcdefghijklmnopqrstuvwx yz 1234567890

VENUS MEDIUM EXTENDED

ABCDEFGHIJKLMNOPQR STUVWXYZ abcdefghijklmnopqrstuvwxyz 1234567890

VENUS LIGHT EXTENDED

ABCDEFGHIJKLMNOPQRSTUVWXYZ abcdefghijklmnopqrstuvwxyz 1234567890

VENUS MEDIUM CONDENSED

ABCDEFGHIJKLMNOPQRSTUVWXYZ abcdefghijklmnopqrstuvwxyz 1234567890

VENUS BOLD CONDENSED

ABCDEFGHIJKLMNTI abcdefghijklmnopqri 1234567890

VENUS EXTRA BOLD EXTENDED

A type designed for optical character recognition machines.

ABCDEFGHIJKLMNOPQRSTU
VWXYZ 1234567890

VIAFONT

A type similar to FOLIO.

ABCDEFGHIJKLMNOPQRSTUVWXYZ&
abcdefghijklmnopqrstuvwxyz$1234567890

VIDEO SPECTRA

ABCDEFGHIJKLMNOPQRSTUVWXYZ&
abcdefghijklmnopqrstuvwxyz$1234567890

VIDEO SPECTRA BOLD

A light titling. The bars of **A** and **H** overhang to the left. In the **M** the middle strokes stop short of the line. **E, N, S** and **T** are narrow and the round letters wide.

Quite different from INTERTYPE VOGUE, which follows lineale style, but has a very unusual **g** in the light and bold versions, and has the CABLE **a**, **e** and **g**, but also FUTURA characters.

ABCDEFGHIJKLMNOPQRSTUVWXYZ
12345678

VOGUE

ABCDEFGHIJKLMNOPQRSTUVWXYZ
abcdefghijklmnopqrstuvwxyz
1234567890 &£

INTERTYPE VOGUE LIGHT

ABCDEFGHIJKLMNOPQRSTUVWXYZ
abcdefghijklmnopqrstuvwxyz
1234567890 &£

INTERTYPE VOGUE BOLD

ABCDEFGHIJKLMNOPQRSTUVWXYZ
abcdefghijklmnopqrstuvwxyz
1234567890 &£

ABCDEFGHIJKLMNOPQRSTUVWXYZ
abcdefghijklmnopqrstuvwxyz
1234567890 &£

INTERTYPE VOGUE EXTRA BOLD WITH OBLIQUE

Designed by Whedon Davis. This type matches others in the normal GOTHIC types of this foundry.

ABCDEFGHIJKLMNOPQRSTUVWX
YZ
abcdefghijklmnopqrstuvwxyz
£1234567890 &

WHEDONS GOTHIC OUTLINE

SCRIPT TYPES

A SCRIPT is a type based on cursive or current handwriting. In the sixteenth century there was a script known as Secretary, which was based on an Elizabethan gothic hand. It has not survived and has not been revived, although a French type, Civilité, of similar style has been. The earliest Latin scripts are the Scriptorials of the Grover foundry which have survived. They appear in Stanley Morison's *Ichabod Dawks*. Towards the end of the eighteenth century scripts were cut based on the engraved copperplate writing. In the end the letters were made to fit so closely as to give the impression of being actually engraved lettering.

A heavy display italic. It is monotone and the letters are not close-setting. Very like ATTRAKTION; the two may be distinguished by the e's; in ACHTUNG the e is italic, in Attraktion it is an inclined roman e.

ACHTUNG

Ludwig & Mayer 1932

viii

ABCDEFGHIJKLMNOPQRSTUV

ABCDEFGHIJKLM

abcdefghijklmnopqrstuvwxyz

ACHTUNG

Designed by Karl Klauss for Geuzsch & Heyse in 1953.

ADAGIO

Bauer

viii

ABCDEFGHIJKLMNOP

QRSTUVWXYZ

abcdefghijklmnopqrstuvwxyz 1234567890

ADAGIO

Designed by R. Hunter Middleton. A pen script with swash caps.

ADMIRAL SCRIPT

Ludlow 1953

viii

ABCDEFGHIJKLMNOPQ

RSTUVWXYZ&

abcdefghijklmnopqrstuvwxyz 1234567890$

ADMIRAL SCRIPT

361

AGITATOR
Typoart 1960

viii

Designed by Wolfgang Eickhoff. Freely drawn capitals of a semi bold script. There is little variation of stress. It is almost an inclined sans serif.

ABCDEFGHIJKLMNOPQR
STUVWXYZ&?
1234567890

AGITATOR

**AKTUELL
or PENFLOW**
Schriftguss 1935

viii

Designed by Walter Schnippering. An informal script of medium weight and with the letters closely set. The alignment is irregular. PENTAPE or ORIGINELL is a heavier face of the same design but an inline conveying the idea of a flowing ribbon.

International European Fairs

Modische Neuheiten für den Herbstanfang

ACTUELLE or PENFLOW

AMANDA
Stephenson Blake 1939

viii

A script of medium weight with flourished capitals and a somewhat stiff lower case. The ascenders are looped. The **m** and **n** have serifs and give an appearance of formality.

ABCDEFGHIJKLMNOPQRSTUV
WXYZ
abcdefghijklmnopqrstuvwxyz 1234567890

AMANDA

AMAZONE
Amsterdam 1959

viii

Designed by Leonard H.D. Smit. A formal script of medium weight. The capitals are flourished. The lower case letters adjoin. Ascenders are looped and tall, as are the descenders.

ABCDEFGHIJKLMNOPQRST
UVWXYZÆŒ
abcdefgijklmnopqrstuvwxyz1234567890£&æœ

AMAZONE

ANDROMAQUE
Anvil Press 1960

viii

Designed by Victor Hammer and cast by *Deberny & Peignot* as a cursive uncial for private press use and originally intended for a printing of Racine's *Andromaque* by the Stamparia del Santuccio.

one light, one ray and it will be the angels' spring:
one flash, one glance upon the shiny pond, and then
asperges me! sweet wilderness, and lo! we are redeemed!

ANDROMAQUE

Designed by A. Drescher. A script with flourishing capitals and a formal lower case. Two sets of capitals, one even more flourished, are provided. The ascenders in the lower case are tall. The **f** and **r** are unusual forms, a number of ligatures are supplied. A heavier face is called ARABELLA FAVORIT.

ABCDEFGHIJKLMNOPQu
RSTUVWXYZ 1234567890
abcdefghijklmnopqrstuvwxyzchck ff fi fl ft ll st ß ttz
ABCDEFGHIJ
KLMNOPQuRS

ARABELLA

ABCDEFGHIJKLMNOPQu
RSTUVWXYZ

viii

abcdefghijklmnopqrstuvwxyz ff fi fl ft ll st ß tt
ABCDEFGHIJ
KLMNOPQuRST

ARABELLA FAVORIT

Designed by G. Zapf-v. Hesse. A set of initials of flowing design with considerable variation of stress. *Cf.* GAVOTTE.

ABCDEFGHIJKLMNOP

ARIADNE

Designed by M. Wilke. A script originally cut in three weights (matrices of the bold were destroyed in the war), with abrupt variation in colour. The capitals are flourished. In the lower case the thin, hair-line upstrokes take off from the feet of the down strokes. Ascenders are of moderate height, and descenders rather short.

ABCDEFGHIJKLMNOPQRSTU
abcdefghijklmnopqrstuvwxyz

ARISTON LIGHT

viii

ABCDEFGHIJKLMNOPQRST
abcdefghijklmnopqrstuvwxyz
1234567890

ARISTON MEDIUM

ARKONA
Genzsch & Heyse 1935

viii

Designed by Karl Klauss. A formal script with considerable variation of stress and slight inclination. Ascenders have no serifs but are thickened towards the top. Descenders are short. It makes an impression of rigidity.

ABCDEFGHIJKLMNOPQRST
UVWXYZ 1234567890
abcdefghijklmnopqrstuvwxyz

ARKONA

viii

ABCDEFGHIJKLMNOPQRS
TUVWXYZ 1234567890
abcdefghijklmnopqrstuvwxyz

ARKONA MEDIUM

ARTISTA
Schelter & Giesecke 1936

viii

Designed by Rudolf Sternberg. A light script with cursive capitals and a lower case which might almost be an italic. There are second varieties of **r** and **s** which are more script-like.

Dresden, the City of Art and Flowers

ARTISTA

ARTSCRIPT
Lanston Monotype 1940

viii

Designed by Sol Hess and based on the writing of Servidori of Madrid, 1798. Servidori was an admirer of the calligraphers of the sixteenth century, and this script is a good revival of an Italian or Spanish Cancellaresca formata of that period. The serifs on the **m**, **n** and **r** are somewhat unusual.

ABCDEFGHIJKLMNOP QRSTUVW
XYZ&
abcdefghijklmnopqrstuvwxyz   fiflff ffiffl   1234567890

ARTSCRIPT

ASHLEY SCRIPT
Monotype 1955

viii

Designed by Ashley Havinden. A heavy monotone brush script with informal sans serif capitals.

ABCDEFGHIJKLMNOPQRST
UVWXYZ 12345

viii

abcdefghijklmnopqrstuvwxyz

ASHLEY SCRIPT

A three-dimensional script.

𝔄𝔅ℭ𝔇𝔈𝔉𝔊ℌℑ𝔍𝔎ℒ𝔐𝔑𝔒𝔓

𝔔ℛ𝔖𝔗𝔘𝔙𝔚𝔛𝔜ℨ

ATLANTIDA

A heavy display italic, monotone in colour. The capitals are of the swash variety. A somewhat condensed version is called BEROLINA.

Noch schneller   **Berolina**

ATTRAKTION   BEROLINA

A strong brush script, designed by Johannes Boehland. The type, which is especially suited for uncoated stock, has a certain similarity to Chinese brush lettering. The lower case **d** and **g** extend over the body. The capital **W** is supplied in two versions, one of these with a strong cross-bar closing the top.

ABCDEFGHIJKLMNOPQRSTUVWX

abcdefghijklmnopqrstuvwxyz

1234567890

BALZAC

A light script of slight inclination of the visiting-card class. The capitals are flowing and the lower-case letters round, with tall ascenders and short descenders. The lower case has thin oblique serifs.

Reise-Erlebnisse aus dem sonnigen Italien

BARBERINA

Designed by Imre Reiner. A bold, informal brush script with irregularly inclined letters and uneven ascender and descender lengths. BRAVO has some similarity to this type.

ABCDEFGHIJKLMNOPQRSTU

VWXYZ abcdefghijklmnopqrstuvwxyz

BAZAAR

Designed by Lucian Bernhard. A heavy informal script, which has the appearance of having been drawn with a brush. The variation of stress is considerable. Ascenders are looped.

The York Times

BERNHARD BRUSH SCRIPT

BERNHARD
CURSIVE
or MADONNA
Bauer 1925
Stephenson Blake

viii

Designed by Lucian Bernhard before the roman and italic, which it now accompanies. The lower case has very tall ascenders and short descenders. **b, d** and **l** have no top serifs, but **h** has a finishing stroke. The vertical strokes of **p** and **q** project high above the bowls. The capitals are flowing pen-forms. There is also a bold face. Stephenson Blake call the type MADONNA RONDE, but their MADONNA BOLD is a different design.

ABCDEFGHIJKLMNOPQ
RSTUVWXYZ

abcdefghijklmnopqrstuvw.xyz 1234567890

BERNHARD CURSIVE

ABCDEFGHIJKLMNOPQ
RSTUVWXYZ

abcdefghijklmnopqrst uvwxyz 1234567890

BERNARD CURSIVE BOLD

Designed by Lucian Bernhard. A stylised script with contrasting bold and hair-line strokes. The **e** is angular, and there are swash capitals.

ABCDEFGHIJKLMNOPQRSTUVWXYZ

abcdefghijklmnopqrstuvwxyz 1234567890

BERNHARD TANGO

Designed by Julius Kirn. A heavy brush script of slight inclination. Ascenders and descenders, as well as capitals, are rather short. The **t** is a slightly inclined cross, cut diagonally at top and foot. The **r** is very narrow; and the **W** follows the lower-case design. BLIZZARD cut by Trennert is identical.

ABCDEFGHIJKLMNOPQRSTUVWXYZ

abcdefghijklmnopqrstuvwxyz

1234567890

BISON

Designed by G.G. Lange. A formal script with much variation of stress. The capitals are flourished and the lower case approaches the English copperplate, but ascenders are short.

ABCDEFGHIJKLMNOPQ

abcdefghijklmnopqrstuvwxyz 1234567890

BOULEVARD

Designed by E.A. Neukomm. A heavy informal script with tall ascenders. The inclination of the letters is irregular, many of them being upright. There are no looped letters and the descenders taper to points. The differentiation of colour is slight. The letters are not close-setting.

$ABCDEFGHIJKLMNOPQRST$

$abcdefghijklmnopqrstuvwxyz\ 1234567890$

BRAVO

Designed by Harold Brodersen. An informal brush script of heavy weight. The lower case letters are close-setting, ascenders and descenders short.

$ABCDEFGH99KLMNOPQRSTUVWXYZ$

$abcdefghijklmnopqrstuvwxyz\ 1234567890$

BRODY

Designed by Robert E. Smith. An informal brush script of heavy weight. The lower-case letters are close-setting and have the appearance of being brush drawn. The set is deliberately irregular. *Cf.* BERNHARD BRUSH and SIGNAL.

$ABCDEFGHIJKLM$

$NOPQRSTUVWXYZ$

$abcdefghijklmn1234567890$

BRUSH

Designed by M. Wilke. A formal script of slight inclination. The lower-case letters are round and the curves have the qualities of pen strokes. Descenders are short and the **g** has an open tail. AMBASSADOR is a second set of plain capitals to accompany BURGUND.

Metropol-Cinema
Schönheit und Kosmetik
BURGUND

Designed by Willy Schumann. A script with flowing capitals and round, broad letters in the lower case. There is only moderate variation in stress. There is also a bold and special initials.

Modehaus Brühl & Co., Dresden
BUTTERFLY LIGHT

Porzellanmanufaktur
BUTTERFLY BOLD

CALLIGRAPH-IQUES

Deberny & Peignot

viii

A copperplate script in the English nineteenth-century fashion, and available from many founders. *Cf.* GRAPHIC SCRIPT, PALACE SCRIPT or COMMERCIAL SCRIPT.

*A B C D E F G H I J K L M M
N O P Q R S T U V W X Y Z Œ*

*abbcdeeffgghijkkllmnopp
qqrrssttuvwxyyzz çœœon
12345 & 67890*

CALLIGRAPHIQUES

CANTATE

Bauer 1958

viii

Designed by J.J. Siercke. A formal script with abrupt variation of colour. Hair lines are frequent. The lower case letters adjoin and ascenders are looped.

*A B C D E F G H I J K L M N O P Q X
abcdefghijklmnopqrstuvwxyzabcdefghk
1234567890*

CANTATE

CAPRICE

Berthold 1939

viii

Designed by M. Wilke. A script of medium weight with freely drawn capitals and a more formal lower case. The pen-drawn characteristic is so pronounced in the larger sizes that the type seems to be almost three-dimensional.

*A B C D E F G H I J K L M N O P Q R
abcdefghijklmnopqrstuvwxyz 1234567890*

CAPRICE

CASCADE SCRIPT

Linofilm 1966

viii

Designed by Matthew Carter.

**ABCDEFGHIJKLMNOPQRSTUVWXYZ
abcdefghijklmnopqrstuvwxyz
1234567890**

CASCADE SCRIPT

CATALINA

Intertype (F) 1955

viii

Designed by Emil Klumpp. An informal script with close-setting lower case and little variation of stress. There are two sets of capitals for this face designed specially for the Fotosetter.

*A A B C D E F G G H I J K L M N O P Q R S T T U V W X Y Y Z
A B C D E F G H I J K L M N O P
Q R S T U V W X Y Z
abcdeffghijklmnopqrstuvwxyz 1234567890$*

CATALINA

368

Designed by G.G. Lange. A script of very informal design and medium weight. There is some variation of colour. The lower case letters are not close-fitting.

ABCDEFGHIJKLMNOPQRSTUVWXYZ

abcdefghijklmnopqrstuvwxyz

1234567890

CHAMPION

Designed by Paul Hayden-Duensing for his private press. The characters have a very low x-height. Many alternative characters are to be added.

ABCDEFGHI JKLMNOPQURSTUVWXYZ

abcdefghijklmnopqrstuvwxyz

CHANCERY ITALIC

Designed by Helmut Matheis. An informal script of medium weight and some variation of colour. The capitals are flowing and the lower case letters are close fitting. There is a set of ranging figures. The bold introduced in 1959, is called SLOGAN but quite different from Nebiolo's SLOGAN.

ABCDEFGHIJKLMNOPQR STUVWXYZ

abcdefghijklmnopqrstuvwxyz

1234567890

CHARME

Designed by Roger Excoffon. A heavy and uniform script. *Cf.* REINER BLACK, but the lettering is even rougher than in that design. In fact it is the most informal of all scripts, although its characters are not as close-setting as those in MISTRAL.

ABCDEFGHIJKLMNOPQRSTUVWXY

abcdefghijklmnopqrstuvwxyz

1234567890

CHOC

Designed by A. Novarese. A formal script heavier in weight than the same founder's CIGOGNA. The capitals are freely drawn and the ascenders in the lower case are without loops.

ABCDEFGHIJKLMNOPQRST UVWXYZÇÆŒ&

abcdefghijklmnopqrstuvwxyzçæœ

1234567890

CIGNO

CIGOGNA

Nebiolo

Designed by A. Butti. This is a script type resembling quill pen lettering. The heavy strokes are finely tapered in some letters. The bowls of the lower-case **a** and **o** are not closed, and the **s** descends below the line. The capital **Q** resembles a hand-written figure 2.

viii

ABCDEFGHIJKLM NOPQQuRSTUVWXYZÇ

abcdefghijklmnopqrstuvwxyzçœœ   1234567890

CIGOGNA LIGHT

viii

ABCDEFGHIJKLM NOPQQuRST
UVWXYZÇÆŒIVX

abcdefghijklmnopqrstuvwxyzçœœ
1234567890

CIGOGNA BOLD

CIVILITÉ

American 1922

viii

Designed by Louis Ferrand. A script with flourished capitals and a formal lower case. There are no serifs.

A B C D E F G H I J K L M N O P Q R S
T U V W X Y Z &

a b c d e f g h i j k l m n o p q. r s t u v w x y z
1 2 3 4 5 6 7 8 9 0

CIVILITÉ

Enschedé

Probably cut by Robert Granjon at Lyons in 1557, although some records seem to indicate that this particular type stems from Plantin's Leyden office, around 1584. It now ranks as a private press type, as it is no longer available from the foundry. The type is heavy, with swash letters, and close setting. M. F. Benton designed a type after this style for American Typefounder's in 1922. *Cf.* LA CIVILITÉ.

viii

R BEG E f GH JJ LL M N O H Q ES T SO SO X Y Z

a b c d e f g h i j k l m n o p q r s t u v w x y z

As Frederic Warde aptly put it, 'as long as we work with the arbitrary figns
of the alphabet, we shall be dependent on the past and-like the Greek vafe

CIVILITÉ

CLIPPER

Française 1951

Designed by M.F. Benton. Based on the French cursive first cut by Robert Granjon at Lyons in 1557. It corresponds to the English SECRETARY. Compared with the original the modern version has been considerably Latinised, especially in the upper case. The **A**, **D**, **R**, **S**, **V** and **W** are Latin forms. The letters are upright and the gothic form of the **d**, with the top stroke inclined to the left, and the **h** with the tail sweeping round below the line, have been preserved. The **m**, **n**, and initial, are other sixteenth-century forms.

viii

ABCDEFGHIJKLMNOPQRSTUV
WXYZ

abcdefghijklmnopqrstuvwxyzœœ 1234567890

CLIPPER

Designed by Helmut Matheis.. An angular vertical script.

ABCDEFGHIJKLMNOPQRSTUVW
XYZ
abcdefghijklmnopqrstuvwxyz
1234567890

COMPLIMENT

COMPLIMENT
Ludwig & Mayer 1966

viii

Designed by Joachim Romann. A light Latin script, similar to GAVOTTE.

ABCDEFGHIJKLMN
OPQRSTUVWXYZ
abcdefghijklmnopqrstuvwxyz
1234567890

CONSTANCE

CONSTANCE
Klingspor

viii

A bold slightly inclined brush script.

ABCDEFGHIJKLMNOPQRSTUVWXYZ
abcdefghijklmnopqrstuvwxyz
1234567890

CONTACT

viii

A bold face of the English copperplate script, similar in style, but not in weight, to MARINA. This is a bolder version of YOUTHLINE.

ABCDEFGHIJKLMNO
PQRSTUVWXYZ
abcdefghijklmnopqrstuvwxyz
1234567890

COPPERPLATE BOLD

COPPERPLATE
BOLD
Stephenson Blake 1953

viii

371

CORONET
Ludlow 1937

Designed by R.H. Middleton. A script very like TRAFTON with freely drawn capitals and a more formal lower case. The descenders are not quite so long as in Trafton; the **d** is not looped, whereas the **l** is, the reverse being the case in Trafton. There is also a bold.

viii

ABCDEFGHIJKLMNOPQRSTUVWXYZ

abcdefghijklmnopqrstuvwxyz

1234567890

CORONET

viii

ABCDEFGHIJKLMNOPQRSTUVW

XYZ

abcdefghijklmnopqrstuvwxyz

1234567890

CORONET BOLD

DERBY
Berthold 1953

Designed by G.G. Lange. A formal script of considerable weight and with pen-drawn characteristics. The lower case has oblique serifs and short ascenders. The lower case resembles TEMPLE SCRIPT, but the capitals are more freely drawn.

viii

ABCDEFGHIJKLMNOPQRSTU

abcdefghijklmnopqrstuvwxyz 1234567890

DERBY

DIANE
Olive 1956

Designed by Roger Excoffon. A modern version of eighteenth-century copperplate scripts with flourished capitals and an angular lower case with joining letters.

viii

ABCDEFGHIJ

KLMNOPQRST

UVWXYZ

abcdefghijklmnopqrstuvw

xyz

1 2 3 4 5 6 7 8 9 0

DIANE

Designed by M. Wilke. A formal script with moderate variation of stress and slight inclination. The capitals are freely drawn. The lower case has no serifs and short descenders. The **f** and **l** are looped.

ABCDEFGHIJKLMNO

abcdefghijklmnopqrstuvwxyz

1234567890

DISCUS

ABCDEFGHIJKLMNO

abcdefghijklmnopqrstuvwxyz

DISCUS BOLD

A visiting-card script. A nearly upright type with curly capitals. The lower case has looped ascenders and long descenders.

The Monotype Corporation's GROSVENOR is a similar design but of larger height and with very short descenders.

ABCDEFGHIJKLMN

OPQRSTUVWXYZ&

abcdefghijklmnopqrstuvwxyz

DORCHESTER SCRIPT

An adaptation of flourished book initials after the Victorian model.

DUTCH INITIALS

373

DYNAMIC
Berthold 1952

Designed by Herbert Post. A heavy, forceful script with several unusual letters. The down strokes of **B** and **P** are crossed by the bottom line of the bowls. The **G** has an open, descending tail, and the **g** an open tail. All down strokes are very pronounced. The bowls of **R** and **e** are open, the upstroke of the **A** descends below the line.

viii

ABCDEFGHIJKLMNOPQRSTUVWZ

abcdefghijklmnopqrstuvwxyz

1234567890

DYNAMIC

ELAN
Stempel 1937

Designed by Hans Möhring. A heavy, informal script resembling SIGNAL. The letters are monotone and close-setting, but the alignment is not so irregular as in Signal.

viii

Besuchen Sie das Seebad

ELAN

ELEGANCE
Ludwig & Mayer 1968

viii

Designed by Karlgeorg Hoefer. A spidery wide script.

ABCDEFGHIJKLMNOPQ
RSTUVWXYZ
abcdefghijklmnopqrstuvwxyz
1234567890

ELEGANCE

EL GRECO
Berthold 1964

Designed by G.G. Lange. An angular pen script.

ABCDEFGHIJKLMNOPQRSTUV

viii

abcdefghijklmnopqrstuvwxyz ij

1234567890

EL GRECO

ELITE
Nebiolo 1968

viii

Designed by Aldo Novarese as a linear script.

ABCDEFGHIJKLMN
OPQRSTUVWXYZ&
abcdefghijklmnopqrstuvwxyz
1234567890%

ELITE

374

Designed by S.H. de Roos. A serifed spidery script, almost an inclined roman but without variation in stress.

Birmingham Industrial Residences

ELLA

Designed by Arno Drescher. A heavy script of monotone colour, with close-fitting letters. It resembles SIGNAL. The alignment is not quite so irregular as in SIGNAL. ENERGOS is a bold version of APPELL.

The Royal Bank of Canada

Sonderschau der Deutschen Graphik

ENERGOS

Designed by Walter Höhnisch. A tall, bold script with even inclination.

ABCDEFGHIJKLMNOPQR STUVWXYZ

abcdefghijklmnopqrstuvwxyz

1234567890

EXPRESS

A fairly heavy, informal script resembling PENFLOW. The lower-case letters are close-setting. There is some variation of stress but there are no hair lines.
 A rather heavier face which is partially shaded, like PENTAPE, is called FLAMME.

ABCDEFGHIJKLMNOPQRSTU VWXYZ

abcdefghijklmnopqrstuvwxyz

1234567890

FANAL

375

FLAIR
Ludlow 1941

Designed by R. Hunter Middleton.

ABCDEFGHIJK
LMNOPQRST
UVWXYZ
1234567890

FLAIR

FLAMME
Schelter & Giesecke 1933

viii

A heavy script, which is slightly shaded. The lower-case letters are close setting. *Cf.* FANAL.

ABCDEFGHIJKLMNOPQR
STUVWXYZ
abcdefghijklmnopqrstuvwxyz&
£1234567890

FLAMME

FLEX
Amsterdam 1937

viii

Designed by George Salter. A ribbon type, or partially shaded script, resembling PENTAPE. The capitals are swash forms and the lower case almost an italic.

Amicable Resolutions Introduced

FLEX

FLORENTINE CURSIVE
Ludlow 1956

viii

Designed by R.H. Middleton. A narrow pen script with tall ascenders and swash capitals.

ABCDEFGHIJKLMNOPQRSTUVW
XYZ&
abcdefghijklmnopqrstuvwxyz 1234567890

FLORENTINE CURSIVE

Designed by A. Butti. A script in which the thin strokes are hair lines starting from the foot of the main strokes.

ABCDEFGHIJKLMNOPQRSTUVWXYZÇŒÆ

abcdefghijklmnopqrsstuvwxyzçœæ

1234567890

FLUIDUM

ABCDEFGHIJKLMNOPQRSTU VWXYZÇ 1234567890

abcdefghijklmnopqrstuvwxyz

FLUIDUM BOLD

Designed by Erich Mollowitz. A script of medium weight and colour with flourished capitals and tall ascenders in the lower case. There are no serifs. Descenders are short. There are also bold face and swash capitals. MERCURY (Stephenson Blake) was copied from the original design. Originally a type designed for Trennert in 1936.

ABCDEFGHIJKL MNOPQRSTUV WXYZ

abcdefghijklmnopqrstuvwxyz 1234567890

FORELLE

ABCDEFGHIJKL MNOPQRSTUV WXYZ

abcdefghijklmnopqrstuvwxyz 1234567890

FORELLE

Designed by R. Hunter Middleton.

ABCDEFGHIJKLMNOPQRSTUV WXYZ&

abcdefghijklmnopqrstuvwxyz

1234567890

FORMAL SCRIPT

A bold script designed by Carl Reissberger. The type has neither kerns nor connecting strokes.

ABCDEFGHIJKLMNOPQRSTUV
WXYZ   1234567890

abcdefghijklmnopqrstuvwxyz

FORTE

Designed by W. Rebhuhn for Genzsch & Heyse in 1955. A heavy brush script of angular design.

ABCDEFGHIJKLMNOPQRSTUVW
XYZ   1234567890

abcdefghijklmnopqrstuvwxyz

FOX

An informal script of medium weight and little variation in colour. The type has a slight but irregular inclination, some letters being upright. Ascenders and descenders are of medium size. The letters are not close-setting.

ABCDEFGHIJKLMNOPQRSTU
VWXYZ   1234567890

abcdefghijklmnopqrstuvwyxz

FRANCESCA RONDE

Designed by Edwin W. Shaar. A formal script of heavy weight and almost monotone. Ascenders and descenders are short. The design is intended to complement the FUTURA range.

ABCDEFGHIJKLMNOPQRSTUVWXYZ
abcdefghijklmnopqrstuvwxyz   1234567890$

FUTURA DEMIBOLD SCRIPT

Designed by Hans Möhring. A formal script of medium weight. The capitals are swash letters. The letters of the lower case are rather wide and ascenders are tall. The serifs are sharp and oblique. There are no looped ascenders.

ABCDEFGHIJKLMNOPQR
STUVWXYZ

abcdefghijklmnopqrstuvwxyz

1234567890

GABRIELE

Designed by Hans-Jürg Hunziker and Matthew Carter as a formal script for phototypesetting.

GANDO
RONDE
Mergenthaler Linofilm 1970

ABCDEFGHIJ

KLMNOPQRSTUVWXYZ

viii

abcdefghijklmnopqrstuvwxyz

$1234567890

GANDO RONDE

Designed by Rudo· Spemann. A light script in which several capitals descend below the line. The ascenders are long. There are also swash capitals.

GAVOTTE
Klingspor 1940

ABCDEFGHIJKLMNOPQR

viii

abcdefghijklmnopqrstuvwxyz

GAVOTTE

Designed by William S. Gillies. A script monotone in colour with flowing capitals and a more rigid lower case. Some of the lower-case letters resemble the italic letters in a sans serif, *e.g.*, the **m**, **n** and **t**; perhaps that trait coupled with the uniform colour accounts for the name Gothic. It is also called FLOTT. There is also a bold version.

GILLIES
GOTHIC or
FLOTT
Bauer 1935

ABCDEFGHIJKLMNOPQRSTUVWXYZ

viii

abcdefghijklmnopqrstuvwxyz *Th*

1234567890

GILLIES GOTHIC LIGHT

ABCDEFGHIJKLMNOPQRSTUVWXYZ

viii

abcdefghijklmnopqrstuvwxyz *Th*

1234567890

GILLIES GOTHIC

Designed by Hans Möhring, originally a Schriftguss type. An informal and heavy brush script.

GLADIATOR
Typoart

As the New Year Opens

viii

GLADIATOR

GLADIOLA
Stempel 1936

Designed by Martin Wilke. An upright and monotone script. The capitals are freely drawn. In the lower case ascenders and descenders are short and the letters are round.

viii

$$Der\ Zauber$$

GLADIOLA

GLENMOY
Stephenson Blake 1931

The Sheffield version of the heavy pen scripts. The letters set closely in a deceptive way. The alignment is more regular than in some of these heavy scripts.

viii

Enterprising Printers

GLENMOY

GLORIA
Gans c. 1930

A formal and rather heavy script, with considerable variation of stress. The capitals are italic swash forms. In the lower case the ascenders have small loops. The **i**, **p** and **q** have large foot serifs, but otherwise there are no serifs. The dots over **i** and **j** are diamond-shaped. The type is also called FULGOR.

viii

ABCDEFGHIJKLMNOPQRSTUV
a b c d e f g h i j k l m n o p q r s t u v w x y z fi ff fl

GLORIA

GONG
J. Wagner 1953

A chalk script of a design similar to the same founder's REPORTER, with mottled shading.

viii

ABCDEFGHIJKLMNOPQRST
UVWXYZ
abcddeemafffffifghchijkckllmnopqrst
tßüowxyzq
1234567890

GONG

GRAFICO
Cooperativa 1965

viii

Designed by Umberto Fenocchio as a pen script of large x-height.

ABCDEFGHIJKLMNOPQR
STUVWXYZ&ÆŒ
abcdefghijklmnopqrstuvwxyzœœ
1234567890

GRAFICO

380

A nineteenth-century copperplate script. *Cf.* CALLIGRAPHIQUES, PALACE SCRIPT, etc. There are two varieties of many letters, the lower-case ascending letters being without loops.

*A B C D E F G G H I J K L
M M N O P Q 2 R S T U V W
X Y Z abcdefghijklmnopqrstuvwxyz e h l r s t z
1234567890*

GRAPHIC SCRIPT

*A A B C D E F F G G H H I
J K K L M M N N O P Q 2 R
S S T U V W X Y Z 1234567890
abcdefghijklmnopqrstuvwxyz e h l r s t z*

viii

GRAPHIC SCRIPT BOLD

Designed by F.H.E. Schneidler (originally cast by Otto Weissert in Stuttgart). A bold, slightly inclined script following the style of other German bold display scripts.

**ABCDEFGHIJKLMNOPQRSTUVWXYZ
abcdefghijklmnopqrstuvwxyz 1234567890**

GRAPHIK

Designed by F.H. Riley. A script of medium weight with considerable variation of stress. In the lower case the thickest parts of the stroke seem to come in an unnatural place. This is also in part true of the upper case.

*ABCDEFGHIJKLMNO
abcdefghijklmnopqrstuvwxyz 12345*

GRAYDA

A light script of the visiting card class. It has a slight inclination, swash capitals, looped ascenders, except the **d**, and short descenders. The lower-case letters are regular and round, and the variation of stress is slight.

For those interested in the Art of fine Printing, there is nothing

GROSVENOR SCRIPT

381

HAUSER SCRIPT
Ludlow 1937

viii

Designed by George Hauser. A heavy brush script like RADAR. The alignment is irregular, but the letters are not close-setting.

ABCDEFGHIJKLMNOPQRSTUVWXYZ&

abcdefghijklmnopqrstuvwxyz 1234567890

HAUSER SCRIPT

HERITAGE
American 1952

viii

Designed by Walter H. McKay. A calligraphic type of slight inclination. The pen-drawn quality is most evident in the serifs. The **a** is unusual in type.

A B C D E F G H I J K L M N O P Q R S T U V W X Y Z Qu &

a a b c d e f g h i j k l m n o p q r s t u v w x y z   ff fi fl ft ffi ffl ft. tt

1 2 3 4 5 6 7 8 9 0

HERITAGE

HOLLA
Klingspor 1932

viii

Designed by Rudolf Koch. A quill pen-drawn script of medium weight. The capitals are freely drawn. **O** and **Q** have an unusual finish at the top of the bowls.

In the lower case ascenders and descenders are short and the letters are somewhat condensed and almost upright. The new version shown here with modified weight was issued in 1951.

ABCDEFGHIJKLMNOPQRSTUV

abcdefghijklmnopqrstuvwxyz

1234567890

HOLLA

viii

BCDEFGIKOUVWY

HOLLA INITIALS

HOYER SCHÖN-SCHRIFT
Stempel

viii

Designed by Hans T. Hoyer. A formal, light script, with flourished capitals and a lower case in which most of the letters are based on the formal Italian hand of the sixteenth century. The inclination is slight. Ascenders are tall and the terminals hooked. The **p** (with an extended upright), the **r**, **v** and **w** vary from the general design.

ABCDEFG

abcdefghijklmnopqrstuvwxyz

1234567890

HOYER SCHÖNSCHRIFT

382

A ribbon script with slight inclination. Fine white hair lines interrupt the black of the strokes where they change from down to up stroke, a suggestion of three-dimensional treatment. Some of the capitals, like the **E**, look as if they fall backwards.

IMPERIO

Nacional

viii

El Escorial situado al pié

IMPERIO

Designed by L. Zimmermann. A heavy script with normal lower case and short thickened ascenders.

IMPULS

L. Wagner; Typoart

viii

ABCDEFGHIJKLMNOPQR STUVWXYZ ADELMORZ abcdefghijklmnopqrstuvwxyzhchchchckffllsstß ttzzenrt 1234567890

IMPULS

A set of calligraphic capitals of the sixteenth century, founder unknown. In 1582 Jan van Hout of Leyden acquired a fount. Enschedé bought them from Ploos van Amstel in 1799.

INITIALS 13

Enschedé

viii

INITIALS 13

An English copperplate script in the traditional style using the caps of MARINA SCRIPT and the lower case of YOUTHLINE.

INVITATION SCRIPT

Stephenson Blake

viii

ABCDEFGHIJKLMNOPQ RSTUVWXYZ

abcdefghijklmnopqrstuvwxyz   1234567890

INVITATION SCRIPT

Designed by Jacoby-Boy. A formal script which is nearly upright and has considerable variation of stress. There are two versions of many of the capitals, italic letters and swash varieties.

JACOBEA

Berthold 1928

viii

Echte Spitzen

JACOBEA

383

JAGUAR
Weber 1967

viii

Designed by Georg Trump. A calligraphic script with very short descenders.

$$ABCDEFGHJJKLMNOPQRSTUVW$$
$$XYZ$$
$$abcdefghijklmnopqrstuvwxyz$$
$$1234567890$$

JAGUAR

JOWA SCRIPT
Wagner 1967

viii

Designed by J. Wagner and following the style of GONG as a light informal pen script.

$$ABCDEFGHJJKLMNOPQRST$$
$$UVWXYZ ÄÖÜ$$
$$abcdefghijklmnopqrstuvwxyz äöü ch ck ff fi fl ß tz$$
$$u en er dell st s g æ œ$$
$$1234567890 &$$

JOWA SCRIPT

JULIET
Nebiolo 1955

viii

Designed by A. Novarese. A light formal script. The capitals are flourished and the lower case has tall ascenders with small loops.

$$ABCDEFGHIJKLMNOPQRSTUVX ÆŒW$$
$$abcdefghijklmnopqrstuvxyzæœw$$
$$1234567890$$

JULIET

JUNIOR
Schelter & Giesecke 1936

viii

Designed by Hans Heimbeck. A light script with a very slight inclination. Pen-drawn qualities are evident in both the freely drawn capitals and the more formal lower case. There are no looped ascenders and descenders are short.

$$ABCDEFGGHIJKLMN$$
$$OPQRSTUVWXYZ$$
$$abcdefghijklmnopqrstuvwxyz$$
$$1234567890$$

JUNIOR

384

Designed by Trochut Blanchard. An unusual script which is nearly upright. Ascenders and descenders are long and the ascenders looped. The lower-case **o** is not closed at the top, and the **r** and **s** are very unusual.

The rotation is continuous and the bottom part touches the color

JUVENTUD

Designed by M.R. Kaufmann. A monotone script of medium weight. The capitals are freely drawn. In the lower case the letters are close-fitting. The **d** is looped. There is also a light face.

ABCDEFGHIJKLMN OPQRSTUVWXYZ&

abcdefghijklmnopqrstuvwxyz

1234567890

KAUFMANN

ABCDEFGHIJKLMNOPQRSTUVWXYZ&

abcdefghijklmnopqrstuvwxyz

1234567890

KAUFMANN BOLD

Designed by W.T. Sniffin. A bold, non-joining, slightly inclined script without serifs. The **Q** almost resembles a figure 2, and **G**, **J**, **S** and **Y** descend below the line. The bowls of many round letters, as for instance, **A**, **B**, **D**, **O**, **Q**, **R**, and some of their lower-case counterparts, are open. The tail of the **y** is vertical and that of the **g** is open.

ABCDEFGHIJKLMNOPQRSTUVWXYZ&

abcdefghijklmnopqrstuvwxyz   *er es is or os Th th tt*

1234567890

KEYNOTE

Designed by Karl Klauss. A fat face pen-script following German handwriting style, notably in the **s** and **f**. The **d** is open and has no spur, and capitals are swash letters.

Reisen in das Mittelmeer

KLAUSS CURSIVE

Designed by Rudolf Koch for children's books and primers to instruct in the German cursive handwriting style then taught in schools.

Winterolympiade in Innsbruck

KOCH KURRENT

KONZEPT
Stempel 1968

viii

Designed by Martin Wilke as an informal script departing from pen or brush script style by using a fibre pen in drawing the original characters.

ABCDEFGHIJKLMNOPQRSTU

abcdefghijklmnopqrstuvwxyz

1234567890

KONZEPT

KÜNSTLER-SCHREIB-SCHRIFT
Stempel 1957

viii

Designed by Hans Bohn. There are three weights of this type and the bold shown here is more rounded and compact than the normal and medium. The script has the design of a copperplate in a bold weight.

ABCDEFGHIJKLM
NOPQRSTUVWXYZ

abcdefghijklmnopqrstuvwxyz

KÜNSTLERSCHREIBSCHRIFT

KURIER
Typoart

viii

Designed by Herbert Thannhaeuser, originally a Schelter & Giesecke face. An informal and heavy brush script, similar to the same founder's GLADIATOR and LOTTO.

ABCDEFGHIJKLM
NOPQRSTUVWXYZ

abcdefghijklmnopqrzsstuvwxyz

1234567890

KURIER

LA CIVILITÉ
Deberny & Peignot

viii

A script based on French sixteenth-century cursive. There are several alternative swash letters The design is very similar to Enschedè's original CIVILITÉ, which is, however, somewhat bolder American Typefounders' CIVILITÉ is less correct in design.

Observez bien la modestie en vous couchant

LA CIVILITÉ

LAPIS
Nebiolo

viii

A pen-script based on Italian writing styles around the turn of the century. Similar types are cast by other Italian founders.

ABCDEFGHIJKLM
NOPQRSEUVXYZWG&

abcdefghijklmnopqrstuvxyzw
1234567890

LAPIS

386

Designed by F.H.E. Schneidler. A script of some distinction. The capitals are flowing. The lower case has long ascenders and descenders and is upright. Some letters, *e.g.*, the **d**, **g** and **h**, together with some second varieties in the capitals, are derived from gothic scripts. The figures are non-ranging.

AABBCDDEFfGHJJKLLMN
OPQRRSSTCUVWXYZTh
abcdefghijklmnopqrstuvwxyz th
1234567890
LEGEND

Designed by W.T. Sniffin. A light, formal script resembling BERNHARD CURSIVE. The capitals are flourished and the variation of stress is considerable. The ascenders are very tall and hooked at the top. The letters are round and the thin strokes take off from the feet of the thick strokes.

ABCDEFGHIJKLMNOPQRSTUVWX
YZ&
abcdefghijklmnopqrstuvwxyz
1 2 3 4 5 6 7 8 9 0
LIBERTY

Designed by Imre Reiner. Not a true script and somewhat reminiscent of TIME SCRIPT.

ABCDEFGHIJKLMNOPQRSTUVW
XYZabcdefghijklmnopqrstuvwxyz&£$!?
aschffffethttSh 1234567890
LONDON SCRIPT

Designed by Herbert Thannhaeuser. An informal and heavy brush script, similar to the same founders' GLADIATOR.

Newspapers and Periodicals
LOTTO

Designed by R.H. Middleton. A medium heavy, informal script. The variation of stress is slight and the lower-case letters are close-setting. The ascenders are short and without loops. *Cf.* ELAN.

ABCDEFGHIJKLMNOPQRSTU
VWXYZ&
abcdefghijklmnopqrstuvwxyz
1234567890
MANDATE

MARGGRAFF LIGHT ITALIC
Schriftguss 1929

viii

Designed by G. Marggraff. Although called a cursive, the type is really a script. There is considerable variation of colour. In some letters, *e.g.*, **g**, **m**, **n** and **r**, the thin upstroke is quite separate from the downstroke, giving the appearance of an inline type. Ascenders terminate in a hook to the left. There is also a bold.

Morgenfeier im Eldorado

MARGGRAFF LIGHT ITALIC*

MARINA
Stephenson Blake 1936

viii

A copperplate script of rather heavier weight than PALACE SCRIPT.

ABCDEFGHIJKLMNOP2RST U V
W X Y Z
abcdefghijklmnopqrstuvwxyz
1234567890

MARINA

MAXIM
Bauer 1955

viii

Designed by Peter Schneidler. A heavy informal script of the brush variety. The inclination is extreme, some letters appearing to be toppling over. The irregularity adds to the informal character of the design.

ABCDEFGHIJ
KLMNOPQRSTU
VWXYZ1234567890
abcdefghijklmnop
qrstuvwxyz

MAXIM

MISTRAL
Olive 1953; Amsterdam 1955

viii

Designed by Roger Excoffon. An informal, true script. The letters of the lower case are joining and the descenders fairly long.

ABCDEFGHIJKLMNOPQRSTUVWXYZ
abcdefghijklmnopqrstuvwxyz
1234567

MISTRAL

Designed by R.H. Middleton. A script of medium weight and sharp variation of stress. The capitals are flourished. In the lower case ascenders are tall and vertical strokes of uniform thickness. The letters are round. *Cf.* BERNHARD CURSIVE BOLD and MERCURY.

ABCDEFGHIJKLMNOPQRSTU
VWXYZ&
1234567890
abcdefghijklmnopqrstuvwxyz

MAYFAIR CURSIVE

Designed by Imre Reiner and drawn with a pen made from bamboo.

ABCDEFGHIJKLM
NOPQRSTUVWYZ
abcdefghijklmnopqrs
tuvwxyz

MERCURIUS

An informal, monotone script of medium weight. The lower case letters are close setting. There are more looped ascenders than in SWING BOLD.

ABCDEFGHIJKLMNOPQRSTUVWXYZ
abcdefghijklmnopqrstuvwxyz 12345

MONOLINE

Designed by E.J. Klumpp. A light script with swash capitals and an informal, condensed lower case. The letters are almost upright.

ABCDEFGHIJKLMNOPQRSTUV
WXYZ& abcdefghijklmnopqrstuvwxyz 1234567890

MURRAY HILL

ABCDEFGHIJKLMNOPQRST
UVWX abcdefghijklmnopqrstuvwxyz
1234567890

MURRAY HILL BOLD

MUSTANG
Stempel 1956
viii

viii

Designed by Imre Reiner. A heavy brush script, less irregular than some similar types.

ABCDEGHIJKLMNOPQRSTUVWXYZ

abcdefghijklmnopqrstuvwxyz

MUSTANG

NOVA SCRIPT
Intertype (New York) 1937
viii

Designed by George F. Trenholm. A script with freely drawn capitals and rather more formal lower case. Ascenders are tall and have slight serifs. The figures are ranging.

ABCDEFGHIJKLMNOPQRSTUVWXYZ

abcdefghijklmnopqrstuvwxyz

1234567890

NOVA SCRIPT

ONDINE
Deberny & Peignot 1954
viii

Designed by A. Frutiger. A formal upright script of heavy weight. There are four additional capitals, including extra wide **M** and **N**.

ABCDEFGHIJKLMNOPQRSTUVW
XYZ QVEMNQu
abcdefghijklmnopqrstuvwxyz
1234567890

ONDINE

ORIENTE
American
viii

A Victorian flourished script.

ABCDEFGHIJKLMNOPQRS
TUVWXYZ
1234567890

ORIENTE

OSCAR
Nebiolo 1966
viii

viii

Designed by Aldo Novarese. A pen script with open bowls to letters and tapered strokes.

ABCDEFGHIJKLMNOPQRSTUVW
XYZ
abcdefghijklmnopqrstuvxyzw
1234567890

OSCAR

An English copperplate script. It is steeply inclined and has abrupt variation in colour. The ascenders are not looped, except the **f**, but there are second looped versions of the **h** and **l**. In combination the letters appear to be engraved and not the impression from type.

EMBASSY SCRIPT (Caslon, 1924) is a similar type. Stephenson Blake have other closely similar copperplates, called MARINA and IMPERIAL. SOCIETY SCRIPT is another, but rather lighter in colour.

PALACE
SCRIPT

Stephenson Blake 1923;

Monotype

viii

*ABCDEFGHIJKLMNOP
QRSTUVWXYZ
abcdefghijklmnopqrstuvwxyz*

STEPHENSON BLAKE PALACE SCRIPT

viii

*ABCDEFGHIJKLMNOPQRST
UVWXYZ abcdefghijklmnopqrstuvwxyz12345*

MONOTYPE PALACE SCRIPT

Designed by Martin Wilke. A strong brush script giving an even black in print. The long descenders are characteristic of some capital letters, as for instance **A, G, M, N, P, T** and **B** have very long upper serifs. The ascender of the **d** is curved backwards.

PALETTE

Berthold 1951

ABCDEFGHIJKLMNOPQRSTUVWX

viii

abcdefghijklmnopqrstuvwxyz

1234567890

PALETTE

Designed by Georg Trump. A script of heavy weight with flourished capitals and an upright lower case. Ascenders are tall and the letters have a pen-drawn quality with little variation of colour.

PALOMBA

Weber 1955

ABCDEFGHIJKLMNO
PQRSTUVWXYZ

viii

abcdefghijklmnopqrstuvwxyz

1234567890

PALOMBA

Designed by Richard Weber. A heavy brush script, without serifs. The counters are circular and the figures non-ranging.

PAPAGENO

Bauer 1958

ABCDEFGHIJKLMNOPQRSTUVW
abcdefghijklmnopqrstuvwxyzabi

viii

1234567890

PAPAGENO

391

PARISIAN RONDE
Stephenson Blake

viii

A faithful reproduction of the common French script of the nineteenth century. It is an upright script with flourished capitals and considerable variation of colour. The lower-case letters are close-fitting, the ascenders looped and fairly tall. Descenders are equally long. The original design was called FRENCH SCRIPT by the Inland Type Foundry and American Typefounders called it TYPO UPRIGHT.

ABCDEFGHIJKLMNOPQRSTUVWXYZ

abcdefghijklmnopqrstuvwxyz

1234567890

PARISIAN RONDE

PARK AVENUE
American 1933

viii

Designed by R.E. Smith. A light script with freely drawn capitals. The pen-drawn quality is very evident in the lower case. Ascenders and descenders are long; the ascenders are bent over at the top. The figures are non-ranging and the capitals are similar to TRAFTON.

A B C D E F G H I J K L M N O P Q R S T U V

W X Y Z &

a b c d e f g h i j k l m n o p q r s t u v w x y z er es rs

1 2 3 4 5 6 7 8 9 0

PARK AVENUE

PARKWAY SCRIPT
Ludlow 1964

viii

Designed by Emil Hirt as a calligraphic script following European contemporary models.

ABCDEFGHIJKLMNOPQRS
TUVWXYZ&

abcdefghijklmnopqrstuvwxyz

1234567890

PARKWAY SCRIPT

PENTAPE
Schriftguss 1935

viii

Designed by Walter Schnippering. An inline script, conveying the idea of a flowing ribbon. The type is also known as ORIGINELL.

ABCEGIKLMOUZ

PENTAPE

PEPITA
Monotype 1959

viii

Designed by Imre Reiner. An informal script of medium weight. The lower-case letters are irregularly aligned and are not close-fitting. There is moderate variation on stress. The figures are non-ranging.

ABCDEFGHIJKLMNOPQRSTUVWXYZ

abcdefghijklmnopqrstuvwxyz

1234567890

PEPITA

Designed by Heinrich Pauser. A script of heavy face. The capitals are of a flowing design. The lower case has tall ascenders and descenders and is almost an italic, with serifs on some letters, *e.g.* **m**, **n** and **u**.

PETRA
Stempel 1954

viii

ABCDEFGHIJKLMNO

abcdefghijklmnopqrstuvwxyz

1234567890

PETRA

Designed by F. Riedinger. A heavy, informal script, but regular in alignment.

PHÄNOMEN
Krebs 1927

viii

Großer Ausverkauf in

PHÄNOMEN

Designed by H. Wieynck. A script with flourished capitals and a lower case which is practically an italic. It has oblique serifs. The **a** is two-storeyed. The **v**, **w** and **y** are script forms.

PHYLLIS or
WIEYNCK
CURSIVE
Bauer 1911

viii

Volkskonzert in der Philharmon

PHYLLIS

Designed by Carl Pohl. A brush script, which is almost upright. The variation in colour is slight, and serifs are all but eliminated.

POLO
Typoart 1960

viii

ABCDEFGHIJKLMNOPQRSTUV
WXYZ&

abcdefghijklmnopqrstuvwxyz?

1234567890

POLO

Designed by E. Lautenbach. A heavy German script, regular in alignment and close setting. Also called SAMSON SCRIPT. *Cf.* SCRIPT BOLD

PRÄGEFEST
Ludwig & Mayer 1926

viii

ABCDEFGHIJKLMNOPQRSTU
VWXYZ

abcdefghijklmnopqrstuvwxyz

1234567890

PRÄGEFEST

PRIVAT

Bauer 1966

viii

Designed by J.J. Siercke as an informal pen script.

AABCDQEEFGHIJKLMMNOPQRS
TUVWXYZ

abcdefghijklmnopqrstuvwxyz
1234567890

PRIVAT

PRIMA

Stempel 1957

viii

Designed by Martin Hermersdorf as a pen-drawn type used by the Moritz Diesterweg educational publishing house in reading primers.

ABCDEFGHIJKLMNOPQRSTU
abcdefghijklmnopqrstuvwxyz
1234567890

PRIMA

PRIMADONNA

Ludwig & Mayer

viii

Designed by Helmut Matheis. A light and formal script with considerable variation of stress. The **m, n** and **p** have roman serifs, which adds to the formality of the design.

ABCDEFGHIJKLMNOPQ
RSTUVWXYZ

abcdefghijklmnopqrstuvwxyz

1234567890

PRIMADONNA

PULIDO

Iranzo

viii

A formal, tall script with pen-drawn qualities and considerable variation of stress.

Competición Internacional de Ajedrez

PULIDO

RADAR

Nacional

viii

A heavy brush script with slight inclination. Descenders are short, and some letters have lower-case handwriting characteristics, as for instance **n, o** and **p**. The cross-beam of the **A** ascends from the right foot of the letter on the line and cuts half-way through the up-stroke. The bowl of the **R** is not closed.

Alpinismo en Navas del Rey

RADAR

Decorated pen-drawn initials in elaborately baroque style, designed by Henk Krijger. The face is characterised by an abundance of pen flourishes.

RAFFIA INITIALS

Designed by Imre Reiner. A strong brush script. *Cf.* CHOC and others. The bowl of the **e** is open at the top and the **r** is curiously shaped.

ABCDEFGHIJKLMNOPQRSTUVW
XYZ& 1234567890

abcdefghijklmnopqrssttthuvwxyz

REINER BLACK

Designed by Imre Reiner. An informal pen script which is almost upright. The variation in colour is slight.

ABCDEFGHIJKLMNOPQRSTUVWXYZ

abcdefghijklmnopqrstuvwxyz

The Quick Brown Fox Jumped Over the Lazy Dog

REINER SCRIPT

Designed by C. Winkow. An informal script of medium weight which is slightly shaded. The capitals are not unlike SIGNAL, and the alignment has a similar irregularity. There are two versions of some letters and a number of tied letters. There is a slight variation of colour. RUSINOL (Fundicion Tipografica National) is identical but has some different alternative letters.

ABCDEFFIGHJJKLMNOPQüRSSchSfLTh
UVWXYZ 1234567890

áãubcdeeiener entf ff fi fl ft ghhch heii ij k ck keit

lllmmunmoopqürsschssst ßt t thHßününsuvwxyz

REPORTER

REPRO SCRIPT

American 1954

Designed by Jerry Mullen. A script of lighter weight than the same founders' BRODY, but equally informal and with close-setting lower-case letters.

A B C D E F G H I J K L M N O P Q R S T U V W

X Y Z &

a b c d e f g h i j k l m n o p q r s t u v w x y z

1 2 3 4 5 6 7 8 9 0

REPRO SCRIPT

RHAPSODY

Ludwig & Mayer

Designed by Ilse Schuele. Mainly intended as a display face, the type was later also issued in the smaller sizes. A modern roman adaptation of Schwabacher. The descenders of **P** and **f** are finely tapered.

ABCDEFGHIJKLMNOPQRSTUVWXYZ

abcdefghijklmnopqrsftuvwxyz

1234567890

RHAPSODY

ROMANY

American 1934

Designed by A.R. Bosco. An upright script bearing a general resemblance to GLADIOLA. There are however many differences in detail. For instance, the **d** has a looped ascender and the **e** an uncial form.

A A B C D E F G H I J K L M N O P Q R S T U V W

X Y Z &

a b c d e a f g h i j k l m n o p q r s t u v w x y z

1 2 3 4 5 6 7 8 9 0

ROMANY

RONDINE

Nebiolo 1948

Designed by A. Butti. A formal script of medium weight. The capitals are freely drawn, and in the lower case the ascenders are tall and looped.

A B C D E F G H I J K L M N O P Qu R S

T U V W X Y Z Ç Æ Œ

a b c d e f g h i j k l m n o p q r s t u v w x y z ç œ œ

1 2 3 4 5 6 7 8 9 0

RONDINE

Designed by Stefan Schlesinger and Dick Dooijes. The flourished capitals have some resemblance to those of the traditional French Ronde, but not the lower case. The variation of colour is small, ascenders and descenders are short and there are no looped letters. The type has a slight inclination. There are two weights.

ABCDEFGHIJKLMNOP
QuRSTUVWXYZ
abcdefghijklmnopqrstuvwxyz 1234567890
RONDO

ABCDEFGHIJKLMNOP
QuRSTUVWXYZ
abcdefghijklmnopqrstuvwxyz
RONDO BOLD

Designed by Karlgeorg Hoefer. An informal Latin script of heavy weight and considerable variation of stress. On the lower case serifs are either stubby or non-existent.

ABCDEFGHIJKLMNOP
QRSTUVWXYZ
abcdefghijklmnopqrstuvwxyz

SALTINO

Designed by Karlgeorg Hoefer. A brush script of slight inclination with strong emphasised down strokes. The capitals are higher than the ascenders of lower-case letters. Some lower-case letters, like **a, n, m** and **u**, have foot serifs on the right, the **h** has a descender with a small spur; the dot on the **i** is a flat stroke.

The Annual Dinner of the Club
SALTO

Designed by Marcel Jacno. An informal and almost monotone script of medium weight, with close-fitting letters in the lower case. Not unlike FANAL, but the letters are more upright.

ABCDEFGHIJ
abcçdefghijklmnopqrs
SCRIBE

RONDO
Amsterdam 1948

viii

viii

SALTINO
Klingspor 1953

viii

SALTO
Klingspor 1952–53

viii

SCRIBE
Deberny & Peignot 1937

viii

397

SCRIPT BOLD

Monotype 1931

A German script based on PRAEGEFEST and also resembling BRUSH SCRIPT or SIGNAL in its informality and blackness. But there is more variation in stress. The small looped tail of **g** and **y** may be noted.

MONOSCRIPT 351 is a rather similar informal and close-setting script, but lighter in weight.

viii

His family has farmed the land for

SCRIPT BOLD

SCRIPTURA

Stempel 1926

Designed by F.W. Kleukens. A light script of slight inclination, with flowing capitals and round letters in the lower case. The ascenders are tall and looped and the descenders short. There is an extra set of open initials.

The type was originally called KLEUKENS SCRIPTURA.

viii

Die Sculptur in Rom

SCRIPTURA

SIGNAL

Berthold 1931

Designed by W. Wege. A heavy script based on an entirely informal hand. It is practically monotone and the letters are deceptively close-fitting. The alignment also is deliberately irregular. The open **o** and irregular **w** may be noted. There are also two lighter weights. Very many German script types resemble this design.

viii

ABCDEFGHIJKLMNOPQRSTUVWXYZ
abcdefghijklmnopqrstuvwxyz

SIGNAL LIGHT

viii

ABCDEFGHIJKLMNOPQRSTUVWXYZ
abcdefghijklmnopqrstuvwxyz 1234567890

SIGNAL MEDIUM

viii

ABCDEFGHIJKLMNOPQRSTUVWXYZ
abcdefghijklmnopqrstuvwxyz

SIGNAL BLACK

SKETCH or SKIZZE

Ludwig & Mayer 1935

viii

Designed by W. Höhnisch. A normal script. The capitals are flourished and the lower case without eccentricity. The **l** is the only looped ascender, the others terminating with hooks.

ABCDEFGHIJKLMNOP
QRSTUVWXYZ
abcdefghijklmnopqrstuvwxyz
1234567890

SKETCH or SKIZZE

Designed by Helmut Matheis. A rather heavy script with considerable variation in colour. The capitals are freely drawn. The lower-case letters are close-fitting and more regular than in other similar scripts. There are ranging figures. Nebiolo's SLOGAN is quite different.

SLOGAN

Ludwig & Mayer 1959

viii

ABCDEFGHIJKLMNOPQR STUVWXYZ

abcdefghijklmnopqrstuvwxyz

1234567890

viii

SLOGAN

Designed by A. Novarese. A brush script with swash letters and rather narrow lower case.

SLOGAN

Nebiolo 1957

ABCDEFGHIJKLMNOPQRSTUV

abcdefghijklmnopqrstuvwxyzææw

1 2 3 4 5 6 7 8 9 0

viii

SLOGAN

Designed by Matthew Carter. Based on the hand of Charles Snell, English writing master and author of *The Pen-man's Treasury open'd* of 1694, whose standard rules for forming letters lend themselves particularly well to phototypesetting scripts. Lower case letters, and some capitals, have joining strokes on the right that run into the following character to allow more than one sort of link than the usual butt joint of the formal script.

SNELL ROUNDHAND

Linofilm 1966

A B C D E F G H I J K L M N O P Q R S T U V W X Y Z

abcdefghijklmnopqrstuvwxyz

1234567890

viii

SNELL ROUNDHAND

Designed by Heinz Schumann. A narrow brush script.

STENTOR

Typoart 1964

ABCDEFGHIJKLMNOPQRS TUVWXYZ

abcdefghijklmnopqrstuvwxyz&

1234567890

viii

STENTOR

399

STOP
Ludwig & Mayer 1939

Designed by Walter Höhnisch. A dry brush script. The shading is irregular and the endings of vertical strokes and arcs are ragged.

viii

ABCDEFGHIJKLMNOPQRS
TUVWXYZ
abcdefghijklmnopqrstuvw
xyz
1234567890

STOP

STRADIVARIUS
Bauer 1945

Designed by Imre Reiner. An unusual script with flourished capitals and a stiff lower case. There is considerable variation of colour. Ascenders are tall and there are no serifs. The rigid appearance is produced by the squaring of the normally round letters. In Germany the type is called SYMPHONIE.

viii

ABCDEFGHIJKLMNOPQ
RSTUVWXYZ
abcdefghijklmnopqrstuvwxyz
1234567890

STRADIVARIUS

STYLO
Française

An informal, monotone script of medium weight. The capitals are flourished and the lower-case is close setting.

viii

ABCDEFGHIJKLMNOPQR
TUVWXYZ
abcdefghijklmnopqrstuvwxyzœæ
1234567890

STYLO

SWING BOLD
Monotype 1955

An informal script of medium weight and monotone in colour. The lower-case letters are joining.

viii

ABCDEFGHIJKLMNOPQRSTUVWXYZ
abcdefghijklmnopqrstuvwxyz 12345

SWING BOLD

400

A pen script lighter in weight and more formal, in the lower case at least, than the brush scripts like SIGNAL, etc. The lower case has oblique serifs. The **o** has a quill-drawn form but such as no quill could manage. There are short-ranging figures.

ABCDEFGHIJKLMNOPQRST
UVWXYZ

abcdeßghijklmnopqrstuvwxyz
1234567890

TEMPLE SCRIPT

Designed by Tommy Thompson. A calligraphic script with slight inclination, in which some lower-case letters, as for instance, the **f**, are almost roman. The **g** has an open tail, and the **p** a slab serif on the foot. Most lower-case letters have no serifs. There are various alternative capital letters.

ABCDEFGHIJKLMNOPQRSTUVWXYZ&

AAEFGHIJKLMNTVW&fh

abcdefghijklmnopqrstuvwxyz

1234567890

THOMPSON QUILLSCRIPT

Designed by G. Trump. An informal calligraphic type with letters of uneven x-height and several capitals descending below the line. Ascenders have spur serifs, which are also found in the **K, N, V, W** and **X**.

ABCDEFGHIIJKLMNOPQRSTU
VWXYZ
abcddefggbijklmnopqrsstuvwxyz
1234567890

TIME

ABCDEFGHIJKLMNOPQR
STUVWXYZ
abcddefggbijklmnopqrsstuvwx
yz 1234567890

TIME MEDIUM

ABCDEFGHIJKLMNOPQ
RSTUVWXYZ
abcddefgghijklmnopqrsstuv
wxyz
1234567890

TIME BOLD

TITANTYPO
Wagner 1966

Originally a Wagner & Schmidt type first cast around 1905, and formerly known as STANLEY. A fat script with rounded letters and tall ascenders. Amsterdam called this type HERCULES and Wagner in the 1927 version TITAN.

viii

ABCDEFGHIJKLMNOPQRSTUVW
XYZ
abcdefghijklmnopqrstuvwxyz
1234567890

TITANTYPO

TRAFTON SCRIPT
Bauer 1933

Designed by H.A. Trafton. A light script with freely drawn capitals. The lower case has long ascenders and descenders and the descenders are looped. There is a considerable gradation of colour, but the vertical strokes are of uniform width. In Germany the type is called QUICK and in France ETOILE.

viii

ABCDEFGHIJKLMNOPQuQRS
TUVWXYZ
abcdefghijklmnopqrstuvwxyz 12345678

TRAFTON SCRIPT

TRIANON
Bauer 1905

Designed by H. Wieynck. A formal cursive script with bold strokes, generally in eighteenth-century design. Some letters are not unlike the italic of TRADITION. Capitals are wide and flourished, and serifs very pronounced. There is also an outline version, TRIANON OPEN.

viii

Haus für Qualitätsdruck

TRIANON

Rheinländer

TRIANON OPEN

Designed by Albert Auspurg. A light script with flourished capitals and a round lower case. The ascenders are tall and nicked at the top. The vertical strokes taper. The **g** has a vertical ear. The **w** is of German design.

Hôtel David Petterson

TROCADERO KURSIV

A ZIRKULAR KARTENSCHRIFT, cut by Wagner & Schmidt in 1926, was cast around 1927 by many foundries. Willy Schumann designed some initials to it for BUTTERFLY of Schriftguss; Georg Belwe another set for L. Wagner (as SCHÖNSCHRIFT MOZART INITIALEN); E. Thiele designed an exclusive series for Haas, TROUBADOUR OPEN, which was also sold by Stempel* and Berthold.* Amsterdam sells this type as GRACIA, Nebiolo as DONATELLO and Berling as HERTHA.

ABCDEFGHIJKLMNOPQRS

abcdefgh.ijklmnopqrstuvwxyz

1234567890

TROUBADOUR

ABCDEFGHIJKLMNOPQR

abcdefghijklmnopqrstuvwxyz

TROUBADOUR BOLD

viii

ABCDEFGHIJKLMNOPQR

abcdefghijklmnopqrstuvwxyz

TROUBADOUR OPEN

viii

Designed by Hildegard Korger. A calligraphic type with some similarity in style to TIME, though narrower and less free in form.

ABCDEFGHIJKLMNOPQRSTUVWXYZ

abcdefghijklmnopqrstuvwxyz

TYPO-SKRIPT

Designed by Joachim Romann. Several letters of this script, with no lower case, resemble the same founder's GAVOTTE. The weight, however, is much heavier, and the contrast between thick and thin strokes much stronger.

ABCDEFGHIJKLM

NOPQRSTUVWXY

VARIANTE

403

VELTRO
Nebiolo 1931

An informal script, very like SIGNAL. It is similar in its irregular alignment, the close setting of the letters, and is also monotone. There are two weights.

viii

ABCDEFFGHIIJKLMNOPQRSSTUV.
abcdefghijklmnopqrsstuvwxyzwçœœ 1234567890

VELTRO

viii

ABCDEFGHIIJKLMNOPQRSS
TUVWXYZÇÆŒ&
abcdefghijklmnopqrsstuvwxyzçœœ
1234567890

VELTRO BOLD

VENTURE
Linofilm 1969

Designed by Hermann Zapf.

ABCDEFGHIJKLMNOPQRSTUVWXYZ

viii

abcdefghijklmnopqurstuvwxyz

1234567890

VENTURE

VERONA
Berthold

Designed by Helmuth Matheis for Genzsch & Heyse in 1958. A script of medium weight and nearly upright.
American Typefounders and Stephenson Blake have quite different types of this name.

viii

ABCDEFGHIJKLMNOPQRSTUVW
XYZ
abcdefghijklmnopqrstuvwxyz
123456780

VERONA

VICTORIANA
Nacional

A formal script with fine up-strokes and bold main strokes. The capitals are higher than the ascenders of lower-case letters. The **r** is slightly higher than other lower-case letters.

viii

Luxemburgo Alemania

VICTORIANA

404

Designed by Hermann Zapf. A fairly condensed formal script with strong hair lines. Descenders and ascenders have been designed to avoid overhanging the kerns whenever possible, thus giving extra strength for printing. There are alternative versions for some letters.

ABCDEFGHIJKLMNOPQu

abcdefghijklmnopqrstuvwxyz

1234567890

VIRTUOSA I

ABCDEFGHIJKLMNOPQuR

VIRTUOSA II

Designed by R. Hunter Middleton.

ABCDEFGHIJKLMNOPQRST UVWXYZ

abcdefghijklmnopqrstuvwxyz 1234567890

WAVE

A non-kerning copperplate script without joins, but very much heavier in weight. Some capitals, as for instance the **Y**, descend below the line. The foot of the **t** is horizontal and has sharp corners. In contrast with other copperplate scripts the letters in this type do not link up. The ascender of the **l** gives the optical illusion of being taller than those of other letters. The type was originally designed for a corsetry brand. Stephenson Blake's COPPERPLATE BOLD (1953) is a bolder version of this type.

ABCDEFGHIJKLMNOPQ RSTUVWXYZ

abcdefghijklmnopqrstuvwxyz 1234567890

YOUTHLINE

Designed by Karl Georg Hoefer. A bold brush script with tinted shading.

ABCDEFGHIJKLMN

abcdefghijklmnopqrst

1234567890

ZEBRA

SOME LITERATURE ON
TYPE & TYPE FOUNDING

Bastien, Alfred. ENCYCLOPAEDIA TYPOGRAPHICA. West Drayton 1953.

Bennett, Paul A. ON RECOGNISING TYPE FACES. In *The Dolphin*, Vol. II, New York 1935.

Berry, W. Turner & Johnson, A. F. CATALOGUE OF SPECIMENS OF PRINTING TYPES BY ENGLISH & SCOTTISH FOUNDRIES, 1665–1830. With an introduction by Stanley Morison. Oxford University Press, London 1935. (Supplement in *Signature*, New Series 16. New edition in preparation by J. Mosley.)

Biggs, J. R. AN APPROACH TO TYPE. Blandford Press, London. 2nd edition 1961.

Bohadti, Gustav. DIE BUCHDRUCKLETTER. Ein Handbuch für das Schriftgiesserei & Buchdruckgewerbe. Ullstein, Berlin 1954.

Burt, Sir Cyril. A PSYCHOLOGICAL STUDY OF TYPOGRAPHY. With an introduction by Stanley Morison. Cambridge University Press 1959.

Carter, Harry. FOURNIER ON TYPEFOUNDING. Soncino Press, London 1930.

Dowding, Geoffrey. AN INTRODUCTION TO THE HISTORY OF PRINTING TYPES. Wace, London 1961.

Falk, V. NUTIDA TYPSNIT, Upkomst & Utveckling. Lagerströms, Stockholm 1956.

Graphic Arts Typographers Inc. GRAPHIC ARTS TYPE BOOK. Reinhold, New York 1965.

Gray, Nicolette. NINETEENTH-CENTURY ORNAMENTED TYPES & TITLE PAGES. Faber & Faber, London 1938.

Hellinga, Wytze & Lotte. THE FIFTEENTH CENTURY PRINTING TYPES OF THE LOW COUNTRIES. 2 vols. Hertzberger, Amsterdam 1966.

SIXTEENTH CENTURY TYPE DESIGNS OF THE LOW COUNTRIES. Hertzberger, Amsterdam 1966.

Hlasta, S. PRINTING TYPES & HOW TO USE THEM. Carnegie Press, Pittsburgh 1950.

Hlavsa, O. & Sedlacek, F. A BOOK OF TYPE & DESIGN. Artia, Prague & Nevill, London. 2nd edition 1961.

Hutchings, R. S. A MANUAL OF DECORATED TYPE FACES. Cory Adams & Mackay, London 1965.

A MANUAL OF SCRIPT TYPE FACES. Cory Adams & Mackay, London 1965.

THE WESTERN HERITAGE OF TYPE DESIGN. Cory Adams & Mackay, London 1963.

Johnson, A. F. TYPE DESIGNS, Their history and development. André Deutsch, London. 3rd edition 1966.

Karch, R. Randolph. HOW TO RECOGNIZE TYPE FACES. McKnight & McKnight, Bloomington, Ill. 2nd edition 1959.

Kelly, R. R. AMERICAN WOOD TYPE 1828–1900 Van Nostrand Reinhold, New York 1970.

Lindegren, Erik. ABC OF LETTERING & PRINTING TYPES. 3 vols. Erik Lindegren Grafisk Studio, Askim 1964–65.

McMurtrie, Douglas C. TYPE DESIGN. An essay on American type designs with specimens of the outstanding types. With an introduction by Frederic W. Goudy. Pelham, New York 1927.

Mores, E. Rowe. A DISSERTATION UPON ENGLISH TYPOGRAPHICAL FOUNDERS & FOUNDRIES (1778). Edited with an introduction by Harry Carter & Christopher Ricks. Oxford University Press, London 1961.

Morison, Stanley. A TALLY OF TYPES. Cambridge University Press 1953.

ON TYPE DESIGNS OF THE PAST & PRESENT. Ernest Benn, London. Revised edition 1962.

Mosley, James. ENGLISH VERNACULA, A study in traditional letter forms. In *Motif*, 11.

Novarese, Aldo. ALFABETA. Progreso Grafico, Turin 1964.

Reed, Talbot R. HISTORY OF THE OLD ENGLISH LETTER FOUNDRIES. Edited by A. F. Johnson. Faber & Faber, London 1952.

Rosen, Ben. TYPE AND TYPOGRAPHY. Reinhold, New York 1963.

Scarfe, L. ALPHABETS. Written and printed letter forms. Batsford, London 1954.

Seemann, A. HANDBUCH DER SCHRIFTARTEN. Seemann, Leipzig 1926 and supplements to 1937.

Spencer, Herbert. THE VISIBLE WORD. Royal College of Art, London 1968, and Lund Humphries, London 1969.

Sutton, James & Bartram, Alan. AN ATLAS OF TYPE FORMS. Lund Humphries, London 1968.

Szántó, Tibor. A BETÜ. 2 vols. Akademia, Budapest 1965.

Thomas, D. TYPE FOR PRINT. Whitaker, London 1939.

Tschichold, Jan. MEISTERBUCH DER SCHRIFT. Otto Maier, Ravensburg 1953.

Updike, D. B. PRINTING TYPES. 2 vols. Harvard University Press, Cambridge, Massachusetts.

SOME TYPE FACE CLASSIFICATIONS

Association Typographique Internationale. CLASSIFICATION INTERNATIONALE DES CARACTERERES D'IMPRIMERIE. Verona 22 May 1962.

Bastien, Alfred. ENCYCLOPAEDIA TYPOGRAPHICA. West Drayton 1953.

British Standard. SPECIFICATION FOR TYPE FACE NOMENCLATURE & CLASSIFICATION BS 2961: 1967. British Standards Institution, London 1967.

Deutscher Normenausschuss DIN 16518. KLASSIFIZIERUNG DER SATZSCHRIFTEN. Beuth Vertrieb, Berlin 1962.

Hostettler, Rudolf. ZUR KLASSIFIZIERUNG DER SCHRIFTSCHNITTE. In *Typographische Monatsblaetter* 5–1963.—A commentary on the various schemes proposed in Europe, with notes pointing out the problems inherent in the schemes suggested.

Mosley, James. NEW APPROACH TO THE CLASSIFICATION OF TYPE FACES. In *British Printer* 3/1960.—A summary of the various schemes then proposed, prepared for the information of a British Standards Institute sub-committee (see above).

Munsch, René H. PHYSIONOMIE DE LA LETTRE CLASSIFICATION DES CRÉATIONS TYPOGRAPHIQUES ET CONSTRUCTION EN VUE D'OEUVRES PUBLICITAIRES. Editions Eyrolles, Paris 1958.

Novarese, Aldo. IL CARATTERRE, Sintesi storica, classificazione, accostamente eststico. Turin 1957.—An application of Vox, with modifications.

Pellitteri, Giuseppe. CLASSIFICAZIONE MORFOLOGICA DECIMALE DEI CARATTERI STAMPA. In *Annunciatore Poligrafico*, May 1962.—Decimal classification based on form or shape.

THE IDENTIFICATION OF TYPE FACES IN BIBLIOGRAPHICAL DESCRIPTIONS. *Journal of Typographic Research* 1/1967.

Schauer, Georg K. KLASSIFIKATION DER DRUCKSCHRIFTEN. In *Linotype Post*, Neue Folge, February 1958.—A German classification governed primarily by form or shape.

Thibaudeau, François. A LETTRE D'IMPRIMERIE. Paris, 2 vols. 1921.

LA CLASSIFICATION DES LETTRES D'IMPRIMERIE. In *Papyrus Typographie*, 1922.

Tschichold, Jan. MEISTERBUCH DER SCHRIFT. Otto Maier, Ravensburg 1952.

Vox, Maximilian. POUR UNE NOUVELLE CLASSIFICATION DES CARACTÈRES (with English translation). Paris 1954.—The basis of BS 2961:1967 and DIN 16518.

Warde, Beatrice. TYPE FACES OLD AND NEW. In *The Library*, September 1935.

Zapf, Hermann. STILGRUPPEN DER ANTIQUA & IHRE CHARACTERISTISCHEN ELEMENTE. In *Gutenberg Jahrbuch*, 1954.

A LIST OF
TYPEFOUNDERS' ADDRESSES

In this list only the addresses of the type foundries are shown. Names and addresses of agents for these founders can be obtained from the offices listed below.

Some founders, whose types are shown in this book, no longer exist or have changed their names. Whenever possible we have endeavoured to indicate names and addresses of the present owners of their matrices and punches, etc.

It should also be noted that the makers of typesetting and type-casting machines (e.g. Linotype, Intertype, Ludlow, Monotype, Nebitype, Typograph) do not normally supply type. In several cases type designs are also available for hot metal and/or filmsetting, and this applies to filmsetting machines made by manufacturers of hot-metal composing machines, and firms making filmsetting devices only.

ADLER TRALDI SpA, 00040 Pavona (Rome), Italy.

AMERICAN TYPEFOUNDERS Inc, 200 Elmora Avenue, Elizabeth, NJ 07207, U.S.A.

AMSTERDAM TYPEFOUNDRY, Bilderdijkstraat 163, Amsterdam-West, Netherlands.

BARNHART BROTHERS & SPINDLER (*this foundry no longer exists. Most of the types are found in the* American Typefounders *catalogue*).

BAUERSCHE GIESSEREI, Hamburger Allee 45, 6 Frankfurt am Main W 13, Germany.

BERLINGSKA STILGJUTERIET, Lund, Sweden.

H. BERTHOLD AG, Mehringdamm 43, 1 Berlin 61, Germany.

BRUCE FOUNDRY (*this foundry no longer exists, but some types are found in the* American Typefounders *catalogue*).

H. W. CASLON (bought by Stephenson Blake in 1937).

DEBERNY & PEIGNOT, 18 rue Ferrus, Paris XIV, France.

Paul HAYDEN DUENSING, 2636 Beethoven Avenue, Kalamazoo, Michigan 49002, U.S.A.

Joh. ENSCHEDÉ & ZONEN, Klokhuisplein 5, Haarlem, Holland.

FONDERIA TIPOGRAFICA COOPERATIVA, Peschiera Borromeo, Frazione Canzo (Milan), Italy.

FONDERIE TYPOGRAPHIQUE FRANCAISE, 31 rue de Verdun, 94 Champigny (Seine), France.

FUNDICIÓN TIPOGRÁFICA NACIONAL, Tomàs Breton 47, Madrid, Spain.

RICHARD GANS, Princesa 61, Madrid, Spain.

GENZSCH & HEYSE (*this foundry no longer exists. Some of the types are held by the* Bauer and Berthold typefoundries).

GRAFOTECHNA, Vrchlickeho 39, Prague-Modrany, Czechoslovakia.

HAAS'SCHE SCHRIFTGIESSEREI, Gutenbergstrasse 1, Basle-Münchenstein, Switzerland.

HARRIS-INTERTYPE Corporation, 360 Furman Street, Brooklyn, NY 11201, U.S.A.

HARRIS-INTERTYPE GmbH, Mariendorfer Damm 1–3, 1 Berlin 42, Germany.

HARRIS-INTERTYPE Ltd, Farnham Road, Slough, Bucks, England.

Dr ing R. HELL, Grenzstrasse 1–5, 23 Kiel 14, Germany.

JOSE IRANZO, Muntaner 176, Barcelona, Spain.

KLINGSPOR (*this foundry no longer exists. Most of the designs, unless discontinued, are found in the* Stempel *catalogue*).

B. KREBS (*this foundry no longer exists*).

LANSTON MONOTYPE Co, 3620 G Street, Philadelphia, Pa. 19134, U.S.A.

LINOFILM (*see* Linotype and Mergenthaler Linotype).

LINOTYPE & MACHINERY Ltd, 21 John Street, London WC1, England.

LINOTYPE GmbH, Hedderichstrasse 106–114, Frankfurt am Main-Süd, Germany.

Ludwig LOEWE GmbH, Huttenstrasse 17–20, 1 Berlin 21, Germany.

LUDLOW TYPOGRAPH Co, 2032 Clybourn Avenue, Chicago, Illinois 60614, U.S.A.

LUDLOW: Ludlow Typograph Co Ltd, 565 Kingston Road, London SW20 England.

LUDWIG & MAYER GmbH, Hanauer Landstrasse 187–189, Frankfurt am Main, Germany.

Elsö MAGYAR Betüöntöde, Dessewffy utca 32, Budapest 6, Hungary.

MATROTYPE Co Ltd, Marshgate Estate, Taplow, Maidenhead, Berks., England.
MERGENTHALER LINOTYPE Co, 29 Ryerson Street, Brooklyn, NY 11205, U.S.A.
MILLER & RICHARD (*this foundry no longer exists. Part of the matrix stock is held by* Stephenson Blake).
MONO LINO Co Ltd, 420 Dupont Street, Toronto, Ontario, Canada.
MONOPHOTO (*see* The Monotype Corporation and Lanston Monotype).
The MONOTYPE Corporation Ltd, Salfords, Redhill, Surrey, England.
Societa NEBIOLO, Via Bologna 47, 10152 Turin, Italy.
NEBITYPE, Via Bologna 47, 10152 Turin, Italy.
Fonderie OLIVE, 28 rue Abbé-Ferraud, 13 Marseilles 5, France.
RCA Graphic Systems, US Highway 130, Dayton, NJ 08810, U.S.A.
J. G. SCHELTER & GIESECKE AG (*nationalised, now called* Typoart).
SCHRIFTGUSS KG (*nationalised, now called* Typoart).
SIMONCINI: Matrotype Co Ltd, Marshgate Estate, Taplow, Maidenhead, Berks, England.
SIMONCINI, Via dei Lamponi 5, Bologna, Italy.
SOFRATYPE, 17 rue Bouret, Paris 19, France.
STAR PARTS Inc, South Hackensack, NJ 07606, U.S.A.
D. STEMPEL AG, Hedderichstrasse 106–114, Frankfurt am Main-Süd, Germany.
STEPHENSON BLAKE & Co Ltd, The Caslon Letter Foundry, Sheffield 3, Yorks., England.
STEVENS SHANKS & Sons Ltd, 89 Southwark Street, London SE1, England.
J. D. TRENNERT & Sohn (*this foundry no longer exists*).
TYPOART, Grossenhainer Strasse 9, Dresden N6, German Democratic Republic.
TYPOGRAPH (*this company no longer exists, but matrices are available from* Ludwig Loewe).
VIATRON, Route 62, Bedford, Mass. 01730, U.S.A.
L. WAGNER AG (*formerly in Leipzig, now in association with* J. Wagner *where some of this foundry's types are cast. Other types now cast by* Typoart).
Joh. WAGNER, Roemerstrasse 35–37, 807 Ingolstadt, Germany.
WAGNER & SCHMIDT (*this foundry no longer exists*).
WARNERY & Cie, 8 rue Jean Dolent, Paris XIV, France.
C. E. WEBER, Immenhofer Strasse 47, 7 Stuttgart 1, Germany.
W. WOELLMER (*this firm no longer exists and most matrices are now in the possession of* Typoart *formerly* Schriftguss KG, *although the majority of the types are no longer available*).

Typefounders' Agents in Britain

AMERICAN TYPEFOUNDERS – DEBERNY & PEIGNOT – STEMPEL: Arnold Cook Ltd, 3 Torrens Street, London EC1.
AMSTERDAM TYPEFOUNDRY – BAUER – HAAS'SCHE SCHRIFTGIESSEREI – LUDWIG & MAYER – NEBIOLO – WAGNER – WEBER: Stephenson Blake & Co Ltd, Upper Allen Street, Sheffield S3 7AY.
BERTHOLD TYPEFOUNDRY: C. F. Moore & Sons Ltd, West Road, London N17.
NEBITYPE: The Monotype Corporation Ltd, Salfords, Redhill, Surrey.

INDEX TO DESIGNERS

413

INDEX TO TYPE FACES

Bold figures indicate pages where the type faces are shown. Other figures are to textual references. The absence of a comma before numerals means that this is part of the typeface name, i.e., Initials 13